FROM CALIGARI TO CALIFORNIA

Erich Pommer's Life in the International Film Wars

Ursula Hardt

Berghahn Books
Providence • Oxford

Published in 1996 by

Berghahn Books
Editorial offices:
165 Taber Avenue, Providence, RI 02906, USA
Bush House, Merewood Avenue, Oxford, OX3 8EF, UK

Library of Congress Cataloging-in-Publication Data
Hardt, Ursula.
    From Caligari to California : Erich Pommer's life in the
international film wars / Ursula Hardt.
        p.   cm.
    Filmography : p.
    Includes bibliographical references and index.
    ISBN 1-57181-025-0 (alk. paper). -- ISBN 1-57181-930-4 (alk.
paper)
    1. Pommer, Erich, 1889–1966. 2. Motion picture producers and
directors--Germany--Biography.   I. Title.
PN1998.3.P66H37   1996
791.43'0232'092--dc20
[B]   96-13245
                                                                    CIP

British Library Cataloguing in Publication Data
A CIP catalogue record for this book is available from
the British Library.

Printed in the United States on acid-free paper

For

Hans H. von Fluegge

and

Allie and Liam Wrubel

CONTENTS

Photos: Private archives of John E. Pommer

ACKNOWLEDGMENTS

My interest in exploring Erich Pommer began with a curiosity about film émigrés from Germany and was rekindled during a Weimar cinema course taught by visiting scholar Thomas Elsaesser at the University of Iowa. Since then, many years of research, journeys to German and U.S. archives, and helping hands of colleagues, friends, and strangers facilitated my original study of Erich Pommer, written in 1989 at the University of Iowa. To them, especially Professors Dudley Andrew, Rudolf Kuenzli, Richard Dyer MacCann, Franklin Miller, and Patrice Petro, the committee members guiding me through the writing of the dissertation, my sincere gratitude.

This book in no way resembles my original study, which covered only a portion of Pommer's career. This is especially true for the biographical aspects I omitted before. Since completing the dissertation, I have been fortunate to have had access to many of Pommer's personal papers graciously provided by the Pommer family. My gratitude for completing the book therefore goes to Pommer's son John and his wife Heidi, without whose generosity I could not have written about a life and career as complex and embattled as Pommer's. Their hospitality toward a stranger from Iowa in the late 1980s and their continued trust and support have given me insight I could not have gained elsewhere. The many conversations and letters between us conveyed to me a personal side of Pommer that guided me throughout the writing process. They were a crucial bridge between the past and the present.

My gratitude also goes to Sylvia Robison for conscientiously reading the manuscript. Her language skills and constructive criticism were largely responsible for making the stylistic transition form dissertation to book; to Heide Fehrenbach, who graciously made her book manuscript on postwar Germany under the occupation powers available to me before publication; and to Professor Winfried Lerg of the University of Münster, Germany, who, like no one else, encouraged me to undertake the original study and its publication. I deeply regret that he did not live to see it in print.

Eric Pommer in RKO Studios Office in 1940

INTRODUCTION

During a show of "This Is Your Life" on American television in 1957, Hollywood star Maureen O'Hara falls to her knees before a wheelchair in which a frail, distinguished-looking man welcomes her embrace and kiss with open arms. "I owe my whole career to Mr. Pommer," she explains, visibly moved by his surprise visit.[1]

The man in the wheelchair was Eric Pommer, appearing in public for the last time before retirement. His long career in the film industries of two continents had come to an end. He had known triumph and defeat on the European side of the Atlantic, success and disillusionment on the other. Born Erich Pommer in Hildesheim, Germany, on 20 July 1889, he was one of Germany's pioneer producers who came to dominate, albeit with interruptions, the film industry of his native country for half a century. As a Jewish émigré after 1933, he fought a valiant battle to establish himself professionally in the United States, which he and his family adopted as home. Between 1907, when he entered the film business in Germany, and 1966, when he died in California, he not only survived the two bloody wars the world's superpowers fought on various fronts, but he also weathered numerous bloodless yet fierce "wars" that national film industries fought on the international battleground. As a result, Pommer fell victim to intrigues, prejudice, and envy, as much as he triumphed in times of power and glory.

---

1. *Das Cabinet des Erich Pommer: Ein Produzent macht Filmgeschichte*. Munich: Klick Film GmbH, 1989, prod. Hans-Michael Bock and Ute T. Schneider.

Many such film battles shaped his life and career. They first erupted among Germans in the Great War during which the chase for dominance in the Balkans pitted the economic interests of German heavy industry against the propaganda strategies of the German military. Assigned military duty in the region, Pommer soon felt the impact of the heated chauvinism between Germans and Romanians, while the German military outmaneuvered its industrial rivals in 1917 in Berlin with the foundation of Ufa, the first film conglomerate on a large scale in Germany. Far from becoming the propaganda apparatus as was first envisioned, Ufa soon placed itself exclusively at the service of entertainment, thus paving the way for its triumphant march to international recognition during the Weimar Republic. The man who was largely responsible for Ufa's ascendence was Erich Pommer, creating movies that were recognized as the "highest achievements in international film art" and "worthy of debate in foreign countries."[2]

Once recognized as an economic power to be reckoned with internationally, triggered by such artistically acclaimed exports as *Caligari*, produced by Pommer in 1919, and *Madame Dubarry*, produced by Paul Davidson the same year, the German film industry was soon drawn into a long-standing trans-Atlantic war over dominance of its market. As production chief and export executive of Ufa, the German film industry's most powerful representative, Pommer was at the forefront. In the early and mid-1920s his strategy of promoting film art was as groundbreaking for Ufa's and the German cinema's international reputation as his policies regulating import and export were crucial for domestic protection. At the height of the German-U.S. film wars, Ufa was on the brink of losing out, partially blaming its financial collapse on production policies "single-handedly" executed by Pommer. The threat of bankruptcy necessitated crippling trade agreements with several major U.S. film companies until total sell-out to the Americans was prevented by the extreme right-wing media czar Alfred Hugenberg. His take-over once again revived the futile contest between propaganda and entertainment, a strife not even Propaganda Minister Josef Goebbels was able to settle to his satisfaction.

The German-American film war was rekindled in all its intensity immediately after the Second World War, under the Allies' occupation of Germany. Pommer, as film control officer of the U.S. military

---

2. "Erich Pommer zurückgetreten," *Film-Kurier*, 22 January 1926. All translations that follow are mine unless otherwise indicated.

government in charge of reconstructing the demolished German film industry in the U.S. zone, successfully warded off the major U.S. film companies which saw a renewed chance in a stunted postwar German film market. Pommer's hard-won victory, however, has long since been reversed. As the history of German cinema has shown, the U.S. film industry of fifty years ago hardly needed to engage in such relentless competition. American films followed their own course overseas, determined by such basic commercial laws as supply and demand. The result is that today, in the mid-1990s, American films are an inextricable part of German life. As German critic and film director Hans-Christoph Blumenberg assessed Germany's first hundred years of filmmaking:

> The German market, in this anniversary year, is more firmly in Hollywood's grip than ever. The battle which the glorious Ufa in Babelsberg had to lead against the aggressive Californian movie giants as early as the 1920s seems finally to be lost. . . Only about one in every ten movie tickets in Germany is bought for entrance to a German film.[3]

But no longer aimed at Germany alone, the film war has escalated to take on the entire European Union. The stakes are much higher now in light of hugely inflated film budgets. With the average production cost in the United States in excess of $50 million per studio picture, few U.S. films are able to recoup their cost from the domestic market alone. For the Americans rescue has to come from the foreign market where, in 1994, theatrical revenues for the first time eclipsed revenues at home.[4] The alarming recognition that Hollywood now "supplies some 80 percent of the full-length films and as much as 60 percent of the television films seen in Europe" was a wake-up call for Europe, especially France, prompting rigid counterattacks to strengthen Europe's own industry while keeping the Americans at bay.[5]

In light of such international battles, Pommer's life and career go far beyond the context of Germany's film industry. Not existing in isolation, this industry was and still is embedded in international

---

3. Hans-Christoph Blumenberg, "100 Years of Movies – or the Story of Monsieur Cinema at a Child's Birthday Party, *Deutschland*, 3 (June 1995): 65.

4. "Average Cost of Making, Marketing Movie Soars," *Los Angeles Times*, 8 March 1995.

5. "European Union Helps the Film Industry Hold Its Own against Hollywood," *The Week in Germany*, 10 February 1995. See also "EU Film, TV Chief Drafts Law to Limit U.S. Rivals for 10 Years," *Wall Street Journal*, 21 March 1995; and "Sunset Boulevard For Jack Valenti?" *Business Week*, 17 January 1994.

trade relations. Pommer doubted that many film industry experts recognized how much the cultural, commercial, and political entanglements of nations affected their film industries.[6] Though German-born, he was an international film producer, trained through his association with the German, French, American and British film industries. His role as a German producer was developed and always maintained from his perspective of international expertise, and his work for Germany was consistently guided by its film industry's need to expand and participate in world markets. As Stuart Schulberg, son of U.S. producer B.P. Schulberg of Paramount, remarked in 1953, it seemed that Pommer's participation as producer in the film industries of four nations had prevented any of these nations from claiming him as its own.[7]

Given Pommer's embattled career, it is not surprising that a comprehensive account of his work does not exist. The price he paid was high, especially for his invaluable postwar reconstruction work that gained him more enemies than friends. As German journalist Paul Marcus (Pem) stated: "It is his personal tragedy that Pommer, the prominent representative of the German cinema, [once] went to war against Hollywood, the only rival and competitor, only to return as representative of the American cinema after the collapse of the Third Reich."[8] But such irony alone hardly explains why Pommer, one of the German cinema's founding fathers and historically its most outstanding producer, was not publicly acknowledged until 1989, the hundredth anniversary of his birth.[9]

Undoubtedly, Pommer made professional decisions affecting the course of his life and career and, ultimately, his image in German film history. But while personal misjudgment and political prejudice against him were decisive factors, inherent bias in film scholarship resulting in a total disregard for producers has been

6. Letter from E. Pommer to Pem (Paul Marcus), 22 March 1964.

7. Stuart Schulberg to the editor of *Films in Review*, 10: 10 (December 1959): 622, following publication of Herbert G. Luft's article on Pommer in the October issue of 1959.

8. Pem (Paul Marcus), "Gedenksprache für Erich Pommer," *Hamburger Filmgespräche, III* (Hamburg: Gesellschaft für Filmkunde, 1967): 39.

9. The impetus came from the Deutsche Kinemathek in Berlin, Federal Republic of Germany. It honored Pommer's hundredth birthday anniversary during the 39th Berlin International Film Festival in 1989. A Pommer retrospective showed thirty-four films; a film about his career, *Das Cabinet des Erich Pommer: Ein Produzent macht Filmgeschichte*, was produced; and a Pommer biography written by Wolfgang Jacobsen, *Erich Pommer: Ein Produzent macht Filmgeschichte*, was published.

another. Apart from producing Germany's silent masterpieces, he was – after all – also the first to produce and perfect the German film operetta, Ufa's entertainment genre *par excellence*. By also advocating the slick and glamorous "Ufa style," Pommer generated commercial success for the company, but little to endear himself to film analysts and historians.

As a producer, Pommer fostered the most splendid and largest number of German "classic" silent films produced in the "golden twenties." That fact is undisputed. Compared with his predecessor at Ufa, Paul Davidson, he channeled the company's art house production (often mistakenly referred to exclusively as "expressionist") into the more serious and Teutonic mode he had successfully explored and perfected at his companies Decla and Decla-Bioscop. One of Pommer's most creative scriptwriters from the *Caligari* period, Carl Mayer, explained:

> Film production in Germany was largely a matter of big-scale historical pictures. [Ernst] Lubitsch was making *Anne Boleyn* and *Dubarry*, [Dimitri] Buchowetzki *Danton* and *Peter the Great*. Such films were really in the tradition of the Italian spectacle films like *Cabiria* and *Quo Vadis?* [Emil] Jannings, [Werner] Krauss, [Conrad] Veidt and Pola Negri were all playing pretentious historical roles. *Caligari* was something completely new and it is to Pommer's credit that he backed it.[10]

Pommer's position at Ufa uniquely situated him between art and commerce, in a film industry backed by substantial private capital, and in a culture abounding with intellectual and creative talent. His artistic judgment and intuition, especially in his choice of, confidence in, and fierce protection of filmmakers such as Ludwig Berger, Fritz Lang, F.W. Murnau, and Robert Wiene, or in his well calculated acceptance of risky film scripts like *Caligari*, were coupled with an astute business sense. Such combination of personal and professional attributes enabled him to mediate between the artistic visions and demands of his film directors and writers on the one hand, and the economic caution and business judgments of Ufa's senior management on the other. Without his exemplary supervision, advocacy, and intervention, films like F.W. Murnau's *Der letzte Mann* (*The Last Laugh*, 1924), *Tartüff* (*The Gilded Hypocrite*, 1925), and *Faust* (1926); Fritz Lang's *Nibelungen* (1924) and *Metropolis* (1925); E.A. Dupont's *Varieté* (1924); Carl-Theodor Dreyer's

---

10. Paul Rotha, "It's in the Script," *World Film News* (London), 3: 5 (September 1938): 204.

Michael (1924); and Ludwig Berger's *Ein Walzertraum* (*Waltz Dream*, 1925) would have been quite different if produced at all. That also is an undisputed fact.

Pommer's critically acclaimed films are presented and studied today at educational institutions almost exclusively as the creation of each individual film director, the *auteur*. Such an *auteur* approach to film analysis has dominated film studies for decades and has consistently obstructed the exploration of other forces that determined film production – producers, studio histories, and economic conditions. As film scholar Richard Dyer MacCann found, "writers and teachers of motion picture history tend to forget about these strong production bosses when they attribute the art of particular films to particular directors."[11] The flood of research conducted on German cinema, especially on Weimar cinema, conspicuously draws attention to the absence of the man without whom the objects of these studies would most likely not exist. Film historians have written extensively about Weimar Germany's film directors and most prominent scriptwriters, whose creative influence on filmmaking is more easily discerned. Conversely, no study exists of Paul Davidson, Erich Pommer, David Melamerson, and Seymour Nebenzahl, to name some of the pioneers in German film production.

Not surprisingly, Lotte H. Eisner, film critic, historian, and author of a thorough and pioneering study of German silent cinema, *The Haunted Screen*,[12] admitted to me her omission of Pommer's role, choosing to emphasize film styles and directors.[13] And yet, she wrote about Fritz Lang and F.W. Murnau, two filmmakers whose careers were generously fostered by Pommer. If film analysis is tantamount to film "art" analysis, and if film art and film industry are seen as mutually exclusive, as film scholar Edward Buscombe contends,[14] directors and producers find themselves in conflictingly divided camps. While an artistically acclaimed film director is showered with praise, the producer is thought to be associated with financing and "mere" film manufacturing and is

11. Richard Dyer MacCann, "The Television Critic's Hidden Agenda," a paper presented at The University of Iowa Symposium and Conference, "Television Criticism: Public and Academic Responsibilities" (April 1985), 6.

12. Lotte H. Eisner, *The Haunted Screen* (Berkeley and Los Angeles: Univ. of California Press, 1973).

13. Letter from Lotte H. Eisner to author, 27 March 1979.

14. Edward Buscombe, "Notes on Columbia Pictures Corporation, 1926–41," *Screen*, 16 (autumn 1975). See also Bobby Allen, "An Alternative to Film History," *AFI Editors Newsletter*, 1:3 (January-February 1980).

relegated to second class status. Aware of the film director's pre-eminence even in the 1920s, Pommer allegedly once complained to F.W. Murnau that he was only the prestige film manufacturer (*Hersteller*), while Murnau was celebrated as a "prestige figure."[15]

The role of the producer is difficult to define. As John Baxter so pointedly expressed:

> On some levels, it means somebody who finds the money and pays the bills. On another, his creative contribution to a film can be as important as that of the director. In general, the two aspects, commercial and artistic, of film production are widely separated, though it was in Hollywood during the Thirties that the techniques of creative production were worked out. There had been producers like this in the European cinema – Erich Pommer, Alexander Korda – but they were rare.[16]

The assumption that producers contribute nothing to the artistic but everything to the business side of a movie can certainly not be applied to Pommer. More than any other producer in Weimar Germany, he produced "art films," thereby providing a strong trump card for Ufa on the international market. He represented characteristics U.S. producer Steven Kovacs considers as absolutely mandatory for his profession, "sufficient respect for the art and craft of filmmaking to do everything in his power to permit the director to achieve his vision."[17] The difficulty, however, lies in the fact that such creative participation in film production can never be accurately determined.

When Kovacs discussed the producer's role in *Sight and Sound* in 1985, he adroitly entitled his article "What Is a Producer, Anyway?" In light of the myriad tasks involved in production, he explained, "the producer credits differ from all others on a picture." While other titles – film director, scriptwriter, cinematographer, set designer, to name just a few from the "jungle of titles" in the credits – specifically state the function that each individual performed, this is not the case when titles refer to producers. According to Kovacs:

> The producers' responsibilities are so great, however, cover so many areas, extend from the seed of an idea through production to the negotiation of distribution and release of the picture, that no

15. Ernst Jäger, "Nicht zur Veröffentlichung: Vergeßnes, Bekanntes und Indiskretes aus deutscher Filmgeschichte," *Der neue Film* (January 1954 ff.), part 31.
16. John Baxter, *Hollywood in the Thirties* (New York: Paperback Library, 1970), 172.
17. Steven Kovacs, "What Is a Producer, Anyway?" *Sight and Sound* (spring 1985): 93.

single person can rightfully claim the title and function for himself. Producer credits are the trophies left after the battles for possession of the picture have been fought. . . As a result, producer credits are the least precise, most confusing credits that can be found on a picture.[18]

This leaves the film historian as detective, hunting for facts that permit insight into conditions that enabled a producer like Pommer, and his teams, to set unprecedented production standards in the German cinema. Unfortunately, neither Pommer nor his peers have left a collection of authentic documents typified by scripts, set and costume design drawings, posters, stills, and budgets; they do not exist for the early industry.[19] They created no *Cahiers du Cinéma*, no film school, and no body of theoretical writings.[20] A film historian therefore often relies for clarification on information supplied by those who witnessed the producer at work. "Many of the most stubborn artistic personalities give great credit to the strong executive figures of those days," Richard Dyer Mac-Cann observed; this statement is assuredly applicable to Pommer.[21]Pommer's son, John E. Pommer, who followed his father's professional footsteps, choosing a career in production, recalls numerous instances in which the creative components of a movie were arrived at by chance, during informal gatherings of film team members at his family's home (See Appendix A).[22] This was especially the case for writing film music, as many of the songs Marlene Dietrich sang in *Der blaue Engel* (*The Blue Angel*, 1930), for instance, were composed in the Pommers' living room. Such a creative contribution arrived at accidentally is hardly reflected in producer credits. Besides, until the late 1920s, producer credits did not exist on German screens, a fact that makes the compilation of a comprehensive filmography of Pommer's work impossible.

Aware of his controversial standing in Germany and in the United States, Pommer refused to leave his own authoritative statement about his career. In California in the 1960s, he collaborated with Siegfried Kyser, son of Ufa scriptwriter Hans Kyser, to

18. Ibid., 91.

19. The beginnings of a film museum can be seen in the Ufa *Lehrschau*, implemented at Ufa by Hans Traub. The most thorough records allowing insight into film production are the minutes of Ufa's senior management (*Vorstand*) meetings, beginning in 1927. They are stored at the Bundesarchiv in Koblenz, Germany.

20. Andrew Tudor, *Image and Influence: Studies in the Sociology of Film* (New York: St. Martin's Press, 1974), 174.

21. Richard Dyer MacCann, "The Television Critic's Hidden Agenda," 4.

22. For a biography of John E. Pommer, see Appendix A.

compile material for his biography, but the younger Kyser's death ended the project.[23] Considering both an autobiography and a film history for a while, Pommer finally concluded that everything about him was written already and that no one wanted to know anyway.[24] He wrote to German journalist Paul Marcus in 1964 that he felt he lacked the journalist's and writer's skills to produce the kind of work he envisioned.[25] Being in poor health, he may have made this decision with a desire for peace, protecting himself from reliving the vicissitudes of a lifetime. Aware of his inaccurate and inconclusive portrayal in the press and in scholarly writing, he elected to remain silent:

> The important facts which I could say about myself have already been published, sometimes accurately, but for the most part incorrectly, by those who were well informed and, unfortunately and more often than not, by those who were not. Often these facts have been reported falsely, with or without intention. Seen in this light, my image sways in film history, and that's how I'd like things to remain. I could correct a lot, and not only in cases where I was unjustly attacked, but also in those where I was undeservedly showered with praise.[26]

Despite Pommer's missing autobiographical statement, he created his own persona, his own "biographical legend," as film scholar David Bordwell called such a biography while writing about Danish film director Carl-Theodor Dreyer.[27] "However subjective," Bordwell contends, "even self-centered, such a legend may appear, that legend has an objective function in a historical situation."[28] An autobiography's absence, or its intended absence,

23. In 1964, two years before Pommer's death, Siegfried Kyser, the son of one of Pommer's scriptwriters at Ufa, Hans Kyser (*Faust*, 1926), began to prepare a Pommer biography. He compiled an extensive inventory of the content of Pommer's *Nachlaß* (his personal papers, photographs, audio cassette tapes, and a list of books and articles with references to Pommer). He also began to tape informal interviews with Pommer conducted in German and English. This material, including the audio cassettes, are part of the Eric Pommer Collection, USC.

24. Victoria Wolff, "Besuch bei Erich Pommer," *Aufbau*, 10 May 1957.

25. Letter from E. Pommer to Pem (Paul Marcus), 22 March 1964.

26. Letter from E. Pommer to Lore and Maurice Cowan, 19 May 1964.

27. This author acknowledges her indebtedness to Bordwell's discussion of the "biographical legend" of Danish film director Carl-Theodor Dreyer, in *The Films of Carl-Theodor Dreyer* (Berkeley, Los Angeles and London: Univ. of California Press, 1981), 9–24. Incidentally, Dreyer's and Pommer's paths merged in 1924 at Ufa, where both worked together on the film *Michael*.

28. Bordwell, *The Films of Carl-Theodor Dreyer*, 9.

is part of that biographical legend. Pommer's own memory, as reflected in interviews and public statements, is both supported, and at times distorted or contradicted, by friends, relatives, film professionals, and the press. This also constitutes and illuminates his legend. By refusing to justify his actions or correct historical falsifications, he willfully allowed this legend to grow and flower. Unlike Siegfried Kracauer whose reactive concern about his legacy caused Theodor W. Adorno to once accuse him "of trying to manipulate his image for posterity,"[29] Pommer intentionally elected to abstain from setting the record straight.

But this cannot satisfy film historians compelled to find and connect the puzzle pieces, although such a puzzle may never be complete. "Take everything you've heard … everything you've ever heard … and multiply it about a hundred times – and you still won't have a picture of John Ford," actor James Stewart once said of the film director.[30] The same is undoubtedly true about Erich Pommer.

29. Martin Jay, *Permanent Exiles: Essays on the Intellectual Migration from Germany to America* (New York: Columbia Univ. Press, 1985), 235.

30. Peter Bogdanovich, *John Ford* (Berkeley: Univ. of California Press, 1970), 6.

Chapter 1

INTERNATIONAL BEGINNINGS

When a specific temperament interlocks with a favorable position, the fortunate individual can extract from the situation a wealth of previously unimagined consequences. This achievement may be denied to other persons, as well as to the same person at a different time. Thus every birth can be imagined as set into play on two wheels of fortune, one governing the allotment of its temperament, and the other ruling its entrance into a sequence.

George Kubler, *The Shape of Time*

The French Connection: Berlin and Vienna

In Berlin's Wintergarten on 1 November 1895, the German brothers Max and Emil Skladanowsky showed the first moving pictures to a paying audience, and the cinema was born. This, of course, is the German claim. Defendable perhaps against the French whose Lumière brothers also presented their invention in the winter of 1895, the German claim most assuredly does not hold up against the Americans whose Thomas Alva Edison beat both Germany and France. Erich Pommer was then a six-year-old schoolboy a few hundred miles away in his native Hildesheim, and so his future career falls into the second generation of film producers in Germany. That first generation, the Skladanowsky brothers, Oskar Messter, and Paul Davidson, were all born a quarter century before Pommer. While Messter alone is recognized as the "father" of German cinema today, he shares credit for the technological innovation with the Skladanowskys and other pioneers. By the time Pommer's career began, Davidson had established a solid reputation as father of the movie palace and owner of Germany's largest chain of movie houses. Davidson had a keen eye for the international market as well. He first imported Asta Nielsen, a mesmerizing actress from Denmark, then collaborated with director Ernst Lubitsch and the captivating Pola Negri from Poland. By the time of Pommer's ascent to power in Berlin after the First World War, Davidson had become the most artistically savvy entrepreneur in the young German film industry. But luck and time were on the younger man's side, giving Pommer the chance to leave his unique mark on German cinema.

In the first decade of the century, Berlin quickly became the major center of film activity in Germany, attracting business entrepreneurs and artists from all over the country and beyond its borders. And while other cities in Germany, Munich for instance, also developed film productivity, they never equalled the capital in importance: "All attempts in the cinema's infancy to become active outside Berlin failed or led already existing companies ... to move to Berlin."[1] The city of Frankfurt/Main, where Davidson had originally set up his theater company in 1906, fared no better. By 1912 Davidson, too, moved to Berlin. Of all the businessmen settling here around the turn of the century, Oskar Messter was by far the most industrious. A year after the Skladanowsky brothers' history-making event in the Wintergarten, moving pictures were shown all over Berlin, but Messter was the first to install one of these exhibition places with state-of-the art equipment, giving Berlin's prominent boulevard Unter den Linden a professionally run, permanent movie theater.[2] He was also the first to produce, as he called it, "acceptable footage" of daily events, working from a production studio on Berlin's Friedrichstraße which soon became the address of choice for aspiring film businesses. A decade later, he founded Messter-Projektion and set up his business on Berlin's Blücherstraße. If ever the term "film factory" (*Filmfabrik*), as the early film businesses were called in Germany, could accurately be applied to a film enterprise at the time, it was to Messter's. He

1. Friedrich von Zglinicki, *Der Weg des Films: Die Geschichte der Kinematographie und ihrer Vorläufer* (Berlin: Rembrandt-Verlag, 1956), 363.

2. Klaus Kreimeier, *Die Ufa-Story: Geschichte eines Filmkonzerns* (Munich and Vienna: Carl Hanser Verlag, 1992), 21.

produced his own film strips, and also built cameras and projec-tors to facilitate production and exhibition. He was clearly setting the earliest example of combined hardware and software produc-tion under one roof.[3]

Soon other German "film factories" came into being. In 1897 Deutsche Bioscop began operation on Berlin's Chausseestraße and later built important studio facilities in Berlin-Neubabelsberg that would come under Pommer's control. Duskes Kinematographen and Filmfabrikations-GmbH operated studios in Berlin-Tempel-hof. The Deutsche Mutoskop- and Biographgesellschaft, formed in 1898 in conjunction with the American Biograph Company, set-tled in Berlin-Lankwitz. Heinrich Bolten-Baeckers's company, the BB-Filmgesellschaft, flourished in the southern part of Berlin and set the first example of German-French cooperation when it shared production sites with the French company Gaumont.[4] Filmmakers and actors, including Wanda Treumann, Viggo Larsen, Stuart Webbs, and Fern Andra, also operated their own studios in Berlin.[5]

Such a cluster of companies involved in the various aspects of filmmaking may paint a deceptively rich and productive picture of an emerging industry well on its way to success. However, Ger-man beginnings were modest indeed, measured against the state of film production and exhibition in France, Italy, Denmark, or the United States. While the problem was primarily economic, it also had deep-rooted cultural causes. Financial backers in Germany were hesitant to invest in a business that showed no clear sign of potential profit and was snubbed by the upper classes. In its early stages, the movie industry, unlike other German arts, did not bear the mark of bourgeois respectability, an attitude actually still apparent in Germany today. The director of a movie theater from those years recalled:

> Ridicule was the worst enemy of the movies. It was considered entertainment for the common and the lowest of men. One tended to laugh at the thought that a cinematographic show could be taken

3. Oskar Messter, *Mein Weg mit dem Film* (Berlin-Schöneberg: Max Hesses Ver-lag, 1936), 56–58. See also Thomas Elsaesser, "Wilhelminisches Kino: Stil und Industrie," in *Kintop 1: Früher Film in Deutschland* (Frankfurt/Main and Basel: Stroemfeld/Roter Stern, 1993), 19.

4. Zglinicki, *Weg des Films*, 347.

5. Hans Traub, *Die Ufa: Ein Beitrag zur Entwicklungsgeschichte des deutschen Film-schaffens* (Berlin: Ufa-Buchverlag, 1943), 9. See also Felix Bucher, *Screen Series Ger-many* (London: A. Zwemmer Ltd., New York: A.S. Barnes & Co., 1970), 117.

seriously. A banker's remark in Düsseldorf is symptomatic. He pinpointed his relationship to the movie theater as follows: I am not embarrassed to enter it, but I am embarrassed to emerge from it after the show.[6]

No one could assess this financial struggle better than entrepreneur and producer Paul Davidson:

> We all, Mr. Messter and Alfred Duskes, started too small, we – against Pathé and Gaumont. Our banks and our press were much too clever to help us little people get going on the right foot. In the beginning, there was the gigantic flood of foreign films. I believe I had the right intuition that we had to go along internationally, or simply die.[7]

It is not surprising, then, that film production companies from outside Germany, especially France, quickly established representatives or subsidiaries in Berlin, which "was not only the seat of foreign film companies, but also – next to its own production studios – the seat of all organizations in the film industry that existed at the time."[8] All three main French companies produced or distributed here, eventually under German names, Pathé under "Literaria," Gaumont under "Deutsche Gaumont-Gesellschaft," and Eclair under "Deutsche Eclair-Film." They operated independently in Germany, guided by French business principles and financed with French capital.[9] Unrestricted by government regulations in prewar Germany, these companies produced at relatively low cost the movies the German market depended on for its growing number of movie theaters. To the public the national origin of a movie was irrelevant; the silent film language was universal.

By 1911, six *Filmfabrikanten* constituted the staple of the Berlin film industry: Messter-Projektion, Mutoskop-Biograph (Germany's oldest company, financed by the chocolate factory Hartwig & Vogel), Vitaskop, Continental-Firma, Deutsche Bioscop-Gesellschaft, and Duskes, which later merged with Pathé.[10] Davidson, who added his Frankfurt-based Union-Film (PAGU) a year later, had already made his presence known in the capital by

6. Fritz Olimsky, "Tendenzen der Filmwirtschaft und deren Auswirkung auf die Filmpresse," Ph.D. diss., Univ. Berlin, 1931 (Berlin: Berliner Börsen-Zeitung, 1931), 22.

7. Jäger, "Nicht zur Veröffentlichung," *Der neue Film*, part 8.

8. Zglinicki, *Weg des Films*, 363.

9. Ulrich Kayser, "Die deutsche Filmindustrie: Entwicklung, Aufbau und volkswirtschaftliche Bedeutung," Ph.D. diss., Univ. Tübingen, 1921, 54.

10. Kayser, "Deutsche Filmindustrie," 52.

building Germany's first movie palace, the Union theater, UT for short, in 1908. But until the First World War, German film production failed to overcome its small trade image. Even Messter, Germany's most prolific producer, was as little able to compete with Pathé, Gaumont, and the other foreign companies in Germany (Alberini, Olsen, and Magnussen) as his female star, Henny Porten, was able to compete with Italian and Danish divas.[11] The power of these non-German companies is evident in the following financial comparison:

> Pathé lists its capital in 1907 at 6 million francs [$1.16 million], in 1912 at 30 million [$5.78 million]. Gaumont, the second largest French company, shows 2.5 million [$482,000] in 1906, 3 million [$578,400] in 1912. The largest northern production company, Nordisk, shows 2 million Kronen [$535,000] in 1912, the Italian company Cines shows 3.75 million lire [$712,125] the same year. The German company PAGU [Paul Davidson's Union-Film] shows a capital of 0.25 million marks [$59,475] in 1911, 1 million [$237,900] in 1912, and 2 million [$475,800] in 1917.[12]

It was figures like these that proved to German banks that an investment in the film business could potentially be profitable.[13] But it was the war with its private and government propaganda efforts that brought profound changes to the organization, productivity, and economics of the film industry. Until then, film exhibition in Germany had meant, to a large degree, the exhibition of international films, many of which were produced in Berlin. Fully 80 percent of the films shown in Germany were foreign-made, mainly by French companies, some by American and Italian ones. Some years this figure rose to 90 percent,[14] or even higher.[15] And so it is not surprising that Pommer began his long film career in the French companies Gaumont and Eclair.

When Pommer's father moved his family, then living in Göttingen, to Berlin in 1905, it was for reasons unrelated to Berlin's

11. Günter Peter Straschek, *Handbuch wider das Kino* (Frankfurt/Main: edition Suhrkamp 446, 1975), 239.
12. Traub, *Ufa*, 9. Pre-WWI exchange rates, here listed for 1913 against the U.S. dollar, provide a basis for comparison: Danish krone = 26.75 cents, French franc = 19.28 cents, German mark = 23.79 cents, and Italian lire = 18.99 cents. Board of Governors of the Federal Reserve System, *Banking and Monetary Statistics* (Washington, DC: National Capitol Press, 1943).
13. Zglinicki, *Weg des Films*, 360.
14. Traub, *Ufa*, 9.
15. Straschek, *Handbuch wider das Kino*, 239.

reputation as a film center. But the young Pommers, Grete, Erich, and Albert, soon became eager participants in Berlin's new industry. As an adolescent growing up in a German middle class Jewish family, Erich had at times considered becoming a physician. Such dreams were unrealistic given his attitude toward formal learning and his less than perfect academic record. He failed to obtain the diploma (*Abitur*) of his secondary school in Göttingen, a necessary qualification for university studies. He twice had to repeat a grade and finally left school for good in 1905, the year his family moved to Berlin. At least in his French class, his lack of motivation was not surprising, for as a friend later reminded Pommer:

> Our teacher Weselmann, who taught us French, lived across the street from you. Most of the time he came to class in the afternoon with liquor on his breath, sat down in the back of the room, hid behind a newspaper, and announced: "If you turn around, I will have you stay after class."[16]

Despite Pommer's voracious appetite for books, his compulsive interest in the theater, and his curiosity and enthusiasm for the movies, he first became an apprentice at Machol & Lewin, a Berlin clothing store specializing in men's fashions. In that respect, his background parallels that of many prominent U.S. film producers with roots in European Jewish family traditions who spent their early years in the clothing business.

Pommer's film career began by chance rather than by choice. He was still undecided about professional goals when his sister Grete became a secretary at Gaumont in Berlin in 1906. A year later the eighteen-year-old Pommer was initiated into the film business, hired as a salesman by Georges Grasset, Gaumont's director in Berlin.[17] About his initial exposure, Pommer said:

> It was here that I first laid eyes on those boxes holding films of 300 meter length. They were then sold to fairground people who showed them while traveling from place to place. I believe I contracted a very special bug at the time, a bug I was never able to get out of my system. Even today, the smell of filmstrip draws me like a magnet when I find myself in editing rooms. That was the reason why medicine lost a candidate and Georges Grasset, director of the

16. Letter from Heinz Bremer, Göttingen, to E. Pommer, 1 June 1959. J. Pommer Collection, Camarillo, CA.

17. This author found three different spellings: Grassi, Grasset, and Grassin. "Grasset" is used by Nino Frank, regular contributor to the French newspaper *Pour vous*, in "30 ans de cinéma: Confidences d'Erich Pommer," *Pour vous*, 11 February 1937.

German branch of Gaumont, agreed to hire as messenger the young boy I was at that time.[18]

Such employment was unheard of in Göttingen's petit-bourgeois circles and smacked of the "forbidden." A friend vividly remembered the visit of the young, elegantly dressed Pommer to Göttingen, a year after he had joined Gaumont in Berlin:

> It must have been in 1908 – you had left school one year early – when you paid me a visit from Berlin … and told me you had joined the film industry. The word film hardly existed at the time, at least not in Göttingen. Here we only knew peep booths. . . Entering them gave us a slight shudder because it was not condoned. However, the attraction was too big [to resist].[19]

Pommer had found his professional calling, learning the trade from the bottom up. Throughout his life he insisted that it was neither specific abilities nor ambition, but pure accident that led to his involvement with the film industry.[20] He was simply in the right place at the right time, witnessing the unfolding of an industry that established itself internationally from the beginning. Pommer was indeed fortunate to experience what George Kubler calls a "favorable entry."

At Gaumont from 1907 on, he was eager to try his hand at anything the company offered, from acting to film projecting, advertising, news editing, and sales. His early sales experiences were often unpleasant but not discouraging. To his customers, many of whom were owners and managers of local fair exhibition booths, neither he nor his product was necessarily welcome:

> Many fair booth operators were among my customers. It was not difficult to sell movies of 300 meter length, the equivalent of one reel. However, complications started when Gaumont began to produce lengthy dramas, two to four reels long. The innkeepers and booth operators had no interest in such long programs, and there were times during these business trips when I found myself kicked out by some of my customers.[21]

Learning the hard way, he soon was known at Gaumont as a shrewd young salesman who beat his customers' ploys to cheat the company out of money. Since it was customary to send, rather than

---

18. Frank, "30 ans de cinéma." Translated by Frauke Ramin.
19. Letter from Bremer to E. Pommer.
20. Frank, "30 ans de cinéma."
21. Friedrich Porges, "Erich Pommers Goldenes Jubiläum," *Aufbau*, 30 April 1959.

deliver, film reels to interested exhibitors, these exhibitors would invariably return a high percentage of the merchandise, declining to purchase the reels although they had obviously shown the movies. Gaumont's success rate increased dramatically when Pommer decided to deliver film reels in person. And his employment enabled him to learn French, which he mastered with a degree of enthusiasm he would have considered impossible during his school years. Most likely he was influenced by his fellow worker and friend, Erich Morawsky, who had learned French while working in Paris.[22] Given the international nature of film in Germany at the time, he was surely aware of the advantages that a foreign language like French would bring him; in his field it was a necessity. But most importantly for his later career, he was introduced to production when Georges Grasset began making movies. In Grasset, Pommer said, he was fortunate to have found an excellent teacher who quickly made him familiar with all the cinema secrets of the time.[23]

The modesty of Grasset's early production attempts is evident in Pommer's recollections:

> His wife was the director, and I remember that a professional actor, Lyon de Beret, played in our first film. The other actors were employees of the house, who played their roles in beautiful costumes and without [receiving] film credit. Between two business trips, I often played the part of an angel, but my career as actor did not last long.[24]

One of the most valuable experiences of his apprenticeship years at Gaumont was the exposure to company policy. Competition between businesses and nations was the daily menu. When interviewed in 1937, he recalled: "You have to remember that Pathé produced in Paris, the Nordisk company in the Scandinavian countries, the Italians had begun to produce, while Bioscop had just started in Berlin."[25] The national origin of individual companies in Germany seems to have been irrelevant. Each company fought for its own survival, and in this struggle Gaumont fought against both its German and its French competitors. In the first decade of the new century, Pommer witnessed both the business

22. See Wolfgang Jacobsen, *Erich Pommer: Ein Produzent macht Filmgeschichte* (Berlin: Stiftung Deutsche Kinemathek and Argon Verlag, 1989), 11.
23. E. Pommer, in a manuscript he typed and revised by hand in 1964, as contribution to Alfred Eibel's work on film director Fritz Lang. E. Pommer Collection.
24. Frank, "30 ans de cinéma."
25. Ibid.

survival strategies of individual companies and the struggle of various national film industries to outwit one another. Working in such an internationally competitive climate, Pommer evolved early as an entrepreneur whose perspective was always, by necessity, international. Had he ever written his autobiography, he once said, it would have mirrored the history of the "international film."[26]

In 1910 Pommer became director of Gaumont's branch in Vienna, with accountability to Gaumont headquarters in Berlin and responsibility for film sales in the entire Austro-Hungarian territory. One year later he was drafted for his compulsory year of military duty. After his discharge as private he could have returned to Gaumont in Vienna, but opted for the director post at Eclair, which planned to establish a branch in Vienna. Pommer's move seems surprising considering that Eclair was less successful in Berlin than its rivals Pathé and Gaumont. But Eclair had begun to expand in 1908, with distribution outlets in Germany, Austria, and Middle-Europe – even in the United States. In 1911 Eclair had severed ties with an unsatisfactory German agent in Berlin, establishing a subsidiary instead. When Pommer became available in 1912, Eclair had just lost its distribution agent in Vienna and was seeking an opportunity to form an Austrian subsidiary.[27] This chance was Pommer, with whom Marcel Vandal, the director and founder of Eclair in Paris, was close friends. Pommer enabled Eclair to build a successful business in Vienna, and Vandal, knowing what to expect of his friend, jumped at this chance when Pommer was eager to leave Gaumont. Vandal also granted Pommer's wish to report directly to company headquarters in Paris, not to the Berlin branch, as was the case at Gaumont. In addition to establishing Pommer's direct contact with France, the nation that produced, to his knowledge, the best films for the European market, the move to Eclair also assured a close working relationship with his friend Vandal.[28] And here his future place in the industry came into clear focus for Pommer:

26. E. Pommer, interviewed in 1964 by Petko Kadiev and Siegfried Kyser. Audiotape. E. Pommer Collection.

27. Eclair's agent in Berlin, Otto Schmidt, was replaced by F. Rudolph Schulz as head when Marcel Vandal and Charles Jourjon formed a subsidiary in Berlin in 1911. In Vienna Eclair was represented by an agent, Alexander Ortony, until 1912. Vandal and Jourjon formed a subsidiary in Vienna in 1913, with Pommer as head. See Lenk, "Lichtblitze," *Kintop 1*.

28. Alexandra Pecker, "Marcel Vandal & Erich Pommer: Pionniers de l'entente Franco-Allemande: Vers une nouvelle formule de diplomatie internationale," *Comoedia*, 9 February 1933.

Here began my collaboration with Marcel Vandal and Charles Jordan [*sic*],[29] which constituted my true training. Vienna was the city from which I conducted the distribution of our movies throughout Middle-Europe. I initiated the construction of film studios in Vienna, which are the Sascha Studios today. I created the *Eclair Journal* and began to produce movies. The "bug" I had caught, escalated and, from then on, I thought of nothing but film production, with some very precise ideas.[30]

As director of Eclair, Pommer jumped at his first chance to produce, aided by Vandal who began to join him for production in Vienna in 1913.[31] The result was nine films, including a few documentaries, which they released under the company name Wiener Autoren Film, apparently Pommer and Vandal's production arm of Eclair in Vienna.[32] Despite Vandal's close collaboration, or perhaps precisely because of his presence in Vienna, this company name seems to indicate relative independence from Eclair's headquarter dictates in Paris. This was especially true for Pommer's success in securing production assignments from outside the company. Apparently the move from Gaumont to Eclair was paying off, as Pommer was able to create a niche in which he felt free from artistic and commercial constraints.[33]

As head of Eclair he oversaw the newsreel production of the *Eclair Journal*, as it was called in Vienna, and at times stood behind the camera himself.[34] He also represented Eclair in the Scandinavian countries and the entire Austro-Hungarian Empire, extending into Hungary, Yugoslavia, and Romania where he built up the distribution of Eclair films at Volta-Film, Eclair's Romanian distribution

29. Correct spelling is Jourjon. Together with Marcel Vandal (both of them Paris lawyers) and Ambroise-François Parnaland, he founded Eclair (Société Française des Films et Cinématographes Eclair) in Paris in 1907 with a starting capital of 150,000 francs. For more information on Eclair, see Lenk, "Lichtblitze," *Kintop 1*, 29–57.

30. Frank, "30 ans de cinéma."

31. See Pecker, "Marcel Vandal & Erich Pommer." The titles of these movies were: *Zu Pferd auf dem Riesenrad* (*A Cheval sur la Grande Roue/With a Horse on a Ferris Wheel*) and *Das Geheimnis der Luft* (*Le Mystère de l'Air/The Mystery of the Air*). Frank, "30 ans de cinéma."

32. For more information on the films produced by Wiener-Autoren-Film in Vienna, see Lenk, "Lichtblitze," *Kintop 1*. Marcel Vandal's interest in production is not surprising considering that the French company Eclair is mainly a production company, including newsreel production. See Richard Abel, *French Cinema: The First Wave, 1915–1929* (Princeton, NJ: Princeton Univ. Press, 1984), 8.

33. Lenk, "Lichtblitze," *Kintop 1*, 48.

34. Letter from J. Pommer to Wolfgang Jacobsen, Berlin, 9 July 1986.

arm in Bucharest.[35] The latter, like all his peacetime work in the Balkans, was excellent preparation for Pommer's military propaganda duties there during the war that erupted soon afterward.

Looking back at his formative prewar years at French companies in Berlin and Vienna, especially at Eclair in Vienna, Pommer concluded during an interview in 1937:

> The French films before the First World War were my most valuable experience, and I will never forget how much I owe to Marcel Vandal. The French cinema was then the only reputable cinema in the world. For everything worthwhile I accomplished in the cinema, I am indebted to the French cinema during my early career.[36]

By August 1914, the Central Powers, Germany and Austria-Hungary, were at war with France and its Allies, Belgium, Great Britain, Russia, and Serbia. The recently married Pommer was inducted immediately and sent to the French front,[37] but the impression he had made during his short involvement in the film industry still echoed in the trade press. The German trade journal *Lichtbild-Bühne*, for instance, published one of his letters from the front in 1914 in which he described the events leading to receiving the Iron Cross, a high military honor for bravery in battle. The journal referred to him as a well-known figure in Viennese and Berlin film circles, who was extraordinarily popular and respected far beyond Eclair's large circle of business associates and friends.[38] Although the war pitted Germany against France, it apparently failed to diminish Pommer's close ties to Marcel Vandal. He was known to warn his fellow soldiers at the French front not to shoot should they encounter an unusually tall Frenchman: "That one is my friend [Marcel Vandal]."[39]

The war brought significant changes for the film industry in Germany. In September 1914, the German police confiscated foreign

35. Jacobsen, *Erich Pommer*, 14.

36. Frank, "30 ans de cinéma."

37. John Pommer gives the following detailed account of his father's army placement at the onset of the war, in his letter to Wolfgang Jacobsen, 9 July 1986: "He was immediately drafted in August 1914 into the third Garde-Armee-Korps, second Infantrie Gardedivision, Kaiser Alexander Garde Regiment number 1, third Bataillon, tenth Squadron. He was immediately stationed at the French front line and received the military medal of honor, *das Eiserne Kreuz*, in October. He is promoted to petty officer. He is wounded in 1915, and the bullet which hit him remains lodged in his leg for the remainder of his life."

38. "Das Eiserne Kreuz," *Lichtbild-Bühne*, 24 October 1914.

39. Pecker, "Marcel Vandal & Erich Pommer." Vandal's (1882–1965) and Pommer's careers continued to intersect, in Paris and in Berlin.

films from companies whose financial base lay in enemy territory, a convenient way to eliminate foreign competition under the pretext of national security. The French companies in Berlin, Pathé (Literaria), Deutsche Gaumont, and Eclair, the latter by then operating as Deutsche Eclair and managed by Pommer's British friend Joseph [Joe] Powell, were no longer allowed to function under French capital in Germany.[40] Their subsidiaries in Germany and Austria-Hungary were placed under military administration.[41] Overnight the German and Austro-Hungarian markets were officially cleared of French films, although unofficially these measures failed to have the overall effect intended by the German government. Apparently the international intertwinement on the German film market was so complete that Gaumont's and Pathé's films were able to enter via harmless-sounding companies routed through neutral foreign nations.[42] Much to the chagrin of German film entrepreneurs, the Danish company Nordisk remained unaffected by wartime restrictions.

On the whole, the war's impact on the German film business was immense. By temporarily providing a nominal market monopoly, it gave birth to a boom in production. Germany was forced to explore and rely on its own resources:

> Overnight the foreign film industry was eliminated as competitor. A few years earlier this would have meant the end of our cinema because we did not have any notable production of our own. But in 1914, a number of studios had just been completed, especially the very large facilities in Tempelhof. Our young film production was about to require effective import regulations, and now the erupted war was much more effective by completely severing the connection with foreign countries. Our film production was suddenly facing the

40. The 1914 production data in Gerhard Lamprecht's silent film catalogues, for instance, reveal abrupt changes in the latter part of the year. Deutsche Gaumont (also called Targa-Film before WWI) disappears from production records, whereas the BB-Film studios, hitherto used by Gaumont, are now used exclusively by "BB-Film." The company "Literaria," actually the production company Pathé, ceases to exist under this name, while the Literaria studios in Berlin-Tempelhof are subsequently used by the newly founded "National-Film" whose first film features are all, characteristically, army burlesques. French distribution companies are cut off as well. There are no production references to Eclair or Deutsche Eclair, but the company is listed for the first time in 1915 under the name "Film-Gesellschaft Holz & Co." in Berlin. The company's first film, *Der Glaube siegt* (*Victory of Faith*), is listed with a probable release date of April 1915. Gerhard Lamprecht, *Deutsche Stummfilme 1903–1931*, 11 vols. (Berlin: Deutsche Kinemathek, 1967–1970).

41. Pommer, Eibel-Manuscript; see also Traub, *Ufa*, 20.

42. Traub, *Ufa*, 20.

undreamed of task of covering the entire demand of the domestic market for feature films. No wonder this favorable situation invigorated our film production.[43]

Following Pommer's departure for military duty, Eclair in Vienna was in the hands of Pommer's deputy Kurt Hubert who was apparently spared military duty. But at stake was Eclair in Berlin, whose British director, Joe Powell, had no chance of remaining in a nation at war with his homeland.[44] When he was interned in late 1914, the former colleagues, Pommer and Hubert, became rivals in the struggle to acquire the rights to the confiscated Berlin company from its government-appointed administrator.[45] Pommer emerged as the successful bidder, aided in his victory by a prewar business association with Fritz Holz, a distributor and owner of movie theaters in Berlin. Holz had contributed financially to Eclair's Berlin subsidiary and was naturally concerned about losing his investment. Holz's financial and Pommer's professional investment in this company were an advantage, supported by the fact that Pommer was favored, over Hubert, for his patriotic service in the military. They emerged as victors. In February 1915, during Pommer's absence, the Decla Filmgesellschaft Holz und Co. came into being; the new company name displayed the affinity to Deutsche Eclair whose assets were subsequently transferred to Decla. Holz and Pommer became co-owners.[46] Pommer's former friend at Gaumont, Erich Morawsky, since 1913 at Eclair in Berlin, remained with the company, and Pommer's brother Albert joined as executive. The company occupied the offices of the former Deutsche Eclair, which continued to exist on paper until its final liquidation in 1917.[47] The events surrounding the end of the former French subsidiary and the beginning of Decla were confirmed by Pommer's son as follows:

> The founding of Decla, as best I know, initially was to preserve the Eclair assets, not to usurp them. Marcel Vandal, the head of Eclair

43. Olimsky, *Tendenzen der Filmwirtschaft*, 23.

44. Close family ties linked the Eclair subsidiaries in Berlin and Vienna, after Joe Powell's sister-in-law, Grace, married Kurt Hubert in Vienna. Powell died in the mid-twenties. Letter from J. Pommer to author, 5 April 1995.

45. See Jacobsen, *Erich Pommer*, 21–24.

46. This date is verified in various sources, despite the fact that the foundation date of Decla is often incorrectly given as 1919. Business reports from Decla to its director Pommer start in 1915. Lamprecht lists 1915 as the date of Decla's first feature film, *Der Glaube siegt* (*Victory of Faith*).

47. Jacobsen, *Erich Pommer*, 24.

in Paris, was my father's best friend, then and later. . . The war seems to have been blamed on England rather than France. My father's other best friend, Powell, was English. He worked for Eclair and Decla in Berlin and was interned. He remained in Berlin after the war. . . As to Decla, obviously it remained German and the French Eclair had nothing to do with it after 1914. So, the use of the name Deutsche Eclair may have had the purpose of maintaining the goodwill created by the French organization which had been managed by my father.[48]

Upon Holz's resignation from Decla in mid-1915, Pommer remained the sole owner, and Hubert, his short-term rival over Eclair in Berlin, became a business associate again, now at Decla.[49]

The company began its road to fame in its studio facilities in Weißensee outside Berlin, while its chief executive officer was on war duty.[50] Pommer's son believes, that his mother was not the acting CEO but corresponded daily with her husband about company business.[51] He is certain, however, that she not only related her husband's instructions but also gave independent opinions when she thought necessary, and that these opinions

48. Letter from J. Pommer to author, 24 March 1987. With the end of its German and Austrian business ventures, Eclair also ceased commercial film production (except the *Eclair Journal*) in France, renting out its studios at Epinay-sur-Seine, and concentrating on camera equipment and film processing instead. See Abel, *French Cinema: First Wave*, 13.

49. Kurt and Grace Hubert survived the Second World War in Berlin; they committed suicide after she was raped by Russian soldiers during the occupation of Berlin. Letter from J. Pommer to author, 5 April 1995.

50. In his letter to the author of 11 May 1985, J. Pommer explains: "In February 1915 my mother wrote a letter on its [Decla's] new stationery, which read: 'Decla-Film-Gesellschaft, Berlin SW. 48, Friedrichstraße No. 22, Fabrikation [manufacture=production] und Vertrieb [distribution] von Decla-Films und Carl-Wilhelm-Films.' The stationery uses the [plural] term 'Film*s*', not 'Film*e*'. Carl Wilhelm was a director and possibly also producer."

51. Letter from J. Pommer to Jacobsen, 9 July 1986. The question of Decla's management during Pommer's absence remains unclear. Pommer's son hypothesizes that Carl Wilhelm, who directed several films at Decla, may in effect have been the guiding creative personality in the first years. Herbert G. Luft claims that "Mrs. Pommer managed it till the war ended," in his article, "Erich Pommer: Germany's Greatest Film Producer Became Such Through Charm and Assiduity," in *Films in Review* 10: 8 (October 1959): 459. However, this is unfounded. The closest to support such a claim is a remark in the third business report from Decla to Pommer, 10 August 1915. While discussing censorship difficulties of a specific film, *Der Herr ohne Wohnung* (*The Gentleman without an Apartment*), the report contains the remark: "Till now no definitive decision has been reached despite your wife's special plea (*Eingabe*). Nevertheless, there is no great chance to free the film for Berlin."

were given serious consideration.[52] Apparently Pommer had input into his company while away from Berlin; he was well informed through regular business reports. For instance, a report dated 10 August 1915, marked as "report number 3," discussed personnel issues, the latest films in production, censorship problems, sales in and outside Germany (Austria-Hungary and Romania), the domestic market, and foreign competition.[53] By the summer of 1916, *Lichtbild-Bühne* praised the absent Pommer for his production company's rapid and successful development and commented favorably on Decla's new status as distribution company. Following in the footsteps of Pathé, Gaumont, Nordische, and Messter, Decla was now the second German *Filmfabrik* to begin selling its product directly to theaters, focusing primarily on Berlin and vicinity and eastern Europe.[54]

The Balkans

For the German government the war created urgent propaganda needs, and it became painfully obvious that Germany had wasted valuable time that had been used wisely for propaganda by the Allies. German efforts to establish efficient and effective propaganda tools were impeded by much more than inexperience in visual propaganda techniques. Political tension between the military and German industries operating in the Balkan and Asia Minor territories for commercial expansion further complicated propaganda. It was here that Germany's heavy industry of the Rhine-Ruhr area competed heavily with the economic interests of the large ship owners and the chemical and electronics industries, all of which were backed by Germany's largest bank, the Deutsche Bank.[55] It was here also that some of the most powerful and influential players in the future German film industry made their first

52. Letter from J. Pommer to author, 27 August 1995.

53. Business Report no. 3 from Berlin to Pommer, 10 August 1915. The report lists four Decla films: *Sein Seitensprung (His Affair)*, *Der Barbier von Filmersdorf (The Barber of Filmersdorf)*, *O diese Männer (Oh, These Men!)*, and *Die Goldquelle (Source of Gold)*. J. Pommer Collection.

54. "Die 'Decla' verleiht," *Lichtbild-Bühne*, 5 August 1916. Head of distribution was Hermann Saklikower.

55. For more details on Ufa's precursors, see Jürgen Spiker, *Film und Kapital: Der Weg der deutschen Filmwirtschaft zum nationalsozialistischen Einheitskonzern* (Berlin: Verlag Volker Spiess, 1975), 18–27.

appearance: the Deutsche Bank's director, Emil Georg von Stauß, publisher Ludwig Klitzsch, financier Alfred Hugenberg, and the military's chief of staff, General Erich Ludendorff.

Klitzsch, the publisher of export magazines and of the *Leipziger Illustrirte* at the publishing house of J.J. Weber, was astutely aware of international market strategies employed by enemy nations, especially through the exploitation of film. He argued repeatedly for intensified German film propaganda. In the spring of 1916, Ludwig Klitzsch suggested to representatives of trade, industry, and transportation a strategy for utilizing film to win the sympathies and secure the support of foreign markets. His call to immediate action did not gain financial support. But Klitzsch's ideas coincided with the politically shrewd Hugenberg, chairman of the steel giant Krupp's board of directors, who authorized him to found and head the Deutsche Lichtbild-Gesellschaft (DLG; Deulig as of 1920). With financing now provided by German heavy industry, Klitzsch apparently found at least the modest fulfillment of his envisioned centralized, large-scale propaganda institution, hoping that this company might be the future umbrella for all German film businesses.

But it was inevitable that the ensuing success of the DLG in the Balkans and Asia Minor caught the wrath of Germany's other industrial capitalists whose financial backer, the Deutsche Bank, pursued similar expansion policies in this area. The bank's director, Emil Georg von Stauß, found unexpected support in his campaign against the DLG in General Ludendorff. Like Klitzsch, Ludendorff envisioned a large-scale propaganda machine in the Reich. While the former's dreams revolved around the DLG, the latter hoped to realize his plans with the Bild- und Filmamt (Bufa), a still picture and film agency established by the military in Berlin in early 1917.[56] With a staff of 450, including its own production facilities, it provided a first link between the young film industry and the military by facilitating and sanctioning eye-witness reportage from the front and film propaganda at home and abroad.[57] Both the DLG and Bufa operated in the Balkans, allegedly representing opposing interests – the DLG seeking primarily economic, and Bufa propaganda goals. The combined forces of the Deutsche Bank, Emil Georg von Stauß, and General Ludendorff,

56. H.H. Wollenberg, *Fifty Years of German Film* (London: The Falcon Press Limited, 1948), 12.

57. See Wilfried von Bredow and Rolf Zurek, eds., *Film und Gesellschaft in Deutschland: Dokumente und Materialien* (Hamburg: Hoffmann und Campe, 1975), 76ff.

however, succeeded in undermining the DLG more and more, finally ignoring it altogether by founding the Universum-Film-AG (Ufa), with private and government financial backing, in December 1917 in Berlin.[58]

Considering the short history of film businesses in Germany, Ufa started on an immense footing, with sufficient financial resources to acquire the most lucrative film businesses in Germany, including the powerful Danish adversary Nordisk.[59] Eventually both of the companies already operative in the Balkans, the DLG and Bufa, also bowed to Ufa. In 1921 the company that was intended as *the* "national" film enterprise for the economic and propaganda needs of all parties involved, was privatized when the Reich withdrew its financial share.[60]

Erich Pommer, too, would play a crucial role at Ufa in the years to come. By the spring of 1916, he had been wounded twice, once on the French, and a second time on the Russian front where he was shot in the leg. He barely escaped death when another bullet pierced the left breast pocket of his uniform but was stopped by a small German-Polish-Russian dictionary and a notebook he carried there.[61] After physicians decided against removing the bullet lodged in his leg, he was released from the Berlin hospital in the summer of 1916 and immediately given new assignments. Following several months of training recruits in Berlin, he was assigned to the newly founded Bufa, which quickly utilized experts from the film industry. This transfer probably came about

58. Accordingly, two scenarios explaining Ufa's foundation, developed after WWII, as Jan-Christopher Horak points out in his M.S. thesis on Ernst Lubitsch: "The first version, based on film histories by Oskar Kalbus, [Hans] Traub, and Siegfried Kracauer, accepted the view that the government initiated the creation of Ufa for propaganda purposes. The second version (appearing in a number of East and West German sources) postulated a theory whereby the Ufa was founded as a result of a corporate power struggle between the reactionary Krupp steel industries and North German banking interests." Horak, "Ernst Lubitsch and the Rise of Ufa 1917–1922," M.S. thesis, Boston Univ., 1973, 39.

59. Besides the Danish Nordisk, the German companies were Messter-Film and Union (Pagu). The various production, distribution (domestic and international), and exhibition branches associated with these firms are too numerous to list here. Messter alone owned Messter-Film, Autor-Film, Hansa-Film Distribution, and one of Berlin's leading film theaters, the Mozartsaal. For more details, see Messter, *Mein Weg mit dem Film,* and Traub, *Ufa.*

60. For an exhaustive history of Ufa, see Hans-Michael Bock and Michael Töteberg, eds., *Das Ufa-Buch* (Frankfurt/Main: Zweitausendeins, 1992), and Kreimeier, *Ufa-Story.*

61. Letter from J. Pommer to author, 28 August 1995. The two booklets with the bullet holes still are in possession of the Pommer family.

through Kurt Waschneck, a friend of the Pommer family, with whom he worked at Bufa, producing news reels, documentaries, and educational films.

But Bufa also distributed films in territories that were occupied by Germany, and in the summer of 1917 Pommer was transferred to Romania where he remained a sergeant in the German army ("out of uniform," as he claims) until he was released from Bufa in November 1918. Romania was known territory to Pommer who had sold films there for Gaumont and Eclair during a time of lively film exchange before the war.[62] But in the year 1915 Romania had ended its alliance with the Central Powers, joined forces with the Allies, and fallen just a few months before Pommer arrived. He was to oversee the film sector of the censorship board of the military administration and to supervise the legitimate stage in Bucharest. The latter had been closed by the military, leaving many artists without work or income. When he reopened the theater on 16 July 1917, the singers and actors thanked him enthusiastically with a letter addressed to "the Honorable Erich Pommer, Director of the Balkan-Orient-Film-Gesellschaft."[63]

This letter reveals Pommer's involvement with a film company in the Balkans. Apparently the Balkan-Orient-Film-Gesellschaft had been founded in December 1916 as a military outlet to promote German propaganda. In 1917, the DLG took command of Balkan-Orient-Film, thus further aggravating the already existing tension with the German government. If the government had initially accepted the DLG's influence in the Balkans, it renounced it in 1917, charging that the DLG did little to further the interests of the German government. Sergeant Erich Pommer, the military's representative in Romania, it was claimed, was the only one doing good work in the area.[64] When Pommer left Romania in late 1918, the Balkan-Orient-Film-Gesellschaft had undergone two name changes, first to "Balkan-Orient-Gesellschaft E. Pommer" and subsequently to "Soarele."[65] It is unclear whether the names reflected legitimate transfer of ownership to Pommer or a strategy to hide

62. E. Pommer, interviewed by Kadiev and Kyser.

63. J. Pommer Collection.

64. Manfred Behn, "Krieg der Propagandisten," *Ufa-Buch*, 29. See also Curt Riess who claims that Ludwig Klitzsch allegedly tried to win Pommer for his DLG, in *Das gab's nur einmal: Die große Zeit des deutschen Films* (Frankfurt/Main, Berlin and Vienna: Ullstein, 1985), vol. 1, 109.

65. The full company name is "Soarele Societta in numen collectiv Beldiman & Co. Bukarest Strada Pictor Grigorescu 7." Letter from E. Pommer to Dr. Theophil Michailovici, 11 February 1919. Ufa file, R109I, Bundesarchiv Koblenz, Germany.

the involvement of the German military. The military nature of Pommer's assignment in Romania would seem to preclude private ownership. It is more likely that Pommer took it upon himself to save the company in the face of mounting hostility toward the occupying Germans, by arranging a fictitious sale to a Romanian citizen.[66] The correspondence between Pommer and his appointed trustee of Soarele reflects the enormous difficulties that arose through repeated and vindictive political pursuit of Soarele following the retreat of the German troops from Romania. German film distribution came to a halt, exhibition in Soarele's own and rented movie theaters was prohibited, and the company's films were confiscated. Soarele was black-listed and business came to a standstill.[67]

Pommer's success in Romania backfired. Since the exhibition and distribution of German films ran smoothly, especially in Bucharest, Pommer's company was pursued more heavily than others that had also been founded and managed with German funds:

> This pursuit was especially aimed at Soarele because it was not only considered an economic enterprise of the Germans, but – to a much larger extent – a political organ. All film theater owners in competition [with Soarele] applied any available method to be reimbursed for the fact that they were hindered, and in part ruined, by Pommer's company. Reports were sent to the Romanian Ministry of War that Pommer had been involved in political propaganda and that he had been an organ of the political Department of the Military in order to assure the effectiveness of his propaganda via film. Furthermore, these statements alleged he had proceeded without scruples against all those affiliated with film and film theaters he considered a German enemy. The financial strength of Soarele was merely a further incitement to take retaliatory action for all economic damages, even in those cases where Pommer had not been responsible.[68]

Notwithstanding the complexity of the company ownership issue, the correspondence between Pommer and the Soarele trustee leaves no doubt that Pommer retained tight financial control over

66. Jacobsen, *Erich Pommer*, 20.
67. Letter from Michailovici to Pommer, 5 February 1919. Ufa file.
68. Letter from Michailovici to Ufa, 25 August 1919. Michailovici claimed to have purchased Soarele from Pommer, together with two other businessmen, Walter Prager and Victor A. Beldiman. Fearing persecution for their association with Germans, Michailovici's associates deserted the company and fled the country when Romanian troops arrived. Ufa file.

Soarele. In May 1919, Ufa enlisted his judgment for determining the validity of claims brought by various businessmen purporting to own the company.[69] In May 1922, with Pommer already at Ufa, Ufa transferred all Soarele rights to a private businessman.

Pommer's involvement in Gaumont, Eclair, Bufa, and Balkan-Orient-Film/Soarele laid the groundwork for his career as company head, export specialist, film politician, and producer. His first decade in the film business was characterized by international coexistence and competition, with domestic and international politics at center stage, in peace- and wartime alike. His early experiences should have prepared him for life-long battles in which national film industries, the government, the military, and local and world politics would continue to return as principal players. Undaunted by wartime intrigues, Pommer transferred his market strategies to peacetime Berlin, where his influence and power continued to grow. His assignment in Romania had given Pommer the opportunity for early contacts with the newly founded Ufa company in Berlin, thereby preparing the path for his future career.

69. Letter from Universum-Film-Aktiengesellschaft [Ufa] to E. Pommer, 30 May 1919. Ufa file.

Chapter 2

BERLIN: POMMER'S DECLA

> The German film industry advances with clock-like prompt-
> ness in a direction that we have already outlined in these
> pages when discussing the genesis of "Ufa." The greater the
> financial power gained by the film industry worldwide, and
> the wider the interest taken in film by society and financiers,
> the more each national industry will strive toward large-scale
> consolidation of enterprises.
>
> "Decla-Bioscop," *Lichtbild-Bühne*, 7 February 1920

Looking Beyond Germany

When Pommer returned home to take command of Decla in Berlin,
he was just barely a producer, but an experienced film businessman with insight into the industry's international implications.
His top priority was Decla's adjustment to postwar market conditions. For a while peacetime gave Germany's film enterprises a
virtual monopoly over the domestic market. This war-induced isolation was soon challenged from outside, this time from the United
States rather than France. As *Filmfabrikant* at the helm of his company, be it as policy maker or head of production,[1] he was soon
forced to focus on the international market. While the international

1. The reported dates when Pommer was in charge of production at Decla differ.
Decla's set designer Hermann Warm maintains that Pommer was Decla's production
head until mid-1919 when actor/director Rudolf Meinert took over. Pommer
resumed this function again in the fall of 1920. See Hermann Warm, "Gegen die

companies coexisting in Berlin before the war had not engaged in overt national chauvinism, postwar competition between German and American companies was at times hostile. German companies saw the opening of Germany's borders to companies abroad with great apprehension. Aggressive business strategies became the defensive mode involving all branches of the industry from production to distribution and exhibition. The consolidation of smaller companies into powerful business combines (*Konzerne*) affected Decla as it did the entire German film industry. On the production level, formulas and strategies most conducive to export, and concepts such as "national" and "international" film, had to be defined. On the distribution and exhibition levels, import issues, which the war years had preempted so effectively and conveniently to the advantage of the German Reich, moved to center stage. These issues provided the testing ground on which Pommer's early experiences in an internationally entwined film industry were to serve him well. He emerged as a prominent industry figure when the confrontation with foreign film industries, especially the Americans, called for action.

Peacetime began in Germany with 145 film companies, producing a total of 1,317 films. Some companies produced no more than two films, and others folded quickly. Production data from mid-1919 reveal the major postwar players: Ufa, in its first full year in business, outshone all others with a total of 269 films, contributing one-fifth of all films shown in Germany that year. But Ufa, of course, was none other than the various companies it had amassed under its umbrella when it was founded in December 1917. Of these, Messter-Film contributed 75 films, Nordisk-Film 76, Oliver-Film 50, and Union-Film 27. Decla was one of five companies outside the Ufa umbrella producing more than 30 films that year; its share was 33, nine more than the previous year.[2] The DLG released 129, Eiko-Film 92, Bufa – in its last year of business – 75, and Bioscop 31.[3] The latter was to merge with Pommer's Decla in the following year.

Caligari-Legenden," *Caligari und Caligarismus* (Berlin: Deutsche Kinemathek, 1970), 11. Meinert was still in charge of production at Decla-Bioscop in October 1920. See *Film-Kurier*, 4 October 1920. According to Decla's press release to *Lichtbild-Bühne* in early December, Pommer succeeded Meinert, who took David Oliver's place in Decla's senior management (*Vorstand*). "Olivers Rücktritt: Die Umgruppierung im Vorstand der Decla-Bioscop," *Lichtbild-Bühne*, 4 December 1920. When Decla-Bioscop merged with Ufa, Meinert resigned from the company. "Rücktritt Rudolf Meinerts: Fusion der Decla-Bioscop mit der Ufa?" *Film-Kurier*, 15 January 1921.

2. "Oliver bei Decla," *Lichtbild-Bühne*, 31 May 1919.

3. "Die Filmproduktion 1918," *Lichtbild-Bühne*, 7 June 1919.

Events at Decla soon reflected Pommer's expansionist policies, and the trade press clearly saw Decla as the emerging leader in the industry, attributing this success to Pommer's "very skillful and goal-oriented leadership."[4] Decla acquired large movie theaters through its newly established theater company, the Decla-Licht-spiel-GmbH, and accumulated more theaters, studio facilities, and distribution channels through mergers with other companies.[5] A particularly newsworthy example was Decla's acquisition of the Circus Schumann in Frankfurt/Main in 1920; converted into a movie theater, it was able to seat 5,000.[6] Clearly Decla was following the growth path demonstrated by Ufa a few years before. But whereas Ufa's amassing of power in 1917 was primarily motivated by wartime propaganda, peacetime expansion was governed by business principles aimed exclusively at competition, prestige, and, ultimately, profit.

In 1919 Decla merged with two companies, Meinert-Film and Oliver-Film, after the latter freed itself from the Ufa umbrella. Both company heads, Rudolf Meinert and David Oliver, became Pommer's coexecutives. Meinert brought his well-known artistic and financial expertise to Decla,[7] and Oliver added international business acumen acquired as the German representative of the Danish company Nordisk. Oliver's move from Ufa to the much smaller

4. "Oliver bei Decla," *Lichtbild-Bühne*, 31 May 1919.

5. The postwar period was marked by accumulations of large movie theaters despite the fact that a wartime government decree of 15 January 1918 prohibited the erection of luxury buildings. See *Lichtbild-Bühne*, 11 October 1919. Nevertheless, Ufa relinquished smaller theaters in order to concentrate exclusively on larger buildings. See *Lichtbild-Bühne*, 1 March 1919. Decla organized its theater acquisition by forming a separate company in August 1919, the Decla-Lichtspiel-GmbH, with a capital of 20,000 marks. See *Lichtbild-Bühne*, 23 and 30 August 1919. For other Decla theater acquisitions see, among others, "Weitere Theatergründungen der 'Decla'," *Lichtbild-Bühne*, 14 June 1919; "Die 'Decla' Lichtspiele," *Lichtbild-Bühne*, 4 October 1919; and "Der ständig wachsende Theaterbesitz der 'Decla'," *Lichtbild-Bühne*, 8 November 1919. These real estate transactions continued to take place despite a debate in the Prussian State Assembly (*Landesversammlung*) that had, in the summer of 1919, upheld the prohibition of using construction material for luxury buildings, under which movie theaters fell. The absence of penalty reinforcement in the past was no doubt due to the recognition that movie theaters were the only places where people could keep warm in winter. See *Lichtbild-Bühne*, 11 October 1919.

6. "Das Frankfurter Riesen-Kino – ein Weltrekord: Das Theater der Fünftausend," *Film-Kurier*, 9 July 1920. See also Paul Monaco, *Cinema and Society: France and Germany During the Twenties* (New York, Oxford, and Amsterdam: Elsevier, 1976), 21; and Kayser, "Deutsche Filmindustrie," 74.

7. "Fusion Decla-Meinert," *Lichtbild-Bühne*, 29 November 1919.

Decla was, judging from press coverage, not considered a step backward but an advantageous association with a company that "possesses an excellent pool of first-rate films, top-notch production facilities, and the best basis for growth and expansion."[8] In addition, Oliver's entry amounted to a substantial concentration of capital for Decla and led to the reorganization of the company.[9]

Not surprisingly, such developments at Decla provoked the suspicion of the trade press. But criticism of unwise business strategies was laid to rest with the conviction that "*Direktor* Pommer is known as a cautious and reserved businessman who would not engage in excessive expansion politics without a sufficient financial basis."[10] Several business agreements in the city of Hamburg followed, one with the Hagenbeck Zoo and another with the Ethnographical Museum founded by Heinrich Umlauff, a relative of the Hagenbeck family. Both were invaluable resources for production, as the vast zoo terrain offered immense possibilities for outdoor shooting, while the museum made its collection available for historical settings.[11]

Bioscop, Decla's future partner, pursued equally aggressive expansion strategies. While Decla expanded into Hamburg, Bioscop merged with the company of producer/director Richard Oswald, who brought in a capital of 30 million marks.[12] With its excellent distribution system and a vast theater circuit (*Theaterpark*) Bioscop would have been comparable to Ufa, were it not for its weaknesses in production, as *Lichtbild-Bühne* was quick to point out:

> The potential for marketing foreign films is guaranteed through a large chain of theaters. This will also provide support for production, which is scheduled to be enlarged. It is important how well the new company will succeed in obtaining first-rate films of quality for its distribution system. Ufa and Decla represent a strong market share of quality products. There will be a heated battle over whatever percentage is left.[13]

8. "Oliver bei Decla," *Lichtbild-Bühne*, 31 May 1919.

9. "Kommanditgesellschaft Decla," *Film-Kurier*, 30 September 1919.

10. "Der Decla-Konzern: Commandit-Gesellschaft [*sic*] mit 15 Millionen Kapital," *Lichtbild-Bühne*, 27 September 1919.

11. "Die Expansion der 'Decla'," *Lichtbild-Bühne*, 11 October 1919. See also Lotte H. Eisner, *Fritz Lang* (New York: Da Capo Paperback, 1986), 33. The resources available through Umlauff facilitated the authentic costumes and exotic sets in Lang's *Harakiri* and *Die Spinnen* (*The Spiders*), and Otto Rippert's *Die Pest in Florenz* (*The Plague in Florence*), all of which were produced in 1919.

12. "Ein neuer 30-Millionen-Konzern! Bioscop-AG.– Oswald," *Lichtbild-Bühne*, 1 November 1919.

13. "Ein neuer 30-Millionen-Konzern!" *Lichtbild-Bühne*, 1 November 1919.

The two smaller companies, Decla and Bioscop, could hardly have won this battle single-handedly, but they would complement each other well should they join forces. Decla was strong in production but lacked Bioscop's strength in distribution and exhibition. Despite Decla's business strides, there were still shortcomings. As Pommer admitted openly, the company

> obviously suffered from the absence of key theaters capable of propagating these kinds of quality films in appropriate and necessary fashion. It also lacked a modern, technically well equipped studio. The Decla studios in Weißensee, which were being used till now, had become too small and outdated.[14]

By merging with Bioscop, Decla would obtain access to Bioscop's forty movie theaters and its gigantic new studio facilities in Berlin-Neubabelsberg, which had been modernized as much as postwar conditions would allow.[15] But Decla still had one crucial advantage over Bioscop, and this was its company head Pommer. When the trade press speculated on Bioscop's new chances in the German film industry, it put its finger precisely on Bioscop's lack of leadership:

> In the final analysis, the decisive factor depends on who is in charge of business politics at the new company. A gigantic, complex enterprise is not the same as an enterprise which consists of a factory [Fabrik] and distribution alone. A gigantic business of these dimensions demands a generous disposition, a quick decision making capacity, and an almost super-human farsightedness undaunted by the unclear situation of our industry. If the new company has men at its disposal who see the world market clearly and who know how to combine domestic considerations and foreign calculations, it will prosper.[16]

In short, Bioscop needed Pommer. In April 1920 Decla and Bioscop merged.[17] Richard Oswald pulled his company out of this newly formed *Konzern* and resumed film production on his own.[18]

---

14. Pommer, Eibel-Manuscript.

15. Alfred Kallmann, *Die Konzernierung in der Filmindustrie, erläutert an den Film-industrien Deutschlands und Amerikas*, Ph.D. diss., Univ. Jena, 1932 (Würzburg: Triltsch, 1932), 21. See also Pommer, Eibel-Manuscript.

16. "Ein neuer 30-Millionen-Konzern!" *Lichtbild-Bühne*, 1 November 1919.

17. This date differs from that in *Lichtbild-Bühne* by one month. It is taken from a report, titled *Gründungsdaten*, n.d., which contains Decla/Decla-Bioscop foundation dates from 1918 to 1925. Ufa file, R109I, Bundesarchiv Koblenz, Germany. Traub lists the merger date as 29 April 1920. See Traub, *Ufa*, 56.

18. "Richard Oswald vor neuen Aufgaben," *Lichtbild-Bühne*, 3 April 1920.

The press dismissed his departure as irrelevant for Decla's success, which it saw in the efficient management by film experts (*Nur-Fachleute*).[19] If experts were Decla's forte, they were apparently absent from Bioscop, which was allegedly forced to consolidate because of lack of management, discipline, and competence. Pommer took no risks when reorganizing the new company. As seen by the press, "[t]he former [Bioscop] company leadership resigns; almost all their positions will be occupied by Decla representatives, especially by the gentlemen Oliver, E. Pommer, Meinert, Baruch, [and] Saklikower."[20] Commenting on Decla's foreign distribution department (*Auslandsabteilung*), *Lichtbild-Bühne* reported: "It goes without saying that an experienced and competent expert belongs at the top of foreign distribution. This position is, quite fortunately, taken by Erich Pommer."[21] In the final analysis, Pommer's company, though merged with Bioscop, remained Decla.[22] The capital then available to Decla-Bioscop was estimated at 50 million marks.[23]

Decla had taken such organizational strides that Pommer felt compelled to defend his expansion policy publicly. He turned to the weekly journal *Das Tage-Buch* to explain "the significance of *Konzerne* in the film industry" as a necessary safeguard for the entire German cinema and not for the promotion of one single entrepreneur. For the same reason, he explained, he eschewed competition with other German companies in favor of a solid front against foreign competition. Without a strong and united German film industry, he argued, foreign market domination of Germany would be easy. He felt that the massive accumulation of capital in the hands of a few privileged film enterprises or, if need be, one single company, was the most effective way to protect Germany's interests:

19. "Der Decla-Bioscop-Konzern," *Lichtbild-Bühne*, 27 March 1920. The journal proclaims only David Oliver and Erich Pommer as experts (*Nur-Fachleute*).

20. "Decla-Bioscop-Konzern," *Lichtbild-Bühne*, 27 March 1920. For more data concerning the two companies' new business organization, see also "Decla-Bioscop," *Film-Kurier*, 4 April 1920.

21. "Decla-Bioscop-Konzern," *Lichtbild-Bühne*, 27 March 1920.

22. It is not uncommon to find references to Bioscop as the "future Decla," as in Asta Nielsen's recollection of her early association with Bioscop. See Renate Seydel and Allan Hagedorff, eds., *Asta Nielsen: Ihr Leben in Fotodokumenten, Selbstzeugnissen und zeitgenössischen Betrachtungen* (Munich: Universitas, 1981), 38. Fritz Lang, for instance, forgets about Bioscop altogether and speaks of the merger of Decla with Ufa in 1921, in *Fritz Lang: Choix de textes établi par Alfred Eibel* (Paris: Présence du Cinéma, 1964), 11.

23. "Decla-Bioscop-Konzern," *Lichtbild-Bühne*, 27 March 1920.

Without the concentration of German capital, foreign countries would be in a position to arbitrarily govern the entire German film industry. They would be able to flood us with their own products and make our competition impossible. Only farseeing policies have enabled the large German companies today to have a decisive voice in all these issues and to exert pressure on the foreign countries. This should not be underestimated. These countries now face a situation that differs entirely from prewar times. They are now forced to take Germany into account, a consideration they would never have imagined, were it not for Germany's large companies. If the German film industry today would still consist of only small individual companies, England, America, France, and Italy would, by virtue of their strength, erase these small splinter groups in the German economy … If benevolent, they would purchase the most valuable ones. But in any case, they would force them under their control.[24]

Thus, when Decla-Bioscop resumed transactions in the Balkans, this move toward the east was simply welcomed and justified in the press as "recapturing lost territory."[25] It was an entirely different matter, of course, when foreign nations seeking business in Germany put forth similar claims.

The cinema's short history of a quarter century showed that peacetime tended to create international battlefields for national film industries while wartime produced conditions of relative domestic stability and growth. Inevitably, Germany became an attractive target for international, especially American, film companies. Under the headline, "German-American Film War," the political weekly journal *Die Weltbühne* astutely proclaimed that the "German-American peace has been declared and the German-American film war has begun."[26] Echoing the prewar entanglement in Germany of French, Danish, Italian, and American film companies, Germany's postwar film industry again erupted in an international "battle," but a much fiercer one than before.

The trade journals reported this economic tug of war in the strongest military language and metaphor. Articles ranged from Germany's paranoia of drowning in foreign films to self-aggrandizing visions of posing a threat to other countries. Headlines, most blatantly those in *Lichtbild-Bühne, Film-Kurier, Tage-Buch,* and

24. Pommer, "Bedeutung der Konzerne in der Filmindustrie," *Das Tage-Buch,* 11 September 1920.

25. "Der Vormarsch des deutschen Films: Decla-Bioscop und National-Film im Baltikum," *Lichtbild-Bühne,* 17 July 1920.

26. Hans Siemsen, "Deutsch-amerikanischer Filmkrieg," *Die Weltbühne,* 1 September 1921.

Weltbühne, were a vivid reflection of this battle. Slogans like "the danger of the foreign film," "the American danger for the film industry," "an assault on the German film industry," "German-American film war," "crisis in the film industry," "fight for the cinema," "fear of the German film," and "beware of the Germans" were the daily menu. The American film industry loomed with financial prowess Germany could only dream of, making domestic strategies for protecting the home market that much more crucial.

The debates reached their peak in the spring of 1920 when the wartime import restrictions of 1916 and 1917 were revived and tightened with greater penalties for import offenders.[27] Not surprisingly, the debate divided the German film industry into import friends and enemies. The most powerful companies with large theater chains and international affiliations – Ufa, Decla, and Bioscop – could not afford to ban foreign imports entirely, while the smaller companies defended a strictly protectionist stance and opposed imports completely. Businessmen like Pommer, with a strong position regarding international exchange, were criticized sharply for advocating even modest import. In an open debate initiated by the trade journal *Film-Kurier*, Pommer took his stance alongside Ufa chief executives (*Generaldirektoren*) Carl Bratz and Paul Davidson.[28] Not surprisingly, Ufa was in favor of "sensible" import regulations, a quota system that kept government interference to a minimum. Clearly stated by chief executive Carl Bratz, Ufa's policy was based on the premise that "film business was international business." Whoever wanted to export German films, Bratz argued, had "to make friends with the thought that foreign countries want to export their films into Germany."[29]

German market conditions were, as Pommer pointed out, still suffering from conditions induced by the war; the loss of former market opportunities in neighboring countries to the east was as devastating as low customs rates and the lack of import restrictions. While the missing Eastern European markets forced Germany to depend for distribution entirely on the domestic and Austrian markets, misguided import regulations opened the gates

27. See reports in *Film-Kurier*, 27, 30, and 31 January; 1 February; and 4. April 1920.
28. See "Generaldirektor Davidsohn [*sic*] über die aktuellen Fragen in der Filmbranche," *Film-Kurier*, 4 June 1920; "Generaldirektor Davidson über die Lösung der Filmeinfuhrfrage," *Film-Kurier*, 17 December 1920; Carl Bratz, "Zur Einfuhr von Auslandsfilmen, *Lichtbild-Bühne*, 28 February 1920; and "Generaldirektor Bratz über den Filmaustausch: Für die kontingierte Filmeinfuhr," *Film-Kurier*, 1 September 1920.
29. Carl Bratz, "Zur Einfuhr von Auslandsfilmen," *Lichtbild-Bühne*, 28 February 1920.

to an American film flood, posing a catastrophe for German film production. Contrary to other German *Filmfabrikanten*, he did not feel threatened by the quality of American films whose theme and content, he felt, would only disappoint German moviegoers.[30]

Pommer actively participated in import and export politics on several levels. Immediately after the war he represented Decla in the Association of German *Filmfabrikanten*. When this group reorganized in 1919 to form a liaison between the public and the legislative body of the government, Pommer was elected one of its chairmen.[31] He also had a decisive voice in import and export issues as member of the Export Commission of the German film industry (*Exportverband*). In August 1920, Pommer and leading Commission members fought a heated debate at Decla, now Decla-Bioscop, wherein Pommer urged members to guard the interests of the *Filmfabrikanten*. He argued that decisions of the Export Commission must neither remove national boundaries nor allow unlimited imports, while a quota to restrict import would be in the interest of the entire German film industry. Narrow-minded protectionism, he warned, would lead to sacrifices in industry labor and wages.[32] In 1920 he represented the *Exportverband* on the newly formed Außenhandelsstelle, an agency of the government's Ministry of Economics, representing the film manufacturers, trade associations, and unions of the German film industry in import and export issues.[33]

Inevitably, Pommer created enemies, a pattern that accompanied him throughout his career. As German film industry spokesman he was held accountable for import constrictions by France, an ironic turn of events given Pommer's early training in French companies, and especially his personal and professional affiliations with Eclair. Following a press conference in Paris after the premiere of Decla's film *Der müde Tod* (*Destiny*, released in France under the title *Les trois lumières*) at the Madeleine theater in 1922, Pommer reported the event with understandable frustration:

> The conversation soon revolves exclusively around German-French film relations. I find myself heavily bombarded with questions and reproaches. I am blamed for German import laws that are interpreted as specifically aiming at the French film industry. There is the

30. Pommer, "Was deutsche Fachleute sagen," *Film-Kurier*, 10 June 1919.
31."Zusammenschluß der Filmfabrikanten," *Lichtbild-Bühne*, 1 November 1919.
32. Fredrik, "Der Kampf um die Filmeinfuhr: Die Sitzung im Decla-Bioscophaus," *Film-Kurier*, 24 August 1920.
33. "Die Gründung der Außenhandelsstelle," *Lichtbild-Bühne*, 4 September 1920.

complaint that not one French film has been shown to Berlin audiences whereas German films are welcome in France ... I can only explain with difficulty to the French that all these measures were the result of the Versailles Peace Treaty, necessitating import restrictions to protect the domestic industry in the postwar transition period.[34]

Despite Pommer's ensuing efforts to influence the legislative body toward liberal import regulations, he saw such regulations as mandatory safeguards for a domestic film market that might otherwise be flooded by inferior foreign films.

The multiple expansion moves involving Germany's film companies seem to reflect an apparent degree of freedom and control for CEOs of large companies. But increasing capital investment in the German film industry came with strings attached. The rapid consolidations of large German companies in the 1920s were not necessarily instigated by the companies and *Konzerne*. The large banks, protective of their film industry investment, especially the Deutsche Bank, exerted substantial pressure toward consolidation. The most blatant example involved Pommer himself. In early 1921 Decla-Bioscop and National-Film were planning consolidation to alleviate Decla-Bioscop's debts. The banks with investments in Pommer's company insisted on a merger with Ufa, despite heavy bidding by National-Film.[35] Fortunately this was also Ufa's strategy, aiming at Decla-Bioscop because of its substantial real estate assets, especially the studios in Neubabelsberg, the core of the later "Ufa city." While Decla-Bioscop favored National-Film, financial dictates forced it to merge with Ufa.

The Deutsche Bank was especially influential. Its president, Emil Georg von Stauß, was chairman of Ufa's board of directors (*Aufsichtsrat*) during the silent film years. His keen interest in the cinema, combined with commendable leadership power, made him a crucial force in film throughout the Weimar era. In his study of Ufa, Jan-Christopher Horak concluded that it was precisely Stauß's "power of persuasion" that "changed the course of film history":

> Prior to the founding of Ufa, no German film company had ever been able to contest the power of the Americans and the French on the international market. [Carl] Bratz and von Stauss were convinced that a German firm with a strong capital base and pecuniary support from respectable banking institutions could successfully

34. Pommer, "Internationale Film-Verständigung," *Das Tage-Buch*, 15 July 1922.
35. Kallmann, *Konzernierung in der Filmindustrie*, 18. See also *Gründungsdaten*, Decla-Bioscop business report.

meet the standards of production set by the majors. Since the German cinema was still protected from foreign competition by a film import ban, they felt the Ufa would be able to develop initially without serious threat... The time seemed auspicious for transferring assets to an industry not subject to confiscation or cut backs in production once the war was over. But, it was von Stauss's track record on the international business market that probably induced the gentleman of high finance to invest in the scheme.[36]

Prominent German production executives like Pommer could not generate monetary investment strong enough to measure up to bank-empowered partners. Rather, Pommer's strength manifested itself internally, in brilliant leadership of his company's creative teams, which he guided through artistic challenges and to international recognition. In the creative domain, banks deferred to the expertise of Ufa's senior management, whose ranks Pommer soon joined. As Horak contends, "as a result the filmmakers at Ufa would enjoy unprecedented artistic control coupled with almost unlimited financial resources."[37]

German Film Art

Film historians tend to dismiss as inferior much of what was produced in Germany before 1919, the production year of such "masterworks" as *Das Kabinett des Dr. Caligari* (*The Cabinet of Dr. Caligari*) at Decla, and *Madame Dubarry* (*Passion*) at Ufa's Union-Film. Earlier indications of an evolving, specifically German film style are often dismissed as exceptions to the rule. Film historian Lotte H. Eisner falls into the same trap. In *The Haunted Screen*, her seminal work on Germany's silent cinema, she states that *Caligari* "was hardly the first film of value ... made in Germany," but then sees *Caligari*'s precursors merely as exceptions.[38] Exceptions or not, these films were nonetheless significant, as film scholar Kristin Thompson finds. They reveal "generic and stylistic developments of the 1910s [which] prepared the way for Expressionism, and *Caligari*, however great its stylistic challenges were, did not appear in a vacuum."[39] *Der Student von Prag* (*The Student of Prague*), directed

36. Horak, "Ernst Lubitsch and the Rise of Ufa," 34–35.

37. Ibid., 79.

38. Eisner, *The Haunted Screen*, 39.

39. Kristin Thompson, "Im Anfang war ... : Some Links Between German Fantasy Films of the Teens and the Twenties," in *Before Caligari: German Cinema,*

in 1913 by Stellan Rye, and Henrik Galeen's *Der Golem* (*The Golem*) in 1914, both produced at Bioscop with stage actor Paul Wegener from the theater of Max Reinhardt, are shining examples of early German film art. Thompson sees them as "background: a set of films which contain stylistic and generic conventions against which we can better understand those of the later set of films."[40] But on the whole, film historian Jerzy Toeplitz is not alone in maintaining that "the majority of [early] German films were imitations of what was fashionable and trendy in foreign films and rather colorless."[41] Apparently German film studios were not concerned about developing a "specifically German film" immediately after the war. But imitations made sense considering the gaiety and charm of the French films to which German moviegoers had grown accustomed in prewar times. As Eisner points out:

> The screens of the German cinema were swamped by the melodramas of Max Mack, Joe May, and Rudolf Meinert, and by simplistic comedies such as those of Bolten-Beckers [*sic*]. Joe May and Rudolf Meinert were later to direct adventure films, but for anything to approach the charm of the films of Louis Feuillade one has to wait until Fritz Lang's *Die Spinnen* [*The Spiders*] (1919).[42]

Given this background it is not surprising that most of the films Decla produced in its first years in business differed little from other mass produced entertainment movies in Germany. Whether production was in Pommer's hands in the immediate postwar years or in Rudolf Meinert's is difficult to ascertain. During Pommer's military service, early Decla film directors like Carl Wilhelm, Alwin Neuß, and Otto Rippert apparently enjoyed a rather privileged role at the company.[43] This was especially the case with Neuß, a former stage actor turned director, long familiar with the film business and under contract with Decla since 1915.[44] His

---

1895–1920 (Edizioni Biblioteca dell'Immagine, 1990), 154. Anyone having attended the German Silent Film Festival in Pordenone, Italy, in the fall of 1990 can attest to the surprising number of quality films produced, though seldom seen and discussed, in Germany before 1919.

40. Thompson, "Im Anfang war ... , *Before Caligari*, 158.

41. Jerzy Toeplitz, *Geschichte des Films* (Munich: Rogner & Bernhard, 1975), 137.

42. Eisner, *Haunted Screen*, 7.

43. See "Einiges aus der kommenden Filmproduktion," *Film-Kurier*, supplement, 26 March 1921.

44. See data on Alwin Neuß in Hans-Michael Bock, ed., *CineGraph* (Munich: edition text + kritik, n.d.).

widespread audience popularity ensured him a degree of company influence, which allowed him to choose film topics and probably also to direct most of the films in which he starred.[45] Eisner singles out Decla's *The Spiders* as the first film to depart from production as usual, and it is tempting to attribute the film's success not to Pommer's hand in production, but to Fritz Lang's own coming of age as film director in 1919, following his rocky start at Decla.

Lang's discouraging beginning did not seem to unsettle his discoverer Pommer, who was rarely disappointed by his intuitive hiring practices. When he hired Lang, an actor with a background in painting and architecture, in Vienna, Pommer liked the intensity of Lang's ideas although he found them "still somewhat 'uncooked' and not always realizable on a practical level."[46] Lang seemed to suffer from a newcomer's "tedious process" of establishing himself in the field, writing scripts that either never became films or were handed to the more experienced directors Alwin Neuß or Otto Rippert.[47] His chance to direct and to use his own script came in 1919 with *Halbblut* (*The Half-Caste*), a film in Decla's star series (featuring Decla female star Ressel Orla). *Die Spinnen* became his road to success at Decla.

By this time Decla's production program proudly featured several popular genres: Decla *Exclusiv* films, a world class series, a woman's series, an adventure series, and a star series, with a masterworks series to follow shortly. Pommer felt that his company "had succeeded, through careful selection of directors, writers, and other artistic and technical collaborators, in establishing an innovative and interesting production base."[48] Film reviews in the press indicated recognizable qualities, particularly more skillful technical production values, as the trademark of Decla. After the 1919 premiere of Decla's *Die Pest in Florenz* (*The Plague in Florence*), directed by Otto Rippert and based on a script by Fritz Lang, reviews focused on its international chances, specifically in the United States.[49] After Lang's *Harakiri*, a *Madame Butterfly* adaptation, premiered successfully in Berlin's Marmorhaus in late 1920,

45. Reinhold Keiner, *Thea von Harbou und der deutsche Film bis 1933*, Ph.D. diss., Univ. Marburg/Lahn, 1983, Studien zur Filmgeschichte 2 (Hildesheim, Zurich, and New York: Georg Olms Verlag, 1984), 61.

46. Pommer, Eibel-Manuscript.

47. Ibid.

48. Ibid.

49. See "Von der Decla," *Lichtbild-Bühne*, 5 April 1919; *Neue Berliner 12 Uhr-Zeitung*, 24 October 1919; and *B. Z. am Mittag*, 24 October 1919, as quoted in *Lichtbild-Bühne*, 8 November 1919.

Lichtbild-Bühne hailed the film as "a weapon worthy to be engaged in a battle against foreign countries":

> It becomes increasingly clear that our film industry does not only strive to appear on the world market, but has also found means and methods to produce films that do not have to fear foreign competition. Financiers and artists are united in the goal to ennoble filmmaking and to produce value and effect creatively.[50]

Such inflated press coverage of German achievements was customary in the immediate postwar years and, as Eisner points out, typical of a nation recovering from defeat. There is no evidence to suggest that Pommer specifically intended *The Spiders* for the international market or that, at the time, he considered Lang to be particularly suitable to direct a film of such scope. The project, initially planned in four parts, was not featured in Decla's world class series, but was part of its adventure series.[51] However, the trade press proclaimed its first part, *Der goldene See* (*The Golden Lake*), to be the beginning of Decla's strategic move toward export, and one critic cited the film as evidence that "the German film industry is well on its way to producing works that will elicit other countries' interest."[52] Another German critic called it an American film in German dress, taking it as proof that German film companies were successfully "Germanizing" the so-called adventure film that was apparently the staple of American film production. Decla's investment in the association with the Hagenbeck Zoo was paying off.[53]

Though these films gave Fritz Lang's future directing career a promising boost, his commitment to the series' second part prevented him from accepting Pommer's offer to direct *The Cabinet of Dr. Caligari*. Instead, he temporarily left Decla after completion of *Das Brillantenschiff* (*The Diamond Ship*), the second part of *The Spiders*, to join Joe May's company, a move allegedly triggered either by disagreements over the use of his scripts at Decla or possibly by a shortage of funds.[54] Whatever Lang's reasons for leaving Decla,

50. "Bemerkenswerte Filme," *Lichtbild-Bühne*, 27 December 1919.

51. Decla produced the first two parts, *Der goldene See* and *Das Brillantenschiff* (former title: *Das Sklavenschiff / Slave Ship*). Parts three and four, *Das Geheimnis der Sphinx* (*The Secret of the Sphinx*) and *Um Asiens Krone* (*For Asia's Imperial Crown*), were not produced.

52. Keiner, *Thea von Harbou*, 65.

53. "Die Uraufführungen der Woche: Die Sensation: 'Der goldene See'," *Film-Kurier*, 5 October 1919.

54. Film review in *Der Film* 7 (1920), quoted in Eisner, *Fritz Lang*, 34.

they took their toll on *The Diamond Ship*, which turned out to be a disappointing film. In 1919, financial problems certainly played a part at Decla and were, ironically, in part responsible for the production of Germany's most astonishing silent film, *Das Kabinett des Dr. Caligari*.

In the case of *Caligari*, speculations over what an individual producer does or does not contribute to a specific film have taken on legendary proportions. It is the key film in Pommer's early career as well as in Decla's young history and in that of the German silent cinema. The film reflects the multiple forces and conditions at work in Weimar culture in 1918/19, primarily the cinema's intersection with the other arts, and the implications such a marriage promised for the domestic and international marketability of films. Since *Caligari* excelled both artistically and commercially, at home and abroad, film historians have refuted earlier claims that its production was purely accidental. There have been repeated attempts to reconstruct the circumstances and conditions of its production, hoping to single out the individual contributions of those involved. Decla's films before *Caligari* certainly bear no resemblance to *Caligari*, thematically or in aesthetic considerations.

Like Pommer himself, this film is surrounded by numerous legends, all of which have become tightly intertwined. There is no doubt that *Caligari* officially gave birth to "cinematic expressionism" although expressionist elements had been visible in earlier films. However, as Lotte H. Eisner reminds us, arguing with hindsight: "The word 'Expressionist' is commonly applied to every German film of the so-called 'classical' period. But it is surely not necessary to insist yet again that certain chiaroscuro effects, so often thought Expressionist existed long before *Caligari* . . ."[55] The expressionism of *Caligari* far surpasses what Eisner calls chiaroscuro effects, a term she borrows from art history and then applies to the display of light and shadow (*Helldunkel*) she associates with early German films. In fact, film scholars today still puzzle over why such a confluence of expressionist elements came together successfully in *Caligari* while other films produced earlier merely contained singular expressionist elements, and later films were mere imitations.

Caligari's multiple expressionist strands were borrowed and adapted from the other arts flourishing in Weimar culture immediately after the war, thematically and stylistically from literature,

---

55. Eisner, *Haunted Screen*, 39.

especially the theater, and visually from architecture and painting. In painting, the term was first used for works appearing in Paris between 1907 and 1909, exhibited in Berlin in 1911. Initially, all artists who were reaching beyond impressionism and realism, no matter how divergent, were labeled expressionists until the term was narrowed to embrace those who expressed their emotions drastically through the distortion of visible reality. Since these feelings reflected deep-rooted inner states, like unrest, despair, and angst, often paired with accusation, rebellion, and social protest, their art is the external representation of an internal reality and, by necessity, dark and brooding.[56] In short, to use Eisner's terminology, "the Expressionist does not see, he has 'visions.'"[57] When *Caligari* was conceptualized, the First World War had just ended. The war's impact on artists was devastating, producing works that reflected disillusionment, hopelessness, and terror. In fact, "expressionism seems particularly to have been associated with madness in Germany, not least by the artists themselves."[58] Presenting *Caligari*'s mad protagonist against a backdrop of painted distorted shapes proved an ingenious blend of theme and style and clearly demonstrated why expressionism did not work in films where this blend was absent.

Caligari's growing historical importance also increased film historians' curiosity about the film's genesis. Such unconventional production, they felt, must have been initiated by specific members of the production team, whether the scriptwriters, Carl Mayer and Hans Janowitz; the set designers, Walter Reimann, Walter Röhrig, and Hermann Warm; film director Robert Wiene; production head Rudolf Meinert; or company head Pommer. At production time Pommer saw himself merely as coparticipant, crediting Robert Wiene with the film's "new style" conception.[59] Hermann Warm, in the late twenties no longer one of Pommer's preferred film architects, was more fortunate in outliving all Decla team members and therefore the last to update *Caligari*'s legend.[60] He attributed the films' making solely to production head Meinert, claiming that

56. Joseph-Emile Muller, *Lexikon des Expressionismus* (Cologne: Verlag M. DuMont Schauberg, 1974), 5–6.

57. Eisner, *Haunted Screen*, 10.

58. Mike Budd, ed., *The Cabinet of Dr. Caligari: Texts, Contexts, Histories* (New Brunswick and London: Rutgers Univ. Press, 1990), 54.

59. Pommer, interviewed by Kadiev and Kyser.

60. Letter by J. Pommer to author, 19 October 1986. Barry Salt, in "From German Stage to German Screen," went so far as to call Warm's account a lie. See *Before Caligari*, 402–23.

Meinert succeeded "despite the objections" of Decla executives, evidently including Pommer:

> The daring execution of the film, which Meinert supervised as head of production, should not be kept a secret or be forgotten. . . The scriptwriters Carl Mayer and Hans Janowitz have never participated in preproduction work or been present during shooting, either in the studio or during meetings. Even Erich Pommer was never present during a meeting. My surprise that these men did not show any interest in this film, especially with respect to its unusual and innovative form, was countered by Meinert with the words that this style of realizing the film was not sanctioned by them.[61]

Meinert's authoritative part in the film's production was initially substantiated by *Film-Kurier*. In its full-page coverage it credited the film's execution entirely to Meinert, and the conception to Wiene.[62] However, just five days later in the same journal, the picture had changed:

> Production head Rudolf Meinert of the Decla-Film-Gesellschaft has asked us to announce that the notice in our journal about the third Decla world class film, *Das Cabinet des Dr. Caligari* [sic], does not correspond to the truth. He is not in charge of the artistic supervision of this film, but Robert Wiene, who is working independently in every respect on this extraordinary film; the claim for the artistic execution of this films has to be his alone.[63]

And coscriptwriter Carl Mayer allegedly felt compelled to disclaim artistic responsibility because film director Wiene had completely diverged from Mayer's concept.[64] Pommer simply attributed the film's style to Decla's economic conditions:

> The studio had a very limited quota of power and light, and on the day when we were notified that we had exhausted the month's quota (several days before the end of the month), my three artists brought in a proposition that seemed to me absurd, and even

---

61. Warm, *Caligari und Caligarismus*, 13.

62. "Expressionismus im Film," *Film-Kurier*, 6 January 1920.

63. "Aus dem Glashaus," *Film-Kurier*, 11 January 1920. Rudolf Meinert's name is consistently absent in future *Caligari* coverage in *Film-Kurier*, and praise is showered on Robert Wiene. See in particular two reviews in *Film-Kurier*, 28 and 29 February 1920. Robert Herlth, Decla film architect not involved in *Caligari*, later claimed that the film director was not in favor, but against the film's expressionist mode, which derived exclusively from the set-designers' initiative. See Warm, *Caligari und Caligarismus*, 5.

64. "Autor und Regisseur: Zum Fall Mayer contra Jeßner," *Film-Kurier*, 13 December 1922.

reactionary – "Why not paint lights and shadows on the sets for the *Caligari* film?"[65]

Caligari's success may have triggered a formula that opened Pommer's eyes to expressionist possibilities, or, as he preferred to call them, stylized "art films." *Die Weltbühne*, for instance, claimed in 1922 that German films like *Caligari* and *Madame Dubarry* (*Passion*) were initially produced without catering to international audience tastes, but instead, surprised their makers by their enormous world-wide success.[66] When interviewed by George A. Huaco in 1962, Pommer explained:

> The German film industry made "stylized films" to make money. Let me explain. At the end of World War I the Hollywood industry moved toward world supremacy. The Danes had a film industry. The French had a very active film industry, which suffered an eclipse at the end of the war. Germany was defeated; how could she make films that would compete with the others? It would have been impossible to try and imitate Hollywood or the French. So we tried something new; the Expressionist or stylized films. This was possible because Germany had an overflow of good artists and writers, a strong literary tradition, and a great tradition of theater. This provided a basis of good, trained actors. World War I finished the French industry; the problem for Germany was to try to compete with Hollywood.[67]

While necessary economizing may have been the propelling force for *Caligari*'s expressionist style, this formula was short-lived. *Genuine* (1920), Decla's second expressionist film, again Mayer-scripted and Wiene-directed, showed that film expressionism led nowhere. Decla's decision to avoid future expressionist films may also have been influenced by strong negative reactions to *Caligari* in France. While in Paris in August 1922, Pommer considered it wise to distance himself from expressionism and apologized for exporting *Caligari* to France as Germany's first postwar

65. *The Cabinet of Dr. Caligari: A Film by Robert Wiene, Carl Mayer, and Hans Janowitz*. Classic Film Scripts (New York: Simon and Schuster, 1972), 28.

66. Roland Schacht, "Filmkrise," *Die Weltbühne*, 21 December 1922. Press reports indicate that international press representatives followed the production of *Madame Dubarry* on the set. See B.E. Lüthge, "Die Entente in Tempelhof," *Film-Kurier*, 3 July 1919. The international stir during *Dubarry*'s premiere at the newly opened Ufa Palace in Berlin is described by Pola Negri, *Memoirs of a Star* (Garden City, NY: Doubleday, 1970), 179–83.

67. Pommer, interviewed in 1962 by Huaco, quoted in George A. Huaco, *The Sociology of Film Art* (New York and London: Basic Books, 1965), 35–36.

representative of "film art."[68] Aware that *Caligari*'s and *Genuine*'s "pathological abnormality" were likely to offend French tastes, he claimed that *Caligari*'s export to France took place over his strict opposition. The film did not represent Germany's cinematic art course, he stated, instead, "caligarism" merely came about by accident. He further maintained that Robert Wiene had no intention of creating this artistic style, even though he is thought to be its "father." To Paul de la Borie, journalist for *La Cinématographie Française* and main *Caligari* opponent, Pommer responded: "No, German art is not to be located here, and caligarism merely constitutes an incident in our production, without significance and without continuance."[69]

On the artistic level, Pommer's role as producer during the Decla and Decla-Bioscop years leaves much room for speculation and interpretation. He was indisputably responsible for choosing the *Caligari* script to be filmed; the fact that scriptwriters Mayer and Janowitz came to Pommer's office unannounced at lunchtime has been reported in several sources. Allegedly Pommer was about to throw them out when something they said caught his interest. The surprise visit then turned into a long meeting that ended with Pommer's on-the-spot purchase of the script, thereby accepting considerable risk. It speaks for his artistic sensibility to have recognized the script's kinship with current cultural trends. Pommer said he decided to acquire it partly because it was bizarre and uncanny, elements prevalent in Weimar cinema: "The mystery and macabre atmosphere of the Grand Guignol was currently in vogue in German films, and this story fitted perfectly."[70]

He also claimed sole responsibility for the film's postproduction care by successfully overturning the film's "initial failure" at the domestic box office through a vigorous advertising campaign:

> There was a big inflation in Germany. We kept our money in foreign currency because the mark was being devalued from day to day. At first *Caligari* was a big box-office flop, but I did not lose money. It cost the equivalent of 18,000 dollars to make *Caligari*, so I could not lose. *Caligari* opened in a Berlin theater, but the audience demonstrated against it and asked for its money back, so after two performances the theater threw it out; and I could not find another theater to show the film. So I forced *Caligari* through a poster and

68. "Nochmals Caligari," *Der Film*, 13 August 1922.

69. Ibid.

70. Pommer, "Carl Mayer's Debut," in *The Cabinet of Dr. Caligari: A Film by Robert Wiene, Carl Mayer. . .*, 28.

publicity campaign. We had very effective, expressionist posters all over Berlin, with Conrad Veidt and the words, "You must see *Caligari*," "Have you seen *Caligari*?" etc. This campaign took six months. Now I approached the original theater and offered 30,000 marks from my own pocket to have them show *Caligari* again. Now the audience had been prepared. The same theater took it and ran it for three months.[71]

This tale of initial failure, though, does not square with eyewitness accounts or reports in *Film-Kurier*. Pommer's advertising campaign story does, but only with respect to preparing the audience *before* the film's initial release. There is no proof of initial audience rejection of the film, but substantial evidence indicating the contrary.

Starting well before the film's premiere in Berlin's Marmorhaus on 26 February 1920, Decla placed sizable advertisements in *Film-Kurier* and *Lichtbild-Bühne*, displaying the film's title and raising reader curiosity by enigmatic invitations to "become Caligari" (*"Du mußt Caligari werden!"*)[72] After four continuous weeks at the Marmorhaus, *Film-Kurier* announced that *Caligari* was held over, due to "hundreds of written requests and inquiries from the audience wanting to see this sensational film over again."[73] On 17 April, the journal announced:

> The Decla Film Company has asked us to announce that the expressionist film *Das Cabinet des Dr. Caligari* [sic] is showing again at the Marmorhaus. The company is unable to respond directly to the countless inquiries regarding schedules and theaters that are showing the film.[74]

And finally, Decla placed an advertisement in *Film-Kurier* announcing *Caligari*'s ninth week and pronouncing the film a "gigantic success."[75]

71. Pommer, interviewed by Huaco, *Sociology of Film Art*, 34. Interestingly, Pommer does not mention the advertising posters' most hypnotic message, *"Du mußt Caligari werden!"* [You must become Caligari!]. All three messages were actually used, as Monaco reported in *Cinema and Society*, 77. Pommer either did not remember or was quoted incorrectly by Huaco from the 1962 interview.

72. Film advertisements of this type in trade journals were customary and ran continuously until the premiere.

73. "Aus dem Glashaus," *Film-Kurier*, 16 April 1920.

74. Ibid., 17 April 1920.

75. *Film-Kurier*, 27 April 1920. See also Walter Kaul's account of *Caligari*'s successful run at the Marmorhaus and other Berlin theaters, in "Bestandsaufnahme 70: Nicht nur expressionistisch und caligaresk," *Caligari und Caligarismus*, 6.

An initial "unsuccessful" *Caligari* premiere must have occurred, as George A. Huaco concluded, in the fall of 1919, a time neatly corresponding to Huaco's hypothesis about the film's historical-political placement. But the film was completed in early February 1920.[76] Pommer's initial failure story, subsequently recorded by film historians, remains a mystery.[77]

Given *Caligari*'s importance in film history, it is not surprising that the surviving participants were interested in the legal rights to the film. According to Mike Budd, both Pommer and Janowitz began "elaborate negotiations through their lawyers" in 1944.[78] Pommer's son remembers that both corresponded with each other but denies that his father intended to pursue his rights in court. Later, after the end of the war, Erich Pommer "fielded numerous inquiries from the lawyers of the Ufa Liquidation Committee (ULC) regarding the rights to many films, including *Caligari*."[79] In the end, Janowitz did not succeed; neither his "extensive treatment for a remake" nor his "script for a sequel" was realized. The rights were acquired, partially from Ufa, by an independent Hollywood producer; his remake, again called *The Cabinet of Dr. Caligari*, was released by 20th Century-Fox in 1962.[80]

Janowitz's belief that he was entitled to the rights again underscores the value and importance placed on film scripts in Germany as early as 1919. Pommer especially always advocated that a film stands or falls with a good script, knowing that production for export would not be successful without giving script selection top priority. As scriptwriter Thea von Harbou's biographer explained:

> In the final analysis, one can begin to speak of a script or script author in Germany beginning with the German film industry approximation to international film production standards. The production of historical costume films, the so-called expressionist films, and the *Kammerspiel* films therefore arose from competition with the American film industry.[81]

76. *Film-Kurier*, 5 February 1920.

77. See, for instance, Paul Monaco, who credits the *Caligari* advertising campaign to Ufa, apparently not realizing that it took place long before Decla-Bioscop and Ufa merged. Monaco, *Film and Society*, 77.

78. See Budd, *The Cabinet of Dr. Caligari*, 32ff.

79. Letter from J. Pommer to author, 27 August 1995.

80. See Budd, *The Cabinet of Dr. Caligari*, 32–33.

81. Keiner, *Thea von Harbou*, 29. Interestingly, trade press articles discussing the quality of American films also revolved around the manuscript as basis for a better film. It was argued that Germany could only counteract the preference for American films by basing movies on better scripts than in the past. See "Eine Gefahr für die Filmfabrikation," *Film-Kurier*, 6 October 1923.

Pommer secured talented writers through affiliations with publishing houses, a strategic move first undertaken in Germany by the much larger Ufa. In the summer of 1920, publisher Franz Ullstein and Decla-Bioscop, for their mutual benefit, formed the Uco film company, granting Pommer's company the exclusive rights to Ullstein's literary publications.[82] Such business connections were sharply criticized because shared financial interests, it was argued, created an incentive to publish biased and favorable film reviews. Subsequently, the liberal political journal *Das Tage-Buch* responded negatively to Decla-Bioscop's first Ullstein film, *Die Kwannon von Okadera* (1920, directed by Carl Froehlich), which was based on an Ullstein novel published in the *Berliner Illustrirte Zeitung*.[83] With the pending merger of Decla-Bioscop with Ufa, then already affiliated with the Mosse publishing house, all major film production firms would have secured the top German publishing houses. Not surprisingly, *Das Tage-Buch* justifiably asked: "Not one word against the personal integrity of individuals. But does this connection leave room for at least a tiny grain of freedom from which an acceptably independent film criticism shoots forth?"[84]

Several Ullstein novels were adapted to films by Decla-Bioscop: Fritz Lang's *Dr. Mabuse, der Spieler* (*Dr. Mabuse, the Gambler*), novel by Norbert Jacques; F.W. Murnau's *Schloß Vogelöd* (*Vogeloed Castle*), novel by Rudolf Stratz, and *Phantom*, novel by Gerhart Hauptmann; and Johannes Guter's *Die Prinzessin Suwarin* (*Princess Suwarin*), novel by Ludwig Wolff. The novelists often wrote or cowrote the scripts.

In 1920, the formation of Russo-Film, a small production company, was another attempt, albeit short-lived, to base films on literary sources. Its purpose was to produce films with Russian motifs, using Russian teams and actors. Three of its six board members came from Decla – Pommer, David Oliver, and Rudolf Meinert. Company records indicate that only three films were completed.[85]

82. Kallmann, *Konzernierung in der Filmindustrie*, 22. See also Decla-Bioscop business report ending on 31 May 1922. Ufa file, R109I. The report lists Uco's goals: Ullstein will promote literary aspects and effectively engage in propaganda, while Decla-Bioscop will undertake Uco film production at its own expense. Pommer and Ullstein were on the board of directors (*Aufsichtsrat*); Pommer's brother Albert was one of two senior managers (*Direktoren*). See also "Fusion Ullstein-Decla-Bioscop," *Film-Kurier*, 8 July 1920.

83. "Mosse- und Ullsteinfilme," *Tage-Buch*, 27 November 1920.

84. Ibid.

85. The company produced three films: *Irrende Seelen* (*Wandering Souls*), based on Dostoyevsky's *The Idiot*, with Asta Nielsen and Alfred Abel, sets by Robert Herlth

The finest scriptwriters of Germany's silent cinema wrote extensively for Pommer. During the 1920s, Thea von Harbou and Carl Mayer, two vastly dissimilar scriptwriters, became his authors. At Decla and later at Decla-Bioscop, Thea von Harbou and Fritz Lang collaborated on a number of films: *Die Vier um die Frau* (*Four Around a Woman*), 1921; *Der müde Tod* (*Destiny*), 1921; and the Uco-Decla-Bioscop production, *Dr. Mabuse, der Spieler*, 1922. Their association continued at Ufa.

Carl Mayer worked with Pommer's film directors, especially Robert Wiene and F.W. Murnau, on several productions; with cowriter Hans Janowitz and Wiene on *Caligari*, 1919; with Wiene again on *Genuine*, 1920; with Murnau on *Schloß Vogelöd*, 1921; *Der letzte Mann* (*The Last Laugh*), 1924; *Tartüff* (*The Gilded Hypocrite*), 1924; and *Faust*, 1926, the last three at Ufa. In Pommer's estimation Mayer was the creator of the "true" silent film, speaking through his scripts with a visual power that freed the moviegoer from relying on titles.[86] Pommer showed his great confidence in Mayer by granting him unusual influence on film production, allowing him shooting and editing privileges and more overall creative participation than his films' directors, cameramen, architects, and actors.[87] Pommer valued him immensely:

> His powerful visual imagination was kept constantly stimulated by close contact with the entire production process – and from *Caligari* can be dated Mayer's well-known awareness of the camera and settings as vital dramatic elements. Other writers wrote (and still write) scripts that have to be translated into film terms. Carl Mayer wrote true film scripts and, in so doing, inspired all film artists who worked in that famous postwar period of German cinema.[88]

Complete license in script conception was so necessary to Mayer that he preferred to return a film contract when he felt his script failed to meet his own high standards, or if employers denied him exclusive script freedom. He would not compromise.[89] Allegedly, "the quiet,

---

and Walter Röhrig, directed by Carl Froelich; *Die schwarze Pantherin* (*The Black Panther*); and *Die Intrigen der Madame de la Pommeraye* (*Madame de la Pommeraye's Intrigues*), with Alfred Abel, sets by Herlth and Röhrig, directed by Dr. Fritz Wendhausen. Decla-Bioscop company report ending on 31 May 1922.

86. Pommer, interviewed by Kadiev and Kyser.

87. Joe Hembus, "Der Autor Carl Mayer," in H.P. Manz, *Ufa und deutscher Film* (Zurich: Sanssouci Verlag, 1963), 38.

88. Pommer, "Carl Mayer's Debut," *Cabinet of Dr. Caligari: A Film by Robert Wiene, Carl Mayer…*, 29.

89. Hembus, "Autor Carl Mayer," *Ufa und deutscher Film*, 38.

shy Mayer was able to blow up and argue passionately over the integrity of a sequence and the strict adherence to his story line."[90]

Though most of the evidence defines Pommer in his early career as entrepreneur and decision maker, the recollections of his associates reveal him as close collaborator and active participant in the production process. Without exception, and extending into periods in which Pommer could do nothing to affect them, his creative team members commended their producer's willingness to go along with experiments, risky and innovative visions, and untested territory. Very few in his position had the confidence and audacity to work in that way. The producer Pommer they knew saw his role as much more than having final authority over his team. Fritz Lang said, "he never tried to interfere or influence me. Authors, set designers, technicians, and other employees were never subordinates but valuable collaborators in his production."[91] Architect and set designer Robert Herlth said:

> Side by side with authors and film directors ... with pioneers of technology ... there was primarily one man without whose initiative and ambition these accomplishments would never have materialized. He not only selected the appropriate team members and allowed them the freedom to work according to their peculiarities, more precisely, their tastes, but, most importantly, he also worked seeing himself as collaborator, unperturbed by his position as production chief responsible for such an enormous business. Through his example he promoted the idealism and urge to explore. Without him there would be no "German era."[92]

The cinema's pioneer years are remembered by those who were involved as "sheer madness" and "fanaticism." Lil Dagover, who signed a three-year contract with Decla and became one of the company's first popular female stars, speaks of the volatile working conditions in the studio where "all these men were terribly excited and nervous, extremely sensitive, prone to feeling insulted easily, and each one thinking of himself as the greatest."[93] According to film director Ludwig Berger, the single dominant force "taming us wild stallions" was Pommer.[94]

90. Hans Feld, "Carl Mayer – der erste Filmdichter," *Caligari und Caligarismus*, 25.

91. Pem (Paul Marcus), "Ein Leben für den Film: Zum Geburtstag Erich Pommers am 20. Juli," *Berliner Allgemeine*, 17 July 1964.

92. Robert Herlth, "Erinnerungen, 1958," *Filmarchitektur: Robert Herlth* (Munich: Deutsches Institut für Film und Fernsehen, 1965), 49.

93. Lil Dagover, *Ich war die Dame* (Munich: Franz Schneekluth-Verlag, 1979), 66.

94. Ludwig Berger, "Der Film kommt durch die Hintertür: Gedanken zur Situation der westdeutschen Produktion," *Tagesspiegel*, 13 March 1966.

Pommer's assessment was simply this: "None of these 'artists' were alike; some lived by economic and commercial considerations, others by purely idealistic ones (or so they thought), but all were egomaniacs."[95] The most possessed of all was Fritz Lang. According to Dagover, "[h]e was obsessed and caused his producer, Erich Pommer, many sleepless nights because he was absolutely oblivious to staying within the budget."[96] The hotbed climate of compulsively driven talents has been called "creative hocus pocus" (*schöpferischer Firlefanz*) by Robert Herlth, who experienced it firsthand: "In those times film was feeding on creative hocus pocus. We invented film. We came to know film. Technically, we were not perfect yet, but we had more imagination."[97] Pommer was known, for example, for rewarding his scriptwriters' imagination during meetings with tossing them a coin for every good idea.[98] Concerning the four-and-a-half weeks of working on *Caligari*, Hermann Warm recalls: "We started work furiously. Even the set workers had fun being involved. We three painters always worked till the middle of the night, as if in ecstasy. It was the new wave of the time, whirling all participants around and holding them up."[99]

The term "magician" was especially pertinent for the pioneering work of the cameraman, then called *Operateur* in the German studio. Herlth credits Decla-Bioscop's three cameramen, Fritz Arno Wagner, Karl Freund, and Carl Hoffmann with discovering the camera as a magic instrument. "One has to realize," Herlth recalls, "that the times lacked the expertise and the means to satisfy the continuous demands that this impatient generation posed for itself on its journey to the realm of the imagination."[100] Pommer repeatedly compared his own obsession with film to catching a contagious disease. According to Billy Wilder:

> Pommer had the same obsession with films, and making them with taste and quality, as Irving Thalberg or Sam Goldwyn. He toiled eighteen hours a day. He had four or five films in work at the same time. He was skinny, sensitive, and nervous; chain-smoked cigarettes; drove everybody relentlessly.[101]

95. Pommer, interviewed by Kadiev and Kyser.
96. Dagover, *Ich war die Dame*, 115.
97. Robert Herlth, quoted in Joe Hembus, *Der deutsche Film kann gar nicht besser sein* (Bremen: Carl Schünemann, 1961), 25.
98. Maurice Zolotow, *Billy Wilder in Hollywood* (New York: G.P. Putnam's Sons, 1977), 44.
99. Warm, *Caligari und Caligarismus*, 15.
100. Herlth, *Filmarchitektur*, 51.
101. Zolotow, *Billy Wilder in Hollywood*, 43.

A glance at the credits of films produced at Decla and Decla-Bioscop reveals that Pommer maintained a stable team of filmmakers, cameramen, set designers, architects, scriptwriters, and actors, all at his ready disposal. Besides the innovatively gifted cameramen, Pommer's set designers and architects Hermann Warm, Rudolf Bamberger, Robert Herlth, Walter Röhrig, Walter Reimann, and Otto Hunte were real members of the Pommer team. Herlth compared his obsessed colleagues to medieval artisans: "The filmmakers and actors, the cameramen and the architects felt a kinship with the lighting crew and stage workers not simply on the basis of comradeship. They depended on each other because each detail of a working process had to become an important moment if the outcome was to be successful."[102]

Pommer firmly believed in team collaboration. He called it his secret success formula, at Decla and subsequently at Ufa as well:

> I have to admit in all modesty that it would never have been possible to make these films if superb set designers, film directors, cameramen, and architects had not been available. I am realizing more than ever that Ufa's success came about because it was possible to create teams. Film is an art species, or an art-related species that cannot be accomplished by a single man but only by artists in close daily cooperation. It can only be accomplished by people who are obsessed by film.[103]

His company's greatest assets, he said, were not funds, but enthusiasm and ingenuity.[104] What Pommer brought to bear was, moreover, faith in the film medium, absolute confidence in his people, willingness to take risks, acceptance of his team's actions as his own, and unusual foresight regarding overall cinema development. When asked about his secret or his formula, or when people, whom he called idealists, approached him with "inflated" and preconceived notions about film aesthetics, he was merely amused and quickly rejected notions of a specific "philosophy" or any specific set of rules. If he had known of any, he said, he would have become a millionaire: "I have always lived by this principle: Everybody wants one thing – above all else he wants to live and support himself and his family. He does not want to become a millionaire (some want to become billionaires), but he has his

102. Herlth, *Filmarchitektur*, 48.
103. Pommer, interviewed in 1950 by Radio Frankfurt, Germany, audiotape, E. Pommer Collection.
104. Pommer, "Carl Mayer's Debut," *Cabinet of Dr. Caligari: A Film by Robert Wiene, Carl Mayer…*, 27.

obligations."[105] Pommer fostered the production of films that were then, and are still today, considered "art films," but he never held elitist film notions. He saw the production team as a family of artisans, film as a craft, knowing that the preferred term in Germany was definitely "art." The German highbrow notion of art became especially obvious, he said, in the attitudes of certain film critics in Berlin, especially theater critic Alfred Kerr, who seemed to consider the reviewing of films beneath his dignity and who felt compelled to attack Pommer.[106] Film theorist Rudolf Arnheim blatantly condemned Pommer's films, and some critics, Pommer said, apparently saw him merely as the producer, "the fellow who does nothing."[107]

Despite the German critics' continued argument against film's claim to be art and despite Pommer's insistence on film as "craft," Pommer's company made specific efforts to assure quality standards that, by the mid-1920s, had evolved into an "art" export strategy. The anticipated postwar invasion of American films provoked and demanded a German film industry response, forcing it to confront German-American film differences. Film scholar Thomas J. Saunders sees American serialized Westerns, social dramas, and slapstick shorts, many of which were dated when first shown in German movie theaters, as Germany's yardstick by which contrasts between Hollywood and Germany were defined.[108] Pommer praised American film characteristics, but saw no need for German film companies to imitate the films of the country whose market they intended to challenge. It was impossible, he believed in 1922, for Germans to imitate Griffith's competence and resources, just as it was impossible to imitate Niagara Falls. The German film industry had different aspirations, he believed:

> The mere admiration that was shown the German script, German direction, German actors, and German artistic resources in Paris and London has proved to us that we have something to offer; on a different level though, but equally inimitable, unique, even unbeatable as America's Niagara. A people has to know where its Niagara, the inimitable, lies.[109]

105. Pommer, interviewed by Kadiev and Kyser.
106. Ibid.
107. Ibid.
108. Thomas J. Saunders, *Hollywood in Berlin: American Cinema and Weimar Germany* (Berkeley and Los Angeles: Univ. of California Press, 1994), 84ff.
109. Pommer, "Internationale Film-Verständigung."

German culture determined its own cinema, whether "expressionist," "*Kammerspielfilm*," "street films," "films of the fantastic," or, as Pommer called them, "stylized" films.[110] Decla made a calculated move toward raising and improving the quality, and ultimately, the status of the cinema. Cross-fertilization of thought, training, and technique within Weimar Germany's culture generated films unlike any other national cinema. In Thomas Saunders's words, "historical authenticity, psychological consistency, the ability to breathe life into myth and legend, and an eye for the uncanny and bizarre: these were the gifts which Hollywood lacked and which could be exploited to challenge it."[111]

When Decla-Bioscop merged with Ufa, Berlin's "roaring twenties" were in full swing. A film premiere was a bigger-than-life spectacle. Berlin audiences felt that the cinema now equaled the stage theater's cultural respectability and that one's social prestige was enhanced simply by attending a premiere. Nothing reflected the development of the film industry more vividly than the splendid movie palaces on Berlin's famous boulevard, the Kurfürstendamm: "In the twenties the baroque of the cinema began. The new palaces of the mass society were built; gigantic theaters with lots of stucco, ushers in livery, and red carpets. The Berlin of the Kurfürstendamm was the Versailles for all smaller cities."[112]

The stage was set for film production, exhibition, and distribution on a scale previously unimagined in Germany.

---

110. Huaco contends that Pommer "sidestepped" genre definition: "For all the serious films done in the 1920–1930 period (*Caligari, The Golem, Dr. Mabuse, Nibelungen, Waxwork, Metropolis*, etc.), we had a different name; we preferred to call them 'stylized' films." Huaco, *Sociology of Film Art*, 5.

111. Thomas Saunders, "History in the Making: Weimar Cinema and National Identity?" Conference Paper, Univ. of Illinois at Chicago, October 1988, 13.

112. "Paläste der Traumwelt," *Magnum* 35 (April 1961): 28–29.

Chapter 3

UFA: SILENT FILM PRODUCTION

At the beginning of the new season, Ufa has primarily secured its own position in Germany vis-à-vis America. Erich Pommer proves, precisely through his unprecedented foresight, that he knows to extinguish American influence at the spot where it would burn most dangerously – in Berlin.

"Die Ufa und Amerika," *Film-Kurier*, 7 August 1925

Berlin Merger: Decla-Bioscop, Union-Film, Ufa

By November 1921,[1] when Decla-Bioscop and Ufa merged, the two forces dominating Germany's film industry were inflation and film export. The devaluation of the mark pushed companies further toward consolidation and market expansion.[2] Inflation led the banks to enormous film industry investments that facilitated immense budgets and films of high quality. Some of the production

1. On 11 October 1921, Decla-Bioscop's stockholders authorized the merger; the contracts are dated 10 and 11 November 1921. See "Auflösung der 'Decla-Bioscop-AG,'" *Film-Kurier*, 9 June 1922, and *Gründungsdaten*, Decla-Bioscop company record. Ufa's stockholders held their annual meeting on 21 November 1921 to vote on the merger with Decla-Bioscop. "Die Generalversammlung der Ufa," *Film-Kurier*, 22 November 1921.
2. Johann-Friedrich Rauthe, "Der Aufbau der deutschen Film-Industrie unter besonderer Berücksichtigung der Konzentrationsbewegung der neuesten Zeit," Ph.D. diss., Friedrich-Wilhelms-Univ. Berlin, 1922.

values of Ufa's films of that period were made possible precisely
by the rapidly decreasing value of the mark. The aim was the international market.[3] Concurrently, Germany's economic chaos discouraged other countries from exporting their films to Germany,
but the income received from foreign distribution of earlier films
became more and more valuable. This condition undisputably
caused the German cinema's spectacular rise in the first half of the
1920s. By juggling expenses in the sinking mark with income from
foreign currencies, Ufa managed to be more stable in financing its
projects than most German companies. The extent of inflation is
evident in the fact that at the end of 1923, one trillion old German
marks were given the value of one new German mark.[4] Such chaos
created a powerful production platform for Ufa executives, especially Pommer, after he inherited Ufa's enormous feature film production network following the merger with Decla-Bioscop.

Trade press reports criticized what they called lunatic film
industry spending, after it became known that the industry operated with a budget of four billion mark in 1920.[5] They argued,
with no subtlety, that the film industry excesses in Germany bore
no relation to the artistic quality of films. They were condemned
as "gigantic, opulent, monstrous, monumental costume spectacles" ("*Riesen-Pracht-Monstre-Monumental-Ausstattungsfilme*") and
dismissed as "pompous and expensive, but boring and empty."[6]
Kurt Tucholsky, writer and critic, argued that the cinema's short
history had produced only one *Caligari* whereas it had inflicted
nine-hundred movies containing nothing but empty kitsch on the
public.[7] When production costs for one single film reached the
amazing sum of two million marks, the banks' involvement was
made accountable for degrading the quality of the cinema: "The
movie with a budget of two million marks is destined to be bad
because it focuses too heavily on that which money can buy while
sacrificing its charm."[8]

3. Kallmann, *Konzernierung in der Filmindustrie*, 15.

4. John Pommer wrote to the author: "I heard from my father that everyone at
the studio was paid weekly, at a rate determined at the beginning of each week. By
the end of the week, the cost of groceries had climbed incredibly. Therefore the studio bought groceries at the beginning of the week and the canteen sold them at the
beginning-of-the-week prices after the employees had been paid so that they could
afford to feed their families." Letter to author, 2 September 1995.

5. Morus, "Decla, Ufa und Valuta," *Weltbühne*, 10 November 1921.

6. Hans Siemsen, "Die Filmerei," *Weltbühne*, 27 January 1921.

7. Peter Panter [Kurt Tucholsky], "Für Hans Siemsen," *Weltbühne*, 10 February 1921.

8. Ibid.

The trend toward high budget films (*Großfilme*) became an investor strategy to protect profits. Germany's market, however, was too limited to recover such high production costs and depended on foreign distribution. Paul Davidson's and Ernst Lubitsch's lavish historical epics, produced with big budgets, had found their way into foreign markets; so had Pommer's and Robert Wiene's relatively inexpensive expressionist film *Caligari*. Counting on these successes, Germany's financially strongest film companies channeled their export production increasingly into "art films." This policy catapulted Ufa into an international race it could not win, dominated, as the company would be, by factors beyond its control. The result in the mid-1920s was disaster.

But in late 1921 the goal was more expansion, enterprise consolidation through the formation of more *Konzerne*, continued *Großfilm* production, and export to the United States, all of which were supported by Germany's increasing inflation. The inevitable amalgamation of Ufa and Decla-Bioscop in 1921 produced the nation's largest concentration of film production, distribution, and theater chains under single control. All production, but especially of films meant for international consumption, shifted into feverish pitch, highly suspect to trade press observers. *Die Weltbühne* was especially biting in its commentary on German film policies at this time: "They cranked out movies as if the whole world was waiting for German films; but it was not."[9] The article took issue with Decla-Bioscop's "victimized" role in the company merger and alluded to the falsification of company records intended to facilitate the takeover by Ufa. Press coverage of the Decla-Bioscop stockholder meeting that decided the company's future indicated that irregularities were indeed at play. During the meeting, stockholders protested and sought in vain to rearrange the meeting's agenda to allow for the discussion of Decla-Bioscop's financial assets. Many felt that it would reveal a more favorable company profile and, subsequently, expose the unfairness of Ufa's bid. Pommer appealed to Decla-Bioscop's protesting senior management (*Vorstand*) not to place obstacles in the proposed company reorganization plans.[10] Pommer's personal account, given years later, affirmed that Decla-Bioscop indeed "did not have much money and could not really compete with Ufa, so Decla-Bioscop was brought into Ufa."[11]

9. Morus, "Decla, Ufa und Valuta." For more data on Decla-Bioscop's financial assets at merger time, see "Die Fusion Ufa-Decla," *Film-Kurier*, 11 October 1921.

10. "Die Fusion Ufa-Decla," *Film-Kurier*, 11 October 1921.

11. Pommer, interviewed by Huaco, *Sociology of Film Art*, 36.

Ufa, Germany's largest *Konzern*, had its own financial and production difficulties at merger time, which are now well docu-
mented.[12] The inflation had a devastating effect on Ufa, magnifying
the ill effects of long-range production investments and fixed distribution rates.[13] Several financial measures were undertaken to
counteract the company's losses from the continuing devaluation
of the mark. Figures from Ufa's business report of 31 May 1922
indicate that the company's base capital of 25 million marks was
increased repeatedly around this time through stock issues: in
March 1921 to 100 million, in November to 200 million, and in
October 1923 to 300 million marks.[14] In addition to financial woes,
Ufa had problems with its most reputable production company,
Union-Film, prompting *Film-Kurier* to announce that Ufa had lost
all significance as a production company.[15] The journal raised the
following question: "No other *Konzern* in our industry has such
powerful means at its disposal as Ufa. How is it possible that it
continues to be unable to once again produce a film which is up to
standards, one to which Ufa and the German film industry can
point with pride?"[16]

In 1921/22, American offers further aggravated Ufa's affairs by
playing havoc with Ufa's Union-Film. In April 1921, Adolph Zukor
of Famous Players (Paramount) allegedly tried but failed to gain 51
percent of Ufa's shares; Ufa declined.[17] Ben Blumenthal and his
American business associate Sam Rachmann, both representatives
of Famous Players (Paramount), evidently attracted to Berlin in
response to the American box office success of Lubitsch's *Madame*

12. For more data, see primarily Traub, *Ufa*; and Rahel Lipschütz, *Der Ufa-Konzern*, Ph.D. diss., Univ. Berlin, 1932 (Berlin: Energiadruck, 1932).

13. Lipschütz, *Ufa-Konzern*, 9.

14. Ibid.

15. "Ufa," *Film-Kurier*, 6 May 1922. The core of Ufa's artistic production, Union-
Film, was hit especially hard since Davidson's successor, Arthur von Gerlach,
proved less successful than what Ufa had expected of this personnel change. The
last collaborative film of the Davidson/Lubitsch/Negri team was *Die Bergkatze*
(*The Mountain Cat*) in 1921. Lubitsch's films *Das Weib des Pharao* (*The Wife of Phar-
aoh*) and *Die Flamme* (*Montmartre*) were already produced for Efa (Europäische
Film-Allianz). Accordingly, Union-Film executives had to admit that their production plans would have been in jeopardy had they not been backed up by Ufa. "Der
Geschäftsbericht der Union," *Film-Kurier*, 24 December 1921.

16. "Ufa," *Film-Kurier*, 6 May 1922.

17. This attempt has been reported in several sources. See, among others, Olimsky, *Tendenzen der Filmwirtschaft*, 44.

Dubarry, were more successful.[18] Negotiations with Paul Davidson, Ernst Lubitsch, their star Pola Negri, and producer/film director Joe May, enabled Union-Film's team financially to split from Ufa. They founded the Europäische Film-Allianz (Efa) in Berlin.[19] The echo in the trade press was pure paranoia, as seen in this *Tage-Buch* report in the summer of 1921, just a few months short of Pommer's association with Ufa:

> The German film industry is trembling. The Americans knock at the door. Behind them the Swedes, the Italians, [and] the British. But the Americans are the most dangerous, because they can bar German films from entering the U.S. The American film appears at a time of crisis for the German industry. Ufa, just deserted by its most successful personnel, fumbles under a new, not yet very secure hand and reduces its production. Decla-Bioscop, just having escaped death through being devoured, is not sure yet how much it can produce, and the Europäische Film-Allianz lacks Ufa's theaters. It has so far only hired a number of big names, who work against each other at times. It will find it impossible to produce for America exclusively, but for Germany this kind of production has become a little too expensive.[20]

The abandonment of Union-Film by its CEO and creative team cut deeply into Ufa, taking a noticeable toll on Ufa's artistic film production, and making a joint venture with Decla-Bioscop that much more urgent. *Film-Kurier* assessed Ufa's production in 1921 accordingly:

18. The 1921 Ufa-Famous Players case evoked an enormous echo in the trade press, especially with respect to Paul Davidson's subsequent resignation and Ufa's reorganization. See particularly *Film-Kurier* in February and March 1921. Leopold Schwarzschild's perspective, less than two years later, when "the American dream" had not materialized as anticipated, is worth noting: "The industry elite was concentrated at Ufa at the time. The four gentlemen begin with arbitrary obsession to hire everything good and expensive away from Ufa – under terms people had not dared dream of before. . . On such a basis contracts are signed with Ufa chief executives [*Generaldirektoren*] [Carl] Bratz and Davidson, with Lubitsch, of course, with Max Reinhardt and Joe May, with Pola Negri, [Emil] Jannings, [Paul] Wegener, [and] about fifty more, who are less famous. All are hired for a company not yet in existence, but with such generosity that the entire industry (not only the now beaten Ufa) mopes around and thinks: 'Now it's over. We can no longer compete with this.'" "Die Vertreibung der Efa aus dem Paradies," *Tage-Buch*, 18 November 1922.

19. According to Horak, Lubitsch persuaded his producer Davidson, set designer Kurt Richter, technical assistant Kurt Waschneck, cinematographers Theodor Sparkuhl and Alfred Hansen, scriptwriter Hans Kräly, and Ufa film director George Jacoby to join Efa. Horak, "Ernst Lubitsch and the Rise of Ufa," 107.

20. "Der amerikanische Film," *Tage-Buch*, 16 July 1921.

Union-Film ranks with those companies that have taken the German cinema to greatness. It has produced films that enabled Germany to conquer the world market. This year's production can only point to the possibility that the trade mark "Union" will be forgotten and that the future Ufa will neither be regarded one of the first, nor the first, film manufacturer.[21]

Evidently Decla-Bioscop's creative team and brilliant young producer were the ideal solution to Ufa's production problems. Besides, gaining Decla-Bioscop removed Ufa's only remaining major competitor in Germany. Both had, as Emil Georg von Stauß, chairman of Ufa's board of directors, later admitted, operated as fierce rivals, primarily through their theaters, and competed to such an extent that they were affecting each other's prices.[22]

At this time, Decla-Bioscop's production looked better than ever. *Film-Kurier*'s article entitled, "The Best Films of the Season: 'Decla-Bioscop' at the Top," showered Pommer's company with praise and highlighted the films of his most prolific film directors as audience and press favorites.[23] Among these were Fritz Lang's *Der müde Tod* (*Destiny*), Ludwig Berger's *Der Roman der Christine von Herre* (*The Christine von Herre Story*), and Johannes Guter's *Zirkus des Lebens* (*Circus of Life*). Also featured was F.W. Murnau, then new at the company, as film director of a three-part adventure story for which Thea von Harbou was to write the script; this project never materialized.[24] Decla-Bioscop's two subsidiaries, Russo-Film and Uco-Film were equally productive. Russo-Film announced two films, Johannes Guter's *Die schwarze Pantherin* (*The Black Panther*) and Fritz Wendhausen's *Die Intrigen der Madame de la Pommeraye* (*Madame de La Pommeraye's Intrigues*), while Uco-Film planned the film adaptation of the novel *Dr. Mabuse, der Spieler* (*Dr. Mabuse, the Gambler*), currently being published in the *Berliner Illustrirte Zeitung*.[25] In addition, Decla-Bioscop's foreign distribution program displayed Swedish and American films.

21. "Die günstigen Aussichten der Ufa," *Film-Kurier*, 24 November 1921.

22. "Die Generalversammlung der Ufa," *Film-Kurier*, 22 November 1921.

23. "Die besten Filme der Saison: 'Decla-Bioscop' an der Spitze," *Film-Kurier*, 19 November 1921.

24. When Murnau came under contract with Decla-Bioscop in January 1921, this move was associated by the press with the departure of *Caligari* director Robert Wiene. See "Ein neuer Regisseur der Decla-Bioscop," *Film-Kurier*, 14 January 1921. The Murnau project refers to a three-part adventure film intended to replace a Fritz Lang project that was not produced either.

25. "Die besten Filme der Saison. 'Decla-Bioscop' an der Spitze," *Film-Kurier*, 19 November 1921.

Such successes increased Ufa's interest in Decla-Bioscop, a company whose strength rested on artistic and technical merits developed by teams that were intuitively selected and orchestrated by their producer Pommer. But Ufa was also forced to settle Union-Film's status through an "official" merger because Davidson, being left out in the cold after the collapse of the Europäische Allianz (Efa), attempted to reclaim Union-Film with a purchase offer. Both Ufa plans for merging were tactics in the company's urgency to preserve and rebuild its artistic film production capacity and its fight for a much needed share in the United States market. Both intended mergers merit a closer look since Pommer, as Davidson's successor, was a reluctant player at their center. For him, repeatedly battling illnesses that were to affect his career until the end, the events could not have come at a less opportune time, as Fritz Lang testified:

> During the filming [of *Der müde Tod*], Pommer became gravely ill. Intrigues arose from all sides and the bizarre attempt was made to integrate Decla into Ufa. Pommer didn't want it. There really were base intrigues to ruin the job for Pommer, and naturally, for me as well. Pommer was ill, and I remained loyal to him.[26]

In the final analysis, the circumstances during the merger highlight the film industry's vulnerability and the fragile nature of company control.[27]

Pommer, as Decla-Bioscop's chief executive, was forced to bow to bank dictates, and preferences he may have entertained about merging with any company, be it National-Film or Ufa, were without

---

26. *Fritz Lang: Choix de textes établi par Alfred Eibel* (Paris: Présence du Cinéma, 1964), 11-12. Translated by Beverly Keim. See also Curt Riess, *Das gab's nur einmal: Die große Zeit des deutschen Films* (Frankfurt/Main, Berlin and Vienna: Ullstein Sachbuch, 1985), vol. 1, 151. Pommer's son remembers a family trip to the Bavarian Alps at the time, which had to be interrupted because his father had difficulty breathing. Although this was Pommer's last bout with asthma, other illnesses soon followed, which his son attributes primarily to his excessive weight, gained from the heavy, fatty meals served especially at Pommer's favorite place, Horcher and Schlichter in Berlin. At the time of the merger, his weight was at least 100 kg, and pictures of the period show it. Later Pommer became more disciplined in his eating habits, especially after doctors diagnosed diabetes.

27. The film industry's vulnerability is echoed in the remark by Dr. Wolffsohn, publisher of *Lichtbild-Bühne*, who referred here to Decla-Bioscop's initial merger plans: "During the merger of Decla-National the press continually claimed that the decisions originated in the film industry and not, as was actually the case, in the bank groups." See "Die Generalversammlung der 'Union'," *Film-Kurier*, second supplement, 1 January 1922.

effect. Not surprisingly, the Deutsche Bank was publicly criticized and accused of exercising its power over the film industry no differently than over other industrial companies, thereby entirely disregarding cultural considerations.[28] The nominal decision over Decla-Bioscop's and Ufa's future depended on the outcome of both companies' annual stockholder meetings (*Generalversammlungen*), whose members represented major banks with large investments in the film industry.

Decla-Bioscop's stockholders met on 20 September 1921. National-Film, to which Decla-Bioscop had turned with merger intentions before, placed a bid for Pommer's company on 26 August 1921.[29] Decla-Bioscop's stockholders rejected National-Film but accepted Ufa's matching bid.[30] On 19 September, one day before the stockholders were to convene again, National-Film increased its bid but was ignored; the Decla-Bioscop merger with Ufa was presented to them as a *fait accompli*.[31] Hans Traub offers this version of the dramatic circumstances:

> Decla was burdened by substantial business difficulties, and it was decided to transfer its capital by sale to the National-Film company. Before this informally agreed-to and concluded plan received formal approval during Decla's stockholder meeting, the new National-Film gentlemen had already physically moved in. However, the banks which had supported Decla-Bioscop up to this point, were, in the meantime, merged with the Nationalbank, which in turn, had shares in Ufa. Therefore Decla-Bioscop was amalgamated at the last minute with Ufa. An attempt was also made to amalgamate National-Film, but Ufa refused.[32]

The trade press was equally dramatic, with reports ranging from the purely speculative to the simply ludicrous. In late October and early November, *Film-Kurier*, for example, announced that the merger between an amalgamated Decla-Bioscop / National-Film

28. "Ufa," *Film-Kurier*, 6 May 1922. The close business connection between the Deutsche Bank and Ufa was underscored by the fact that Ufa held its annual stockholder meetings at the bank, which had equipped its new conference room with "Ufa of AEG [Allgemeine Elektrizitäts-Gesellschaft]" facilities for movie projection. "Die Generalversammlung der Ufa," *Film-Kurier*, 22 November 1921.

29. *Gründungsdaten*, Decla-Bioscop business report.

30. Ibid.

31. Ibid.

32. Traub, *Ufa*, 56. The identical names of the company (National-Film) and the bank (Nationalbank) do not represent business associations. For a more sarcastic account of National-Film's dismissal, see Morus, "Decla, Ufa, und Valuta"; and Kallmann, *Konzernierung in der Filmindustrie*, 18.

company with Ufa had already been consummated by the banks.[33] Other articles knew of complications, allegedly caused by Decla-Bioscop's debts to other German film enterprises. On 5 December 1921, a new headline spoke of *Konfusion* rather than *Fusion*, and finally, a full month after the actual merger, a headline stated that plans had failed altogether.[34]

The merger proved costly for Ufa. The stockholder meeting seven months later revealed that 66 million marks had to be invested, partly for a decrease of Decla-Bioscop's bank debts, partly for production.[35] As a result, the German film industry now comprised one major vertically integrated firm (with governmental, industrial, and banking support) and various new independent firms,[36] with Ufa holding a near-monopoly in domestic film commerce but still watching the American advance nervously.[37] From the vantage point of its newly strengthened position, Ufa devised its own production strategy to ward off American competition, resorting to "monumental films in grand style," whose production peaked during the mid-1920s.[38] No producer, either at Ufa or outside of it, could with more brilliance and confidence fulfill Ufa's ambitious production aspirations than Pommer. No one's competence offered greater promise for Ufa and the German film industry, as was publicly affirmed by *Lichtbild-Bühne*:

> It is our opinion that no one but Pommer could even be considered for this post which had been deserted since the departure of Davidson-Lubitsch. We are convinced that the company trademarks "Union," "Messter," and "Ufa" will rise again to the splendor it once knew.[39]

33. "Die Zukunft der Decla und National: Selbständigkeit innerhalb der Ufa," *Film-Kurier*, 31 October 1921; and "Die Zukunft der Decla und National," *Film-Kurier*, 1 November 1921.

34. See *Film-Echo*, supplement to *Berliner Lokal-Anzeiger*, 5 December 1921; and "Die Fusion Ufa-Decla gescheitert," *Film-Kurier*, 30 December 1921.

35. "Die Generalversammlung der Ufa," *Film-Kurier*, 5 January 1923.

36. Douglas Gomery and Janet Staiger, "The History of World Cinema: Models for Economic Analysis," *Film-Reader*, 4 (1979). Besides Germany's four core postwar companies, Ufa, Decla, Bioscop, and Deulig, all of which were to engage in merger policies, the authors list the following small competing companies already in existence, or formed by entrepreneurs between 1919 and 1922: Westi, Emelka, Prometheus, Phoebus, Terra, Sofar, Sokal, Neptune, Jessner, and Oswald.

37. David Bordwell, *The Films of Carl-Theodor Dreyer* (Berkeley, Los Angeles, and London: Univ. of California Press, 1981), 18.

38. Lipschütz, *Ufa-Konzern*, 11.

39. "Erich Pommer im Vorstand der Ufa: Kurswechsel bei der Universum-Film AG," *Lichtbild-Bühne*, 10 February 1923.

At Ufa, Pommer continued in his role as Decla-Bioscop's CEO in addition to assuming production command of Union-Film and Messter-Film in February 1923.[40] He was placed in charge of feature film production and appointed to Ufa's *Vorstand*.[41] He was responsible for foreign distribution and in this capacity the ideal candidate for negotiations with France's Etablissement Aubert in 1924. The press had nothing but praise for Ufa's new member (*Direktor*) of the *Vorstand*:

> Pommer is recognized as one of those who always know what they want and who pursue a goal with an energy rarely found today. Through this energy and his personal popularity he has achieved international connections which can hardly be claimed today by anyone else in the German film industry.[42]

One can speculate whether Pommer's entry into Ufa would have occurred differently had Davidson remained, but not whether he would or would not have entered, since the merger was inevitable.[43] These two top German film producers were much alike in their international market strategies, their company expansion, and production policies, but only one could occupy the top production position unless some power sharing scheme were implemented. On

40. Both *Film-Kurier* and *Lichtbild-Bühne* reported that Ufa had counted on state theater head Dr. Hagemann, Wiesbaden, as Arthur von Gerlach's successor at Union-Film. *Lichtbild-Bühne* even claimed that Hagemann had assumed production responsibilities at Ufa before his status was cleared in Wiesbaden. The negotiations failed because of Hagemann's commitments to Wiesbaden. "Wichtige Veränderungen in der 'Ufa': Direktor Erich Pommer übernimmt die Oberleitung der gesamten Produktion," *Film-Kurier*, 8 February 1923; and "Erich Pommer im Vorstand der Ufa," *Lichtbild-Bühne*, 10 February 1923.

41. Contrary to the term board of directors (*Aufsichtsrat*, that is, supervisory board, in German), U.S. corporate law has no equivalent to the German *Vorstand* or *Direktorium*, which represents the senior management of a corporation (*Aktiengesellschaft*=AG). At Pommer's start at Ufa, four senior managers (*Direktoren*), representing their respective departments, constituted the *Vorstand*: finances, production, distribution, and exhibition. At times the *Vorstand* was also headed by a CEO (*Generaldirektor*). The situation changed after Alfred Hugenberg's take-over of the company. In German business, *Aufsichtsrat* and *Vorstand* are rigidly separate bodies within a corporation whereas in the U.S., a board chairman can also assume the top management role of CEO, and board members can be inside-members from senior management. Pommer himself, and subsequently his son, used the term "board of directors" when referring to "*Vorstand*" (most likely taking the term "director" from British business law. I find it essential to preserve the German terms while also providing approximate U.S. equivalents.

42. "Wichtige Veränderungen in der 'Ufa'," *Film-Kurier*, 8 February 1923.

43. By 1924, four senior managers constituted the *Vorstand*, each one responsible for his respective domain: Erich Pommer for production, Siegmund Jacob for distribution,

the other hand, their coexistence in powerful Ufa positions might have led the company to a greatness even surpassing Ufa's production success under Pommer's tenure. As it happened, Pommer rose to the top while Davidson's power declined. The latter, left behind empty-handed and not willing to follow Lubitsch to the United States, founded the Davidson-Film company (D-Film) in Berlin in 1924, which eventually became associated with Ufa as a production and distribution company.[44] Once Germany's most important production chief, he "would sink into obscurity, following Lubitsch's departure, and the liquidation of the Efa [company]."[45] While Davidson's and Pommer's companies, Union-Film and Decla-Bioscop respectively, had clearly operated as rivals prior to Pommer's Ufa affiliation, Pommer now controlled both.

The tug over Union-Film in 1922 revealed much more than internal turmoil, financial and otherwise, at Ufa. The tenacity employed by Ufa in keeping its dethroned production chief Davidson at bay was deeply rooted in nationalism and triggered by the fear of losing control over the German film industry. During the bidding for Union-Film by Ufa, Davidson, and his American business associate Ben Blumenthal, the looming specter of American capital involvement far outweighed the fact that Davidson had abandoned his former company. On 7 August 1922, Ufa CEO Felix Kallmann definitively stated Ufa's judgment and policies during Union-Film's decisive stockholder meeting that led to Davidson's rejection:

> Davidson's bid is another matter. It is American money. We cannot blame the Americans for taking advantage of the favorable exchange rate when they find people who are for sale. Ufa also received such offers. It received repeated offers to be taken over by an American enterprise paying horrendous sums. But it is not in

---

Alexander Grau for exhibition, and Eugen Stauß (not to be confused with Emil Georg von Stauß of Ufa's *Aufsichtsrat*) for finances. They managed the day-to-day company affairs without a CEO (*Generaldirektor*) following Felix Kallmann's departure, until Ferdinand Bausback was appointed in 1926. "Bei der Ufa machte man es so: Kino – das große Traumgeschäft," *Der Spiegel*, 6 September 1950.

44. In February 1927 Davidson severed his Ufa association, allegedly to go to the United States. He committed suicide in Munich in July of the same year. Obituaries, finally appearing more than a month later, listed a heart attack as cause of death. Davidson-Film was liquidated. *Jahrbuch der Filmindustrie 1923/24*; *Jahrbuch der Filmindustrie 1926/27*; and *Jahrbuch der Filmindustrie 1928* (Berlin: Verlag der Lichtbild-Bühne, 1924, 1927, and 1928).

45. Horak, "Ernst Lubitsch and the Rise of Ufa," 120.

the German interest to have its most important industries fall into foreign hands.[46]

Ufa rejected foreign financial involvement by overruling both Davidson's financially attractive offer and Blumenthal's, which was even higher. The rejection was based on the intention "to continue to work in the interest of Germany's industry and to demonstrate what this industry can do on its own."[47] In the early 1920s, Ufa was still in the position to decline.

The history of Union-Film and Decla-Bioscop, and their respective production chiefs, reveals conditions in the early twenties that made successful German film production possible. Both companies succeeded at the artistic level with similar internal structures: both were in the capable hands of an industry-trained production head and could rely on the presence of long-term team collaboration. When either structural component was absent, artistic film production declined, as Union-Film demonstrated. Union-Film's most productive early period occurred under Davidson and Lubitsch, and prior to that, under Davidson, Urban Gad, and Asta Nielsen. Deprived of his teams, Davidson was not successful. But deprived of Davidson, Union-Film failed completely, despite Ufa's efforts to revive a tradition that once included Max Reinhardt, Weimar Germany's most ingenious theater impresario.

Ufa's steps to remedy this situation did not occur without detours. Before Pommer became production chief at Ufa, Felix Kallmann, then *Vorstand* CEO, felt that Union-Film's former productivity and artistic reputation could best be restored by entrusting the company into the care of a former stage director. In 1921, theater impresario and stage director Arthur von Gerlach became Davidson's successor and Union-Film's new production head. Although he appeared the right person to guide the company to artistic success, his lack of Davidson's film industry expertise soon became evident, and he was repositioned as an Ufa film director.[48] When a second attempt to hire a theater impresario failed in February 1923 and Pommer received his Ufa appointment, it was immediately interpreted by the press as a diversion from Kallmann's "disastrous" policy of barring film industry experts from

46. "Die Fusionsversammlung der 'Union'," *Film-Kurier*, 8 August 1922.
47. Ibid.
48. Arthur von Gerlach directed *Zur Chronik von Grieshuus* (*The Chronicle of Grieshuus*) under Pommer's supervision for Ufa's Union-Film in 1924/25. He was planning *Der Prinz von Homburg* (*The Prince of Homburg*) when he died on 4 August 1925, at age 49. "Arthur von Gerlach +," *Film-Kurier*, 5 August 1925.

senior management.[49] Pommer was welcomed as "the right man in the right place."[50] Union-Film under Pommer produced some of Germany's *Großfilme* for the "art" movie theater audience, albeit not in such profusion as Ufa's Decla-Bioscop, where most of Germany's "classic" silent films originated. Likewise, Union-Film's artistic accomplishments were never repeated by Davidson's later company, Davidson-Film (D-Film).

Decla-Bioscop's advantage was uninterrupted production under Pommer's continuously advancing leadership skills, including his ability to assemble new teams. This company never relied too heavily on any single film director. Ludwig Berger, Johannes Guter, Fritz Lang, F.W. Murnau, and E.A. Dupont all directed well under Pommer's guidance. Decla-Bioscop did not decline when one of its top filmmakers left for Hollywood, as the departure of Berger, Murnau, and Dupont proved. One of Pommer's most valuable skills was his ability to work equally well with any film director. Conversely, a film director worked best specifically when supervised by him and developed, as British film critic C.A. Lejeune so aptly describes it, "qualities of forces and imagination that seem to evade him in his other films."[51] It took more than capital, a vertically organized enterprise, excellent technicians, stars, and artistic personnel to produce films successfully. A production head with a strong vision, able to incite while guiding well-selected production teams, made the system work. When Steve Neale lists Ufa's "strategies" and "strengths," both domestically and abroad, as partial causes for Germany's postwar film production boom, he disregards the fact that strategies need an originator and executor without whom they would not exist.[52]

Pommer's Rise to Power

Pommer's and Decla-Bioscop's reputation rested firmly on the European and American successes of films like *Caligari* and *Der müde Tod*. *Caligari* proved that "art films," intersecting as they did with other aspects of German culture, could actually bring profit alongside prestige. For Andrew Tudor the preconditions in the German film industry could not be isolated from *Caligari*:

49. "Erich Pommer im Vorstand der Ufa," *Lichtbild-Bühne*, 10 February 1923.
50. Ibid.
51. Lejeune, *Cinema* (London: Alexander Maclehose & Co., 1931), 128.
52. Steve Neale, "Art Cinema As Institution," *Screen*, 22:1 (1981), 22.

They needed only a trigger, and that was provided by this sudden proof that the new style had commercial potential. The safes were unlocked, as aesthetic, moral, political, and commercial interests joined hands over the grotesque somnambulist's coffin. The German style began its mobilization, and continued in full flood to the middle of the decade. Its expansion was paralleled by that of the industry itself, and Pommer rode his support of *Caligari* to control of Ufa.[53]

Ufa's feature film production under Pommer's reign apparently exceeded all expectations. Fritz Lang's *Dr. Mabuse, der Spieler* premiered in the spring of 1922 and became enormously successful with German audiences and, more importantly, achieved international success. Attending its London premiere, Pommer and Lang were repeatedly called on stage by an enthusiastic audience.[54]

Considering Ufa's dependence on "art film" production, it should not surprise anyone that it treated Decla-Bioscop, as it treated Messter-Film or Union-Film before, as an "artistic and technical collaborator." Ufa encouraged these companies "to make use of past experiences while, at the same time, covering new ground in new film creation."[55] Unlike Ufa's centralized management, production remained individualized and decentralized.[56] This also remained true for Decla-Verleih and Bioscop-Verleih, Decla-Bioscop's two distribution arms.[57]

Ufa's international catalogue of 1924 listed the impressive former achievements of Union-Film (*Madame Dubarry, Sumurun/One Arabian Night, Anna Boleyn/Deception*); Messter-Film (*Golem*); and Decla-Bioscop (*Caligari, Der müde Tod/Destiny, Dr. Mabuse, Phantom, Ein Glas Wasser/A Glass of Water*). Ufa proclaimed these films the pillar of its new production: "The traditions of the past manifested in these

53. Andrew Tudor, *Image and Influence: Studies in the Sociology of Film* (New York: St. Martin's Press, 1974), 175.

54. "Der Erfolg des 'Dr. Mabuse' in London," *Film-Kurier*, 9 March 1923.

55. Ufa Publicity Booklet, Berlin (December 1923): 21.

56. Kayser, "Deutsche Filmindustrie," 68. By the end of May 1922, six months after the merger with Ufa, Decla-Bioscop no longer operated as corporation [AG= *Aktiengesellschaft*], but as limited liability company [GmbH=*Gesellschaft mit beschränkter Haftung*]. Decla-Bioscop's assets were transferred to Ufa, liquidation did not take place. Pommer's company operated as one of Ufa's departments until 1 June 1924, after which it merged with Ufa's central administration. See *Gründungsdaten*, Decla-Bioscop business report; and "Auflösung der Decla-Bioscop-AG," *Film-Kurier*, 9 June 1922. Decla-Bioscop still appeared as AG beyond 31 May 1922 because this change was not entered in the commercial register-general (*Handelsregister*) until later.

57. Traub, *Ufa*, 56.

films has been the guiding star for this year's productions of the united Decla-Bioscop, Messter, and Union companies."[58] Pommer's former company became, as David Bordwell calls it so pertinently, the "artistic wing" of Ufa.[59] Though it had lost its financial power before merging, it had joined Ufa with its artistic reputation intact. *Film-Kurier* reported that "Ufa intends to enable Decla-Bioscop to unfold its productive forces," which had evidently improved Ufa's domestic and international reputation.[60] When in early 1923 Ufa's stockholders reviewed the merger with Decla-Bioscop, the executives' decision was reaffirmed by Pommer's production skills, which also promised success for the much desired foreign distribution.[61] In the spring of 1923, Decla-Bioscop's Neubabelsberg facilities, which were used primarily for outdoor shooting, and the Tempelhof studios were a bustling "film city.[62] The production of four *Großfilme* was in progress: Fritz Lang's Germanic epic, *Die Nibelungen*; Ludwig Berger's fairy tale, *Der verlorene Schuh* (*Cinderella*); Arthur von Gerlach's *Zur Chronik von Grieshuus* (*The Chronicle of Grieshuus*); and Benjamin Christensen's *Wilbur Crowfords wundersames Abenteuer* (*Wilbur Crowford's Strange Adventure*).[63] Referring to Neubabelsberg, Ufa boasted: "Without fear of being contradicted one may proclaim the Ufa Decla-Bioscop film plant the biggest and best equipped film city of the entire European continent."[64]

Ufa's facilities were immense, as Alfred Hitchcock said, recalling his first impression of the Ufa studios after arriving in Berlin in 1924: "The studio where I worked was tremendous, bigger than Universal is today. They had a complete railroad station built on the back lot. For a version of *Siegfried*, they built the whole forest of the *Nibelungenlied*."[65]

58. "Our Artistic and Technical Collaborators," International Ufa Publicity Booklet, n.d. (1924?), 21.

59. Bordwell, *Films of Carl-Theodor Dreyer*, 18.

60. "Auflösung der 'Decla-Bioscop-AG'," *Film-Kurier*, 9 June 1922.

61. "Die Generalversammlung der Ufa," *Film-Kurier*, 5 January 1923.

62. For a detailed description of the Ufa studios in Berlin-Tempelhof, see A. Kossowsky, "Die Berliner Ateliers," *Kinotechnische Rundschau*, 4: 21, supplement of *Film-Kurier*, 2 October 1924; and Bock and Töteberg, *Ufa-Buch*.

63. "Neues vom Ufa-Konzern," *Film-Kurier*, 10 May 1923. Christensen's film is not listed in this author's Pommer filmography, unless it is hiding under the title *Seine Frau, die Unbekannte* (*His Wife, the Stranger*), which Christensen directed for Pommer in 1923.

64. Ufa Publicity Booklet, 17.

65. Bob Thomas, "Alfred Hitchcock: The German Years," *Action* (January–February 1973), 23.

Even the inflation's end in 1924 did not interrupt Decla-Bio-scop's bustle. When German film manufacturers were hit hard by the shortage of capital, Ufa's Decla wing was singled out by the trade press as the only exception:

> The picture is the same everywhere. Nobody produces, everybody is desperate for money, for funds to fulfill the smallest routine obligations. Nothing is going on anywhere. Decla is the most lively factor. The film *Nibelungen* was a huge success, at the box office as well. There are strategists who dare place everything on one card. Erich Pommer is one of these very few. Ufa's moguls, Kallmann, von Stauß, and Jacob have to realize this after all.[66]

By the end of 1924 Ufa clearly favored Decla-Bioscop, placing a full-page advertisement in *Film-Kurier* displaying their respective company emblems side by side as Germany's "leaders." The ad proudly lists company resources like "the best German producers, the favorite stars, the best artistic collaborators, the best German films, consequently the only helpful chanel [*sic*] of selling German films in foreign countries, the best means of distributing foreign films in Germany."[67] Under Pommer Ufa produced the most expensive and largest number of Weimar Germany's artistically acclaimed "classic films." But not every film produced at Ufa in the early twenties was an "art film," and other companies produced "art films" as well. The Ufa trademark was by no means synonymous with "the German classic cinema" or "Weimar cinema."[68] On the whole, Ufa's annual film production was the popular, well-made entertainment film that provided the financial base for artistically more demanding films. Only the latter are known today and, given the emphasis on canons, the others are all but forgotten. As Karl Klär deplored, "today we merely remember the top artistic productions and hardly the mass of mediocre movies which were produced in the majority."[69]

---

66. "Berliner Selbstbewußtsein," *Süddeutsche Filmzeitung*, 27 June 1924. Felix Kallmann was *Vorstand* CEO, Siegmund Jacob was in charge of Ufa's distribution. Emil Georg von Stauß was chairman of the board of directors (*Aufsichtsrat*) and CEO of the Deutsche Bank.

67. *Film-Kurier*, export edition, English segment, 30 December 1924.

68. As an example, see Roger Manvell's selection of "masterworks of the German cinema." Of the four films he lists, only one, *The Golem* of 1920, is an Ufa production. *Masterworks of the German Cinema* (New York, Evanston, San Francisco, and London: Harper & Row, Icon Editions, 1973).

69. Karl Klär, *Film zwischen Wunsch und Wirklichkeit* (Wiesbaden: Verlagsgesellschaft Feldt & Co., 1957), 109.

Pommer certainly differentiated between these two production modes and established personal priorities. He divided feature film production into *Großfilm* production for international distribution and *Mittelfilm* production, Ufa's bread-and-butter output for domestic theaters. The former, referred to as Ufa's "own" production (*Eigenproduktion*), took place primarily in the original Decla-Bioscop, Union-Film, and Messter-Film companies at Ufa. Production of smaller budget films was assigned to non-Ufa affiliated German production companies (*Auftragsproduktion*).[70] The economic advantage of such differentiation was obvious, even to those opposing such a policy.[71] It enabled Ufa "to concentrate all its energies on what it considered to be its real task," which was unmistakably the export market, understood by Ufa to be the cornerstone of the film industry.[72] Like Irving Thalberg at Metro-Goldwyn-Mayer, Pommer handpicked Ufa's "prestige" films and gave them his foremost attention. Though he considered run-of-the-mill productions to be Ufa's economic backbone, he relied on his producers "to grind those out."[73] Delegating them to outside companies was economically wise and freed him to focus on "prestige" films instead:

> Ufa is primarily equipped to handle quality film production. Considering its high general expenses, etc., it is practically impossible to produce really inexpensive movies. Ufa will be in the position to operate much more safely when it continues to assign its middle budget production to those companies that produce according to prices and conditions which were agreed upon in advance. . . This way Ufa is able to determine precisely how much production will cost, without burdening its administration or without diffusing its interests. These production companies [*Herstellungsfirmen*] march along a rigidly delineated path, with limited freedom of movement, so that truly unpleasant surprises cannot occur. When Ufa follows the principle of decentralization, the final risk factor is eliminated from a quantitatively substantial portion of its production.[74]

70. In the mid-1920s these were: May-Film, Davidson-Film (D-Film), Messter-Ostermayr-Film, Sternheim-Film, Rex-Film, Ellen-Richter-Film, BB-Film, and Maxim-Film. See "Zur neuen Produktion: Das Programm der Ufa," *Film-Kurier*, 5 January 1925.

71. For an opposing view of Ufa's division into *Eigenproduktion* and *Auftragsproduktion*, see Kurt Pinthus, "Die Film-Krisis," *Tage-Buch*, 7 April 1928.

72. Pinthus, "Film-Krisis."

73. Huaco, *Sociology of Film Art*, 51.

74. "Amerikanisierung der Ufa?" *Lichtbild-Bühne*, 9 January 1926.

Conversely, smaller production companies also derived economic advantages from this association that guaranteed them loans and subsidies through Ufa and enabled them to produce films of higher quality.[75]

Some critics claimed that such delegation to smaller production companies caused a quality decline in Ufa's average film production, subsequently accelerating Ufa's financial ruin, a problem discussed, for instance, by film director Ludwig Berger in his memoirs. Großfilme, he explained, with a budget between 800,000 and 1 million marks, often returned their investment in addition to establishing foreign acclaim. Small budget movies, costing around 150,000 marks, were no risks and proved, if popular, extremely profitable.[76] But mid-range budget films were problematic because they were neither inexpensive nor quite internationally marketable and therefore risky if they failed in Germany. If Pommer was blamed for attempting to raise the quality of the Mittelfilm, Berger argued, such criticism originated from those who begrudged him his success at Ufa: "People accused the young, fanatically striving Ufa chief of jeopardizing Ufa because of his ambition, which drove him to raise 'entertainment films' of mid-size budgets to too high a level."[77]

But while Pommer's "art production" policy undisputably worked successfully on an artistic level, bringing him critical acclaim, it often failed to be profitable. Artistic acclaim alone could not refill Ufa's pockets, and it soon became clear that films that were expected to soar at the box office because of their artistic merit were soon forgotten.[78] Some of Germany's "art films" were assured box office success neither in Germany nor in the United States. Critic Friedrich Porges calls this dilemma the "tragedy of film production," deploring the incompatibility of art and profit, without naming film titles, in 1924:

> During these last weeks, three German film directors have experienced such disappointments. Three German Großfilme, produced with high hopes, including the "film industrialists'," have been bypassed by success. One of them by local success, the second by

75. Hanns Hellmich, "Die Finanzierung der deutschen Filmproduktion," Ph.D. diss., Schlesische Friedrich-Wilhelm Univ. Breslau, 1935, 91.

76. Ludwig Berger, Theatermenschen: So sah ich sie (Velber/Hanover: Friedrich Verlag, 1962), 72.

77. Ibid.

78. This situation was discussed repeatedly in the trade press toward the mid-twenties. See, for instance, "Die Sorge um den Film," Süddeutsche Filmzeitung, 21 March 1924.

world success, the third most likely by both. This is happening despite the fact that each film represents in itself an immense achievement, artistic intention, and competence. Each is, doubtlessly, the result of immeasurable work ... having swallowed exorbitant sums of money.[79]

Since Germany's American debut, *Madame Dubarry*, was such an enormous success, American audiences were allegedly disappointed when subsequent German movies did not always match the standard set by director Ernst Lubitsch. Karl Klär offers the following comments:

> In the years 1924 to 1930 Ufa produced an average of eighteen films in its *Eigenproduktion*. These numbers fluctuated between 15 and 20 each year. Of these 15 to 20 Ufa-produced films, only three films per year became world successes. Only during one year, with a production of 20 films, this number rose to 4. Even if those companies are added which competed with Ufa on the world market, the total of all actual internationally profitable successes does not exceed fifteen percent.[80]

Caligari was an exception, bringing more money abroad than at home. Murnau's *Faust* only brought in 75 percent of its cost in 1926, one-third of it in Germany, two-thirds outside.[81] Only one of Pommer's "art films" of the 1920s, Ludwig Berger's *Ein Walzertraum* (*Waltz Dream*), produced in 1925, supposedly grossed its production cost at home box offices.[82] Berger also lists *Die Nibelungen* and *Der letzte Mann* as films that recouped many times their investment.[83] As Robert C. Allen found when examining Murnau's Hollywood work, critical success certainly did not assure profit, although it did establish some German directors' reputation through their "highly artistic pictures."[84] And at times Pommer compromised to guarantee box office success. For instance, he added a happy ending to *Der letzte Mann* (*The Last Laugh*) "because without it the film would have been too much like real life and would have been a commercial failure."[85] He also changed the ending of *Michael*, a film the Danish director Carl-Theodor Dreyer

79. Friedrich Porges, "Tragödie der Filmarbeit," *Film-Kurier*, 10 January 1924.

80. Klär, *Film zwischen Wunsch und Wirklichkeit*, 109.

81. Ibid., 108.

82. Ibid.

83. Berger, *Theatermenschen*, 72.

84. Robert C. Allen, Douglas Gomery, *Film History, Theory and Practice* (New York: Alfred A. Knopf, 1985), 96-99.

85. Huaco, *Sociology of Film Art*, 55.

made for him at Ufa.[86] The first part of *Die Nibelungen* (*Siegfrieds Tod*), was shown to audiences in England with a different ending as well.

Weimar Germany produced its cinematic "milestones" through filmmakers who were generously supported by Pommer. Between 1923 and 1926, F.W. Murnau directed *Die Austreibung* (*The Expulsion*), *Die Finanzen des Großherzogs* (*The Finances of the Grand Duke*), *Der letzte Mann, Tartüff* (*The Gilded Hypocrite*), and *Faust*. Ludwig Berger made *Ein Glas Wasser, Der verlorene Schuh*, and *Ein Walzertraum*. E.A. Dupont made *Varieté*, Arthur von Gerlach *Zur Chronik von Grieshuus*, and Carl-Theodor Dreyer, a Danish visitor to Ufa, made *Michael*. Fritz Lang made the two *Nibelungen* films (*Siegfrieds Tod / Death of Siegfried* and *Kriemhilds Rache / Kriemhild's Revenge*), and *Metropolis*. Pommer's principle was to produce *Großfilme* by adhering to the highest standards of technical quality while simultaneously producing "art." It was not uncommon to see film reviews refer to his films as "Pommer films."[87] Even hard-to-please German critic Herbert Ihering paid tribute to him after he saw *Der letzte Mann*.[88] Willy Haas spoke of him enthusiastically as "the businessman who knows that which so many don't know, and who again and again has the courage to stand by his own conviction and who is therefore to all of us at least as important as the greatest artist."[89]

Pommer could financially go over budget because in his capacity of senior manager of Ufa (*Vorstandsdirektor*) he knew that the board of directors (*Aufsichtsrat*) would eventually support his position. He could afford and was willing to accept a substantial loss to produce "art," because he knew this loss would be sanctioned to gain the company prestige that "art films" brought to Ufa and Germany. Such prestige helped gain the Deutsche Bank's financial approval and Emil Georg von Stauß's benevolent support.[90] In the decade's second half, especially toward the transition from silent to sound film, the banks would not and could not concur with such extravagances.[91]

86. Herbert G. Luft, "Erich Pommer: Part II," *Films in Review*, 10: 9 (November 1959), 518. See also Bordwell, *Films of Carl-Theodor Dreyer*, 18.

87. "Drei neue Ufafilme: Dazu 2 Pommer-Filme und 6 Auftragsfilme," *Film-Kurier*, 15 April 1926.

88. Herbert Ihering, *Berliner Börsen-Courier*, 24 December 1924, quoted in *Film-Kurier*, 29 December 1924.

89. Willy Haas, "Der Tag der großen Premiere: 'Der letzte Mann' im Ufa-Palast am Zoo," *Film-Kurier*, 24 December 1924.

90. Berger, *Theatermenschen*, 72.

91. John Pommer, interviewed by author on 7 January 1985 in Camarillo, CA.

The press expressed diverse opinions on Ufa's extreme production budgets. *Lichtbild-Bühne* condemned these practices, while *Film-Kurier* praised them, saying they displayed a certain producer's courage to dare forego profit and other business concerns:

> Do we want to repeat all formulas that have proven to be wrong since 1919 just to make sure that they were indeed wrong? Don't we have enough businessman-produced commercial movies that lose him money just as easily as if he had made the craziest expressionist experiment? Wouldn't we rather build on the honest and clean foreign successes of *Ein Glas Wasser, Der letzte Mann, Der müde Tod,* and *Die Straße* [The Street]?[92]

Pride Before the Fall

Pommer and Ufa's course toward even more spectacular prestige film production reached unimagined dimensions by the mid-twenties. Production furor, spectacular home premieres, and international recognition in England, France, and the United States formed part of a show intended to exhibit Ufa's excellence to the world. The marketing of a *Großfilm* took up a substantial portion of the budget. Pommer's hand in promoting these films was crucial for Ufa's export. He did it in grand style. He was known for inviting critics at his expense to a banquet following a film's premiere in Berlin. He personally took charge of *Der letzte Mann*'s London premiere: "Erich Pommer took care that *Der letzte Mann* received the frame which its representation in London deserved … It will be shown in the newest and most modern theater, and Emil Jannings will introduce himself to the audience at the London premiere."[93]

He also personally fought against what he called the Americans' "boycott" of German films, especially with respect to *Der letzte Mann*. When he realized that no reputable American film distributor intended to see or distribute this film, he staged a special press screening at his own expense to "sell" it to the United States. The enthusiastic audience and press response incited America's interest in the German film industry, he said, but only for this specific film.[94]

---

92. "Nur Theorie – !" *Film-Kurier,* 28 October 1925.
93. Ejott (Ernst Jäger), "Rund um die Woche," *Film-Kurier,* 23 February 1925.
94. Alexander Saklikower, "Amerika und wir," *Film-Kurier,* 12 February 1925. See also Richard Dyer MacCann, "Erich Pommer: Film Leadership on the Old Scale," *Christian Science Monitor,* 27 October 1959.

Banquets were another promotional technique. In March 1924, for instance, Ufa invited high-ranking political figures to a banquet providing a chance to witness the shooting of the final scene of Lang's second *Nibelungen* film, *Kriemhilds Rache*. Ufa exploited the shooting of the scene's gigantic fire for a public spectacle, thereby turning the Ufa propaganda wheels without digging substantially into its advertising budget.[95] It was not unusual to see high government officials at the Ufa studios. Special invitations were issued by Ufa and, on occasion, by SPIO (*Spitzenorganisation der deutschen Filmindustrie*), the industry's professional representative body, to Reich government and Berlin officials, foreign diplomats, and other public dignitaries. Even Chancellor Gustav Stresemann and President Friedrich Ebert participated in such events, which involved studio tours, public addresses, and banquets. Members of Ufa's board of directors and SPIO's top executives used opportunities like these to air their industrial concerns to government dignitaries and the press. Pommer strongly favored such communication:

> When at times we were faced with problems at Ufa, we were able to speak with the government directly. Our contact with the government was continuous and such that Stresemann would ask me to meet him informally for dinner. That provided the opportunity to disclose our problems and wishes at the highest level. And our political speaking partners were extremely well informed.[96]

For the Pommer-Murnau film *Faust*, produced in 1925/1926, Ufa invited artists to participate in a *Faust* poster design contest. Since Ufa already had its own design, this contest was a shrewd advertising ploy and received considerable press coverage.[97]

Ufa's exhibition strategy for Berlin was predetermined by individual film budgets. In the twenties Ufa owned six "first-run" movie palaces. The largest was the Ufa-Palast am Zoo, which had opened on 18 September 1919 with the premiere of *Madame Dubarry*. In the mid-twenties this theater underwent controversial changes when the American businessman Samuel Rachmann

95. "Die Beendigung des Nibelungenfilms," *Lichtbild-Bühne*, 18 March 1924; "Nibelungen-Dämmerung," *Lichtbild-Bühne*, 20 March 1924; and "Brand in Neubabelsberg," *Film-Kurier*, 21 March 1924.

96. Helmut Müller, "Zwischen Hamburg und Hawaii," *Filmecho/Filmwoche*, 8 June 1965.

97. Heinrich Heining, *Goethe und der Film* (Baden-Baden: Neue Verlags-Anstalt, 1949), 73.

attempted its conversion to "New York show" standards.[98] There was the Gloria-Palast, the UT (Union theater) Kurfürstendamm, the Universum, the Ufa-Pavillon, and the UT Königstadt.[99] According to Zglinicki, the selection from among first-run movie theaters for the premiere of a large budget film was determined by type and importance of the film. This choice then decided the necessary star propaganda, which at times consumed up to 10 percent of the production cost.[100] For the opening of the Gloria-Palast with the Pommer-Murnau "art film" *Tartüff* on 25 January 1926, little porcelain figurines of Emil Jannings and Lil Dagover, the film's leading players, were specifically designed by a German professor and produced in the Staatliche Porzellanmanufaktur Berlin.[101] Given the existing hierarchy of first-run movie theaters, a theater's designation endowed a film with prestige: "A premiere at the Gloria-Palast," Zglinicki wrote, "imprinted on the film the label *Spitzenfilm* [film of the highest quality]."[102] Not surprisingly, this process was criticized and condemned as large company politics, predisposing moviegoers in favor of films: "Whether an Ufa film is good or bad," one critic complained, "whether it affects the audience or not, a large number of viewers is always guaranteed."[103]

When *Siegfrieds Tod* premiered on 14 February 1924 in Berlin's Ufa-Palast am Zoo, opening night resembled a stunning night at the opera. The elite of German society, government representatives, the foreign press, and representatives of the international film industry attended this event, resulting in a triumph for Ufa, its film director Fritz Lang, and scriptwriter Thea von Harbou. The Austrian, English, and French reviews of the Berlin premiere paid particular attention to Germany's film industry, Ufa, Decla-Bioscop,

98. Zglinicki, *Weg des Films*, 441. For a detailed account of Rachmann's remodeling of the Ufa-Palast am Zoo, see "Gegen die Amerikanisierung des deutschen Kinos! Hat Rachmann Geheimverträge?" *Film-Kurier*, supplement, 8 October 1925; "Film: Ufapalast," *Tage-Buch*, 3 October 1925; "Film," *Tage-Buch*, 7 November 1925; and Heinrich Stürmer, "Deutscher oder amerikanischer Film," *Tage-Buch*, 14 November 1925.

99. Zglinicki, *Weg des Films*, 435.

100. Ibid.

101. Eberhard Spiess, "Werbung für den Film: Ein Anfang ohne Ende," *Filmkunst* 91 (1981): 30.

102. Zglinicki, *Weg des Films*, 438.

103. Rudolf Arnheim, "Betrübliche Filme," *Weltbühne*, 12 January 1932. Arnheim habitually attacked what he called Pommer's commercialism. In this article he claimed: "A film produced for 100,000 marks by a small company outside mainstream film production, which wins nobody's attention and brings in no money, can seem more remarkable to us than an entire year's worth from Pommer's mill."

and its production head Pommer. For instance, the French praised Pommer's visible intelligence, vitality, and extraordinary energy and referred to him and Ufa CEO (*Generaldirektor*) Felix Kallmann as "the soul of the gigantic cinematographic organization," which had no parallel in France.[104] The French cultural magazine *Comoedia* attributed the film's success to German work ethics, remarking that people do not play but work in the Tempelhof studios, where production head Pommer provides his film directors with all required money and all necessary means.[105]

Siegfrieds Tod seemed the epitome of Pommer's vision. Following its release in London, Paris, and New York, the film was hailed as "specifically German," "ambassador between nations," and Germany's "messenger of peace through art." It could not have been produced without Pommer's mediating position between his team and Ufa's top management. After the premiere, Ufa executives spoke of the difficulties resulting from tension between those controlling the budget and those defending their creative vision, in short, the chasm between businessman (*Kaufmann*) and film expert (*Fachmann*). Like no other film *Nibelungen* had exposed this dichotomy during the planning stage. Initially no agreement could be reached between the business and production sectors, and "the very heated debate fought with great tenacity on both sides resulted in victory for the film experts at Ufa."[106] CEO Kallmann publicly admitted that his politics had been wrong and that the film expert deserved victory over the businessman.[107]

The Munich premiere a few weeks later was no less spectacular. Here Emil Georg von Stauß, chairman of the board of directors, provided unusual insight in company politics:

> Perhaps it took some optimism, or better, frivolousness on the bankers' part, to nurture an enterprise of Ufa's kind. . . I believe that tonight proved the justification for taking film seriously, as an industry and as an art that reaches the entire world. . . A film can never recover its costs in one country. It can only survive on the world market, given its enormous cost and large resources that were allocated for its production. . . We have to aim for the best if we want to survive.[108]

104. Paul de la Borie, in *Cinématographie Française*, 23 February 1924, printed (in trans.) in *Film-Kurier*, second supplement, 1 March 1924.
105. "Fritz Langs Pariser Erfolg," *Film-Kurier*, first supplement, 26 March 1925.
106. "Der Wendepunkt," *Lichtbild-Bühne*, 16 February 1924.
107. Ibid.
108. "Die Nibelungen," *Süddeutsche Filmzeitung*, 14 March 1924.

The genesis of the *Nibelungen* films clearly reveals Pommer's understanding of his role as producer. As production chief and *Vorstandsdirektor* he was uniquely positioned to mediate between the executive/financial and the cinematic/creative sectors, in short, between business and art. Had he not fully supported film director Lang's artistic vision, he would not have provided the financial backing. Customarily a producer did not cater to the financial demands of a film director, who is habitually oblivious to film expenses in the realization of a personal film vision in the studio. Yet, in this era at Ufa, the film director was "the dictator" and Pommer strongly believed in the director's power. The film's creator, he believed, was the director, not the producer, because once everything is prepared, "the director will go on stage, with the author."[109] Perhaps this was particularly true for the collaboration between Pommer and Lang at Ufa. Lang admitted he never would have been able to make the films of the twenties without Pommer.[110] One anecdote about their collaboration has become part of the Pommer legend. During the filming of *Kriemhild's Revenge*, Pommer, concerned about the budget, allegedly suggested to Lang to omit a scene that – according to Lang – required hundreds of extras and horses. After thinking it over, Lang was ready to comply, but was surprised by Pommer who had thought it over as well; the scene remained.[111] Pommer also knew he would have been unable to attract and hold top visionary and highly motivated filmmakers like Lang, Murnau, and Berger had he been less than generous with funds. Big American film companies were always ready and eager to offer Germany's most talented filmmakers and stars more than Germany could pay, a fear openly acknowledged by *Film-Kurier*: "Hopefully the contracts between Ufa and Murnau and Lang are such that we must not fear America's temptations in the near future. In any case, the

109. Pommer, interviewed by Kadiev and Kyser.
110. Viege Traub, journalist and widow of Ufa's Hans Traub, interviewed by author on 2 January 1985 in Los Angeles.
111. Quoted in Eisner, *Fritz Lang*, 80. John E. Pommer, a young boy at the time of the shooting, remembers being present during this particular sequence: "At the time I was impressed that the Huns were riding bare-back, although I assume that flat saddles were hidden under the rags on which the Huns were sitting. But they had no stirrups; only Etzel had large wooden clogs in which he placed his feet. I did not think it fair, but now I wonder whether that really made it easier for [Rudolph] Klein-Rogge [who played the King of the Huns]. The wild rides caused several accidents. I remember a few extras being cared for in a tent hospital." Letter from J. Pommer to author, 2 September 1995.

German film industry ought to watch out so the best men are not being snatched up."[112]

At least for a while Pommer attracted and held his top film-makers with generous offers. For instance, Lang resisted American opportunities, though he may have been motivated by other factors as well: "I was in America," he said, "and it felt like being in exile."[113] Murnau's case was different. No producer in the German film industry had ever supplied as much money for a director/scriptwriter team as Pommer had for Murnau and Carl Mayer, much to the chagrin of director Lupu Pick, for whom Mayer had previously worked, but who simply could not pay as much as Pommer.[114] And yet in 1925, despite Pommer's generosity, just when Ufa was wrestling financial disaster, Murnau accepted an invitation to the United States, and Pommer allegedly felt betrayed.[115]

In the mid-1920s, of course, Ufa executives did not greatly oppose extravagances, especially those demanded by a film director like Lang, since his monumental film productions precisely reflected Ufa's, some insist Pommer's,[116] policy of international market expansion. Ufa executives apparently failed to recognize that the company's economic situation demanded thrifty production policies. On the contrary, they hoped for successful export business and were eager therefore to expand distribution channels by exerting influence on foreign companies, especially theaters. The objective was to beat American competition with their own weapons, the "superfilm," the expensive *Monumentalfilm*.[117]

Pommer believed, however, in national film production and vehemently rejected the notion of a film "with an American look," as was suggested by Samuel Goldwyn while visiting Ufa. Pommer defended national filmmaking precisely as a counterbalance to America and as a mandatory precondition for an understanding among peoples.[118] He compromised neither his belief in "nationally specific" films nor his desire to remove national boundaries through the cinema. Just as *Der letzte Mann* was recognized in France as "thoroughly German," it was celebrated in

112. "Amerikanische Filmchronik," *Film-Kurier*, 30 December 1924.
113. "Fritz Langs Pariser Erfolg," *Film-Kurier*, first supplement, 26 May 1925.
114. Jäger, "Nicht zur Veröffentlichung," *Der neue Film*, part 33.
115. Ibid., part 31.
116. "Die guten Freunde," *Lichtbild-Bühne*, 20 May 1926.
117. Spiker, *Film und Kapital*, 42.
118. "Goldwyn bei der Ufa," *Film-Kurier*, third supplement, 17 January 1925.

Germany as a "world film." *Der letzte Mann* proved that "Pommer's production mode opened the door to a 'world cinema.'"[119] *Die Nibelungen* continued in this tradition. As Steve Neale concluded in his exploration of art cinema, Pommer's policy was a "concern with national culture, the national economy, the national industry, and with national cinematic traditions."[120]

In October 1924, Lang, Pommer and his wife Gertrud crossed the Atlantic to attend the New York City premiere of *Die Nibelungen*. They continued to Hollywood, accompanied by Ufa CEO Felix Kallmann and Frederick Wynne-Jones, Ufa's American representative. The German trade press hailed this trip as an exploration of American film production facilities and a visit to Ufa's recently established office in New York.[121] But the press also speculated on the trip's potential effect on Ufa's production. *Lichtbild-Bühne* expressed hope that Pommer would not change his production mode at Ufa after his return.[122] *Film-Kurier* was less optimistic, speculating that Ufa's new production program would undoubtedly be affected by American experiences.[123] Had the American film industry conspired to undermine affairs at Ufa, they could not have planned it better; the trip was to have long-lasting reverberations. Lang's and Pommer's overwhelming impression of New York's skyline, when their ship entered the harbor, created the vision for their next film, *Metropolis*, and the rest is history.

Metropolis was the beginning of the end, at least for Ufa's "golden era" of silent film production. While *Die Nibelungen* soared, taking with it Pommer, and intoxicating its makers, *Metropolis* became, in many respects, a "death film" for Ufa and for Pommer. While the first film was a manifestation of Pommer's

119. "Das Welt-Echo des 'letzten Mannes'," *Film-Kurier*, 17 April 1925.

120. Neale, "Art Cinema as Institution," 34.

121. It was customary at Ufa to send representatives to foreign countries, sometimes on very specific assignments. The minutes of Ufa's *Vorstand* meetings contain repeated references to such trips. During the 12 March 1929 meeting, with special attention given to the advance of sound film in the U.S., the following decision was made: "The gentlemen [Ernst Hugo] Correll, Pommer, and Joe May will, as soon as possible, go on an exploratory trip to the U.S. An extension of this trip to Hollywood is, if possible, to be avoided." Extensive trips were also authorized for contract negotiations, especially when Ufa was highly interested in an actor (Emil Jannings, for example), a novel, or a script. This occurred in March 1931 when Ufa sent Pommer and an Ufa attorney to Paris to obtain the rights for the film operetta *Bomben auf Monte Carlo* (*Monte Carlo Madness*) from novelist Heltai Jenö. Ufa file R109I.

122. "Pommers Reise nach Amerika," *Lichtbild-Bühne*, 30 September 1924.

123. Ejott, "Rund um die Woche," *Film-Kurier*, 23 February 1925.

power at its peak, the latter – consuming even bigger, more gigantic sets, a still larger cast, and a continuously increasing budget – pulled the rug out from under him. While, thematically, *Die Nibelungen* plunged deeply into the heart of German folklore and saga-laden forests, intending to restore audience confidence in Germany's past history, *Metropolis* alienated with the futuristic landscape of foreign skyscrapers. *Die Nibelungen* became the epitome of German filmmaking in its national specificity; the utopian city of *Metropolis* constituted a betrayal in its departure from Pommer's and Lang's vision of a "German" film. European and American reception of *Die Nibelungen* showered Ufa with praise and thrust Ufa still more toward expensive "prestige" film production. *Metropolis* was accused of being not only "almost American, but more American than most of the American films."[124] Deprived of Pommer's editing skills due to his resignation from Ufa and robbed of its important secondary plot,[125] it came to puzzle and annoy critics, bringing Ufa's *Großfilm* production to a painful halt.[126] "Modern cinema's monstrous cathedral," as Luis Bunuel called the film, contradicted Pommer's previous course.[127]

Ufa's Hans Traub justifiably interpreted *Metropolis* as Ufa's desire to create a film style equal to America's and therefore capable of winning in the American market. He called it

> a magnificent film in terms of the means and possibilities of film as artistic craft, but a cold, almost – it could be said – mechanical film. Compared to the romantic, often monstrous [*monströs*] sweep of *Die Nibelungen*, it exaggerates in demonstrating the influence of

124. Riess, *Das gab's nur einmal*, vol. 2, 19.

125. The subplot, which is the basis for the deadly rivalry between the industrialist and the inventor, consists of a love affair between the latter and the industrialist's wife, Hel. For the film's U.S. opening, censors allegedly found the name's resemblance to "hell" unacceptable and, instead of changing the name and the subtitles, cut out the entire secondary plot. Ufa later followed suit and did not restore the film's original version. Enno Patalas, before his retirement as director of the Munich Film Museum, was able to remedy some of the damage by using stills and various copies he located, primarily in Australia. He then reconstructed the storyline from a copy of the original music score. Letter on audiocassette from J. Pommer to author, 7 July 1993.

126. *Das Tage-Buch* published an especially nasty review, condemning *Metropolis* as a "gigantic, hollow, twisted, dishonest *Metropolis* monster" and giving the film the dubious distinction of quintessential "world failure." L.S., "Am Wrack der Ufa," *Tage-Buch*, 2 April 1927. See also Lucien Bourdet, "Deutscher Stacheldraht," *Tage-Buch*, 10 September 1927.

127. Ilona Brennicke and Joe Hembus, *Klassiker des deutschen Stummfilms 1910-1930* (Munich: Goldmann Verlag, 1983), 136.

American realism. Two films, in concept and mentality each at one extreme end of the wide spectrum of artistic film production of those years, lead the silent film toward its perfection and toward its termination.[128]

Fall from Grace

Pommer's rise and fall mirrored Ufa's. Ufa gave Pommer the means and power to use his brilliance to produce "highly artistic motion pictures." While Pommer led the company to unprecedented world-wide prestige, his power ride was expensive and growing more so with every film. Ufa's resources and income could no longer support his extravagant spending, albeit company-condoned, and the gain in prestige was overwhelmed by economic reality, that is, loss of funds. While in 1925 production of *Metropolis* was in full swing, Ufa's board of directors had to admit that the *Konzern* was on the brink of bankruptcy. Company assets no longer covered the enormous debts that were then listed as 36 million marks. The situation leading to the German-U.S. Parufamet (Paramount/Ufa/Metro-Goldwyn-Mayer) agreements was so unfavorable that even negotiations with the German government and other large German non-film enterprises proved unsuccessful.

After Ufa obtained another loan of 15 million marks, debts were no longer covered by Ufa's 45 million mark base capital.[129] Emil Georg von Stauß's suggestion to the board to sell the company was vetoed by their majority. As Ufa's feature film production head and *Vorstandsdirektor*, Pommer was at the forefront of negotiations with the two American film giants, Famous Players-Lasky (Paramount) and Metro-Goldwyn-Mayer. And as with Decla-Bioscop in 1921, when financial difficulties necessitated a structural move to which he was opposed,[130] Pommer again found himself confronting a situation without alternatives. He was overruled by Ferdinand Bausback, Ufa's new *Generaldirektor*. As head of foreign distribution Pommer cosigned three of the five agreements, as the

---

128. Traub, *Ufa*, 53.
129. Spiker, *Film und Kapital*, 42.
130. Fritz Lang recalls that Pommer opposed the merger with Ufa for which negotiations were prevalent during the filming of Lang's *Der müde Tod*, in *Fritz Lang. Choix de textes établi par Alfred Eibel*, 10. As to Pommer's role in the Parufamet agreements, see Zglinicki, 414. John Pommer has confirmed Zglinicki's assertion in an interview with the author.

Parufamet documents show.[131] None of these was signed by Pommer alone, yet he was unjustly blamed by some critics for having authorized these loans himself.[132]

The Parufamet agreements were a complex entanglement of loans and entitlements between Ufa and Paramount on the one hand, and Ufa and Metro-Goldwyn-Mayer on the other, the sum of which was believed to provide Ufa at the end of 1925 with desperately needed financial resources. But the loans came with costly strings attached. The agreements stipulated a ten-year loan of 2 million dollars from each company (amounting to about RM 17 million)[133] in exchange for a mortgage on Ufa's downtown office building in Berlin, Haus Vaterland, and the distribution of ten Ufa films in America. Additionally, the contracts gave a huge German market share to the United States, forcing Ufa to accept twenty films from each company for distribution. But the most devastating stipulation concerned Ufa's theaters. Ufa was obliged to reserve half of its theater slots for exhibiting the films of these U.S. companies, a requirement Ufa could hardly survive.

And yet, the German-American agreements were initially interpreted by some as an advantage to Ufa, as Germany's long-awaited chance to exhibit films in American theaters on a regular basis.[134] Pommer's negotiations received the trade press's stamp of approval, interpreted, as they were, as saving the company from surrendering to U.S. ownership. Far from signaling Ufa's

131. The following three agreements were signed by Pommer in his capacity as head of foreign distribution: 1. Agreement of 29 December 1925 between Universum-Film AG (Ufa) and Famous Player-Lasky Corporation and Metro-Goldwyn Pictures Corporation, regarding a $2 million loan from each company. Repayment was scheduled to begin 1 January 1928 in monthly installments of $20,833.33 on account of principals plus interest. *Vorstandsdirektoren* Pommer and Eugen Stauß signed. 2. Agreement of 31 December 1925 between the same partners, regarding Ufa film distribution in the United Sates. Pommer and *Vorstandsdirektor* Siegmund Jacob signed. 3. Agreement between Universum-Film AG (Ufa) and Ufa Film-Vertriebsgesellschaft mbH (Ufa's distribution company) regarding distribution in Germany. Pommer and *Vorstandsdirektor* Alexander Grau signed. Two other agreements, both between Ufa's distribution company and each of the two American partners regarding the distribution of their films in Germany, were not signed by Pommer whose responsibility was foreign distribution. These agreements were dated 31 December 1925. Ufa file, R109I.

132. See Charles Ford's consistently incorrect claims in "Grandeur and Decadence of Ufa," *Films in Review*, 4: 6 (June-July 1953): 267.

133. Kallmann, *Konzernierung in der Filmindustrie*, 27. See also "Die Generalversammlung der Ufa," *Film-Kurier*, 30 December 1925.

134. See Curt I.C. Anderson, *Über die deutsche Filmindustrie und ihre volkswirtschaftliche Bedeutung unter Berücksichtigung ihrer internationalen Beziehungen*, Ph.D.

demise, the agreements were interpreted as an intensification of Ufa's business relations with big American firms:

> But Ufa reserves for itself a free hand in the current year. It was surprisingly able to intensify its business relations with the "big" American companies. Erich Pommer's trip to the United States last year is certainly not going to be his last one. But we are convinced that Ufa's big art films of 1925/26 will attract even more attention among the American film industry than has been the case with *Die Nibelungen* and *Der letzte Mann*. When the time comes that Erich Pommer is going to present the new Ufa-films in America, he can do so in the proud realization that American film production is dependent upon him in Germany.[135]

But soon such initial enthusiasm diminished, and America's intervention was interpreted as overtly forcing its German competitor into the role of economic dependent.[136] For instance, Ufa was barred from making its own selection of American films, whereas the Americans had the right to refuse German films as they pleased. While American films had to be shown in Ufa's largest and best theaters in Berlin, Ufa films were not shown at the Roxy, but in Yorktown, New York City's German section.[137] Not surprisingly, of interest to the American audience were exactly those films which Pommer had produced at Ufa for this market (*Faust, Metropolis, Varieté*) whereas the average German fare was considered either boring or pathetic.[138]

In 1926, while Ufa was already severely disabled by Parufamet agreements, rising costs during production of *Metropolis* merely intensified press criticism about Ufa business policies. "Nobody wants to take the blame for the current condition of the German film industry," *Film-Kurier* stated on 16 February 1926.[139] It was easy for Ufa to blame its disastrous financial dilemma before and after the Parufamet agreements on the extravagance of its production chief Pommer and his director Fritz Lang, who, together, were held

---

diss., Univ. Munich, 1927 (Munich: Weiss, 1929). He praised the German-American "film exchange" through the Parufamet agreements as commendable model for two equal film industry partners. Likewise, Ufa felt to have shielded itself from its American partners by keeping them out of its board of directors (*Aufsichtsrat*) and senior management (*Vorstand*). See "Der gute Wille," *Film-Kurier*, 16 January 1926.

135. "Die Ufa und Amerika," *Film-Kurier*, 7 August 1925.
136. See also Spiker, *Film und Kapital*, 43.
137. John Pommer, interviewed by author.
138. Zglinicki, *Weg des Films*, 418.
139. "Mohrenwäsche ["Dirty Laundry"]," *Film-Kurier*, 16 February 1926.

responsible for spending 5 million marks on their last joint project, *Metropolis*. Likewise, it was easily forgotten that his expansion policies at Ufa had earlier been assessed as "necessary and victorious." As the press was quick to point out:

> Let us not forget a fact which evolves more clearly every month: that the Ufa film has become the world competitor for America on all foreign markets with respect to its artistic reputation. (What laurels and hymns of praise would have been showered on a man like Erich Pommer for such a victory at different times or in another industry or art!)[140]

Other irregularities at the company notwithstanding, the issue of accountability was passed between the chairman of Ufa's board of directors, Emil Georg von Stauß, and the head of production, *Vorstandsdirektor* Erich Pommer, the final burden of responsibility resting with Pommer, the film expert.[141] The political magazine *Das Tage-Buch* came to Pommer's rescue:

> It is futile to continue playing the well-known circle of guilt displacement. Futile especially in view of the fact that Ufa's top leadership has never changed. The real leader, or whatever the chiefs called themselves, was the Chairman of the *Aufsichtsrat*, [Emil Georg von] Stauß, who simultaneously represents the creditor Deutsche Bank. Whenever he said, "produce," Ufa produced; whenever he said, "reduce," Ufa reduced.[142]

Stauß was indeed in control and no justification existed for delegating the blame to Pommer except for saving face. Filmmaker Ludwig Berger confirmed this, stating that since the merger of Decla-Bioscop and Ufa, an executive concerned with the financial aspects of negotiations had always been present, not Pommer alone.[143] This person proposed Berger's future film project and negotiated the salary with him, while Pommer held a mediating

---

140. "Zur Situation der Ufa," *Film-Kurier*, 17 February 1926.

141. On 22 July 1927, Pommer, then working in the U.S. film industry, wrote to his family that he had learned about a lawsuit by Ufa against one of its senior managers accused of having squandered 16 million marks. "If this is true," Pommer writes, "it would give me great satisfaction since it would mean the public affirmation that not my department but another one at Ufa was accountable for the company's million mark loss." Letter from J. Pommer to author, 15 August 1993. See also "Blindbuchen und Zweischlagerprogramm müssen beseitigt werden," *Film-Kurier*, 1 March 1929, which refers to legal proceedings against former *Vorstandsdirektor* Siegmund Jacob.

142. "Die notleidende Ufa," *Tage-Buch*, 18 December 1926.

143. Ludwig Berger, *Wir sind vom gleichen Stoff aus dem die Träume sind* (Tübingen: Wunderlich Verlag, 1953), 168.

position.[144] Clearly in at least some business negotiations practiced at Ufa, Pommer's position was not that of unsupervised financial decision maker. When Ufa top executives made its production head largely responsible for the consequences of the company's expansion policies, it actually undermined Stauß's power by placing the burden exclusively on Pommer's shoulders. If Pommer indeed had the power to cause that much damage to company finances, the board of directors conspicuously neglected to use its supervisory function. Accordingly, the trade journal *Lichtbild-Bühne* had no problem seeing it this way. In an attempt to dismantle the "halo" that press favoritism had placed around Pommer, the journal claimed: "Who was head of production in Ufa's *Vorstand*? Erich Pommer! If this is the case, any discussion of who was responsible for the production policy is superfluous."[145]

Others came to Pommer's rescue by pointing to his enormous work load, which far exceeded any single production chief's human potential. Despite Ufa's production division between *Eigenproduktion* and *Auftragsproduktion*, it was impossible for Pommer as head of Ufa's entire feature film production to maintain close oversight of all films. Justifiably, the question concerning Pommer's responsibilities was raised after his resignation. "I have been told in Germany," Charles Davy wrote, "that Pommer failed because he attempted too much himself. Originally at the head of the administrative side of the business, he undertook also the general production supervision as well."[146] *Das Tage-Buch* was equally sympathetic: "Is the production head who carries the world film in his heart also in the position to show an equally strong interest for the cheap film which is intended for small town audiences? Would it not have been better to separate categories of production?"[147]

The opinion expressed in *Lichtbild-Bühne* hinted at Pommer's failure to establish priorities:

> We never disavowed Pommer's qualities. The source of the fiasco
> lies in Pommer's personal expansion ambition, insisting on doing

144. The film project was Berger's *Der verlorene Schuh* whose Cinderella theme did not immediately meet either executive's approval, but became a very successful film. *Süddeutsche Filmzeitung* praised its cinematography and its insight into the "wonders of technology." It claimed the film would alert foreign countries to the high standard of German technology. "Kritische Filmschau," *Süddeutsche Filmzeitung*, 11 January 1924.

145. "Die guten Freunde," *Lichtbild-Bühne*, 20 May 1926.

146. Charles Davy, ed., *Footnotes to the Film* (London: Lovat Dickson Ltd. Readers' Union Ltd., 1937), 195.

147. *Tage-Buch*, 18 December 1926.

everything alone. Instead of focusing all his strength exclusively on his production, he took on representative obligations, had advertising in his hands, undertook time-consuming travels, led difficult negotiations, and finally, also handled foreign sales. This diffusion of energy has to result in a distraction from his actual task, and production had to suffer.[148]

In January 1926 Pommer resigned from Ufa; increasing frustration with the policies of the new CEO Ferdinand Bausback left no other choice. He also resigned from two other organizations, the Association of Film Industrialists and SPIO, whose first president he had become.[149] The German film industry thereby lost one of its top spokesmen, but Pommer strongly felt that his SPIO presidency was contingent upon his post as Ufa *Vorstandsdirektor*.[150] Most tragically for the German cinema, Pommer's departure from Ufa was interpreted in the press not so much as Ufa's but as Germany's loss. Stefan Großmann commented in *Das Tage-Buch*: "Pommer's departure is not only the fall of a man but the fall of the big art film, which can hold its own on the world market and which causes the Americans some discomfort. . . Without Pommer, the German cinema of the next ten or twenty years will be shaky."[151] In the wake of Pommer's resignation, Ufa terminated four hundred employees in an obvious survival move toward rationalization.[152] In March 1926, *Die Weltbühne* reported:

> The season is at its peak. Nearly all of the new movie palaces [*Großkinos*] are open. Six premieres a day are no rarity. But behind this opulent activity the demolition of the German industry progresses rapidly. The production base of Ufa has, through the dismissal of almost all film directors, architects, cinematographers, qualified clerks, [and] actors under contracts, been reduced to the status of a mid-sized enterprise.[153]

To Ufa's chagrin, Lang refused to opt out of his Ufa contract. In an apparent move to curb his astronomic spending, Ufa renegotiated

---

148. "Die guten Freunde," *Lichtbild-Bühne*, 20 May 1926.

149. For more details about Pommer's instrumental role in SPIO's foundation, see *Film-Kurier*, 6, 11, 20, 22, and 27 October 1923. SPIO's successful joining of film manufacturers and film industrialists after their earlier rift was considered a major accomplishment.

150. "Erich Pommer scheidet aus der Spitzenorganisation," *Film-Kurier*, 28 January 1926.

151. Stefan Großmann, "Erich Pommers Sturz," *Tage-Buch*, 30 January 1926.

152. "Zur Situation der Ufa," *Film-Kurier*, 17 February 1926.

153. Axel Eggebrecht, "Filmkunst und Filmgeschäft," *Weltbühne*, 2 March 1926.

Lang's position within the *Konzern*. The result was the Fritz Lang Film Company within Ufa, which enabled Ufa to recover part of the production cost for Lang's future films from the film director.[154]

The legacy of Pommer's early career was astounding. *Film-Kurier* called him the most popular personality in the German cinema, one of Germany's few high-calibre film politicians who represented, as did no one else, the German cinema in Germany and vis-à-vis its European neighbors: "Through his doing, Erich Pommer has given the Ufa trademark a name in the world. That means he has presented exemplary works on the world market with a twofold effect: the German film became worthy of debate in foreign countries, and the Ufa films received world recognition as highest achievements in international film 'art.'"[155]

154. See *Fritz Lang. Choix de textes établi par Alfred Eibel*, 217. For more information on the ensuing drama involving Lang's company and Ufa, see Michael Töteberg, "Nie wieder Fritz Lang!" in *Ufa-Buch*, 218–23.

155. "Erich Pommer zurückgetreten," *Film-Kurier*, 22 January 1926.

Chapter 4

AMERICAN INTERLUDE

It is my privilege now to be in Hollywood to aid in the introduction of some phases of European technique into American picture making, but at the same time I am learning much
that I hope I may some day use for the improvement of pictures abroad.

Erich Pommer, "Hands Across the Sea
in Movie Development"

Hollywood

A call to Hollywood was inevitable given Pommer's reputation at
home and abroad as Germany's most brilliant young producer. In
Berlin, the pending premieres of his last Ufa films, especially *Faust*
and *Metropolis*, kept his name very much alive.[1] Such fame apparently caused his former employer justifiable trepidation that he
might remain in Germany and join forces with another German
company, thereby securing a competitive position vis-à-vis Ufa.[2]
The trade press speculated wildly about Pommer's future moves.
Lichtbild-Bühne, for instance, claimed to know of Pommer's plans
to produce in Germany independently, and predicted good chances

1. At Pommer's resignation, the following films were completed: *Der Geiger von
Florenz* (*The Violinist of Florence*), *Die Brüder Schellenberg* (*The Schellenberg Brothers*),
and *Die drei Kuckucksuhren* (*Three Cuckoo Clocks*). Not completed were *Faust and
Metropolis*. "Erich Pommer zurückgetreten," *Film-Kurier*, 22 January 1926.
2. See Riess, *Das gab's nur einmal*, vol. 2, 14–15.

for success if he would adhere to "reasonable" budgetary restrictions and choose his team "wisely."[3] *Film-Kurier*, on the other hand, speculated on the possibility that Pommer might produce for one of Ufa's Parufamet partners in Berlin, but reported on Ufa's and Paramount's inability to agree on the nature of Pommer's production activity in Germany.[4] For the time being, however, Pommer's choice was Hollywood. In early 1926 he crossed the Atlantic several times until negotiations with Adolph Zukor's Famous Players-Lasky Corporation (Paramount) were finalized during Pommer's February trip to New York.[5]

Ufa had not only given up its top producer but was also losing several members of Pommer's production and acting team, who opted to follow him to Hollywood.[6] It did not take long for the question to surface whether the German film industry was healthy enough to weather such decimation of talent.[7] *Film-Kurier* remarked: "Pommer's remaining in Germany would perhaps have provided an incentive for many film directors, who have now left for America, to remain in Germany. The exodus of our best and most competent film directors is the hardest blow the German film industry had to endure."[8] Trade press reaction to Pommer's U.S. contract was mixed, especially in light of the German-American Parufamet agreements.[9] Press paranoia was inevitable, as for instance in *Weltbühne*'s proclamation that Pommer "is organizing in Hollywood a good portion of the American invasion whose final victory he might some day take back home."[10] Other voices, less warlike, interpreted Pommer's work in Hollywood as a possible indication of future German-American cooperation. The overall consensus

3. "Pommers Ausscheiden aus der Ufa," *Lichtbild-Bühne*, 23 January 1926.

4. "Erich Pommers Abreise," *Film-Kurier*, 6 April 1926.

5. The *Jahrbuch der Filmindustrie* (Berlin: Verlag der *Lichtbild-Bühne, 1928*) cites February 1926 for Pommer's contract with Paramount. Pommer boarded the "Olympic," sister ship to the "Titanic," in New York on 26 February 1926 "in order to settle his personal affairs" in Berlin. "Pommer und Paramount," *Film-Kurier*, 27 February 1926. In April the same trade paper reported his stop-over in Paris from where he planned to travel to New York and Los Angeles. "Erich Pommers Abreise," *Film-Kurier*, 6 April 1926. He was accompanied on this trip by his wife and son.

6. Following Pommer to Hollywood were film directors Ludwig Berger, Paul Leni, E.A. Dupont, Lothar Mendes, and William Dieterle; and actors Conrad Veidt, Emil Jannings, and Lya de Putti. See Jäger, "Nicht zur Veröffentlichung," *Der neue Film*, part 28.

7. Großmann, "Erich Pommers Sturz," *Tage-Buch*, 30 January 1926.

8. "Erich Pommers Abreise," *Film-Kurier*, 6 April 1926.

9. "Amerikanisierung der Ufa?" *Lichtbild-Bühne*, 9 January 1926.

10. Axel Eggebrecht, "Film im Jahreswechsel," *Weltbühne*, 11 January 1927.

was that his motives were always the best. *Film-Kurier* commented: "We are convinced that Erich Pommer's work for Paramount will not be conducted without taking the interests of the German and European cinema into account." The journal also reported, "Pommer is convinced that Paramount will do everything in its power to advance the German film industry and to support the German film."[11] Such faith in Pommer's loyalty is remarkable considering that he was joining the enemy's ranks. His future in the States seemed full of opportunities for Pommer and a triumph for the U.S. film industry.

After only a few months, Pommer's start at Paramount appeared promising enough to justify selling the house he had purchased in Berlin in 1925 and shipping his household belongings to Hollywood. He rented a house on 1725 Camino Palmero from the widow of Douglas Fairbanks's brother Jerry. With many European filmmakers and actors employed in Hollywood, Pommer seemed to fit right in. It made sense to place them under the supervision of a European producer, especially when they proved to be difficult to work with. His initial six months' contract with Paramount specified the production of three feature films. For his first film, the First World War story *Hotel Imperial*, Pommer chose Mauritz Stiller, a Swedish film director already present in Hollywood. Allegedly, Stiller had a reputation for being difficult, strange, and eccentric, which accounted for Metro-Goldwyn-Mayer's willingness to free him for Pommer's film at Paramount.[12] The female star of Pommer's Paramount films was to be none other than Pola Negri, once one of German producer Paul Davidson's biggest box office attractions at Union-Film and now under contract at Paramount. Knowing that Pommer would produce her films for Paramount, she wrote in her memoirs that his supervision would guarantee "that all of the production values would be of the highest order."[13]

Contrary to his work in Germany where the producer's name did not appear in the credits, his first Hollywood film, *Hotel Imperial*, gave Pommer full name recognition. The U.S. trade paper *Variety*, in reviewing the film after its 1926 New Year's Eve premiere in Paramount's newly opened theater in New York, granted considerable publicity to the producer, especially his collaboration with Stiller. Acknowledging that "Stiller and Pommer have

11. "Pommer und Paramount," *Film-Kurier*, 27 February 1926.
12. For more on Stiller, see Pola Negri, *Memoirs of a Star* (Garden City, NY: Doubleday, 1970), 255; and Norman Zierold, *Garbo* (New York: Stein and Day, 1969).
13. Negri, *Memoirs*, 289.

done their work well," *Variety* concluded that good direction and supervision were of no avail because the film lacked a good story. If "great things" were expected of the "two master craftsmen of the industry imported from abroad," they did not materialize, at least not for this American reviewer.[14] Unfortunately, the review does not give credit to the film's outstanding camera work. Pommer, Stiller, and cameraman Bert Glennon designed the most up-to-date camera that was able to move in two planes simultaneously. As described by Pommer's son John, "it was a metal scaffold built along a stage wall, whereby the camera could roll along a horizontal track while simultaneously rising or falling along a vertical plane."[15]

Pommer's second Hollywood film, *Barbed Wire*, was again a story from the Great War, directed by the American film director Rowland V. Lee. Like its predecessor, it failed to win over U.S. audiences despite its promising opening night. This time *Variety*'s reviewer no longer singled out the European producer but focused almost entirely on Pola Negri's unconvincing performance. The film's central theme, its pacifism, was pure Pommer. The reviewer stated that *Barbed Wire* was "no offense whatsoever to any nationality seeking neither to place the blame of the war on one people or another."[16]

In early 1927, *Variety* reported Pommer's dissatisfaction in Hollywood and remarked that he "is not having any too smooth sailing."[17] Apparently things went wrong during the planning stage of Pommer's third Paramount film, *The Man Who Forgot God*, to be again directed by Mauritz Stiller, and starring Ufa's Emil Jannings. Allegedly Stiller and Pommer disagreed with studio executives over the conception of the film. Stiller was relieved of his task and Pommer opted to resign. *Variety* reported that "Pommer was to have continued as supervisor of the unit but due to the fact that the story as it is to be made did not meet with his approval, he did not think it advisable for him to continue with the organization."[18]

Several factors contributed to Pommer's difficulties at Paramount. Whether it was a matter of economics, studio politics, or

14. Fred., "*Hotel Imperial*," *Variety*, 5 January 1927.

15. Letters from J. Pommer to author, 6 July 1993 and 20 November 1993. See also the production still from *Hotel Imperial* in Arthur Knight, *The Liveliest Art: A Panoramic History of the Movies* (NY: Macmillan Co., 1957), 98.

16. "*Barbed Wire*," *Variety*, 10 August 1927.

17. "Eric Pommer Leaves F.P.; Couldn't Agree on Story," *Variety*, 26 January 1927.

18. Ibid.

clashing personalities and production concepts, the U.S. film industry was no less affected by financial dictates than the one Pommer had left behind. His short months at Paramount coincided with a number of efficiency and economy measures, the opening of Paramount's new theater in New York City notwithstanding. In late 1926, for instance, Paramount's production chief, Ben P. Schulberg, eliminated the mediating positions of the company's editorial production supervisors, insisting on personal participation in story construction and conferences with the writers.[19] Jesse L. Lasky, executive head of production, cut back production of road show films and announced that the company would henceforth concentrate on a weekly change program. Lasky reasoned that "the picture which holds the attention of the public from two to seven days is the foundation upon which the film industry is built."[20]

There was also mounting friction between Pommer and Schulberg. Though Schulberg's son Stuart later claimed that his father had given Pommer "carte blanche" in the twenties at Paramount, nothing could be further from the truth.[21] According to Pommer's son, Adolph Zukor tried to persuade Pommer to stay, apparently toying with the idea of replacing Schulberg: "But my father was still in his 30's, young and impatient, and decided to leave, especially since there was the possibility of going to MGM."[22]

Like Paramount, Metro-Goldwyn-Mayer (M-G-M) offered Pommer a six months' contract. Apparently, Pommer was felt to be the producer best able to handle the company's difficulties with its obstinate Swedish star, Greta Garbo.[23] Hired to supervise all units involving foreign directors, he began preparations for the Tolstoy adaptation *Anna Karenina*, with Garbo as star. Shooting was scheduled for April, with the Russian-born Dimitri Buchowetzki as director. Apparently, production began with "language and other difficulties with the director and problems of temperament with the stars."[24] Buchowetzki was replaced by the British Edmund Goulding with whom Pommer established a good rapport.[25] But eventually Irving Thalberg, second-in-command at M-G-M after

19. "F.P.'s Editorial Supervisors Eliminated by Schulberg," *Variety*, 17 November 1926.
20. "Less Road Show Films in '27–'28, Says Lasky," *Variety*, 26 January 1927.
21. Stuart Schulberg, letter to the editor, *Films in Review*, 10: 10 (December 1959), 632.
22. Letter from J. Pommer to author, 7 July 1993.
23. "Pommer with M-G-M; Can Handle Greta," *Variety*, 9 February 1927.
24. Zierold, *Garbo*, 67.
25. See "Miss Garbo Still Stubborn," *Variety*, 23 March 1927; and *"Love,"* *Variety*, 7 December 1927.

Louis B. Mayer, took over the film's production, and the film was released under the title *Love*.

Organizational and economic changes were also under way at M-G-M. In July 1927, *Variety* announced the company's appointment of David Selznick as associate producer, listing Pommer as one of M-G-M's seven producers.[26] The scenario and writing staff was cut from seventy-two to forty-two in one week, followed by drastic payroll deductions.[27] At a meeting with the directors' branch of the motion picture industry's Academy of Arts and Sciences, Jesse Lasky and Louis B. Mayer told the directors "that production costs greatly exceed revenue and that curtailment is necessary; that there must be no ifs, buts, ands or don'ts, but that everyone was expected to help readjust conditions by taking the cut."[28] In August 1927, *Variety* reported that "a general cut in production costs, in line with new plans laid for film producing, results in approximately twenty-five percent reduction for program releases with Metro-Goldwyn-Mayer, Paramount, First National, Universal and Warner Brothers."[29]

At M-G-M Pommer also experienced difficulties, with problems stemming primarily from disagreements over his script proposals. *Variety* attributed these to producer Harry Rapf:

> On each of them it became necessary for him to consult with Harry Rapf, another producer. The latter did not see any of the stories that Pommer submitted, with the German producer becoming quite indignant, claiming that Rapf could give any reason for turning down the stories.
>
> Pommer is reported to have complained to the executive heads at M-G-M over the attitude of Rapf and it is said unless he is given full sway in getting production on the way or another executive to confer with, he will step out.[30]

While European film directors like Stiller and Buchowetzki were simply relieved of assigned films, an imported producer found himself transferred to unacceptable working conditions.

26. Besides Pommer, the producers were David Selznick, Irving Thalberg, Harry Rapf, Hunt Stromberg, Eddie Mannox, and Bernie Hyman. "David Selznick Appointed Asso. Prod. for M-G-M," *Variety*, 20 July 1927.

27. "MGM Cut 30 Off; Still Largest Staff," *Variety*, 8 June 1927; and "Cut So Far, $350,000 Wkly," *Variety*, 29 June 1927.

28. "Cut So Far, $350,000 Wkly."

29. "Some Producers Have Effected 25% Cut in Production Cost to Date," *Variety*, 31 August 1927.

30. "Pommer Dissatisfied; May Walk Out on M-G," *Variety*, 23 May 1927.

The assignment of a Tim McCoy western to Pommer at M-G-M was a curious development indeed, and even *Variety* pointed out that Pommer's experiences were in dramatic productions and not with frontier or western pictures.[31] Pommer's legacy as head of Ufa's feature film production was certainly no secret to American studios; one prestigious Ufa "art film" after another was released in the United States and reviewed in *Variety*. Their reception by American audiences and critics was mixed, but at least *Walzertraum* evoked the compliment that "this German Ufa bunch knows how to make pictures." And even *Faust*, predicted by critics to be rejected as "art for art's sake," surprised by doing well at the box office.[32] None of the reviewers commented on the fact that the films' producer was presently working in the American film industry. On the contrary, *Variety* made this statement in March 1927:

> Every effort is being made to save the Ufa trade mark because of its value in the foreign market, though it is stated by those interested that American producers have advised them that it is the director and the star pulling at the box office, with the public paying but little attention to the company (producer).[33]

Meanwhile Berlin briefly relived the splendor of the Pommer era when his last German film, *Metropolis*, and his first one from Hollywood, *Hotel Imperial*, released as *Hotel Stadt Lemberg*, simultaneously premiered in January 1927. In what amounts to a reassessment of the "ousted" Ufa production head, film critic Kurt Pinthus took this occasion to illustrate Pommer's important role as international entrepreneur. Stating that Pommer's last German film was a "utopian world film" while his first American film was the product of the "utopian world USA," he saw what they had in common: "Even if these films had amounted to nothing, at least they had created the new word 'world premiere,' which both experienced in Berlin as Ufa presentations. They were greeted with an excitement that the most important theater premieres have not enjoyed in a long time, perhaps never before."[34]

31. "Pommer Gets Western," *Variety*, 6 April 1927. Reviews of Tim McCoy westerns in *Variety* in 1927 do not specify producers. Pommer could have supervised either of the following: *California*, directed by W.S. Van Dyke (reviewed in *Variety* on 29 June 1927); and *The Frontiersman*, directed by Reginald Barker (*Variety*, 26 October 1927).

32. "*Waltz Dream*," *Variety*, 28 July 1926; and "*Faust* Hits in Frisco; $26,000 for Ufa Film," *Variety*, 19 January 1927.

33. "No Ufa Subsidy From German Gov't," *Variety*, 23 March 1927.

34. Kurt Pinthus, "*Lemberg* und *Metropolis*," *Tage-Buch*, 15 June 1927.

Interestingly, Pinthus now saw the ill-fated *Metropolis* as "the last, the greatest, and, for a long time, the unrepeatable triumph" of Ufa, Germany, and Europe.[35] The U.S.-produced *Hotel Stadt Lemberg* also evoked positive responses, faring much better in Germany than in the States. Critic Axel Eggebrecht proclaimed it "cinematically perfect" and saw it as "the continuation of German film production with more effective means."[36] Of the films depicting the Great War, which were shown in Germany in the late 1920s, Pommer's Hollywood-produced *Hotel Stadt Lemberg* and *Stacheldraht (Barbed Wire)* stood out as "peace films." Like other U.S.-produced war films of the time, Pommer's films compared favorably to those produced by Ufa. Where Ufa "treat[ed] war as history," Hollywood emphasized the emotional impact of war: "So skilful was their blend of romance and suspense, and so successful was the blend at avoiding national pique, that both achievements attracted critical comment."[37]

At M-G-M Pommer's situation apparently improved, because his family correspondence in 1927 contained references to the development of a number of scripts and the supervision of several films, without mentioning exact titles. The contract between Pommer and M-G-M gave the company the right (*Option*) to renew Pommer's employment with a substantial raise by 1 July. While still anticipating M-G-M's decision, he wrote to his wife Gertrud, who was on her way back to Europe with their son, on 28 June:

> [Benjamin] Christensen finished his film last night. I hope it will be good. I expect editing to take three weeks. . . I will cable you as soon as I know what M-G-M has decided on 1 July regarding the *Option*. At the moment a lot of measures are being taken to save money (everyone is affected by salary cuts, from the producer, director, and star down to the last worker). There is a lot of agitation in *all* film studios. They have not approached me yet but will most likely do so when negotiating the *Option* of my contract. . . Meanwhile, I am preparing the next [John] Gilbert film (Monte Bell, director) and the next Garbo film ([Victor] Seastrom, director), but will hardly see

35. Ibid.
36. Axel Eggebrecht, "Film im Februar," *Weltbühne*, 15 March 1927. See also "Am Wrack der Ufa," *Tage-Buch*, 2 April 1927, in praise of American films: "And from America came at least twenty unforgettable compositions, from *Goldrausch* [*Gold Rush*] to *Schwarzer Engel* [*Black Angel*], from *Ehe im Kreise* [*The Marriage Circle*] (which the good Lubitsch could never have made in Germany) to *Hotel Stadt Lemberg* [*Hotel Imperial*]."
37. See Thomas Saunders, "Politics, the Cinema, and Early Revisitations of War in Weimar Germany," *Canadian Journal of History*, XXIII (April 1988), 38–40.

the studio for another seven weeks since both are working on *Anna Karenina*. I don't know what my next project will be, probably a film with Christensen, who has done very good work. (That is, if everything will work out with the *Option*, a fact I can't know yet.) Should that not be the case, I am convinced that I would be able to find something appropriate.[38]

The film Danish film director Benjamin Christensen completed in June 1927 must have been *The Mockery* starring Lon Chaney. In a letter written 22 July, Pommer spoke of the successful preview of a Lon Chaney film on 20 July 1927 and wrote that the responses to the film praised it for its "very good entertainment" and called it "one of Chaney's best works."[39] Pommer also mentioned exceptionally successful previews of a film he produced with Norma Shearer, the bride-to-be of M-G-M's Irving Thalberg. This film may have been *The Demi-Bride*, directed by Robert Z. Leonard. But he also wrote to his wife that M-G-M had not made a move on 1 July. In view of the cordial treatment he continued to receive at the company, especially from Irving Thalberg, he interpreted M-G-M's silence as an oversight. His bargaining position in the U.S. film industry that summer was apparently advantageous; he received inquiries from First National and United Artists, even from Paramount where Adolph Zukor, Jesse Lasky, and Walter Wanger wanted him back. Pommer's renewed negotiations with Paramount finally failed because of Schulberg's firm opposition. He then negotiated with Louis B. Mayer, and although the latter wanted to retain him for his company, Pommer failed to secure a pay raise. Pommer was justifiably afraid that his acceptance of Mayer's terms would be interpreted as weakness, resulting in less important assignments should he stay on. He opted for an uncertain future and severed ties with M-G-M, following the fulfillment of his contractual obligations. Mayer rejected his offer to stay two more months to complete the Gilbert and Garbo films, but Thalberg asked Pommer to remain one week beyond 1 August 1927, which Pommer did.[40] Already on 20 July 1927, *Variety* reported

38. Letter from E. Pommer to his wife, 28 June 1928.

39. Letter from E. Pommer to his wife, 22 July 1927. Of interest in this context is actor Lon Chaney's assessment of film directors, especially Scandinavian ones, expressed in an interview conducted by *Photography* magazine. According to Chaney, Tod Browning, Victor Seastrom, and Benjamin Christensen were "truly great directors" who had "finer values" than other U.S. directors. See Don Whittemore and Philip Alan Cecchettini's Anthology, *Passport to Hollywood: Film Immigrants* (New York: McGraw-Hill Book Co., 1976), 267.

40. Letter from E. Pommer to his wife, 22 July 1927.

that "Pommer finishes up at the Metro-Goldwyn-Mayer lot in a few days and will not return."[41]

Surely the adamant positions during negotiations between Mayer and Pommer were not motivated by finances alone. As Pommer's son speculates, "it looks as if my father's seemingly dubious decision to turn down Mayer was based, at least in part, on his being uneasy at MGM and especially with Mayer. That may have been mutual."[42] The younger Pommer also debunks the myth of cordial immigrant support:

> Despite the fact that most of the founders of the American industry were immigrants themselves (but not from Germany and arriving at early ages), my father indicates the difficulties of Europeans (mainly directors) working in Hollywood in those years, although that may apply mostly to Germans. World War I was still in the minds of many. Of the German directors then working in Hollywood, no one remembers Ludwig Berger, Paul Ludwig Stein, Paul Leni or E.A. Dupont for their American work. Only F.W. Murnau is recalled; perhaps because of his untimely death after his first film. There were only two producers: Lubitsch and my father. Lubitsch then was considered mainly to be a director or a producer/director; several of my father's letters indicate that Lubitsch also had problems and even considered putting his house up for sale. My father had the additional burden of having proved that he could run a major studio. That made him persona non grata with Schulberg and Thalberg. The situation improved for Lubitsch by the end of the 1920s, and the advent of Hitler made the later émigrés seem more like anti-Nazis than Germans; they did not have the same problems.[43]

In late summer Pommer wrote to a friend in Germany about promising negotiations with United Artists, but he simultaneously expressed strong reservations regarding a foreigner's chances in the U.S. film industry:

> Judging from my experiences, it is difficult for Europeans to be accepted. Time and again we will merely be tolerated as foreigners and unwelcome rivals. Competition here is much stronger than abroad. An American producer [*Produktionsleiter*] has to be guarded at all times to stay in control. Therefore he must keep capable competitors at bay. Are you surprised, then, that my thoughts lean more than ever toward working abroad again at some point in the future?

41. "Pommer Moving," *Variety*, 20 July 1927.
42. Letter from J. Pommer to author, 17 August 1993.
43. Ibid.

That I want to apply [over there] my experiences, my knowledge of all advantages and disadvantages of U.S. production?[44]

Precisely at this time, Ludwig Klitzsch, the newly appointed CEO of Ufa (*Generaldirektor*) after the company's acquisition by Alfred Hugenberg, toured the United States promoting Ufa's cause. The trip was watched closely by *Variety*. Emphasizing Ufa's financial dilemma, the trade paper predicted that less expensive film production in Berlin would lead to the absence of international "specials" and to an increase of "bread and butter" films. The United States' commercial attaché in Berlin agreed: "In spite of the present series of "bread and butter" films there will always be a German industry. . . Specials may have been stopped but the German citizens demand a goodly percentage of German films, even if of poor quality, mixed with the best of the American."[45]

In New York, conspicuously avoiding Hollywood, Klitzsch discussed the possibility of increased distribution of German films in America and suggested the realization of this goal through the production of "Americanized" films.[46] *Variety* summarized Klitzsch's visit in 1927 with these words: "Not having learned how Americans make good pictures the German boys came over to see how they make money and, if possible, arrange a 'deal.'"[47] German producers, it was felt in the United States, did not "have the right slant on the kind of pictures suited for American box offices, with but rare and costly exceptions."[48]

From his Hollywood perspective, Pommer predicted that these German-American negotiations were destined to fail, despite Klitzsch's undeniable business acumen and negotiation skills. Lacking first-rate German films for U.S. distribution, Klitzsch had nothing to offer that the Americans had not already secured through the Parufamet agreements. In fact, Pommer felt that Ufa would continue to fail in film production for the U.S. market unless production were put in the hands of a European producer with American experience.[49] The management at the new Ufa was

44. Letter from E. Pommer to Hugo von Lustig, Berlin, 30 August 1927. J. Pommer Collection.

45. "German 2 For 1 Plan Continued," *Variety*, 20 July 1927.

46. "Par.-M.-G. Turn Down Ufa Deal. Foreigners Wanted 12 or 15 More Films Distributed," *Variety*, 17 August 1927.

47. "Germans-Hays Talk While Loew-Zukor Keep On Gazing," *Variety*, 10 August 1927.

48. "Par.-M.-G. Turn Down Ufa Deal. . ."

49. Letter from E. Pommer to Lustig.

obviously aware of this problem, as the minutes of a *Vorstand* meeting in late 1927 reflect. They read: "As production head for a group of films we are considering first of all Erich Pommer. It is decided to examine next what offer can be made to Mr. Pommer."[50]

The invitation to return to Germany was totally unexpected for Pommer. He was approached by Klitzsch at a time when he saw his immediate future, no matter how insecure financially, in the States. He was committed to a long-term rental agreement and planned to become a permanent resident. An immigration visa could not be issued inside the United States, which he and his family had entered the previous year with visitor's permits. While he planned to obtain his own papers from Canada, he had sent his wife and son to Germany to obtain immigration visas there. Though planning to remain in the States, his vision for the future did include Germany, but not in the course envisioned by Klitzsch and Ufa. Pommer's personal correspondence from that period clearly indicates plans to produce in Germany at a later time in his career. But he envisioned a system of artistic and financial cooperation involving Germany *and* the United States.[51] He strongly believed in 1927 that such collaboration between American and European producers, distributors, and exhibitors was inevitable. "One day we will see a complete internationalization of the cinema, and that must be wonderful," he said.[52]

Pommer accepted Klitzsch's offer; the personal feelings concerning Ufa, however, which he expressed in a letter to his family in Germany, were illuminating: "To say the least, I am not too optimistic regarding Ufa. Do I know who holds the reigns besides Mr. Klitzsch and who else is there with whom I would have to deal? But I also know now that I can work with the least likeable people, given my experiences in the United States."[53] He returned in late October 1927; the household goods were shipped from Hollywood back to Germany. His acceptance of Ufa's offer decisively affected his life and career. He gave up a clear opportunity to become part of the American film industry in the late 1920s. Ernst Lubitsch had shown that Germans could be successful there; others, like Henry Koster, Douglas Sirk, or Robert Siodmak, though directors rather than producers, proved it later. Hollywood would

50. Minutes of *Vorstand* meeting, 23 September 1927.
51. Letter from E. Pommer to Lustig.
52. "Internationalisierung des Films ist nur noch eine Frage der Zeit," *Film-Kurier*, 10 September 1927.
53. Letter from E. Pommer to his wife, 17 September 1927.

eventually have given him the financial stability he lacked throughout his career, especially since his ensuing health problems were
going to swallow a substantial portion of his earnings.[54] Apparently personal reasons played a more decisive role than financial
considerations. Given his controversial parting with Ufa in early
1926, he must have seen this invitation as a personal and professional vindication. On the professional level, his decision to return
home was not necessarily disadvantageous, either for him or the
German cinema, as the films he produced during his second tenure at Ufa were to prove.

Bringing Hollywood to Berlin

Ufa offered the returning Pommer $1,000 weekly, two-thirds what
Louis B. Mayer had paid, and a 10 percent profit share. His position
was that of independent producer (*Produktionsleiter*, or *Herstel-
lungsleiter*)[55] in Ufa's most prestigious new production unit. Ufa's
contracts with Pommer from this time on were through his personal services corporation, Producers Service Corporation in New
York.[56] The Berlin press credited this decision primarily to Klitzsch's
trip to New York where Americans had reminded him that Pommer, then in the American film industry, was responsible for Ufa's
high reputation in the United States.[57] And indeed, Pommer's recall
was part of Ufa's remedy for its production dilemma, wanting to

54. Letter from J. Pommer to author, 15 August 1993.
55. The German terms *Produktionschef, Produktionsleiter, Produzent,* and *Herstellungsgruppenleiter* are used inconsistently in German language film studies. I
prefer to use the term *Produktionschef* (production head or chief) for Pommer's
position at Ufa till 1926 and for Correll's as of 1928. This term is in line with Pommer's own concept of his position. Conversely, I am using the term *Produktionsleiter*
(producer-in-charge) for his position at Ufa from 1928 on, although the more precise professional term should be *Herstellungsgruppenleiter*, because he was responsible for a steady number of films in his own production unit (*Herstellungsgruppe*).
In his business correspondence, Pommer referred to his position from 1928 on as
independent producer. For the organization of Ufa's production in the late 1920s,
see also Rudolf Oertel, *Filmspiegel: Ein Brevier aus der Welt des Films* (Vienna: Wilhelm Frick Verlag, 1941).
56. The three year contract between Producers Service Corporation, New York
(Pommer's company) from 1 December 1930 to 30 November 1932, which was
extended one year, provided for an annual salary of RM 300,000, payable semi-
monthly. In addition, the contract stipulated profit participation of 10 percent until
180 percent of costs were received, and increased to 15 percent profit participation
thereafter. Letter from J. Pommer to author, 9 September 1995.
57. "Pommer bleibt in Berlin," *Film-Kurier*, 24 November 1927.

secure from outside Germany, especially from across the Atlantic, film stars and personnel with world reputations. The U.S. press, however, criticized the American film industry for failing to grasp Pommer's possibilities and for failing to provide a place for "the greatest brain in pictures."[58] And yet, his American interlude, short as it was, amounted to more than what has been assessed as "a minor interruption in a career marked by extraordinary achievements."[59] It proved a tough school with significant consequences for Pommer's German and international film production. Though Hollywood had refused to learn from him, the returning Pommer made extensive use of what he had absorbed in Hollywood.

Back at Ufa, he made no secret of his leanings toward a more "Americanized" or "democratic" production view for the domestic and world markets, now emphasizing purely materialistic concerns.[60] His press statements at the time clearly indicated that his post-American production approach stressed profits, not art, as the film industry's first law. The new conditions at Ufa certainly demanded thriftier production measures, but Pommer's remarkable change was not merely the adaptation to a new company course. He could not help being influenced by conditions prevalent in American film production. In Hollywood, he and his Swedish colleague Mauritz Stiller had to realize that, while they had been "trained in an entirely different school," they were surrounded by "American shop methods and formulas."[61] As during his first trip to the United States in 1924, Pommer was eager to learn and was especially interested in "the definite interchange of ideas and methods in production between Europe and America."[62]

Above all, he wanted to keep abreast of technological advances that were of utmost interest to him throughout his career. In 1924, for instance, he had discovered the superiority of American lighting and returned to Germany with "one of every kind of light I had found in the United States."[63] With the same tenacity he pushed for Kodak products at Ufa whose business connection

58. *The Film Spectator*, 15 October 1927.

59. Saunders, *Hollywood in Berlin*, 210.

60. Friedrich Porges, "Nur das Beste ist gut genug für das Publikum: Ein Leben für den Film: Gespräch mit dem fünfundsiebzigjährigen Erich Pommer," *Die Welt*, 25 July 1964.

61. Lewis Jacobs, ed., *The Compound Cinema: The Film Writings of Harry Alan Potamkin* (New York: Teachers College Press, 1977), 343.

62. Pommer, "Hands across the Sea in Movie Development," *The New York Times*, 16 January 1927.

63. Ibid.

with Agfa, it was argued, prohibited competition. Thus opened the door for Kodak, and Eastman Panchromatic negative film was used for shooting and Eastman positive for most of the copies.[64] At Paramount in 1926 and 1927, he was introduced to the shooting schedule developed in 1926 by Mel Templeton, head of the company's budget department. It consisted of a very large sheet of paper on which each sequence had a vertical column indicating the set, scene numbers, the members of the cast involved, and other pertinent information. According to John Pommer, entries were made by pen and were the basis for typing a condensed shooting schedule. In case of schedule changes, the entire schedule had to be laboriously entered on a clean sheet.

Erich Pommer promptly implemented this system in Berlin, not without causing a stir. The schedule board was at Ufa to stay. Meanwhile Hollywood had already switched to schedules laid out on boards made of solid plywood about three feet high and five or six feet long, holding movable celluloid strips for each sequence on which information was entered with colored grease pencil. By the time Pommer's son John came to Germany in 1950 as production manager on Anatole Litvak's *Decision Before Dawn*, Hollywood had switched again, and the celluloid strips were now replaced by disposable cardboard strips of various colors, with information entered by colored ballpoint pens. But in Germany, John Pommer made a peculiar discovery:

> I found to my amazement that the schedule form introduced by my father in the 1920s still was used totally unchanged in Germany, whereas in Hollywood it had gone through numerous improvements. . . . The American production staff worked with the latest U.S. boards but the German assistant directors insisted that the shooting schedule be transferred to this very large sheet of paper based on what my father had brought over in 1927, and that it be recopied each time we altered the schedule. In effect, they created an almost full-time job throughout the film for one assistant director.[65]

Erich Pommer was impressed by the sheer size of American studio facilities. "The American studio," he explained in 1927, "has room to build all its sets before producing the picture, insuring more methodical work, a certainty in outlining the details of

---

64. Letter from W. Langfeld of Kodak, Stuttgart, to E. Pommer, on the occasion of Pommer's 75th birthday, 19 August 1964.

65. Letter from J. Pommer to author, 7 July 1993.

a picture."[66] He welcomed the opportunity to move from one set to another without having to dismantle the one built before. By comparison, German studio limitations permitted the construction of only one set at a time, leading to enormous time loss if shots had to be taken over at a later time. He also recognized that America's market advantages allowed higher star salaries:

> When Europe has made a star Europe cannot long retain that star – for a very simple reason – money. Europe cannot now, nor, I fear, for some time, pay the salaries America can – because Europe cannot get that salary back in box office returns. The possibilities of profit, until a better organization of the foreign market [can be achieved], are too restricted.[67]

He praised the United States for its better sense of showmanship and felt that Germany could learn much from American modes of advertising. Above all, he expressed his admiration for the American motto of "business first":

> America's studios operate with the mechanical precision of any other great industry, and the commercial side is equally efficient. With all understanding of the artistic side, business first is the motto followed and respected by not only the operative side, but by stars, directors, and writers.[68]

Under such strict focus on business, Pommer's major film directors were never again to attain the influence on production they had enjoyed in the first half of the twenties. On the other hand, a case could also be made that Pommer's self-image as producer was affected by his work in Hollywood. He may have favored the American system, which clearly withheld from film directors the level of control earlier given to a director such as Fritz Lang at Ufa.[69] Placing himself on the business side of film production and distancing himself from his former Ufa course, he proclaimed:

66. "International Co-Operation (As Eric Pommer Sees It)," *Variety*, 3 August 1927. A translated version appears later under the headline "Internationalisierung des Films ist nur noch eine Frage der Zeit," in *Film-Kurier*, 10 September 1927. *Variety*'s use of the American version of Pommer's first name is premature, as he did not legally change it until 1944 when becoming a U.S. citizen.

67. "International Co-Operation (As Eric Pommer Sees It)."

68. Ibid.

69. This would explain film director Wilhelm Thiele's claim that Pommer was jealous of Thiele's success with the enormously profitable film operetta *Die Drei von der Tankstelle* in 1930. See Jan-Christopher Horak's 1975 interview with Wilhelm Thiele in *Middle European Emigrés in Hollywood (1933–1945): An American Film Institute Oral History* (Beverly Hills, CA: Louis B. Mayer Foundation, n.d.).

Who has made films here during the last years? Almost always the film director alone, without the *Produktionsleiter* [production supervisor]. In all but few cases he enjoyed the secure backing of an organization, and when he did, even greater difficulties were caused at work. . . . His goal, especially here in Germany, is aimed at making artistically perfect films, knowing that they guarantee success among the educated. In this respect he instinctively imagines himself in the same position as the director of the stage.[70]

Pommer's change was most striking and the American influence most visible when he took issue with the concept of educating the audience. He now distanced himself from the art formula of his earlier German films and attributed such concept solely to his film directors. In Hollywood, he had watched the American response to his earlier Ufa "art films." At the same time, he had the opportunity to make American films and to observe why they were successful with audiences. "The Americans," Pommer declared in early 1928, "have given us excellent models for making world successes."[71] Though these films may appear trivial, childish, and naive in plot, he saw their appeal in beautiful countrysides, talented and good-looking actors, top-notch photography, and the highest technical perfection. This formula guaranteed success at the box office, with huge ticket sales actually making the film industry profitable, not just self-supporting.

In 1929, in an article entitled "Artistic Entertainment Films," he attempted a synthesis of film art and entertainment by leaning heavily on the American model.[72] While the Americans achieve profits with their films, he explained, the Germans are preoccupied with art, thereby often sacrificing profitability. While American films reach a large audience through entertainment, German films aim at educating the public through art. He again took issue with German film directors, claiming they produced for the screen what stage directors produced in the theater. He shifted drastically from his earlier approach by implying that art is not as essential for the cinema as for the theater:

> The concept of educating the audience through films is beautiful in theory, but in practice only slowly realizable, and certainly not in the terms which are imagined by some of us over here. If this goal could be attained at all, it would more likely happen in a strong film industry that can occasionally tolerate the luxury of producing

70. Pommer, "Film, Filmgeschäft und Weltmarkt," *Der Film*, 23 May 1928.
71. Ibid.
72. Pommer, "Künstlerische Unterhaltungsfilme," *Reichsfilmblatt*, 20 April 1929.

films, which fail to become box office hits. It cannot be accomplished in a film industry where individual companies are shaken to their foundations after two or three box office flops.[73]

Pommer felt, however, that the American and German cinema had succeeded in cross-fertilizing one another, each with what it understood best. He was convinced that films like *Caligari* and *Der letzte Mann*, though perhaps not enormous financial American successes, made American studios aware of artistic filmmaking. More importantly, both films had gained respect for German cinema abroad and increased its export opportunities. He felt that the American film provided an effective and workable formula and was convinced that this formula was also transferable to German filmmaking: "It is better after all that a film is too light than that it is too heavy."[74] A film producer, he asserted, could not afford to ignore the first law of film production, the need for profit, which, in turn, depends on popular films:

> Those are certainly right who demand a higher status of the cinema. But those are even more right who expect it to be profitable. After all, they are the ones who make film production possible through the allocation of funds. We don't speak of the film industry in the entire world for nothing. Film is not an affair of those few who constitute the intellectual elite of a nation.[75]

Such purely commercial concerns also justified films that would not win critical acclaim. Reproached by a journalist, who argued that some of his films lacked artistic merit, Pommer is known to have replied politely: "What do you want, we made a lot of money with them."[76]

More than ever, American films showed Pommer a model for international filmmaking:

> The commanding importance of the American film on the world film market cannot sufficiently be explained merely by the gigantic monetary means which Americans have at their disposal and which they use with such skill. The explanation can be found moreover in the mentality of the American film, which apparently comes closest to the taste of the international movie audience, all attacks and opinions to the contrary notwithstanding. This recognition is not a value judgment at all, either in an artistic or in a technical

73. Pommer, "Film, Filmgeschäft und Weltmarkt."
74. Pommer, "Der internationale Film," *Film-Kurier*, 28 August 1928.
75. Pommer, "Künstlerische Unterhaltungsfilme."
76. "Impressionen rund um den Film," *Der Film*, 15 March 1930.

sense. The peculiarity is simply that the naiveté, the lack of complexity and of problems in the American film, which is attacked and seen as trivial – that precisely these characteristics are its main strength in the battle on the international film market.[77]

Pommer's first opportunity to apply his Hollywood experience was *Heimkehr (Homecoming)*, a film whose Great War story completes the trilogy he began at Paramount with *Hotel Imperial* and *Barbed Wire*. Joe May, his former colleague, directed. Pommer saw *Heimkehr* as a film fully reflecting his ideas about the "international film":

> Important is not the exterior frame, but the inner language, the workings of the soul, which have to be comprehensible to everyone. During my almost two years in America, I had the opportunity to convince myself of the validity of this theory. And when I returned to Germany to produce here for Ufa, it was an especially pleasant surprise for me to find in my old friend Joe May absolute approval of the transferral of my American experiences to German modes of production.[78]

The film production models were no longer exclusively his earlier German films, although he singled out *Der letzte Mann* and *Varieté* as exceptions, but also his American films, especially *Hotel Imperial*. He preferred plot simplicity and universal conflicts: "In my view, the requirements of a *Großfilm* today seem to be the intensive combination of plot, acting, and setting, in all their effects, on the inner emotions of man."[79] Interestingly, Pommer listed as mandatory international film components precisely those themes he had advocated in his early career at Decla and Decla-Bioscop, especially when working with scriptwriter Carl Mayer. Insisting on a limited number of principal characters – in *Heimkehr* there are three – and their deeply felt psychological conflict, Pommer was returning to the early 1920s' *Kammerspielfilm*.

But even universal themes did not necessarily guarantee foreign accessibility, as his experience of *Heimkehr* showed. Ufa's New York office head, Frederick Wynne-Jones, suggested that the film be reshot with a specifically American ending for U.S. release, and Pommer compromised, as he had done before.[80] The need for export, he felt, justified and necessitated such compromise:

77. Pommer, "Der internationale Film."
78. Ibid.
79. Pommer, "Visuelle Handlung oder Milieu," *Reichsfilmblatt*, 30 March 1929.
80. Ufa's *Vorstand* approved the funds for three additional studio days. Minutes of *Vorstand* meeting, 30 March 1928.

Film is export merchandise. The German film industry cannot live from German movie theaters alone. It must export in order to be able to continue production. This further demands that the German film producers take the mentality of other nations into account, without falling into the habit of blind imitation.[81]

Adopting the American notion of "entertainment value" while retaining Germany's art heritage, he suggested, "the task of the film industry in the year 1929 is not so much the cultivation of the absolute artistic film, as it is the raising of the artistic level of the entertainment film."[82] And German audiences had also changed. They were familiar with American entertainment films and able to compare and choose (see Appendix B). They also knew that the German cinema was capable of art; it no longer needed to prove its respectability. Gone were the days of such national spectacles as *Nibelungen* and *Metropolis*, the German answer to Hollywood. The last silent films Pommer produced, using his new insight, became extremely popular. Of the sixteen films Ufa produced in 1928, *Heimkehr* was one of the most successful.[83] Pommer's films *Asphalt*, *Ungarische Rhapsodie* (*Hungarian Rhapsody*),[84] and *Die wunderbare Lüge der Nina Petrowna* (*The Wonderful Lie of Nina Petrowna*) all made the 1928/29 list of Germany's most popular films. Not surprisingly, so did Fritz Lang's films *Spione* (*The Spy*) and *Die Frau im Mond* (*Woman in the Moon*), produced by Lang's independent production group at Ufa.[85] The ultimate approval came from abroad. When *Asphalt* was shown in the United States, *Variety* proclaimed it so well produced that it was "entertainment" indeed.[86]

81. Pommer, "Künstlerische Unterhaltungsfilme."

82. Ibid.

83. Winfried B. Lerg, "Die Publizistik der Weimarer Republik," in *Presse im Exil: Beiträge zur Kommunikationsgeschichte des deutschen Exils, 1933–1945* (Munich, New York, London, Paris: K.G. Saur, 1979), 46.

84. Pommer called *Ungarische Rhapsodie*, which he produced in late 1928, his first "sound film." He produced his first "all-talking" film, *Melodie des Herzens*, in the following year; it premiered in December 1929. Luft, "Erich Pommer, Part II," *Films in Review* 10: 9 (November 1959), 523.

85. Monaco, *Cinema and Society*, 166–68.

86. *Variety*, 7 May 1930. Of interest is *Asphalt*'s rediscovery in 1995. It was screened at the 1995 Berlin Film Festival, accompanied by a newly composed score by Karl-Ernst Sasse and played by the Brandenburg Philharmonic of Potsdam. Richard Trauber, the reviewer of *Asphalt*, far preferred this score to the original score of *Metropolis*, which he heard a few days earlier in the former East Berlin. About *Asphalt*, Trauber writes: "Another special event was the screening of *Asphalt*, with an orchestra, at the huge Zoo Palast, just after this year's awards were announced. The 1929 Ufa production, directed by Joe May, was recently discovered

Pommer's last silent films were intended to be, and were recognized by critics, as a synthesis of both cinematic traditions. The
gap was narrowing.[87] It was safe to incorporate art into entertainment, to bring Hollywood to Berlin.

---

in its most complete state at the Gosfilmofond archive in Moscow. This triumph of
the silent era, made at a time when German film was at an expressive and artistic
zenith, received a tumultuous ovation and – expectedly – made most of the new
films, German or otherwise, seem fairly puny." Richard Trauber, "Berlinale '95,"
Films in Review (July/August 1995): 32. Not surprisingly, the producer's name is
not mentioned in the review.

87. See Siegfried Kracauer, *From Caligari to Hitler: A Psychological History of the
German Film* (Princeton: Princeton Univ. Press, 1947), 190; and John Baxter, *The Hollywood Exiles* (New York: Taplinger Publishing Co., 1976), 57.

Chapter 5

UFA: TRANSITION TO SOUND FILM

When the stabilized currency forced us to calculate, even on the basis of the penny, the lack of a person with the ability to find a common denominator for the commercial and the artistic demands became obvious. The deflation therefore created a new profession, that of the *Produktionsleiter*.

Ernst Hugo Correll, "Die Arbeit des Produktionsleiters"

The New Ufa

The "horrible Bausback Ufa" of the late silent film era, headed by Ferdinand Bausback as *Vorstand* CEO (*Generaldirektor*), was short-lived and completely revamped by the time Pommer returned. Nonetheless, a flashback to company developments during his U.S. years is in order to better illuminate Ufa's motives for rehiring its former production head Pommer. Bausback, Ufa board director and former head of the Stuttgart branch of the Deutsche Bank, did not lead Ufa to new domestic or international glory.[1] Neither did Alexander Grau, who had succeeded Pommer as head of feature film production and *Vorstandsdirektor* after having led Ufa's successful documentary and educational film production (*Kulturfilmproduktion*). The two separate production categories, feature and nonfeature films, were joined during Pommer's absence

1. See "Vor großen Entscheidungen: Das Amerika-Ufa-Abkommen – Der Nachfolger [Felix] Kallmanns," *Film-Kurier*, 29 December 1925. Kallmann left his CEO post on the *Vorstand* on 28 February 1925. See also Kurt Mühsam and Egon Jacobson,

and placed under the supervision of a single *Vorstandsdirektor*, Major Grau.[2] With the *Vorstand's* leadership now in the hands of a novice to the film industry (Bausback), and with production entrusted to a former German Army major turned head of *Kulturfilmproduktion* (Grau), Ufa's feature film production became a shadow of its former self. Devoid of Pommer's flamboyancy, financial support, and artistic guidance, there were no "milestones" of film history among the films Ufa offered for exhibition from its 1926/ 27 production but films for every taste, primarily those of Ufa's *Auftragsproduktion*.[3]

Ufa had returned to most modest film production, readopting pre-1924 standards, as critic Axel Eggebrecht claimed.[4] Allocating as little as 100,000 marks for individual film budgets was a far cry from Pommer's pre-American Ufa films whose budgets were ten to sixty times higher. Eggebrecht had nothing but disdain for the industry as a whole:

> Awakened abruptly from all film-imperialist dreams, the German film industry becomes the petty bourgeois among the film producing nations. Under the old motto of "cheap and bad," the domestic market is now flooded with products unsuitable for export. What a difference to the years 1920 to 1924 when every little corner-*Fabrikant* produced "for Broadway."[5]

Conspicuously gone were the days of the Pommer era, with their artistic and technological risk-taking. As one critic remarked, Ufa resembled a "giant" whose apparatus produced "dwarves"; apparently there was no company consensus regarding the types of films to be produced.[6] In the spring of 1927, *Die Weltbühne* deplored that "reading the announcements of German films for the coming season is enough to make one feel sick."[7] Even expensive films, occasionally

---

Lexikon des Films (Berlin: Verlag der *Lichtbild-Bühne*, 1926). Ferdinand Bausback was appointed in December 1925. About allegations that his appointment had contributed to Pommer's decision to resign from Ufa, see Riess, *Das gab's nur einmal*, vol. 2, 14. Herbert G. Luft commented on Bausback's appointment, " … and when the Deutsche Bank appointed a watchdog committee, headed by Dr. Ferdinand Bausback to okay all major expenditures, Pommer did not ask for the renewal of his contract in March '26." Luft, "Erich Pommer: Part II," *Films in Review*, 10: 9 (November 1959), 522.

2. *Jahrbuch der Filmindustrie, 1928*, 16. See also Ufa file R109I/1026a.

3. Zglinicki, *Weg des Films*, 422.

4. Axel Eggebrecht, "Filmsommer 1926," *Weltbühne*, 10 August 1926.

5. Ibid.

6. "Am Wrack der Ufa," *Tage-Buch*, 2 April 1927.

7. Axel Eggebrecht, "Deutscher Filmfrühling 1927," *Weltbühne*, 10 March 1927.

still produced in Germany, yielded little quality.[8] Eggebrecht expressed little respect for Ufa's production plans:

> Based on the latest policy, all films representing an "experiment," that is, an artistic risk, are to be avoided. This does not sound unreasonable considering the unfortunate experiments of *Faust* and *Metropolis*. But basically this amounts to a total abandonment of any plan for improving today's miserable production. It is almost an offensive acknowledgment of the stingy, cheap, trashy type of film that dominates current programs.[9]

Ufa, of course, was not unique in presenting films of poor quality to the public, as the following survey shows. During Pommer's first year in the United States, the entire German film industry produced 185 films. Critic Kurt Pinthus pronounced three-fourths of these unfit for exhibition in larger cities because of low quality, and considered three-fourths of the remaining films simply "bad." Holding up two of Pommer's earlier films as production models, E.A. Dupont's *Varieté* and Ludwig Berger's *Walzertraum* (*Waltz Dream*), he deplored the industry's practice of imitating American motion pictures and of cheaply copying operetta productions modeled on Berger's film.[10] And across the Atlantic the trade paper *Variety* announced "at the time Americans accepted '*Variety*' [*Varieté*], '*Waltz Dream*' and the others, Germany had already stopped producing specials."[11] Many of the German low budget films were "quota quickies," mediocre films produced in exchange for those imported from the United States. And indeed, the most popular films in 1926 were American imports. After the popular *Ben Hur*, Pinthus reported, German audiences favored Charlie Chaplin, Douglas Fairbanks, Mary Pickford, and Buster Keaton. Evidently, "the remaining mid-quality productions from the United States show better distribution and audience figures than the same year's entire German film production."[12] Commenting on the growing market for American films in Germany, a Berlin report in *Variety* portrays this picture in late 1926:

> American films are being better received here this season, although the whole film situation seems to be suffering from inflation due to too many houses. The general acceptance of the American pictures is to be practically ascribed to the lack of any native hits. Up to now

8. Kurt Pinthus, "Die Film-Krisis," *Tage-Buch*, 7 April 1928.
9. Eggebrecht, "Deutscher Filmfrühling 1927."
10. Pinthus, "Die Film-Krisis."
11. "German 2 For 1 Plan Continued," *Variety*, 20 July 1927.
12. Pinthus, "Die Film-Krisis."

the German film industry has failed to deliver anything with a punch. Even the long heralded "Faust" has done nothing to boost the box office. Its artistic qualities are appreciated but do not seem to attract paying visitors.

Of the American films the big successes are "Ben Hur" and Lillian Gish in "Boheme." The Gish picture at the Gloria Palast has been nothing short of a sensation. Miss Gish has a real following here. They attend her every picture and the critics always rave. The reception of this picture has been more enthusiastic here than it was in N. Y.[13]

Critics ridiculed Ufa's 1926 Christmas present to German audiences, the 1.5 million mark mountain film, *Der heilige Berg* (*The Holy Mountain*), directed by Arnold Fanck. Conversely, they had nothing but praise for a comedy, *Madame wünscht keine Kinder* (*Madam Desires No Children*), produced for the U.S. Fox Film Corporation in Germany by the Hungarian, just returned from America and soon to be British producer/director Alexander Korda. Under a *Tage-Buch* headline, "A Big, Expensive, Bad Movie, and a Little, Inexpensive, Good One," Pinthus upheld Fox's film as a shining example of high quality, achieved on a shoe-string budget to boot: "Men of Ufa, have a look at what the American competition (Fox) has managed to accomplish with 100,000 marks in less than three weeks through Alexander Corda [*sic*] in Germany!"[14]

Obviously no Ufa leader was considered an artistic "giant." Even *Variety* remarked that "there is not a single long-visioned leader who could again put German pictures on the international map."[15] In the spring of 1927, *Weltbühne* and *Tage-Buch* took issue with Ufa's troubled administration. *Die Weltbühne* seemed to know that "Ufa's board directors [of the *Aufsichtsrat*] are implored every day by well-meaning experts to replace the banker Bausback, or at least Major Grau, who controls production, with film experts."[16] And *Tage-Buch* wrote:

---

13. "Berlin Likes 'Sparrows' and Gish's 'La Boheme.' 'Ben Hur' Beyond Expectations – 'Stella Dallas' Not Over," *Variety*, 17 November 1926.

14. Kurt Pinthus, "Ein großer, teurer, schlechter und ein kleiner, billiger, guter Film," *Tage-Buch*, 25 December 1926.

15. "Ufa's Passing May End German Films as International," *Variety*, 4 May 1927.

16. Axel Eggebrecht, "Film im Februar," *Weltbühne*, 15 March 1927. The deemphasis of the "artistic" side of film production was evident at the Paris Film Congress in late 1926. Whereas even the smallest film producing nation was represented in Paris by equal numbers of artists and industrialists, Germany sent two artists (film director Karl Grune and writer H.E. Jacob) and fifty-five industrialists. Axel Eggebrecht, "Filmwinter 1926," *Weltbühne*, 7 December 1926.

And when we rack our brains today over the question who on earth should head Ufa, we come to the conclusion that in all of Germany literally *not one man* can be found who would provide more than simply a weak emergency solution. We are already raising the question in all seriousness whether one should not employ an American, which would not be the worst solution.[17]

More than anything, Ufa desperately needed to settle its financial affairs. And in this sector, Germany offered few acceptable solutions to Ufa's board directors to save the company from either total collapse or foreign sale.[18] Negotiations with two potential German buyers, the Reich's Ministry of Economics and the two leading Jewish publishing houses, Ullstein Brothers and Rudolf Mosse, led nowhere. In the end, the urgently required "savior" did emerge from within Germany. He was Alfred Hugenberg, head of the right-wing National People's Party and owner of Germany's leading non-Jewish publishing house, August Scherl. In April 1927, Hugenberg purchased Ufa, supported in his take-over by the Deutsche Bank.[19] Organizationally and financially, Hugenberg left nothing to chance, especially with Ufa's *Aufsichtsrat* and *Vorstand*. For the first time in company history, the chair of the board of directors was no longer held by Deutsche Bank CEO Emil Georg von Stauß. Hugenberg took his place as *Aufsichtsrat* Chairman, and Stauß was demoted to second-in-command. Ludwig Klitzsch, the trusted CEO of Scherl, Hugenberg's publishing house, joined Ufa. Klitzsch remained in charge of Scherl but was also, for all practical purposes, at the helm of Ufa, taking over the reigns from the ill-fated Ferdinand Bausback. In August 1931, Klitzsch became the "official" head (*Generaldirektor*) of Ufa's *Vorstand*, finally realizing a dream he had harbored as far back as 1917.[20] Battling Ufa's American obligations, Klitzsch became an enormously important company asset, skillfully negotiating Ufa's release from the Parufamet agreements and finally freeing the company from its U.S. dependency in 1932.[21]

Hugenberg's acquisition of Ufa was exclusively governed by his urge to preserve Ufa's national status; the thought of Ufa in American or Jewish hands was out of the question. Not surprisingly,

17. "Am Wrack der Ufa."
18. Spiker, *Film und Kapital*, 43.
19. For more details about the business transfer to Hugenberg see Traub, *Ufa*; and Spiker, *Film und Kapital*.
20. Spiker, *Film und Kapital*, 295.
21. Traub, *Ufa*, 78.

developments at Ufa were severely criticized in Germany by the film industry and intellectuals. The German left, especially, condemned such a powerful hold on both the motion picture and the print media, fearing an outpour of films infused with right-wing ideology. As expected, Hugenberg's arrival also evoked justifiable curiosity across the Atlantic where the media tycoon was quickly seen as the counterpart of America's William Randolph Hearst.[22] As *Variety* reported, "the press is still waiting for a definite statement from the Hugenberg concern as to just what its coming program will comprise."[23] Ufa promptly refuted the American supposition that Hugenberg's reign would result in exclusively military films not suitable for export. Emphasizing Klitzsch's over Hugenberg's role in the company, Ufa assured *Variety* of Klitzsch's nonpolitical stance: "As a business man he knows that the ... public does not wish to see pictures with political tendencies but rather all films."[24] Judging from the Ufa files, the *Vorstand* had to take measures to curb overt criticism of Hugenberg from within the company. In early 1928, the *Vorstand* reached the following consensus: "Various incidents force us to abstain from hiring or otherwise employing personnel – and this applies primarily to artistic production personnel – who have publicly and in ugly fashion attacked *Geheimrat* Hugenberg personally, have participated in such attacks, or intend to do so."[25]

The rationalization measures undertaken in the wake of the Hugenberg/Klitzsch take-over resulted in tighter budgetary policies and organizational changes in the production sector. The *Vorstand* began holding daily meetings to facilitate smooth cooperation between the four Ufa departments.[26] The meetings were meticulously recorded, and thus production can be traced in detail from the time of Pommer's return to Berlin till his dismissal in 1933.[27] The new *Vorstand* was quick to implement a production reserve fund to avoid past financial disasters.[28] Having learned from earlier mistakes, it reserved the right to approve all financial

22. "German 2 For 1 Plan Continued."

23. "Ufa's Statement on Its War Pictures," *Variety*, 22 June 1927.

24. Ibid.

25. Minutes of *Vorstand* meeting, 22 February 1928.

26. The four departments were administration, production, domestic and foreign distribution. Traub, *Ufa*, 68.

27. The records, kept in proverbial German accuracy, are stored today at the Bundesarchiv in Koblenz, Germany. Ufa file R109I.

28. See Zglinicki, *Weg des Films*, 421. The Ufa files from 1927 to 1933 show that decisions about this account were made especially for Pommer's productions.

decisions, insisting on precalculation for each film. Permission to overshoot the budget was only granted under exceptional circumstances. Earlier conditions of the mid-twenties, as described here by Hans Traub, were now out of the question:

> The manufacturing methods which came into play under the inflation's heavy influence, did not facilitate long-term supervision and certainly did not enforce proper production. Conditions had been untenable. A film's cost was at times initially estimated at RM 800,000, then raised to RM 1,000,000 during shooting, and the film finally completed with a budget of RM 2,200,000, more than double the amount of the second estimate. The number of studio days was set at sixty but the film shot in 194 days.[29]

As Fritz Lang deplored, there was no chance to "spend too much." Like Pommer, Lang was working as an independent producer for Ufa in 1929. His comment during the shooting of *Die Frau im Mond* (*Woman in the Moon*) assessed production at Ufa well: "The Klitzsch era had begun, and we were placed in financial straight jackets."[30] Compared to the astronomical budgets of *Nibelungen* and *Metropolis*, this was certainly true, but Lang was not faring badly. The Ufa files indicate that the *Vorstand* allocated 1,132,000 marks for *Die Frau im Mond*, far exceeding the original sum of 800,000 marks. Apparently, Ufa's strict new business principles were sometimes challenged by former visions of international success, justifying Lang's additional expense in anticipation of "an extraordinary film."[31] Pommer, to whose production unit the biggest budgets were to be allocated, was occasionally reminded that overspending was unacceptable and found his requests for additional funds denied. At other times, he negotiated successfully, and Ufa dipped into the production reserve fund.

In 1928, Ernst Hugo Correll, former head of the Phoebus Film Company, took over Pommer's former responsibility for all of Ufa's production, with appointment to the *Vorstand*.[32] With production

29. Traub, *Ufa*, 69.

30. Ludwig Maibohm, *Fritz Lang – Seine Filme, sein Leben* (Munich: Wilhelm Heyne Verlag, 1981), 132. After *Metropolis* Lang formed his own production unit within Ufa, the Fritz Lang-Film GmbH. Ufa listed this company as its second most important production unit, following the Erich Pommer Produktion. Lang was featured as Ufa film director. "Das Produktionsprogramm der Ufa: 10 europäische Produktionsmarken – 21 Filme," *Film-Kurier*, 4 May 1928.

31. Minutes of *Vorstand* meeting, 23 October 1928.

32. Correll represents an interesting case in the German film industry, and not only because of his past involvement in the controversial film company Phoebus. Contrary to Pommer, the Jewish Correll remained at Ufa until 1939 when his discharge

sectors now divided and clearly defined, Pommer was finally able
to center exclusively on Ufa's international production.[33] He was
now conspicuously separated from management by not being reap-
pointed to the *Vorstand*. He also abstained from serving again as
president of SPIO, the industry's professional representative body.
Ludwig Klitzsch took Pommer's former SPIO position, with Ufa
Vorstand chiefs Correll (production) and Wilhelm Meydam (distribution) also aboard. Such heavy Ufa representation, of course, guaranteed the company's influence on SPIO and the film industry.[34]

Now feature film production was shared by a number of production groups, each one in the hands of a producer-in-charge
(*Produktionsleiter*) with full economic and organizational responsibility. The importance of Pommer's new position is underscored
by his entitlement to have his name appear in film credits where
Ufa's Erich Pommer Produktion now appeared as production
company, with Eberhard Klagemann, Max Pfeiffer, or Carl Winston named as assistant or associate producer.[35] In addition to
receiving screen credit, Pommer was also entitled to a 10 percent
profit share from his films.[36]

---

was masked as voluntary resignation. In his role as chief of production, he was,
as Klitzsch insisted, indispensable for Ufa's survival. Klitzsch was able to delay
Correll's dismissal for several years despite constant pressure from Goebbels,
who tried repeatedly to replace Correll with his own candidates. See Spiker, *Film
und Kapital*, 291.

33. Wolfgang Jacobsen, author of a Pommer biography in Germany, came to the
same conclusion. Letter from Jacobsen to author, 19 September 1988.

34. Spiker, *Film und Kapital*, 71–72.

35. Carl Winston arrived with Josef von Sternberg, oversaw Hanns Schwarz's
Bomben auf Monte Carlo (1931), and remained as supervisor of the English language
versions. His counterpart for the French versions was André Daven. Pfeiffer was in
charge of *Stürme der Leidenschaft* (1931/32) and *Quick* (1932), both directed by
Robert Siodmak. Klagemann came aboard as production assistant shortly before
Der blaue Engel, taking on more and more responsibilities after Pfeiffer left. He
worked on Siodmak's *Der Mann, der seinen Mörder sucht* (*The Man with the Scar*,
1930/31), Eric Charell's *Der Kongreß tanzt* (1931) and almost coproduced *FP1*. In
April 1932, the *Vorstand* decided to omit several production crew names from film
credits, among them the names of these assistant and associate producers (*Ge-
schäftsführer*). Minutes of *Vorstand* meeting, 5 April 1932.

36. About profits, see Excerpt from the Production Agreement between Ufa and
Pommer, 16/18 August 1930, and letter from the Ufa Liquidating Committee, 17
April 1951, E. Pommer Collection.

Erich Pommer Produktion

Pommer took charge of the most prestigious of Ufa's ten newly established production units, named Erich Pommer Produktion.[37] Fritz Lang's unit was second in Ufa's production hierarchy.[38] Ufa scheduled twenty films for 1928/29, Pommer's first year back in Berlin. Six were planned as *Großfilme* with well-known stars, four of these in Pommer's new unit, and two in Lang's.[39] At Ufa, a *Großfilm* was an international film, often produced by Pommer himself. Its sizable budget meant that an international star like Emil Jannings could appear only in a Pommer film.[40] If Jannings were unavailable, the film might not be produced as a Pommer *Großfilm* but as a *Superfilm* supervised by one of the producers in Pommer's unit.

Ufa's new outlook on production and the role of the producer-in-charge (*Produktionsleiter*) was widely discussed in the trade press at the time, with two of Pommer's film directors, Joe May and Hanns Schwarz, and production head Correll featuring as principal speakers.[41] In defining the role of the *Produktionsleiter*, which was now Pommer's, as a bridge between art and industry, May and Schwarz merely reiterated a concept practiced by Pommer throughout his career. The difference lay in the fact that Pommer was now accountable to Correll as head of production. May's and Schwarz's claim that the studio is the film director's exclusive domain, over which the producer-in-charge has no authority, was sharply contradicted by Correll:

37. "Das Produktionsprogramm der Ufa. . ." In the same issue, Ufa listed its European production units as Erich Pommer Produktion, Fritz Lang Film GmbH, Ciné Alliance, Henny Porten Froelich Produktion, Reinhold Schünzel Film GmbH, Richard Eichberg Film GmbH, Ring Film AG, Albatros Film S.A., and the English production companies associated with Gaumont-British: Gainsborough Pict., W.& F. Service, and Ideal. *Produktionsleiter* were Noë Bloch, Richard Eichberg, Dr. Nicholas Kaufmann, Max Pfeiffer, Erich Pommer, Dr. Gregor Rabinovitsch, Dr. Ulrich K.T. Schultz, Reinhold Schünzel, Günther Stapenhorst, Hans von Wolzogen and A.E. Esway, and Alfred Zeisler.

38. Ufa's production agreement with Lang was short-lived. On 14 June 1932, the *Vorstand* decided to abstain from further production association with Lang because former disagreements had resulted in a substantial loss for Ufa.

39. "Blindbuchen und Zweischlagerprogramm müssen beseitigt werden," *Film-Kurier*, 1 March 1928.

40. Minutes of *Vorstand* meeting, 10 July 1928. The collaboration of Jannings and Pommer, scheduled for Pommer's first post-American year at Ufa, fell through because Jannings was not available until November. This date was considered too late for the beginning of a Pommer film.

41. Joe May and Hanns Schwarz, "Was ist ein Produktionsleiter?" *Film-Kurier*, 4 May 1928.

About eight years ago, in the blissful times of the inflation, the film director was the self-appointed commander. His interest was one-sided. He only cared to succeed with all his might in his artistic vision, oblivious to financial concerns. He did not have sufficient training and capabilities in technical and organizational affairs. These deficiencies were especially felt and typically present in cases where a talented film director was involved, and not a mediocre or a bad one. His one-sidedness was usually his advantage, even though this was not always true for the company that employed him.[42]

Correll now held Pommer's earlier position as mediator between the production team and the *Aufsichtsrat*. Pommer, as *Produktionsleiter*, held the balance between the artistic and business sides of production for his unit, with responsibility for team selection, script supervision, and strict adherence to the approved budget. According to Correll, the *Produktionsleiter* was "for all team members, whether technician, artist, or businessman, the highest place of authority, and he imprints on the film, although his activity has its professional limits, the mark of his personality."[43]

Although Correll spoke of "professional limits," Pommer's vast experience in film policy and technology continued to make itself felt. In the late 1920s, he again became a prominent spokesman for the German film industry. Believing firmly in the marketing concept of a "film Europe," he advocated stronger trade relations among the film producing nations of Europe.[44] In *Exporting Entertainment*, film historian Kristin Thompson refers to Pommer "as a

42. Ernst Hugo Correll, "Die Arbeit des Produktionsleiters," *Die Woche*, special issue of "Der Tonfilm," 4 July 1931.

43. Ibid.

44. The notion of "European film" was not new in 1928. It had been discussed in the mid-twenties, primarily by French film industrialist Louis Aubert who came to Berlin in 1924, strongly pursuing to establish French-German relations through an agreement with Ufa. In this respect he had been successful with Sascha-Film of Austria before. Interviewed in Berlin, Aubert said: "I take it for granted that the film industry of a certain nation can only flourish and grow today if it not only depends on the domestic market, but also on foreign countries. This is especially true for the European countries that absolutely must depend on export and that are not in the fortunate position, like America, to recuperate the production cost in their own countries. Here, perhaps, also lies the key to the solution of the much debated American competition question. Not the French, German, or Italian film can meet this competition successfully, but only the European film. I imagine here – in a loose association of course – a type of 'European block' which is able to regain its cost through business on the European market to the same extent that the Americans succeed on theirs." See "Deutsch-französischer Filmaustausch: Ufa-Etablissement L. Aubert," *Film-Kurier*, 22 May 1924, and "Interview mit Louis

potential leader in a new pan-European industry."[45] Pommer contended, "it is necessary to create 'European films,' which will no longer be French, English, Italian, or German films; entirely 'continental' films, expanding out into all Europe and amortising their enormous costs, can be produced easily."[46]

France and Germany initiated several international conferences, but by 1928 it had become clear that these business negotiations would not yield the success expected of a "film Europe."[47] The arrival of sound film technology finally destroyed all notions of close European collaborations, plunging national cinemas into challenges of an entirely different nature, with new demands placed on production, distribution, and exhibition.

At Ufa, Pommer represented Klitzsch in several special missions to New York, Hollywood, London, and Paris.[48] And when the conference for cinema and photography (Kipho) opened in Berlin in the fall of 1930, he represented the German film industry as the keynote speaker, addressing an audience of such notables as the Minister of Culture, the Mayor of Berlin, and the Secretary of State. Pommer's speech was a plea to government to unburden the German film industry from such restrictions as censorship and entertainment tax. As models he cited the supportive intervention of the U.S and British governments.[49]

Pommer also made artistic and technical suggestions when attending *Vorstand* meetings, though these were at times rejected when the company did not foresee a profitable venture. For example, Pommer requested Professor Max Reinhardt from the Deutsche Theater as film director but was told that, while Reinhardt's direction skills might prove very interesting, he was considered too much of a risk because he was a novice to film.[50]

Aubert," *Film-Kurier*, 24 May 1924. See also Kristin Thompson, *Exporting Entertainment* (London: British Film Institute, 1985), 112–18. Had it come about, the collaboration with Aubert would have brought Pommer's career to full circle. Coproducing with Aubert's associates, Marcel Vandal and Charles Delac of the company Film d'Art, would have renewed Pommer's old friendship and business association with Vandal of the Eclair years in the teens.

45. Thompson, *Exporting Entertainment*, 113.

46. Ibid.

47. For more details, see Staiger and Gomery, "The History of World Cinema. . ."

48. Frederick Kohner, Erich Pommer Biography for Foreign Film Seminar, USC, no date, J. Pommer Collection.

49. "Der Sinn der Kipho: Die Ansprache Erich Pommers," *Film-Kurier*, fifth supplement, 26 September 1930.

50. Minutes of *Vorstand* meeting, 12 September 1930.

Always on the cutting edge of technology, Pommer insisted, for example, on using Kodak film stock, thereby establishing business relations between Ufa and the Kodak company, which Ufa had resisted in the past.[51] And again, as in 1926, he alerted Ufa's *Vorstand* to the new sound film technology, asking for funds in early 1928. During his two years abroad he had witnessed the American film industry's experiments with sound and the 1927 premiere of *The Jazz Singer*. Back in Berlin, he suggested that Ufa's theaters use the German-developed Tri-Ergon sound system, but he was told that the uncertainty of this venture did not immediately warrant such an astronomical investment.[52] But a year later, in March 1929, Ufa's top management realized the urgency for conversion to sound, after it was learned that silent film production was already on its way out in the United States.[53] Subsequently, Ufa's sound film production was scheduled to begin in Pommer's unit, and the *Vorstand* promptly sent Correll, Pommer, and Joe May on an exploratory trip to the United States.[54]

As we know today, the transition from silent film to sound could have occurred much earlier in Germany. As early as 1922, Germany had its own sound invention, "Tri-Ergon," developed by Joe Engl, Joseph Massolle, and Hans Vogt. Ufa had used it as early as 1925 in a feature film, *Das Mädchen mit den Schwefelhölzern (The*

51. Although the minutes of the *Vorstand* meetings clearly indicate the top management policy of tight control over film production, Pommer's requests with respect to personnel hiring and technical improvements did not go unheard. A letter from an old friend, Board Director of the Kodak company in Stuttgart, dated 19 August 1964, testifies: "I am indebted to you personally (as is my son), because it was you who, in 1927, established business relations between my company and Ufa. At the time, I had made ceaseless attempts to establish business contacts with the company which had just been acquired by Hugenberg, but the leading authorities Klitzsch, Lehmann, and Meydam all replied Ufa's connection with Agfa prohibited the purchase of Kodak's product. Not until you took over the production unit of Ufa so successfully and insisted that Eastman Panchromatic negative film had to be used for shooting, and Eastman positive for most of the copies, the ice was broken and my company, the Kodak-A.G., became a steady Ufa supplier, very much to the chagrin of my old late friend Walter Strehle (Agfa)." W. Langfeld of Kodak, Stuttgart, letter to Eric Pommer, Encino, California, on the occasion of Pommer's 75th birthday, 19 August 1964. J. Pommer Collection.

52. Minutes of *Vorstand* meeting, 28 March 1928. Ludwig Berger, Pommer's former film director working in the American film industry in 1929, published a *Tage-Buch* article entitled "Sound Film Does not Have to Be Trash." Berger's intent was "to expose the disgrace that valuable time is wasted in Germany," while in Hollywood initial experiences and attempts led to decisions in less than a year. Berger, "Tonfilm muß nicht Dreck sein," *Tage-Buch*, 10 August 1929.

53. Minutes of *Vorstand* meeting, 12 March 1929.

54. Ibid.

Girl With Matches), and in several short features. The screening was unsatisfactory, however, and all further experimentation with sound was abandoned.[55] But sound film technology had come to stay, igniting legal entanglements and battles among major inventors in Germany, other European countries, and the United States in the late twenties and early thirties.[56] In Germany, forces quickly joined to create a stronger bulwark against the United States. The warring parties were the Tonbild Syndicate AG (Tobis), which had acquired the Tri-Ergon patents, and the Klangfilm GmbH, which was founded by two of Germany's largest electrical manufacturers, AEG and Siemens. In March 1929 Tobis and Klangfilm buried their patent rivalry and merged. They subdivided the enormous sound conversion task, with Tobis focusing primarily on film production and Klangfilm on equipment installation in film studios and movie theaters.[57] Obtaining the Klangfilm system monopoly in Germany, Ufa became the country's first company to convert to sound.[58] But in 1929 the racing Americans beat Ufa in the newly resumed exhibition battle in Germany. On 3 June 1929, Warner Brothers' *The Singing Fool* premiered in Berlin's Gloria-Palast.[59] Ufa was also outrun by Tobis, which premiered a sound documentary in the spring of 1929, and by the German production team of Fellner and Somlo, which showed *Das Land ohne Frauen* (*Land Without Women*), an 80 percent sound film, in Berlin's Capitol Theater on 30 September 1929.[60] With the help of its Klangfilm alliance, however, Ufa soon caught up and again assumed the dominant position in the German film industry.

55. Walter Strohm, *Die Umstellung der deutschen Filmwirtschaft vom Stummfilm auf den Tonfilm unter dem Einfluß des Tonfilmpatentmonopols*, Ph. D. diss., Univ. Freiburg/Breisgau, 1935 (Freiburg: Kehrer, 1934), 18.

56. See especially Dudley Andrew, "Sound in France: The Origins of a Native School," and Douglas Gomery, "Economic Struggle and Hollywood Imperialism: Europe Converts to Sound," both in *Yale French Studies*, 60 (1980); Douglas Gomery, "Tri-Ergon, Tobis-Klangfilm, and the Coming of Sound," in *Cinema Journal*, 16: 1 (fall 1976); Fritz Heinrichs, "Die Entwicklung der Tonfilmindustrie", in *Technik und Wirtschaft*, 23: 10 (October 1930); and Strohm's dissertation, on the German role in the sound film patent wars of the time.

57. Strohm, *Die Umstellung der deutschen Filmwirtschaft.* . ., 45.

58. Ibid.

59. Warner Brothers by then owned the stock majority of the German company National-Film, which it used as distributor for its sound films. In May 1929 Warner Brothers leased Ufa's Gloria-Palast and equipped the theater with Western-Vitaphone sound equipment. Despite the German court injunction to prevent the premiere of *The Singing Fool* because of licensing infringement, the film opened in Berlin. Strohm, *Die Umstellung der deutschen Filmwirtschaft.* . ., 31–32.

60. Tobis produced *Die Melodie der Welt* (*World Melody*), a travelogue/*Kulturfilm*, in conjunction with Hapag. See Strohm, *Die Umstellung der Filmwirtschaft.* . ., 46. On

Conversion to sound caused Ufa and the entire German film industry enormous market problems. In Pommer's words, "the invention of the sound film seemed to instantaneously destroy the artfully established film export."[61] National film industries tried various approaches to maintain foreign market shares. The Americans, for instance, "ran" subtitle translations of English dialogue on the screen. But this system was accepted by German audiences only during the novelty period of sound film.[62] Pommer spoke of the need to reestablish for the sound film the broad international basis the silent film was enjoying.[63] "The German sound film," he said, "will have to go entirely different paths if it wants to succeed internationally. It will become necessary for the German film industry to create a new international sound film style."[64] The German concept of international sound films differed completely from its silent film concepts. With the beginning of sound, Pommer said, all film-producing nations began to divide their production plans according to national and international films, while a silent film's suitability for export was sometimes determined later.[65] Because of their big budgets and stars, Pommer's films were planned as international sound films from the beginning.

The sound film conversion proved a painful process, costing nearly 20 million marks, in addition to higher production expenses and a decrease in export opportunities.[66] Judging from the minutes of Ufa's *Vorstand* meetings, top management placed tremendous pressure on its producers during this transition. Initially, the *Vorstand* ordered that shooting costs remain within the year's allocated budget. In March 1929, after learning that Tobis, not Ufa, had completed the first German sound film, the *Vorstand* decided on immediate production of two German all-sound films, in the minutes referred to as "all talkies." The fact that the new sound film studios were still incomplete and insufficiently

the first German sound film, *Das Land ohne Frauen*, and other German developments in 1929, see "Ein Jahr deutscher Tonfilm: Imposante Leistung der deutschen Film-Industrie," *Film-Kurier*, 27 September 1930.

61. Pommer, "Der deutsche Film hat Weltgeltung," *Reichsfilmblatt*, 20 February 1932. In referring to export problems, Pommer used the adjective "artful" (*kunstvoll* in the original German text).

62. Pommer, "Der deutsche Film hat Weltgeltung."

63. Pommer, "Artistical Form and Sound-Film Problems of International and National Films," *Der Film*, international ed., 14: 11 (June 1929).

64. Pommer, in *Film-Kurier*, special 10th Anniversary issue, 1 June 1929.

65. Pommer, "Artistical Form and Sound-Film Problems. . ."

66. Olimsky, *Tendenzen der Filmwirtschaft. . .*, 66.

equipped by Klangfilm and Tobis did not deter Ufa from giving orders "to shoot anyway." While perfection was not expected, the company was counting on considerable success and figured that shooting with sound would provide valuable and much needed practice for production in the future. Costs were to be kept as low as possible.[67]

While other production units at Ufa, among them Fritz Lang's, continued to shoot primarily silent films, Pommer's unit became Ufa's cell of sound film production.[68] He said initial experiments with sound made everyone in his unit feel that the floor was moving underneath.[69] While in the middle of shooting *Melodie des Herzens* (*Melody of the Heart*) in Hungary, Pommer received orders to convert to sound. The pressure on Fritz Thiery, Ufa's first sound master, and his team, battling obstinate machinery in the Berlin studio, was enormous. It was a vexingly tall order, driven by intense political pressure to win German and European market supremacy. "We *had* to produce German sound film equipment, because the Americans already had it and because they intended to use it to turn the German film industry into their vassal," Pommer recalled in 1964.[70] The Americans, he said, had acquired all the patent rights that were once Ufa's, and there was intense pressure to compete in the race. Ufa was totally dependent on Klangfilm, as Pommer's words made clear:

> Siemens and Telefunken had promised that they could produce sound equipment for me within three weeks. It was madness what we did ... Our millions were running away from us, there were already six sound films, and we had none. The English had made one with American equipment. We were far behind. It was a national affair. We tried and tried. Theoretically and technically, everything should work, but we didn't get sound.[71]

Night turned to day, with everyone working in the studio at a fever pitch. The breaking point finally came, in the middle of the night. Pommer remembered Thiery's voice yelling in his office, "*Herr* Pommer, wake up! We've got it, we've got it, we've got it." Looking back, Pommer did not believe that *Melodie des Herzens*

---

67. Minutes of *Vorstand* meeting, 26 March 1929.

68. Kreimeier, *Ufa-Story*, 215.

69. Pommer, "Dichter und Tonfilm," quoted in Anton Kaes, ed., *Weimarer Republik: Manifeste und Dokumente zur deutschen Literatur 1918–1933* (Stuttgart: J.B. Metzlerische Verlagsbuchhandlung, 1983), 236.

70. Pommer, interviewed by Kadiev and Kyser.

71. Ibid.

was a good film in technical terms, affected as it was by the fact that "we had to stop every time a plane went by," but it was a beginning.[72] From then on, Pommer said, they made films at Ufa with relatively good sound but nothing compared with later standards. "Today," he said in 1964, "we would be run out of the theater."

Ufa's first sound feature film was as much a transitional film as it was ground-breaking. It was also exhibited as a silent film, since many theaters lacked sound film technology. As sound film, it generated the formula Ufa would use for its international prestige films for some time to come – foreign version shooting. With its original cast, *Melodie des Herzens* was also shot in English, French, and Hungarian.[73] The musical nature of the film led Pommer in a direction that was to prove enormously successful for Ufa. Whether by intuitive insight or by accident, the use of song and dance elements in *Melodie des Herzens* gave way to a new genre, the film operetta (*Operettenfilm*). To Pommer, this concept with its own symbiotic formula seemed the perfect response to the demands of sound film technology. *Melodie des Herzens* thus not only led to an immensely popular German genre but also one perfectly suited for international audiences. The film operetta was a light entertainment film, the German answer to the American musical, mixed with Viennese charm.[74] It seemed the perfect synthesis of art and entertainment, successfully integrating Pommer's production concepts from two continents.

But before the Pommer unit produced its string of frothy film operettas, it produced the starkly contrasting *Der blaue Engel* (*The Blue Angel*). Based on the 1905 novel *Professor Unrat* by the radical left-wing German author Heinrich Mann, it looked like a return to the realism and social criticism of some of Pommer's earlier films. But dramatic plot aside, the film's plentiful musical numbers sung by the then relative newcomer Marlene Dietrich, clearly offered a taste of the film operettas that were soon to follow in such profusion.

Der blaue Engel was as groundbreaking in the emerging sound film era as *Madame Dubarry* and *Caligari* had been in the silent era, repeating, with new technology, Germany's international success of a decade earlier. The film became another of Ufa's key films on the international market and established Ufa anew as a world

72. Pommer, interviewed by Kadiev and Kyser.
73. Hans-Michael Bock, "Keine dramatischen Maggiwürfel: Die Einführung des Tonfilms," *Ufa-Buch*, 257.
74. For a detailed discussion of this genre, see "Le parlant en Allemagne," "L'effort Allemand," "l'apport allemand," and "Berlin capital viennoise," in *Les Cahiers de la Cinémathèque*, 13, 14, 15 (1975).

competitor.[75] Reminiscent of Pommer's international prestige film strategy of the early and mid-twenties, Ufa willingly allocated production funds of pre-Hugenberg dimensions. The originally approved budget of RM 1,250,000, then raised to RM 1,279,000,[76] was still in line with Pommer's other *Großfilm* productions of the thirties.[77] By the end of production, however, the budget had climbed to RM 2,367,322, making *Der blaue Engel* Ufa's most expensive early thirties film, to be surpassed only by Pommer's *FP1 antwortet nicht* in 1932/33. The advertising budget alone was close to RM 34,000.[78] The *Vorstand* compensated for the budget in part by dropping several medium-budget films (*Mittelfilme*) from its production plan for the following year.

The enormous budget guaranteed production values of the highest quality, including the top star of the German silent cinema and an internationally renowned film director imported from abroad. German actor Emil Jannings and U.S. film director Josef von Sternberg were celebrities in the American film industry; and Ufa apparently counted on the export chances of their film.[79] Using a Hollywood film director also assured experience in sound film production, which Ufa badly needed. When asked what he was bringing with him from the United States, Sternberg's answer supposedly was, "one-and-a-half years of sound film experience."[80]

By Sternberg's standards, the technical state of the sound film studio equipment at Ufa was still crude when he arrived in Berlin. Encountering what he called "insurmountable" preparatory problems but an eager and capable production crew, he found that the Germans "had neither the proper equipment nor the experience to make a film with sound."[81] Though Sternberg claimed he was interested in the film because of Jannings, he also expressed a longing for making an artistically challenging film, and he felt that Pommer

75. See Kurt Pinthus's review, *"Der blaue Engel,"* *Tage-Buch*, 5 April
76. Minutes of *Vorstand* meeting, 4 November 1929.
77. *Melodie des Herzens* cost RM 1,532,522, *Liebling der Götter* (*The Great Tenor*) RM 1,050,768, *Der Kongreß tanzt* RM 1,913,173, to be topped by *FP1 antwortet nicht* with RM 2,215,277. Herstellungskosten und Erlöse für die Filme der Erich Pommer Produktion 1929/30 to 1932/33.
78. Minutes of *Vorstand* meeting, 24 March 1930.
79. The minutes of the 22 July 1929 *Vorstand* meeting show that Ernst Lubitsch was originally invited to direct a Jannings film. The *Vorstand* voted on Sternberg's contract after Lubitsch declined. Sternberg was to receive $30,000 instead of $40,000.
80. Josef von Sternberg, *Film-Kurier*, 16 August 1929, quoted in Renate Seydel, *Marlene Dietrich: Eine Chronik ihres Lebens* (Berlin: Henschelverlag, 1984), 94.
81. Josef von Sternberg, *Fun in a Chinese Laundry: An Autobiography* (New York: Macmillan Publishing Co., 1965; Collier Books, 1973), 138.

would guarantee that.[82] Evidently, he expressed his admiration for Pommer by stating: "Thank God for Erich Pommer. Without him, nothing would be possible … If we had more producers like him – what films we could make! He has taste *and* understanding of the creative process. Such a rarity in our business."[83] *Film-Kurier* reported: "The film's scope is guaranteed by producer Pommer's name. It will be world class, a *Spitzenfilm*, by virtue of its solid production base."[84] Interestingly, as if Pommer had never before applied his U.S. experience in Berlin, art was again the focus of one of the film's reviewers, who paid special attention to the producer: "Erich Pommer who produced this film for Ufa – the last of this year's four *Großtonfilm* productions – consciously pursued a strategy to raise the film to high level. He and his collaborators intended to create a piece of art from the beginning. . ."[85]

Numerous aspects of this film's making were unusual. Given Hugenberg's political background, Ufa's use of a film script based on the novel of an author who was, in essence, Hugenberg's ideological nemesis, was remarkable. Allegedly, author Heinrich Mann was not rejected by Ufa because the administrators mistook him for his brother Thomas, who, in 1929, was still politically acceptable to Ufa. A script by "Mann" meant Thomas Mann, not Heinrich. More credible is the possibility that Ufa's new *Generaldirektor*, Ludwig Klitzsch, overruled political concerns in favor of business finances.[86] Slanted remarks in the Hugenberg press about the author, claiming that "the film is not a film with Heinrich Mann, but against him," prompted Pommer to a public statement. On the day *Der blaue Engel* premiered, the newspaper *Berliner Tageblatt* published a letter in which Pommer risked everything for principle. Rebutting the allegations of the Hugenberg press, Pommer stated emphatically that he had never, throughout his entire career, allowed a film to be produced against agreements initially made with an author. *Der blaue Engel*, he stated, was no exception: "Not only the script's completion, but also the film's production has taken place by being in close touch with Heinrich Mann."[87] The film's domestic and international success apparently smoothed ruffled feathers among Ufa's top management.

82. Seydel, *Marlene Dietrich*, 94.

83. Maria Riva, *Marlene Dietrich* (New York: Alfred A. Knopf, 1993), 66.

84. Quoted from *Film-Kurier*, 17 August 1929, in Seydel, *Marlene Dietrich*, 95.

85. Eugen Santmari, "*Der blaue Engel*," *Berliner Tageblatt*, 2 April 1930.

86. Kreimeier, *Ufa-Story*, 224.

87. Pommer, "Eine Erklärung," *Berliner Tageblatt*, 1 April 1930. Despite Pommer's claim that the film had Mann's total approval, Ufa was criticized for having worked

Today, *Der blaue Engel* is considered by many the greatest film to have come out of Weimar Germany's Berlin; in 1930, it won audiences as quickly as Marlene Dietrich had seduced costar Emil Jannings in the film. However, Ufa executives erred on another account. Failing to assess the market value of the film's sensational new star, Marlene Dietrich, they opted not to renew her contract, thereby enabling her to emigrate and to continue her career in the United States. Responsibility for the casting of Dietrich, of course, produced numerous legends, some even by the star herself. If we elect to believe Sternberg's version, she was chosen despite the objection of nearly everyone on the team, because "Pommer quietly settled the matter by stating that the choice of the cast was my responsibility and that it was his responsibility to support me."[88] Lastly, although Ufa's policy reserved the right to alter the completed film, including editing,[89] Sternberg credited Pommer with having ensured that the completed film was not altered in any way after he left Berlin.[90] Not surprisingly, the film still showed traces of silent film technique, as evident in a remark by the prominent theater director Max Reinhardt:

> It is not altogether a talker nor yet a silent. It's an in-between situation. Jannings does nothing, says nothing, but expresses much. The only shortcoming that the film has, or at least the only criticism I have concerning this is that the technical reproduction of the sound produces a needle-scratching or a hum which disturbs just these silent portions wherein the players motivate. This, of course, will be readily corrected.[91]

---

against Heinrich Mann in turning a novel that lives off its sparkling satire into a watered-down, sentimental portrayal of a bourgeois existence. Carl von Ossietzky, editor of *Weltbühne*, published a biting Ufa critique on 29 April 1930, titled "The Film against Heinrich Mann," in which he proclaimed Dietrich's Lola portrayal to be the only redeeming factor of the film: "The only event remains Marlene Dietrich. Heaven knows whether this woman can achieve this a second time, but this here cannot be equalled by anyone in several continents' studios. This magnificently lascivious face, this haggard, long-legged figure with the shabby silk panties and the incredible black elastic garters is one of the few truly great film images in years. Here, and only here, is that wit of thought that justifies the novel's screen adaptation by transcending subject matter. Dietrich alone defends the spirit of Heinrich Mann in this film against Heinrich Mann." Quoted in Carl von Ossietzky, *Rechenschaft: Publizistik aus den Jahren 1913–1933*, ed. Bruno Frei (Berlin & Weimar: Aufbau-Verlag, 1970), 180.

88. Sternberg, *Fun in a Chinese Laundry*, 237.

89. This policy was discussed at the 3 June 1927 *Vorstand* meeting and applied to contracts of actors, directors, cinematographers, and architects (referred to as "artists") hired by Ufa.

90. Sternberg, *Fun in a Chinese Laundry*, 139.

91. Abel Green, "Germans Slam Hollywood: Reinhardt with Molnar – Pommer," *Variety*, 7 May 1930.

In the spring of 1930 Pommer became an enthusiastic spokes-man for sound film production in the German trade papers, espe-cially after the production of *Der blaue Engel* had given his unit the experience and confidence of shooting with sound.[92] By early 1932, Pommer felt comfortable stating that

> Ufa's method to produce its own films for the large French-and English-speaking markets has come through with flying colors. In typical German thoroughness, "version shooting" has become a big, important aspect of the German sound film. Its export proceeds today constitute a significant and unmistakably positive role for the German economy.[93]

Pommer's new films, *Der blaue Engel, Liebeswalzer (Love Waltz), Die Drei von der Tankstelle (The Three from the Filling Station), Der Kongreß tanzt (Congress Dances), Bomben auf Monte Carlo (Monte Carlo Madness), Stürme der Leidenschaft (Storms of Passion),* and *Ein blonder Traum (Happy Ever After),* were all produced with multi-language versions for the international market.[94] Pommer's guid-ing hand in Ufa's success was acknowledged in Germany and France alike. In Germany, *Film-Kurier* attributed it entirely to Pommer's creation of the sound film operetta.[95] In France, he was praised for excelling in films whose technical qualities "place them on the same level as their American competitor."[96] And another French source remarked: "It is primarily in the domain of the operetta, Viennese that is, in which the efforts of the produc-ers and mainly of the powerful Ufa are visible, inspired by Erich Pommer, George [*sic*] Stapenhorst, [Gregor] Rabinowitsch. . ."[97] The "Viennese" authenticity of the *Operettenfilme* coming out of northern Germany is debatable, at least judging from the re-sponse to the Viennese premiere of *Der Kongreß tanzt,* whose plot actually does take audiences to Vienna. The premiere was such a

---

92. See the following texts by E. Pommer: "Der Tonfilm und seine Technik," *Reichsfilmblatt,* 15 February 1930; and "Wie eine Tonfilm-Szene gedreht wird," *Film-woche,* 9 April 1930. See also these accounts of E. Pommer interviews: "Der stumme Film ist erledigt: Gespräch mit dem Produktionsleiter der 'Ufa,' Erich Pommer," in *Filmwoche,* 12 March 1930; and Green, "Germans Slam Hollywood. . ."

93. Pommer, "Der deutsche Film hat Weltgeltung."

94. See Pommer's own account of the films of his production unit in "Der deutsche Film hat Weltgeltung."

95. "Der Sieg des Tonfilms," *Film-Kurier,* second supplement, 27 September 1930.

96. "Le parlant en Allemagne," 124.

97. "Berlin capitale viennoise," 169.

disappointment that Pommer hastened to arrange the immediate Berlin premiere before Viennese reviews could reach Berlin and negatively affect audiences there. The German premiere at the Ufa-Palast am Zoo was successful, reportedly because the audience there was transported to "Vienna, tasted the wine, relived the past and its splendor."[98]

In his unit Pommer perfected a formula with no cinematic precedent, adapting song and dance to cinematic form. In fostering this genre, he again entrusted projects to filmmakers who brought with them experiences unrelated to film. He could reliably trust his own judgment as much as the talents of those he chose. Wilhelm Thiele, Hanns Schwarz, and Eric Charell were film directors who demonstrated that Pommer's approach worked well and that it led to both artistic acclaim and commercial success. Ufa considered Pommer's discovery, Eric Charell, such a box office guarantee that it allowed him budgetary exceptions.[99] Thiele, film director of the enormously profitable *Die Drei von der Tankstelle* became so successful that he felt he apparently provoked Pommer's jealousy.[100]

The foreign language versions were not copies of German originals with French or English sound, but versions that were shot with international stars entirely for the foreign market, a practice soon taken up by Hollywood. Pommer's son John, who began his career in the U.S. film industry at the Fox Film Corporation in 1934, remembers how systems differed:

> They did it a little different than my father ... In Germany they had the three sets of actors, necessary directors, dialogue people and so forth, and shot each scene as they were in the set. At the Fox Western Avenue, they finished the English picture and, having plenty of stages between Fox Western Avenue and Fox Hills, let the sets stand and then afterwards went in and shot the film with the Spanish cast. These separate language versions were done as long as the sound track was optical. When magnetic sound came in, that's

---

98. Riess, *Das gab's nur einmal*, vol. 2, 178.

99. Minutes of *Vorstand* meeting, 30 December 1932.

100. Horak, *Middle European Emigrés in Hollywood (1933–1945)*. This negative statement may stem from disagreements between Pommer and Thiele over the innovative style of the operetta. According to John Pommer, his father almost fired Thiele until he agreed to shoot the film the way Pommer wanted. *Die Drei von der Tankstelle*, with total production cost of RM 1,138,224, had grossed RM 3,090,761 by 31 May 1932, more than *Der blaue Engel* (RM 2,866,015). See Herstellungskosten und Erlöse für die Filme der Erich Pommer Produktion.

when dubbing started, and that is – naturally – when American films practically took over the world. . .[101]

Minutes of Ufa's *Vorstand* meetings show Ufa's ambition to employ multilingual stars who guaranteed international success for the company's foreign language versions. A prime example was the British-born actress Lilian Harvey, who became Ufa's most popular star of the 1930s and who rose to international stardom on the wave of Pommer's film operettas. The voice of Emil Jannings, lacking Harvey's language skills, was sometimes dubbed when playing the lead in international versions. Despite Ufa's concern for efficiency and rationalization, the *Vorstand* made no compromise in the quality of films for the international market. For example, for Pommer's sound film *Bomben auf Monte Carlo*, the *Vorstand* would approve the English language version if Pommer found a qualified actress because business with America, it was argued, required absolutely first-rate films.[102] International distribution also demanded that a foreign language film's ending differ at times from the original version. For foreign language versions, separate budgets were approved at the *Vorstand* meetings.[103] To assure a market for its sound films, Ufa was eager to get in touch with "suitable foreign business allies" to negotiate their participation in the foreign version costs. In October 1930, for instance, the *Vorstand* decided to show the French version of the enormously popular film operetta *Die Drei von der Tankstelle*[104] in the Gloria-Palast, merely to prove "that we in Germany are capable of producing foreign language films."[105]

In addition to the prolific film operettas, Pommer's unit produced a surprising variety of other genres. In his history of Ufa, film scholar Klaus Kreimeier correctly states that these are easily overlooked, overshadowed as they are by the sheer number of commercially and critically successful Ufa operettas. In the fall of 1930, Pommer announced, "the three top films of my next season

101. Letter from J. Pommer to author, 7 July 1993.

102. Minutes of *Vorstand* meeting, 10 March 1931.

103. The budget for a foreign language version ranged from RM 250,000 to RM 408,000 (RM 250,000 for the French version of *Die Drei von der Tankstelle*; RM 375,000 for the English version of *Bomben auf Monte Carlo*; RM 408,000 for the French version of *Der Kongreß tanzt*).

104. In a compilation of production cost and profit regarding Pommer's Ufa films from December 1929 to December 1932, *Die drei von der Tankstelle* (premiered on 30 September 1930) had brought in a total of RM 2,425,574 by 31 May 1931. Production cost had been relatively low, at RM 1,138,224.

105. Minutes of *Vorstand* meeting, 2 October 1930.

will differ from each other in subject matter and every other respect."[106] There were comedies, with and without music, adventure films, and the psychologically intriguing films of his new film director Robert Siodmak, which defy any genre definition. All of them display production values inextricably linked to Pommer's name. An adventure film like *FP1 antwortet nicht* (directed by Karl Hartl), Pommer's last Ufa film, was as popular with audiences as the musical comedy *Quick*, with film operetta star Lilian Harvey. Actors from the silent era, such as Emil Jannings, were still starring, but new ones, such as Hans Albers, were also emerging. Robert Liebmann was now one of Pommer's favorite scriptwriters. Friedrich Holländer, of *Der blaue Engel* fame, was his preferred composer of film music. Pommer's return to Germany was paying off indeed. *Variety*, assessing his success in Germany, commented that, though he was "known to Hollywood," he was "content to remain the production chief of UFA in Berlin."[107]

Though this appeared to be true in 1930, it was certainly no longer tenable by 1932 when political events in Germany began to trigger the exodus of Germany's Jewish population, hundreds part of the film industry. Seeing the writing on the wall, Pommer began to negotiate with the American Fox Film Corporation, with the understanding that he was to produce for them in Germany or – should that become politically impossible – anywhere else in the world. With Hitler's ascent to power a *fait accompli* in January 1933, Pommer signed a contract with Fox's Sidney Kent while in Hollywood. It was to take effect in the fall of that year. At Ufa two films were still to be produced in his unit. When Pommer approached Klitzsch, allegedly saying, "Herr Klitzsch, if you want me to resign at this point, it makes no difference to me," he was assured of Ufa's nondiscriminatory stance. A year later, Pommer did not hesitate to refresh Klitzsch's memory in writing, reminding him of his emphatic statement as late as the spring of 1933 that the company did not differentiate between Aryan and non-Aryan personnel and that it had no intention of parting with its Jewish "friends."[108] So Pommer remained at Ufa, preparing the production of *Odysseus' Heimkehr*, a John Erskine adaptation of Ulysses's

106. E. Pommer, "Richtlinien der neuen Produktion," *Film-Kurier*, second supplement, 27 September 1930.
107. Green, "Germans Slam Hollywood. . ." Note that *Variety*'s reference to Pommer as Ufa's production chief does not correspond to his post at the time. Production chief then was Ernst Hugo Correll.
108. Letter from J. Pommer to author, 6 July 1993; and letter from E. Pommer, Paris, to Ludwig Klitzsch, 19 August 1933, J. Pommer Collection.

homecoming, to be directed by Eric Charell. The next film was to
be *Ljubas Zobel*, but neither film was ever produced. In its 29
March 1933 meeting, the *Vorstand* decided the fate of Ufa's Jewish
"friends." The dismissal was aimed especially at those who enjoyed
a high profile at the company; Klitzsch was present at the meeting.[109] Simultaneously Ufa authorized that two films of "purely
German character" be given immediate production priority over
previously scheduled French versions.

Judging from Klitzsch's sudden change of heart, developments
leading to this decision occurred rather abruptly at Ufa. This is
clearly traceable in the minutes of earlier *Vorstand* meetings, which
indicate that both Pommer and his film director Eric Charell were
highly favored in the *Vorstand* at the time the decision was finalized. Charell, for example, was still able to "sell" the Odysseus
idea to Ufa's *Vorstand* in February. Pommer's overspending on the
Odysseus script was also still approved on 7 March 1933. The minutes of the fateful late March meeting also reveal a most curious
selection process in which the decision to dismiss Ufa's Jewish
personnel was certainly not carved in stone and at times even
reversed to benefit production at Ufa. A typical example was Pommer's film director Ludwig Berger, who was retained, though only
temporarily, to direct the film *Walzerkrieg* (*Waltz War*) whose production in Pommer's unit was then in the scriptwriting stage.[110]

Quite clearly, Ufa may have acted too zealously in dismissing
Pommer. Soon afterward he was contacted by the Foreign Office,
where he had many prominent friends, a step most likely encouraged by Propaganda Minister Joseph Goebbels though Pommer
never met with him. In an attempt to retain Pommer for the German film industry, Goebbels was apparently willing to circumvent
party politics and overlook Pommer's Jewish heritage, promising
to make him an honorary Aryan. Several dinner meetings took
place in Pommer's home. As John Pommer remembers:

> During the third week of April a letter arrived summoning me to a
> meeting in the school auditorium to acquaint all students as to their
> role in the May Day parade. The next day a newspaper article
> informed that Jewish students would be forbidden to participate in

109. Minutes of *Vorstand* meeting, 29 March 1933, regarding the issue of Ufa's
Jewish employment.

110. Minutes of *Vorstand* meeting, 29 March 1933. The film was completed under
Produktionsleiter Günther Stapenhorst who took over Pommer's tasks in March
1933. It premiered at the Ufa-Palast am Zoo on 4 October 1933. *Filmkundliche Hefte*,
5: 1 (Wiesbaden: Deutsches Institut für Filmkunde, 1972), 25.

the parade. At the next meeting Pommer showed both documents to the negotiators and said: "Gentlemen, how can you expect me to work in a country where my son is told that he is not good enough to march with his peers. Please get me an exit permit." The next day his passport had the necessary endorsements.[111]

Pommer left Germany that evening on the Berlin-Paris Express. Not trusting Goebbels, he sent his car and driver to Hanover where he left the train. They drove to a little known border station and crossed into France without a problem.

Throughout the 1930s, though no longer in Germany, Pommer received preferential – and totally unsolicited – treatment from the German government. Unlike his wife, who was denied the new German passport she applied for, Pommer was granted a renewal as late as 19 September 1935 by the German Consulate General in New York. It did not identify him as Jewish, apparently in the hope that he might change his mind to return to Berlin.[112]

Pommer chose to immigrate to France because he could work for Fox's subsidiary in Paris; he had left the work he was preparing for Fox's German production in the hands of his assistant producer Eberhard Klagemann. His departure, however, had grave financial consequences for him and his family. Through a tax the government imposed on the property of German refugees (*Reichsfluchtsteuer*) Pommer lost his house, his savings, and the value of a life insurance policy taken out in U.S. dollars convertible to ounces of finegold.[113] Though barred from taking money out of Germany, Pommer received permission to move his furniture to Paris where it was stored and later confiscated when the German Army invaded the city. Ufa also made an unsavory attempt to deny him and other Jewish colleagues the payments due them from partial ownership of a German movie theater they had sold to Ufa. When Pommer insisted on his rights in a letter to Klitzsch, Ufa's *Aufsichtsrat* retaliated, threatening a lawsuit "for defamation of character" if Klitzsch approved. The legal firm representing Ufa was none other than that of Dr. Donner of Ufa's board of directors. Donner's procedure was vetoed by Klitzsch.[114] In 1934, Pommer and his family finally returned to the United States, not with

111. Letter from J. Pommer to author, 9 September 1995.
112. Letter from J. Pommer to author, 6 July 1993.
113. Letter from J. Pommer to author, 8 July 1993.
114. Ownership of the movie theater in Beuthen, Upper Silesia, goes back to 19 September 1919 when it was acquired by Adolf Stern, Jr., with Pommer and others as limited partners. After the theater's sale to Ufa, the former owners were entitled

tourist permits but with immigration visas, and this time he was there to stay.

Throughout the 1920s, especially before the advent of sound film made language a factor to be considered along with technique, the American film industry eagerly absorbed top German film industry talent, eroding German competition. The Nazi regime not only robbed the German culture and film industry of many vital talents by forcing them into exile, it also played into the hands of the American film industry. German émigrés attempted to build or rebuild new careers in exile, first in neighboring European countries, such as Austria, England, and France, and finally in the United States. Many in the American film industry sympathized with the Hitler émigrés' situation, as Jan-Christopher Horak found in his study of the German film émigrés after 1933. Horak also recounted their difficulties, disappointments, setbacks, and failures.[115] Pommer's own story in exile in many ways mirrored the ups and downs of his fellow countrymen. Like Ulysses, hero of the film Pommer was unable to produce, Pommer's travels eventually led him back to the country of his birth. But not until 1946, when Germany was no longer home.

---

to payments, which Ufa, conveniently aided by its policy against Jews, attempted to avoid. For details describing the "Stern/Beuthen" affair, see letter from E. Pommer to Klitzsch, 19 August 1933, J. Pommer Collection; and minutes of *Vorstand* meeting, 22 September 1933.

115. Jan-Christopher Horak, *Fluchtpunkt Hollywood: Eine Dokumentation zur Filmemigration nach 1933* (Münster: MAKS Publikationen, 1986).

Göttingen 1897 with siblings. From left: Albert Pommer, Erich Pommer, Otto Pommer, Ina Pommer, Grete Pommer.

Gaumont Berlin office party, New Year's Eve, 1908. Erich Pommer is seated on floor at right (with top hat), sister Grete Pommer is standing in doorway.

Sergeant in German
Army, 1915.

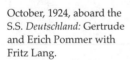

October, 1924, aboard the
S.S. *Deutschland:* Gertrude
and Erich Pommer with
Fritz Lang.

In the Garden of Winklerstrasse, Berlin-Grunewald estate, 1925. From left: John Pommer, Gertrud Pommer, father Gustav Pommer, and Erich Pommer.

Berlin Zoo Railroad Station, August, 1929. Arrival of von Sternberg to direct *Rasputin*. *The Blue Angel* was substituted. From left: Ruth Landshoff, Carl Vollmueller, Riza Royce von Sternberg, Erich Pommer, Josef von Sternberg, Paramount or Ufa official, Emil Jannings, Sam Winston.

Babelsberg Studios lot, 1932 – Erich Pommer. Note the sign: "Rauchen Streng Verboten!"

On board the *SS Paris* 1933 for discussions with New York Fox executives.

In garden of London
residence, 1936 – John
Pommer, Erich Pommer.

Royal Benefit opening of *Vessel of Wrath (The Beachcomber)* at Regal Theatre,
London, February, 1938 – Charles Laughton and Erich Pommer.

Attending preview of *Dance Girl Dance* 1940 – Gertrude Pommer, Eric Pommer.

Los Angeles, California, 1943 – Staff Sergeant John Pommer on leave during World War II visits his parents. From left: John Pommer, Gertrude Pommer, and Eric Pommer.

Berlin-Dahlem, 1946 –
Eric Pommer in U.S.
civilian uniform as
Chief, Motion Picture
Branch, Information
Services Division, Office
of Military Government
(U.S.).

Munich-Geiselgasteig Studios, 1947. The first two producer licenses are issued in
the American Zone. From left: French Film Officer Colin Revel, Eric Pommer,
Günther Stapenhorst, Fritz Thiery, interpreters in background.

Encino, California, 1957. Eric Pommer and John Pommer review reedit of *Sons, Mothers and a General*.

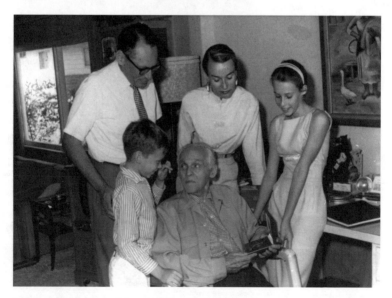

Encino, California, 1959. Family examine the Order of Merit from the German Federal Republic. Standing from left: grandson Eric Stephen Pommer, John Pommer, Heidi Pommer, granddaughter Nina Pommer, seated Eric Pommer.

Chapter 6

EXILE AND IMMIGRATION

Now the so-called "European Colony" ... Frederick Hollander is now with Warner Brothers, Franz Waxman still very successful with M.G.M. Joe May and especially Hanns Schwarz are in a very bad shape. Both haven't worked for practically over one year. The "European Colony" is growing daily by continuous arrivals of directors, actors and writers who used to work in France until the collapse. A lot is done for them by the various film funds and charity organizations and you can imagine that you see here now more misery than ever before.

Erich Pommer, letter to Lore and Maurice Cowan,
31 January 1941

Paris

Before the United States became the final destination for most of the refugees fleeing National Socialism, especially those from the film industry, countries closer by, even the Soviet Union, had become temporary homes. Austria, France, Great Britain, and Hungary offered the best chances for employment in the film industry.[1] After Pommer had arrived in France, Paris became a

---

1. For a closer look at Germany's émigrés, see Jan-Christopher Horak, Anti-Nazi-Filme der deutschsprachigen Emigration von Hollywood, 1939–1945 (Münster: MAKS Publikationen, 1985); and *Fluchtpunkt Hollywood: Eine Dokumentation zur Filmemigration nach 1933* (also MAKS, 1986).

refuge for many of his fellow émigrés from Berlin. In his essay "Pathos and Leave-Taking," Thomas Elsaesser appropriately speaks of Paris as a "waiting room," a station before embarking for Hollywood or, perhaps, before returning to Germany whose Fascist government many a refugee considered to be short-lived.[2] Paris was more than hospitable to these émigrés with respect to film production. They were able to make the transition in part because they had trained and worked in a film industry that was international from the beginning. Assessing Pommer's role in Paris, Elsaesser finds:

> The producers, for their part, could mount projects in such apparently difficult conditions, despite the political turn of events in 1933, precisely because of the long-established and initially uninterrupted competition by co-operation between the German and French industries. Having already set up, supervised and marketed French-language versions of most major German productions, [Seymour] Nebenzahl, Pommer, Eugen Tuscherer and a few others moved into original film production with relative ease.[3]

For Pommer, production in Paris meant continuation of the work he had begun in Berlin for the American Fox Film Corporation (soon to become 20th Century-Fox). It was also a return to the Eclair years of the 1910s and his Viennese collaboration with Marcel Vandal, now coproducer of *Liliom*, Pommer's second film in French exile.[4]

For each of his French films Pommer chose a film director ousted from Berlin. Max Ophüls directed Pommer's first film, the musical mystery-comedy *On a volé un homme* (*The Stolen Millionaire/A Man Was Stolen*), and Fritz Lang directed the bitter-sweet love story *Liliom*. Ophüls was a relative newcomer to the film industry and on the verge of establishing himself in Germany as film director for Ufa and other studios when Hitler came to power. He had left Germany as quickly as Pommer and Lang, just at the moment when his first major success, the Arthur Schnitzler screen adaptation *Liebelei*, opened in German theaters. Judging from Ophüls's memoirs, Pommer may have assigned the wrong film to each director. "Had we exchanged the films," Ophüls wrote, "Lang most likely would have made an extraordinary mystery

2. Thomas Elsaesser, "Pathos and Leave-Taking: The German Emigrés in Paris during the 1930s," *Sight and Sound*, 53:4 (autumn 1984): 279–83.

3. Elsaesser, "Pathos and Leave-Taking."

4. Letter from J. Pommer to author, 24 March 1987.

and I a very good romantic comedy."[5] He was amused by Pommer's determination to transfer Teutonic working conditions from Berlin to Paris. Pommer, though familiar with French film and with the language, apparently made no allowances for cultural differences, expecting his French crew and cast members to sit through the same lengthy script sessions he was accustomed to in Berlin. Allegedly puzzled when one after the other got up and left during a late afternoon session, Pommer asked the first cameraman for an explanation. He received an unmistakably French answer: "*C'est l'heure de l'apéritif, Monsieur ... j'ai une femme – une maitresse et des enfants.*"[6]

As with *On a volé un homme*, the production crew of *Liliom* was a congregation of fellow émigrés: Fritz Lang was the director, Robert Liebmann the scriptwriter, Rudolf Maté one of the cinematographers, and Franz Waxmann one of the composers. While it may well have been, as Elsaesser wrote, that the émigrés were forced to economize because of limited budgets, Waxmann recalled the use of relatively expensive technological efforts reminiscent of Erich Pommer Produktion at Ufa:

> We engaged the best Symphony Orchestra available in Paris at that time: the orchestra Straham. At my suggestion we rented the Theatre des Champs Elysée for the recording; a movable projection machine was installed in the theater to synchronize the music with the action on the screen ... I wanted the accompanying music to have the kind of spacious sound which today is produced through artificial echo, which, at that time, was virtually unknown ... Apart from the full Symphony Orchestra I also employed three electronic instruments, called the "Ondes Martenot" (named after their inventor Martenot).[7]

Liliom, immortalized long since by the American musical *Carousel*, tells the story of an ill-fated relationship involving an innocent girl and an incorrigible merry-go-round operator who pays for his sins with an untimely death.[8] Perhaps the protagonist's early death contributed to the poor reception of the film by French audiences

5. Max Ophüls, *Spiel im Dasein* (Stuttgart: Henry Goverts Verlag, 1959), 177.
6. Ophüls, *Spiel im Dasein*, 178.
7. Letter from Franz Waxmann to Herbert G. Luft, 4 October 1959, J. Pommer Collection.
8. According to Lotte H. Eisner, U.S. film director Frank Borzage wanted to make the film as *Carousel* in 1929, but was discouraged by Sol Wurtzel, head of the original Fox studio, who did not want "a picture where the hero dies in the middle." Eisner, *Fritz Lang*, 158. Borzage did make the film, however, in 1931.

despite its favorable contemporary reviews.[9] But because of the film's depiction of heaven, it also ran into problems with the Catholic Church, resulting in protests from militant Catholic youth organizations. Fox did not distribute it to the States where Fox had released a U.S. produced film by the same title, directed by Frank Borzage, in 1931.

While production conditions may have been favorable for the German émigrés, and their technical sophistication welcomed by French studios, the films resulting from such foreign collaboration did not fare well. Anti-German sentiment inevitably contributed to the failure of Pommer's two French films at the box office, as was the case a few years later, during the German occupation.[10] Elsaesser also pointed to stylistic differences between French and German films, which were apt to affect French audiences negatively. Moviegoers may also have resented seeing some of their screen favorites, such as Charles Boyer in *Liliom*, cast against type.[11] And, of course, Pommer's French films lacked the world-wide distribution channel of his earlier films. The Nazis' advance across Europe gradually cut off all European markets, starting with Germany and Italy, while the U.S. market was not conducive to showing European films at this time. Today, Ophüls's film is considered lost while Lang's enjoys occasional revivals in art movie houses.

In the personal realm, Pommer's exile in France was marked by serious health problems; the strict diabetes diet he had been following since 1928 had helped him lose weight but done little to control his illness. While working on *On a volé un homme* and *Liliom* in Paris, Pommer underwent surgery for colon cancer. Though the operation was successful, a colostomy followed, and on his journey to the United States in early 1934 he was still under the care of a French medical student. The deterioration of his health certainly contributed to the lack of success in his second Hollywood period in 1934.

Pommer's departure from Paris was brought on by developments in world economics. By 1934 Fox's French business ventures were no longer profitable. As John Pommer explained, "the adverse currency ratio of the dollar to the French franc when the

9. Eisner, *Fritz Lang*, 158.
10. See Alan Williams's thoughts on the reception of both Pommer productions in Paris, in *Republic of Images: A History of French Filmmaking* (Cambridge, MA and London: Harvard Univ. Press, 1992), 211.
11. Elsaesser, "Pathos and Leave-Taking."

US went off the gold standard caused Fox to discontinue production in France and to bring my father in 1934 to its studio in what is now Century City."[12] Unfortunately, most of Pommer's household goods stayed behind in storage. As it turned out, he was not going to see them ever again. The personal belongings he took with him to Hollywood, his files, the family's silver, chinaware, and half a dozen art objects, were all he saved from Germany until they, too, were lost.

Hollywood

In Hollywood as in Paris, Pommer's contract enabled him to provide work for a number of his fellow émigrés. *Music in the Air*, produced for Fox in the summer of 1934, was almost entirely the product of German émigré collaboration. Director Joe May, co-writer of the script Billy Wilder, and musical director Franz Waxmann were all working in the U.S. for the first time. But Joe May as director was probably the wrong choice, overburdening a film already steeped in Bavarian folklore with too much of a European flavor. John Pommer, apparently reflecting his father's thoughts, feels that an American director would have assured a product more palatable to U.S. audiences. Hollywood was not Paris, and inevitably this foreign collaboration on a single project created studio problems. Even the fact that the film was based on the 1932 Broadway musical hit by Jerome Kern and Oscar Hammerstein could not save it; *Music in the Air* failed miserably.[13]

Production suffered from a number of adversities, some of them stemming from Pommer's illness. Pommer's son attributes many problems to casting and to studio politics at a time when Fox, led by Sidney Kent and Winfield Sheehan, was struggling to ward off a take-over by 20th Century. Pommer's suggestion to cast the then unknown American actress Grace Moore was vetoed by Winfield Sheehan, head of production at Fox. Unfortunately history was to prove Pommer right. Moore's film, *One Night of Love*, produced by Columbia but not yet released during the planning stage of *Music*

12. Letter from J. Pommer to Wolfgang Schivelbusch, author of *Vor dem Vorhang: Das geistige Berlin, 1945–1948* (Munich and Vienna: Carl Hanser Verlag, 1995), 1 April 1995, J. Pommer Collection.

13. Letter from J. Pommer to author, 12 August 1988. See also Gloria Swanson's perception of her role in the film she calls a "flop," in *Swanson on Swanson* (New York: Random House, 1980), 434–36.

in the Air, made her a star overnight and earned her an Academy nomination. Instead, Sheehan insisted on Gloria Swanson, an actress Pommer considered to be too old for the role, which then also required the casting of an older leading man. Obviously Pommer was at the mercy of studio heads who had obligations to other Hollywood studio heads. In the choice of Swanson, Pommer's son claims, Sheehan was apparently influenced by M-G-M's Irving Thalberg who "had a commitment that he wanted to shove off on somebody else."[14] Still recuperating from surgery performed less than a year earlier, Pommer lacked his proverbial energy and well-known ability to override executive decisions.

And so *Music in the Air* remained the only film Pommer produced in Hollywood in 1934. Fox was soon acquired by Joseph M. Schenk and Darryl Zanuck's 20th Century, and Pommer was apparently included in the company's future plans. He left, however, as Zanuck seemed "to have taken a personal dislike" to him, which continued for the next two decades. Perhaps it was true, as Pommer's son speculates, that Zanuck, then just starting as studio head, did not want a potential studio rival around.[15]

Again Pommer explored Hollywood for assignments, talking to several U.S. film companies, none of which was major. And as in 1928, he undermined his chances in Hollywood by following a call back to Europe. He received an offer from British film producer Alexander Korda to join his London Film Productions at Denham Studios. They negotiated the details of their work and had, as John Pommer called it, a handshake deal, when Louis B. Mayer contacted Pommer, who was then in New York, to return to M-G-M. Pommer felt that his understanding with Korda had gone beyond the point where he could withdraw ethically and turned Mayer down. With hindsight, this choice is hard to understand. Pommer may have had reservations about entering into competition with Irving Thalberg at M-G-M, unaware that the relationship between Mayer and Thalberg had become strained. Perhaps Mayer knew that Thalberg, whose contract with M-G-M was to expire in 1937, planned to resign as production head of M-G-M to go into production on his own.[16] These plans never materialized, because Thalberg died unexpectedly in 1936, at age thirty-seven.

14. Letter from J. Pommer to author, 8 July 1993.

15. Letter from J. Pommer to Wolfgang Schivelbusch, 1 April 1995.

16. Frederick Kohner, *The Magician of Sunset Blvd: The Improbable Life of Paul Kohner, Hollywood Agent* (Palos Verdes, CA: Morgan Press, 1977), 88.

Pommer's rejection of Mayer's offer at this time may have aggravated Mayer beyond Pommer's expectations; it certainly had devastating consequences for Pommer's future in the U.S. film industry and was probably the greatest mistake of his career. Mayer never gave Pommer another chance, and Pommer's son speculates that he may have placed Pommer on his private blacklist. When one of Pommer's Ufa cinematographers, Karl Freund, tried to intervene on his behalf in Hollywood in 1942, Mayer allegedly declined, saying: "Pommer left me once and turned me down when I gave him a second chance. In my book, you are out after the second strike."[17] A few years short of becoming a U.S. citizen, Pommer must have been aware that his British adventure was going to complicate his naturalization plans. Resident aliens, such as the Pommers, could be issued a reentry permit valid up to one year. The renewal necessitated a return to the States, long enough to complete the paperwork for a new reentry permit. If a reentry permit expired while aliens were abroad, they would have to apply for a new immigration visa that was almost impossible to obtain. Such travels took a deep bite into the Pommers' finances.

His return to Europe just a few years short of the Second World War was a most unfortunate career move with dire consequences.

London

One can only speculate on Pommer's reasons for joining Alexander Korda. He may have been propelled by his disappointment over developments at 20th Century-Fox, or by his aversion to M-G-M, which may have evoked mixed memories of his Hollywood

17. Letter from J. Pommer to author, 15 August 1993. Karl Freund was one of the most creative and successful cameramen of the Weimar cinema. The period knew other outstanding cameramen, such as Axel Graatkjaer, Carl Hoffmann, Franz Planer, Günther Rittau, Eugen Schüfftan, and Fritz Arno Wagner. But none worked as closely with Pommer as Freund after they first met at Gaumont where Freund was the regular projectionist. He joined Pommer's team as cameraman on *Die Spinnen* and worked on many films at Decla, including *Der letzte Mann* and *Metropolis*, materially advancing moving camera techniques. In the late 1920s he immigrated to the United States and eventually settled at M-G-M, receiving an Oscar for *The Good Earth* in 1937. According to John Pommer, he developed the three-camera television film technique for the *I Love Lucy* series. While continuing on the show, Freund established the Photo Research Corporation that developed early lenses for the U.S. government to be used on the U-2 and spy satellites. He was a good friend to both Pommer generations. Letter from J. Pommer to author, 12 September 1995.

experiences in 1927/28. He may also have wanted to participate in the British film industry, which, in the thirties, experienced a considerable production boom and had strong connections with the German film industry.[18] Gaumont-British, for instance, was producing musicals modeled after Pommer's Ufa film operettas, and even some remakes, backed by a 1932 production agreement with Ufa.[19] If any European film studio was able to realize the market strategy of a "film Europe" that Pommer had so fervently advocated, it was Korda's London Film Productions and his Denham Studios, built with substantial backing from the Prudential Assurance Company.[20]

Welcoming filmmakers from Germany, France, and other European countries, the Korda empire, small as it may have been by U.S. standards, was the most cosmopolitan British film enterprise of the time. Aiming at the world market, Korda was producing on a grand financial scale not unlike Pommer when he pursued Ufa's international art strategy of the mid-twenties. And the producers appeared to be kindred spirits in their interest in putting national history on the screen. As Pommer had given German audiences their glorified past with historical epics like the *Nibelungen*, Korda fulfilled the British appetite for wanting to relive the nation's past. With London Film Productions' *The Private Life of Henry VIII*, the film that secured British actor Charles Laughton a Hollywood career, Korda had conquered moviegoers in the States as well as in Britain. In Laughton, Korda had found his Emil Jannings – while the fascination lasted – and it was only a matter of time before Pommer and Laughton were to meet and join forces.

Pommer was certainly not motivated by financial rewards in accepting Korda's call. While he had been paid $2,000 weekly at Fox in 1935, his annual earnings in England between 1936 and 1939 averaged only $25,000.[21] But his London Films contract guaranteed the same 10 to 15 percent profit participation as his Fox contract had for his European films. Such income expectations, however, were

18. For a closer look at German filmmakers in the British film industry of the 1930s, see the *CineGraph* publication *London Calling: Deutsche im britischen Film der dreißiger Jahre*, Hans-Michael Bock, Wolfgang Jacobsen, and Jörg Schöning, eds. (Munich: edition text & kritik, 1993).

19. Andrew Higson, "Way West: Deutsche Emigranten und die britische Filmindustrie," *London Calling*, 48.

20. For more details on Korda, see Higson, "Way West," in *London Calling*, 42–54; and Paul Tabori, *Alexander Korda* (London: Oldbourne Book Co., 1959).

21. Letter from J. Pommer to author, 15 August 1993.

again cut short by Nazi politics, and the beginning of the Second World War in 1939 ended Pommer's London excursion.

Pommer began his British production work with two films for Korda's London Films, drawing from British history in both. *Fire Over England*, directed by William K. Howard in 1936, took audiences to England under the reign of Queen Elizabeth I. *Farewell Again*, directed by the Irish-American Tim Whelan in 1936/37, was based on an incident in recent British history. Both films were intensely British, reflecting Pommer's belief in "nationality" and possibly his desire (shades of Bufa and its propaganda goals) to strengthen British resolve against the growing Nazi menace. Committed in Germany to producing purely German films in spirit and atmosphere, he now transferred this belief to England. Aware of the inherent contradiction of such a belief from "a confirmed wanderer about the globe," he said: "I am interested in making 'English' films, because I feel strongly that each country should produce films of its own, with a strong national flavor."[22]

He also saw no contradiction in the fact that *Fire Over England* was achieved through an entirely international effort. The producer was German, the film director American, the cameraman Chinese, the scriptwriter British, her cowriter Russian, and the cast of actors British. "I do not say it is a good film, a bad film, a great film, a weak film," Pommer said, "but I do claim that it is an *English* film."[23] And his films were apparently convincing. *Farewell Again* proved that Korda and Pommer, two foreigners in the British film industry, "could tackle an intensely British subject and do it without a single false note."[24] Both films were released in the States by United Artists, *Farewell Again* under the title *Troopship*. *Fire Over England* did especially well, counting as "one of Korda's most successful pictures" and winning the Gold Medal of the International Committee for Artistic and Literary Diffusion by the Cinema.[25]

While preparing *Fire over England*, Pommer met Charles Laughton, then starring in Korda's *Rembrandt*. Evidently neither saw a future at London Film Productions and both were looking for alternatives. Laughton, especially, felt disillusioned after Korda pulled the rug from under his film, *I, Claudius*, an ill-fated product of Denham Studios, suffering intense difficulties arising from the

22. Pommer, "Films Over England," date and source unavailable, despite BFI search.
23. Ibid.
24. Tabori, *Alexander Korda*, 196.
25. Ibid., 188.

mutual dislike between Laughton and the film's director, Josef von Sternberg. With his London Films contract coming to an end in April 1937, Laughton joined Pommer in planning a business venture in which they would be co-owners, featuring Laughton as star and absorbing several of the Denham Studios' employees. Laughton was especially interested in Pommer's former association with German silent film star Emil Jannings and evidently saw a chance for greater control over the script, direction, and roles in his future films.[26]

Pommer, convinced that he could handle an actor as difficult as Laughton, apparently saw him as another Jannings. By that time, Laughton was an international star, having completed *Les Miserables* for 20th Century and *Mutiny on the Bounty* for M-G-M in 1935. He was an asset Pommer could apparently count on without risk. In 1937 they formed a production company, jointly owned by Laughton's company and Pommer's British holding company, Rosemullion Pictures Corporation Limited. In partnership with John Maxwell, chairman of Associated British Pictures Corporation Ltd. (ABP), they committed themselves to three films, each to cost between 90,000 and 100,000 English pounds. Since they also intended their films for the U.S. market, they named the company Mayflower Film.[27] Not surprisingly, Mayflower's mission statement evokes Pommer's Ufa concepts of the late 1920s and early 1930s:

> We believe it is possible to break away from conventional ideas in film entertainment and that there is big money in pictures that answer the call for something fresh. But, while we will endeavour at all times to maintain a high artistic standard in our product, our aim and object is also to make films that have definite box-office value and attract both the popular audiences and also those people who fail to patronise the cinema because they regard the average film entertainment as lacking in intelligent appeal.[28]

The promised art and entertainment formula was evident in the fact that two of Mayflower's three films were based on the works of popular novelists, *Vessel of Wrath* by Somerset Maugham and

26. For an overview of Laughton's career, see Simon Callow, *Charles Laughton: A Difficult Actor* (London: Methuen, 1987); Charles Higham, *Charles Laughton: An Intimate Biography* (Garden City, NY: Doubleday, 1976); Elsa Lanchester, *Charles Laughton and I* (New York: Hartcourt, Brace and Co., 1938) and *Elsa Lanchester Herself* (New York: St. Martin's Press, 1983); and Kurt Singer, *The Laughton Story: An Intimate Story of Charles Laughton* (Philadelphia and Toronto: John C. Winston, 1954).

27. Letter from J. Pommer to author, 15 August 1993.

28. Pommer, "The Mayflower," Mayflower Publicity Booklet, n.d., J. Pommer Collection.

Jamaica Inn by Daphne du Maurier. Quite clearly Laughton envisioned Mayflower's productions as a writer's cinema where authors would do for the screen what Shakespeare, Molière, and Chekhov had achieved for the stage.[29]

With *Vessel of Wrath*, released in the States under the title *The Beachcomber*, Pommer began a number of films shot almost exclusively on location. The Somerset Maugham South Seas tale was shot in southern France, where Pommer's old friend Marcel Vandal joined him in organizing and handling the production of the exterior settings.[30] It would be the last joint effort of a collaboration that had spanned thirty years. Production, however, began with a shock for Pommer. Almost immediately it became obvious that the film's director, the writer Bartlett Cormack, was not up to the task of directing, and he agreed to be replaced by Pommer. *Vessel of Wrath* became the first and only film Pommer directed, a task he absolutely disliked. A producer through and through, Pommer did not share other producers', especially Korda's, oscillation between directing and producing. Shortly before, after *Fire Over England* was completed, Pommer had emphatically stated: "I am a producer, and not a director; I have never been a director, never wanted to be, possibly could not be if I tried; anyway, I prefer not to put it to the test."[31] According to his son John, Pommer felt that, "while doing a competent job of directing, he would have preferred to concentrate on producing; he believed that he would have obtained a better film."[32]

Interestingly, as a director Pommer apparently did not practice what he had preached so emphatically throughout his career. The many months of script conferences during the summer of 1937 notwithstanding, Laughton admitted the improvisational quality of the film: "We did not adhere strictly to the original scenario. Pommer produced the picture from behind the camera and although we followed the basic outline of the story we made many inventions as we went along."[33] While Laughton saw no problem in allowing his protagonist's character to go his own way, resulting in slapstick where the intention had been dramatic, critics felt different. As Mayflower's first production, *Vessel of Wrath*

29. Callow, *Charles Laughton*, 122.
30. Letter from J. Pommer to author, 27 July 1995.
31. Pommer, "Films Over England."
32. Letter from J. Pommer to author, 15 August 1993.
33. Charles Laughton, in *Film Weekly*, 19 February 1938, reprinted in Callow, *Charles Laughton*.

was not only received enthusiastically by audiences, but also judged by the British press with unusual scrutiny. Especially John Grierson of *World Film News* took issue with Laughton's tendency to cram every aspect of his enormous talents into one single role. In what amounted to a warning for him and Pommer, Grierson stated:

> I like Laughton very much, for he is a brilliant fellow, but I like the future of British films even more ... See the film as, nearly, in the category of Laurel and Hardy, and you will see *Vessel of Wrath* at its best. But this does not absolve Pommer and Laughton from making up their minds more decisively next time.[34]

Pommer never directed a film again, although he did receive offers to direct and could have pursued a directing career. But the experience of directing *Vessel of Wrath* and the film's reception confirm John Pommer's impression of his father:

> I believe that he felt that he could exercise sufficient creative input by actively participating in all areas of preproduction, comments during shooting, and especially in the cutting room and postproduction phase. That way he could work on several projects at once without being tied down to a single film for a protracted period. He also asserted that a director can do better work on the set if he has the creative filter of a strong producer available to him.[35]

With the second Mayflower film, *St. Martin's Lane*, later renamed *London After Dark* and released in the States under the title *The Sidewalks of London*, Pommer and Laughton returned to location shooting in England. According to scriptwriter Clemence Dane, they chose London's West End, planning to make "a classic of London street life, so that everybody should cry out: 'This is home!' 'This is the true London!'"[36] Alexander Walker, in his biography of the film's young star Vivien Leigh, drew an interesting line to some of Pommer's German films when he wrote:

> Tim Wheelan was a Hollywood director, but it was Pommer's Teutonic attachment to the detailed realism of German films like *Varieté*, as well as Laughton's appetite for wolfing down heaped helpings of humiliation like Jannings in *The Blue Angel*, which gave the film its sense of pitiless destiny ... Not until Chaplin

34. John Grierson, quoted in Callow, *Charles Laughton*, 124–25.
35. Letter from J. Pommer to author, 4 May 1991.
36. Callow, *Charles Laughton*, 125.

made *Limelight* in 1952 was the same kind of *milieu* presented quite so picaresquely.[37]

The authenticity of the exterior scenes notwithstanding, there were several reasons why *St. Martin's Lane* was disappointing. Laughton's biographer, Simon Callow, blamed the film's script. Laughton, Pommer, the film's director, and coscriptwriter changed it so often that Dane renounced her authorship. Not surprisingly, Callow raised the question of how Laughton and Pommer, "with their avowed sense of the central significance of the script," could "have gone into production with such a hodge-podge."[38] There were also problems with the film's director, Tim Whelan, but not, as has been claimed, because he was an alcoholic. Pommer had worked with Whelan before, on *Farewell Again*, and evidently considered him a suitable director. In the final analysis, the film pleased primarily for one reason – leading lady Vivien Leigh, with whom Pommer had worked on *Fire Over England* and who was on loan to Mayflower from London Films. It was allegedly after seeing an unfinished work print of *St. Martin's Lane*, sent to M-G-M's David Selznick at the request of Harry Ham of the London Myron Selznick office, that David Selznick gave Leigh the role of Scarlett O'Hara in *Gone with the Wind*.[39]

If the first two Mayflower films had their share of problems with film directors, the third film, *Jamaica Inn*, proved no exception. *Jamaica Inn*, directed by Alfred Hitchcock, was the director's last British film before resuming his career in Hollywood. Pommer and Hitchcock had worked together before at Ufa, where the latter worked as writer and art director on *Die Prinzessin und der Geiger* (*The Blackguard*, 1924).[40] Apparently Hitchcock hated *Jamaica Inn* and considered the story "absurd." In fact, he criticized everything, from Pommer whose knowledge of the English language he questioned, to Laughton whom he considered an amateur. Allegedly he said, "it isn't possible to direct a Charles Laughton film, the best you can hope is to act as referee."[41] Though Hitchcock acknowledged Laughton as an artist and a genius, he would have preferred a "craft professional." Their personal dislike was mutual.

---

37. Alexander Walker, *Vivien: The Life of Vivien Leigh* (New York: Weidenfels & Nicolson, 1987), 103.

38. Callow, *Charles Laughton*, 126.

39. Letter from J. Pommer to author, 15 August 1993.

40. François Truffaut, *Hitchcock* (New York: Simon and Schuster, A Touchstone Book, 1967), 87.

41. Callow, *Charles Laughton*, 130.

Again a young actress was the most redeeming feature of the film. As with Korda's discovery of Vivien Leigh, it was now Maureen O'Hara's turn, discovered by Laughton and Pommer.

After three films the Mayflower partners were running into financial problems. Their films had not been box office hits. *St. Martin's Lane*, for instance, received "decent notices and a stupendous première at the Odeon Leicester Square, at which 5,000 people massed for the arrival of the stars," but it fared no better than the other two films.[42] *Jamaica Inn* was even called a disaster. Mayflower's fourth project, *The Admirable Crichton*, never had a chance of becoming a film. Pommer's son places the blame for some of the company's financial problems on poor distribution:

> While ABP [Associated British Pictures Corporation Ltd.] was a good distributor in England, the German-language market at the time was non-existent for a Pommer production. In the U.S., the films were distributed by United Artists who were not the power house that they had been earlier and were to be again ten years later. They were ill equipped to handle British pictures, as Korda's experience, except for *Henry VIII*, shows.[43]

The year 1939 put an end to Pommer's British film production. John Maxwell, Mayflower's principal financial source, backed out of his commitment, forcing Pommer and Laughton to look elsewhere for financing.[44] When Laughton received an offer from RKO Radio Corporation to star in *The Hunchback of Notre Dame*, Pommer spent the month of June in New York, attempting to parlay RKO's interest in Laughton into the possibility of financing and distribution for Mayflower films. On 18 August, two weeks before the outbreak of the war, he arrived in New York again in order to bring distribution negotiations with RKO to an end. Luckily, his wife was with him since she also needed a reentry permit. With Pommer in possession of a German passport, there was no way to return to England, or even to risk going on the high seas.[45] The Pommers stayed in the United States. Their return from Europe dealt them another financial blow. His long-time secretary in London had stored their personal belongings in the M-G-M offices, which were destroyed by fire and water when hit by a bomb during the London Blitz.

---

42. Ibid., 128.
43. Letter from J. Pommer to author, 15 August 1993.
44. Higham, *Charles Laughton*, 94.
45. Letter from J. Pommer to author, 15 August 1993.

With Laughton's approval, the Mayflower Company went into hiatus, and the partners both signed employment contracts with RKO while reserving the right to continue as Mayflower directors. O'Hara's seven-year Mayflower contract was also taken over by RKO.[46] Laughton and O'Hara were to star in *The Hunchback of Notre Dame*, directed by German émigré William Dieterle. Pommer was to produce *Dance, Girl, Dance* and *They Knew What They Wanted*. His salary, $1,250 when he began working for RKO in October 1939, increased to $2,000, as it had been at Fox Film before.[47]

Hollywood Again

RKO was a studio in constant flux and hardly the guarantor of an immigrant producer's Hollywood career. According to *The RKO Story*, "RKO existed in a perpetual state of transition: from one regime to another, from one set of production policies to the next, from one group of filmmakers to an altogether different group."[48] By the time the Mayflower partners joined RKO, it had gone through five presidents and six production heads in ten years. Pommer was hired by George Schaefer who had recently taken over as corporate president from Leo Spitz. As detailed in the *RKO Story*, "Schaefer was determined to turn RKO into a 'prestige' studio, emphasizing quality productions based on respected literary and theatrical properties."[49] When studio head Pandro S. Berman left RKO after completing *The Hunchback of Notre Dame* with Laughton and O'Hara, the company was left with Schaefer in charge of all business and creative decisions.[50] During Schaefer's tenure – he resigned in 1942, leaving an almost bankrupt company – RKO's production concept was nothing short of schizophrenic:

> On the one hand, he cultivated prestige offerings such as *Abe Lincoln in Illinois*, *They Knew What They Wanted*, *Citizen Kane* and *The Magnificent Andersons*. On the other, he approved a giddy collection of "B" efforts for the hoi polloi ... The lamentable fact was that

46. See Louella O. Parsons, "Laughton, Pommer Bring Their Mayflower Unit to Hollywood," *Los Angeles Examiner*, 20 October 1939.

47. Summary of Contract between Pommer and RKO Radio Pictures, Inc., 1 April 1940, E. Pommer Collection.

48. Richard B. Jewell and Vernon Harbin, *The RKO Story* (New York: Arlington House, Octopus Books Ltd, 1982), 10.

49. Ibid., 12.

50. Ibid.

Schaefer's amalgam of the high and low didn't work – mostly because the majority of the "A" specials were paybox failures.[51]

Pommer, hired as the European producer *extraordinaire*, was intended precisely for the prestige films Schaefer envisioned for RKO. His contract specifically stated that Pommer was "only required to work on 'A' feature length pictures." This was especially true for *They Knew What They Wanted*, "purchased by RKO for $50,000 in the studio's continuing effort to raise the quality and eminence of its product."[52]

But it seems to have been Pommer's fate that none of his U.S. production work went smoothly. His first film for RKO in 1940, *Dance, Girl, Dance*, was no exception. It was based on a novel by the well-known author Vicky Baum. Maureen O'Hara starred as a ballet student and Lucille Ball, early in her film career, as a burlesque queen. Roy Del Ruth was hired to direct because of his experience with musicals. But his ideas clashed with those of Pommer, who had established a different kind of musical with Ufa's film operettas in the early 1930s. Unlike Del Ruth, Pommer was not interested in another clone of M-G-M's *Broadway Melody*, especially not after his disappointment with the earlier *Music in the Air*. Despite their discussions and Del Ruth's agreements to all terms, the latter persisted in guiding *Dance, Girl, Dance* along standard M-G-M musical lines.[53] When production came to a halt with the death of Maurice Moscovitch, who was playing the ballet master in the film, Pommer used the opportunity to fire Del Ruth and replace him with Dorothy Arzner, "who tossed out Del Ruth's footage and began anew."[54] He gave Moscovitch's role to Maria Ouspenskaya, who was available, had the right Russian accent, the appropriate age, with acting talent and marquee value equal to that of Moscovitch.[55]

Much has been read into the replacement of a male actor with a female counterpart, especially after the film was discovered by feminist film theorists in the 1970s. Film scholar Judith Mayne, for instance, approaching *Dance, Girl, Dance* exclusively from a feminist perspective, called this gender change so crucial that she made it accountable for giving the entire film a new focus.[56] Clearly

---

51. Jewell and Harbin, *RKO Story*, 140.
52. Ibid., 152.
53. Letter from J. Pommer to author, 19 January 1995.
54. Jewell and Harbin, *RKO Story*, 150.
55. Letter from J. Pommer to author, 7 February 1995.
56. Judith Mayne, *Directed by Dorothy Arzner* (Bloomington and Indianapolis: Indiana Univ. Press, 1994), 143.

contradicting what Pommer's son remembers of the film's production, she claimed "the most significant change made *by Arzner* was to transform the head of the dance troupe from a man to a woman, from 'Basiloff' to 'Basilova.'"[57] In Mayne's book on Arzner, Pommer barely exists. Mayne's placing Arzner centerstage unrealistically credits creative aspects like scriptwriting, choreography, and editing, to the film's director. Indicative of her agenda is the caption under a photo showing Arzner, Ball, and Pommer in discussion, which merely states "Dorothy Arzner and Lucille Ball on the set of *Dance, Girl, Dance* (1940)."[58] Pommer's son was amused: "My father would have liked to know that in 1940 he made the feminist film of the 1970s."[59] An unexpected turn in film theory and reception has revived a film that "took a severe drubbing from reviewers and audiences alike when it was first released," allegedly causing RKO a loss of $400,000.[60] Evidently the relationship between Arzner and Pommer was positive. In 1949 she initiated a business venture with Pommer and his son. They formed Signature Pictures, a production company, with guaranteed financing from a friend of Arzner's. However, through untimely speculation by this financial backer, Signature Pictures never got off the ground despite the fact that it was developing projects with talents such as Billy Wilder and Walter Reisch.[61]

Pommer's second RKO film, *They Knew What They Wanted*, ran into problems barely encountered with the earlier films. The story, based on the Pulitzer Prize-winning play by Sidney Howard, involved an aging Italian immigrant winegrower in California's Napa Valley and his mail-order bride who falls for someone else. But Joseph Breen, then director of the Production Code Administration, objected to the film's marriage of Laughton to Carole Lombard, the "fallen woman." The Hays Office in 1941 did not permit films featuring women with questionable pasts to have "happy endings." John Pommer wrote:

57. Mayne, *Dorothy Arzner*, 143. Emphasis added.

58. Ibid., 141.

59. Letter from J. Pommer to author, 7 February 1995.

60. Jewell and Harbin, *RKO Story*, 150.

61. Letter from J. Pommer to author, 7 February 1995. Austrian-born Billy Wilder started as a scriptwriter in Berlin and became one of the most successful émigrés to Hollywood, writing the script for Ernst Lubitsch's *Ninotchka* and directing Paramount films such as *Sunset Boulevard*, *The Apartment*, and *Some Like It Hot*. Walter Reisch was a successful scriptwriter (with E. Pommer in Berlin and also for *Ninotchka*) and film director at M-G-M and 20th Century-Fox.

When Laughton and my father, with Schaefer's approval, picked *They Knew What They Wanted* as a change of pace for Charles, they must have underestimated censorship problems. After long negotiations they had to sacrifice a satisfactory ending; Joseph Breen and the Catholic Church would not allow such a marriage.[62]

That was unfortunate, as the success of the later Broadway musical version by Frank Loesser, called *The Most Happy Fella*, showed. It had the "happy ending" that the film should have had.[63]

Production also suffered from animosity among the various players involved. Director Garson Kanin disliked Laughton, and Laughton disliked his leading lady, Carole Lombard. According to John Pommer, "in their search for a second important marquee name, Schaefer and my father also discounted or did not know of the aversion Laughton and Carole Lombard felt for each other from having worked together previously. There is no rapport between the two in the film."[64] And Laughton's wife, Elsa Lanchester, testified to her husband's aversion to Lombard: "Charles begged Pommer to replace Lombard – he felt he had suffered through *White Woman* with her – but Pommer and RKO refused."[65] With much of the film shot in Napa Valley, Pommer, who worked at the studio, was not available on a daily basis to smooth ruffled feathers.[66]

Apparently never able to overcome his frustrations during the shooting of *They Knew What They Wanted*, Kanin took revenge.[67] His recollection of Pommer in his memoirs, written more than two decades later, was nothing short of a vicious personal attack. No wonder – the authors of *The RKO Story* assessed *They Knew What They Wanted* in these words: "When the picture was finally finished, George Schaefer, Harry Edington, and other company executives probably wished Joseph Breen had stopped them from making it in the first place ... The eventual loss was $291,000."[68] However, the financial losses of *Dance, Girl, Dance* and *They Knew What They Wanted* should be seen, as John Pommer rightly points

62. Letter from J. Pommer to author, 15 August 1993.
63. Letter from J. Pommer to author, 20 November 1993.
64. Letter from J. Pommer to author, 15 August 1993.
65. Lanchester, *Elsa Lanchester Herself*, 166.
66. Letter from J. Pommer to Patrick McGilligan, author of a forthcoming book on Fritz Lang, quoted in letter to author, 19 January 1995.
67. Garson Kanin, *Hollywood: Stars and Starlets, Tycoons and Fleshpeddlers, Moviemakers and Moneymakers, Frauds and Geniuses, Hopefuls and Has-Beens, Great Lovers and Sex Symbols* (New York: Limelight Editions, 1984).
68. Jewell and Harbin, *RKO Story*, 152.

out, in the context that few RKO films that year were in the black: "For example, *All That Money Can Buy* lost $53,000 in its initial run, and even *Citizen Kane*, violently denounced by Louella Parsons and William Randolph Hearst, lost $160,000."[69]

By early 1941 Pommer had five films in preparation, with scripts completed for three of them.[70] In a letter to friends in British exile, Pommer voiced his frustration over the many obstacles postponing production of each film. He wrote:

> Although I had to work very hard I was not able to bring many pictures on the floor, but nor was any other producer of this lot. There were plenty of small and bigger worries that I had to overcome. In addition I had the most difficult task of clearing up the whole Mayflower business and Mayflower's relationship to John Maxwell. With George Schaefer's help I was pretty successful in this in spite of the difficulties in dealing with such a strange personality as poor old J. M. was and of the complete lack of understanding that Charles [Laughton] always shows in business matters. But still I have no reason to complain and I believe that fate has been very kind to me.[71]

He especially cited difficulties with Laughton who, without explanation, suddenly refused to star in *Mister Pinkie* when it was ready for shooting. He wrote to his British friends: "Charles' strange behavior in this and other matters has created plenty of trouble for me from the day on when I arrived in New York in August 1939. It would take volumes to write you all about it."[72] But more than revealing personal problems with his former partner, Pommer's letter shows a keen sense of the limitations of the studio for which he was working in particular, and of the means it would take to achieve success in the U.S. film industry in general. Discussing RKO's attempt to substitute "one real box-office name by a combination of three good names" for *The Unexpected Uncle*, he explained:

69. Letter from J. Pommer to author, 15 August 1993.

70. The films were *Two On An Island*, based on Elmer Rice's play; *Water Gypsies*, based on A. P. Herbert's novel; *Mister Pinkie*, original story, script by Louis Bromfield and John Van Druden; *Weekend For Three*, original story, script by Dorothy Parker and Alan Campbell; and *The Unexpected Uncle*, magazine story by Eric Hatch, script by Demar Daves. Letter from E. Pommer to Lore and Maurice Cowan, 31 January 1941, J. Pommer Collection.

71. Letter from E. Pommer to L. and M. Cowan.

72. Ibid.

The possibility, however, of securing real box-office stars or 'established' directors is a very dark chapter in present day picture making in Hollywood.

This studio which is still in the middle of a complete re-organization has not the talent-buying power as some other major studios. And as to the 'established' directors they are just as difficult to get on account of their being able to form their own independent units and dictate their terms. The foreign markets are gone and the picture stands and falls with its domestic success. For assuring success in USA you must have box-office names ... This studio here is very poor in established talent.[73]

And yet, the letter reflects his confidence "to get this studio really going." He writes about his good rapport with both Schaefer and Edington, two company executives in apparent conflict with each other.

In April 1941, all of Pommer's plans came to an abrupt halt when he suffered a coronary thrombosis. A chain smoker until then, as is visible on many of his photographs and production stills, he never smoked again. But the damage was done, and eventually he developed atherosclerosis. George Schaefer took advantage of Pommer's illness to fire him from RKO under a health clause. His contract with RKO stipulated that his employment could, at the company's discretion, be terminated if illness exceeded three out of fifty-two weeks.[74] Pommer's attempts to avert his dismissal by holding production conferences at his home within three weeks of his heart attack were in part sabotaged by RKO. A settlement attained by Pommer, granting him production of at least one more film, was broken by RKO. He sued the company and reached a new settlement regarding salary, office, and a secretary. But he was not given the opportunity to produce another film. Tay Garnett, an experienced director hired by RKO in the meantime, took over the production of *The Unexpected Uncle* and *Weekend For Three*, neither one with success.[75]

The heart attack left doubts in Hollywood about the state of his health. His dismissal from RKO, coupled with the possibility that Louis B. Mayer had placed him on his "blacklist," made a future career for Pommer in the U.S. film industry virtually impossible.

73. Letter from E. Pommer to L. and M. Cowan.

74. Letter from J. Pommer to author, 19. October 1986; and contract between Pommer and RKO, 1940.

75. Letter from J. Pommer to author, 15 August 1993. See also Jewett and Harbin, *RKO Story*, 156 and 166.

"In Hollywood," John Pommer stated, "you are only as good as your last film, and for various reasons he had not produced a real money maker in several years."[76] And there may have been an additional factor. By 1942 Pommer and his wife had not been able to become citizens because immigration regulations required five years of uninterrupted residency in the States, and the British interlude had pushed their eligibility date up to 1944. That they now were "enemy aliens" may have aggravated Pommer's situation further. It is entirely possible, as John Pommer thinks, that it left a negative impression on prospective employers in the U.S. film industry who thought the Pommers lacked patriotism because they had not become citizens in 1939, five years after their immigration. Such thinking is also indicated in Jan-Christopher Horak's study of German immigrant filmmakers in Hollywood during the war, which states that immigrant producers did not feel comfortable with American film genres until after they had produced an anti-Nazi film.[77] An anti-Nazi film under one's belt may very well have opened doors to a future Hollywood career, and this is precisely the route Pommer attempted in collaboration with Max Ophüls in Hollywood after his dismissal from RKO.

As a result, the years between 1942 and 1946 were, psychologically and financially, the most devastating of Pommer's life and career. There were a few projects on which he worked, some even for pay, but eventually they went into production without him. And then there were turndowns. There were medical bills and taxes to pay, resulting in financial and legal choices he and his wife regretted later. The most devastating decision involved their house. When 1941 income taxes became due in early 1942, they were unaware of the possibility of deducting as a war loss the household goods still stored in Paris. Pommer's wife Gertrud, in whose name the house had been bought, insisted on selling the house to pay the taxes. In a bad housing market the house brought little more than the $20,000 for which they had bought it in 1940.[78] They rented a small apartment and lived off the proceeds from the sale of personal valuables. They were aided by two close friends,

76. Letter from J. Pommer to author, 15 August 1993.

77. Horak, *Anti-Nazi-Filme*, 32.

78. The Pommers' house was at 1721 Angelo Drive, in one of the best areas of Beverly Hills. The garden in the rear shared the fence with part of Jack Warner's large estate on the next street. In the mid-1960s, the house was sold for about $2,000,000. In the late 1980s, David Geffen purchased the adjoining Warner estate for well over $50,000,000. Letter from J. Pommer to author, 14 September 1995.

Fred Pinkus, a former business manager from Berlin, and his wife, silent movie star Eliza La Porta. John Pommer remembers that "they bought chinaware and glasses, handpainted them and sold them to better-class department stores. My mother helped with the painting, my father for a time alternated with Pinkus working the baking ovens."[79] In the final analysis, few producers who immigrated to Hollywood from Hitler's Germany were successful. As Jan-Christopher Horak pointed out, their situation depended on access to capital, their own or borrowed, or on the copyright to a story. Horak found:

> Of those who emigrated [from Europe] after 1939, [Hermann] Millakowsky, [Seymour] Nebenzahl, [Arnold] Pressburger and [Gregor] Rabinowitsch were the most successful because they invested the capital they had been able to transfer from France in an independent production. The exorbitantly high cost of U.S. production, however, meant that they were rarely able to overcome the level of second-rate B-films. Pressburger was the only exception.[80]

In May 1944 the Pommers finally became U.S. citizens and changed their names to Gertrude and Eric. They were never able to reclaim their household goods from Paris. After the liberation of Paris, they were informed that they had been taken by the Germans in the first days of the occupation and that nothing had been recovered at the end of the war. Instead, they received a detailed inventory and appraisal, carefully stamped "Confiscated [*beschlagnahmt*] by the Wehrmacht." After wrangling a few years with the IRS, the Pommers eventually received substantial refunds plus interest.[81]

With peace in 1945 came the opportunity for Pommer to embark on a new and highly successful phase of his career, though in many aspects controversial. He was asked by the United States government to reorganize the demolished German film industry in the U.S. zone. After years of unemployment, any call to action was invigorating. Though aware of difficulties awaiting him in Germany, he could hardly have predicted the battles he was going to have to fight anew.

79. Letter from J. Pommer to author, 15 August 1993.
80. Horak, *Anti-Nazi-Filme*, 32.
81. Letter from J. Pommer to author, 14 September 1995.

Chapter 7

GERMANY REVISITED

The victims are the German filmmakers. Perhaps a man can help them when he finally decides whether he will build production in the future as Mr. Eric Pommer or as Erich Pommer.

"Der Vater der Film-Dekartellisierung,"
[The Father of Film-Decartelization]
Oberbayerisches Volksblatt, 12 January 1952

Postwar Germany

May 1945: the Second World War was over and Germany defeated and in ruins. The remainder of the former German Reich was split among eastern and western Allies. The western part, the future Federal Republic, was divided among the American, British, and French occupation powers. So was West Berlin, situated like an island in an East German zone occupied by the Soviets.

Germany's Ufa, since 1942 part of Propaganda Minister Josef Goebbels's gigantic state-controlled Ufi *Konzern*, was divided between the Soviet occupation power in the East and the three Allies in the West. Unlike the East, the western part of the Ufi *Konzern* was prevented from reviving as a monopoly. Gone was the era of Weimar Germany's vertically integrated film conglomerates and Nazi Germany's centralized state-controlled film industry. Instead, the western Allies

intended the total disentanglement and liquidation of the Ufi capital. Film production and distribution were to develop outside of the formation of cartels and independently of state interference by competing freely and by benefiting from the Ufi assets. The military governments therefore prohibited the inception of a new monopoly.[1]

The revival of the film industry in the West was delayed, obstructed by the fact that victors and vanquished were all determined to play out their political, ideological, and economic ambitions. Of the western Allies, the Americans (occupying Bavaria, except for Lindau on Lake Constance, parts of Baden-Württemberg, Hesse, and Bremen) held a key position in western reconstruction. Whatever was left of Ufi's former production sites in the West was on American-occupied territory: Ufa's Tempelhof studios in Berlin, stripped bare by the Soviets, and Bavaria Film's Geiselgasteig studios, the former Emelka studios, in Munich, the latter still used, at the time, for military purposes. The British zone in the North (Schleswig-Holstein, Hamburg, Lower Saxony, and Northrhine-Westphalia) soon merged with the American, forming an economic "double zone" in which filmmakers were able to use British and American licenses interchangeably.[2] The French, whose zone (Lindau in Bavaria, parts of Baden-Württemberg, and Rhineland-Palatinate) contained no notable Ufi assets except movie theaters, occupied a back seat in the reconstruction process.

The reconstruction goals of the western Allies stood in sharp contrast to those of the Soviets controlling the East. They also clashed with West German government officials, who had a strong interest in reviving a German film monopoly and who argued that the Ufi assets were too small to be divided further after having been split already between East and West. On paper, the western portion of the Ufi *Konzern* remained the same monopoly that had emerged from the Third Reich. But apart from studio facilities, laboratories, and movie theaters suitable for repair and rebuilding, the confiscated Ufi assets accounted for little in the western

1. Spiker, *Film und Kapital*, 241.
2. Peter Pleyer, *Deutscher Nachkriegsfilm, 1946–1948* (Münster: Verlag C. J. Fahle, 1965), 43. The British zone became more important after 1950 when Ufi's administration was moved to Wiesbaden. For a detailed account of the German film industry under occupation administration see also Michael Dost, Florian Hopf, and Alexander Kluge, *Filmwirtschaft in der BRD und in Europa: Götterdämmerung in Raten* (Munich: Carl Hanser Verlag, 1973); Heide Fehrenbach, *Cinema in Democratizing Germany: Reconstructing National Identity after Hitler* (Chapel Hill: Univ. of Carolina Press, 1995); Georg Roeber and Gerhard Jacoby, *Handbuch der filmwirtschaftlichen Medienbereiche* (Pullach/Munich: Verlag Dokumentation, 1973); and Christoph Weisz, ed., *OMGUS-Handbuch: Die amerikanische Militärregierung in Deutschland, 1945–1949* (Munich: R. Oldenbourg Verlag, 1994).

German film industry's revival and regrowth and remained virtually outside the newly emerging film production. In the final
analysis, the western portion of the Ufi *Konzern*, although legally
divided according to occupation territories, remained untouched,
held together by the western Allies as an occupation *Konzern*, their
strict decartelization guidelines notwithstanding. As such, it was
allowed neither to play an active role in production, distribution,
and exhibition nor to help finance the newly licensed independent production companies. On the contrary, Ufi's capital grew,
once the exploitation of its various assets got underway by the
granting of licenses. Its dissolution and reprivatization were delayed, first by the Allies and later by the German government, to
such an extent that it was never really integrated into the private
film industry.[3]

The motives governing occupation policies, primarily those of
the Americans, were a mixture of missionary zeal, paranoia, and
imperialism. With the largest of Germany's former film production sites under U.S. control, the task of rebuilding the film industry was directed by the Information Control Division (ICD),
accountable to the Office of the U.S. Military Government for Germany (OMGUS). Initially, ICD officials, led by General Robert
McClure, were less interested in a quick reactivation of German
film production than in the democratic reeducation of filmmakers.
Newsreels, documentaries, and carefully selected U.S. feature
films were used as means to confront Germans with past Nazi
atrocities and to lead them toward a democratic future. For this
purpose, film activity began in 1945 with the production of *Welt im
Film*, an Anglo-American newsreel for Germany and Austria, produced first in Berlin and soon afterward in Munich's Geiselgasteig
studios. Five camera teams alone covered the four sectors of Berlin, often running into difficulties in the Soviet sector where

3. By the time the *Konzern* was "turned loose" and ready for production again,
backed by the Deutsche and the Dresdner Bank, it was too late to combat American supremacy and the rise of television. The Ufi "ghost monopoly" was not
affected by the Federal Republic's Constitution (*Grundgesetz*) in 1949 nor by the
end of the licensing system a year later and the abolishment of monopoly restrictions in 1953. Reprivatization was not initiated until 1956 when, for the first time
since the war's end, West Germany's film industry finally saw a joint basis. But the
government's goal of an actual communication monopoly did not materialize until
the ascent of television in the early 1950s. After undergoing various organizational
changes, the remaining Ufa "new" company and the Ufa-Theater AG came into
ownership of the Bertelsmann publishing group in the 1960s. Elsaesser, *New German Cinema*, 19. For a more detailed account, see Roeber and Jacoby, *Handbuch*.

cameramen "would suddenly find themselves locked up for no good reason, and we would have to go down and argue them out."[4]

Another early activity was the production and dubbing of official U.S. documentary films intended by ICD to lead Germans, their ideological exhaustion and entertainment craving notwithstanding, in a new political direction. American feature films, carefully screened for their political suitability, were also dubbed early on. Regrettably for German moviegoers, the Motion Picture Branch of ICD had no control over the choice of these films. Eric Pommer, after taking over film production initiatives, explained:

> I wish to make it very clear that this office is not responsible for the choice of films shown in Germany. They are selected in the States and all we can do is protest when the films get here. We are sometimes able to reject a film on political grounds, but that does not happen very often. The U.S. motion picture industry feels that if a film was a success in the States, it should be a success everywhere, and they resent all criticism of their selections.[5]

Unlike their fellows in the British zone, who were able to see old German movies in their theaters, Germans in the U.S. zone soon tired of films whose language and plots became a source of irritation.

For the major American film companies Germany was a promising market. The films, imported with little cost to their U.S. producers, were hopelessly outdated, at least by American standards, and had amortized their production costs long ago.[6] The Americans were in no hurry to undermine their market potential and were holding back more contemporary quality films for economically more opportune times in Germany.[7] A frustrated Austrian

4. Report from E. Pommer to Carl Winston, 23 August 1947, E. Pommer Collection. From 1946–49 Carl Winston was Chief, Berlin Sector, Motion Picture Branch, and eventually became Pommer's successor. Carl and his brother Sam first came to Germany with Josef von Sternberg to work on *Der blaue Engel*. Afterward Carl stayed in Berlin with the Erich Pommer Produktion of Ufa and returned to the U.S. where he was associate producer at Paramount. A close friend of Pommer, he followed him to Germany to assist him in OMGUS activities. His brother Sam was Sternberg's regular editor; in postwar Germany he supervised the Anglo-American newsreel *Welt im Film*, first in Berlin and, after the Russian blockade in 1948, in Munich. Letter from J. Pommer to author, 15 September 1995.

5. The films ready to be dubbed were: *Our Town, Our Vines Have Tender Grapes, Song of Bernadette, Bells of St. Mary, Sister Kenny, Gaslight, Rhapsodie in Blue, Spiral Staircase*, and *Lost Weekend*. His comment was: "These titles may sound ancient to you, but they are brand new as far as Germany is concerned. No American films were shown here after 1941." Report from E. Pommer to Winston.

6. See Fehrenbach, *Cinema in Democratizing Germany*, for a listing of these films.

7. Ibid., 54–55.

film producer, for instance, was told by U.S. authorities in Vienna that his request for a license was withheld on American orders because they wished to delay the development of a new film industry in Austria and Germany until American distributors had established their hold in these countries. Allegedly he heard that "Erich Pommer has the same orders in Germany."[8] True or not, it soon became obvious that the U.S. military government's policy of reviving the German film industry clashed with the American film companies' intention to pursue economic objectives in western Germany. While the U.S. government believed in a "program of reinformation and indoctrination,"[9] the major American film companies were determined to succeed in winning the battle over Germany's potentially profitable market. The Motion Picture Export Association (MPEA), founded immediately after the war's end as the export branch of the Motion Picture Association of America (MPAA), soon figured prominently in reviving the long-standing film war with Germany.

Allowing Germans to take matters into their own hands was dependent upon the tedious denazification process enforced by the Allies according to political rather than professional considerations. Though valuable time was lost to get production under way, procrastination in initiating German production was easily justified by the assumption that the politically untrustworthy Germans were not yet able to undertake film production on their own.[10] As historian Felix Gilbert assessed the postwar situation, "a 'political pause' was considered to be necessary. Germans were not to be allowed to form political parties, to edit newspapers, nor to embark on any kind of political activities."[11] Once film production got

---

8. Géza von Cziffra, *Kauf dir einen bunten Luftballon: Erinnerungen an Götter und Halbgötter* (Munich and Berlin: F.A. Herbig Verlagsbuchhandlung, 1975), 336.

9. Robert Joseph, "Our Film Program in Germany, I: How Far Was It a Success?" *Hollywood Quarterly*, 2: 2 (1947): 123.

10. Pleyer, *Deutscher Nachkriegsfilm*, 37. The revised U.S. military government regulations stated: "Information Control will provide the Germans with information, which will enable them to understand and accept the United States program of occupation, and to establish for themselves a stable, peaceful, and acceptable government. Such information will impress upon the Germans the totality of their military defeat, the impossibility of rearmament, the responsibility of the individual German for war and atrocities, the disastrous effects of the structure and system of National Socialism on Germany and on the world, and the possibility that through work and cooperation Germany may again be accepted in the family of nations." Quoted in Pleyer, *Deutscher Nachkriegsfilm*, 25.

11. Felix Gilbert, *A European Past: Memoirs, 1905–1945* (New York and London: W.W. Norton and Co., 1988), 202.

under way, it developed totally without the Allies' financial support. The first phase of new German film production – the onerous "license phase" – unfolded entirely without state funds. In his report on the film control officer's tasks he was to commence after his arrival in Germany, Pommer confirmed that the reconstruction of the German film industry was a German affair: "The films are produced with German capital by German producers, German scriptwriters, and German actors. Even the first, very difficult reconstruction tasks were accomplished without an American cent."[12]

In granting licenses to those working in the press, radio, and film, the Allies selected Germans "first on the basis of their records of opposition to Nazism. Secondary consideration was given to their professional qualifications."[13] Not surprisingly, this created hardships especially in the area of film production where nearly everyone who had stayed in Nazi Germany, from the entrepreneur to the last technician, from the filmmaker to the actor in the smallest role, whether a Nazi or not, had once been forced into membership in Goebbels's Film Chamber, the *Reichsfilmkammer*.[14] Restriction was eventually eased and "passive" former party members were exempted, a realistic recognition of the fact that most postwar filmmakers in Germany were left-overs from the pre-1945 film industry. For Pommer, once he came to be in charge of screening license applicants, the choice was extremely limited. As he had indicated to the chief of the Film-Theatre-Music Control Section before leaving for Germany, he could be sure of only one producer of his Ufa years, Günther Stapenhorst, while he had reservations about the others.[15] Once in Germany, he regretted that "several vital key men within the former Ufa" had to be dismissed despite their excellent work, their devotion, and the fact that they were difficult to replace: "I do not employ any person who is not carefully vetted and confirmed by Intelligence."[16] He

12. DENA (Deutsche Nachrichten-Agentur)-Sonderdienst 3, 7 February 1947, E. Pommer Collection.

13. Henry P. Pilgert, *Press, Radio and Film in West Germany, 1945–53* (1953), quoted in Pleyer, *Deutscher Nachkriegsfilm*, 29.

14. "From now on a work permit depended without exceptions on the membership in the *Kammer*. This way it was able to withhold the permission for any continuation of work from opponents and especially non-Aryan people and those companies which they controlled." Spiker, *Film und Kapital*, 106.

15. Letter from E. Pommer to Heinz Roemheld, Chief of the Film-Theatre-Music Control Section, ICD, 27 October 1945, E. Pommer Collection.

16. Letter from E. Pommer to his wife and son, 25 December 1946. This and all other family letters cited in this chapter are part of the J. Pommer Collection.

assured his family: "I can simply tell you that I have not gone soft nor have I forgotten the past ... The whole denazification problem is so complicated that it cannot be explained by letter. Additionally, nearly each case is different. The problem cannot be solved by Hollywood views ... In many cases we even have to compromise, simply because the intended reconstruction here cannot proceed otherwise."[17]

After extensive "vetting" through Intelligence Information Control, several of his former Ufa colleagues obtained U.S. licenses in the West: Günther Stapenhorst, in the 1930s the highest ranking Ufa producer after Pommer, was the first to be issued a license to start production. Fritz Thiery, Ufa's first sound master, had become a producer and was indispensable in the reconstruction of the Geiselgasteig studios in Munich. Eberhard Klagemann, assistant producer in Ufa's Erich Pommer Produktion, founded a production group. So did Robert Herlth, set designer for such Murnau films as *Der letzte Mann* and *Faust*, and Günther Rittau, one of the cameramen on the *Nibelungen* and *Metropolis* sets at Ufa during the 1920s.[18] In his correspondence to his family in California, Pommer wrote: "Certainly all of them have been proven to be no Nazis. Eberhard Klagemann seems to have been cleverly able to also stay away from the Nazis. He surely is an opportunist and therefore should be handled with care. Too bad, because he knows more about our business than all the others."[19] As it came to pass, former Ufa filmmakers dominated Germany's new film production until the sixties, a fact that often caused returning film émigrés to feel unwelcome in Germany.[20]

17. Letter from E. Pommer to his family, 23 November 1946.

18. For a discussion of postwar filmmaking according to prewar aesthetic traditions, see Pleyer, *Deutscher Nachkriegsfilm*, 45.

19. Letter from E. Pommer to his wife and son, 20 August 1946. Two months later, he wrote to his family: "Klagemann is certainly an opportunist. Nevertheless, at the moment he is the only German of real help to me in Berlin, as is Fritz Thiery in Munich. Believe it or not, he is making a lot of financial sacrifices by helping me in my reconstruction work. Who cares as long as he tries hard to prove to me that he was always loyal. Concerning most of the others, they were as much opportunists as Klagemann. At least he stayed far away from Mr. Goebbels and made only escapist pictures with Jenny Jugo for all these years, until he got seriously in conflict with Goebbels and was inducted into the army. Then he was smart enough to get out again within a few months. He is the only real producer in Berlin of whom it can be said that his shirt is about clean. On the other hand, Jenny Jugo is blacklisted with us. She probably will work soon for the Russians in Johannesthal." Letter from E. Pommer to his wife and son, 14 October 1946.

20. Horak, *Fluchtpunkt Hollywood*, 36.

As was to be expected, denazification was a touchy subject for Germans and, in more than one sense, a costly one for the Allies. Germans holding responsible positions in denazification offices faced enormous hostility, especially in their employment search afterward when unemployment was high around 1948. As Justus Fürstenau revealed in his examination of the Germans' denazification trauma, "it was already extremely difficult in 1946 to enthuse people for this task for which – as was to be expected – they were later kicked in the rear by the state off whose shoulders they had taken such [a] thankless task."[21] Hostility of this nature was felt by Americans in charge of denazification many times over, especially in cases where Americans were former Germans, now in U.S. uniform, exercising authority over Germans, as Pommer's experiences were to show. Frank Stern, author of *The Whitewashing of the Yellow Badge*, pointed out:

> The practice of appointing returning emigrés [*sic*] to official posts, a policy instituted by the occupying powers, was criticized "because these emigres [*sic*] have lost the contact with the people; they have not endured the hardship of war and of anti-Nazi fighting, but have lived comfortably and safely in neutral or allied countries. They are estranged from their people and have lost their confidence."[22]

Pommer, for instance, did not endear himself to Germans with his decision to deny licenses for political reasons to two of Weimar Germany's best-known and most gifted actors, *Caligari*'s Werner Krauß and Emil Jannings, the latter a former close friend to whom Pommer never spoke again.

Unlike their compatriots in the West, East Germans did not face such political and economic battles. Reconstruction was not hampered by time-consuming and cumbersome licensing procedures. The Soviet occupation power allowed and even encouraged political activity; political parties were formed, and newspapers, for example, were published, written, and edited by Germans.[23] The

---

21. Justus Fürstenau, *Entnazifizierung: Ein Kapitel deutscher Nachkriegspolitik* (Neuwied und Berlin: Luchterhand, 1969), 100.
22. OMGUS, report USFET (19 November 1945), NA. Rg 260, quoted in Frank Stern, *The Whitewashing of the Yellow Badge: Antisemitism and Philosemitism in Postwar Germany*, trans. William Templer (Oxford, New York, Seoul and Tokyo: Pergamon Press, 1992), 88.
23. Gilbert, *A European Past*, 203. For a closer look at the relatively problem-free transition to a constructive daily work routine in the Soviet-controlled East, see also Fürstenau, *Entnazifizierung*, 23.

film industry therefore experienced a relatively quick start in 1946 when the Soviet zone's centralized film company DEFA (Deutsche Film-AG) was formed in East Berlin. The foundation for such speedy reconstruction was readily available: the Neubabelsberg studios, the former Tobis studios, and the still functional raw film stock company Agfa, all of them staples of the Ufi *Konzern*.[24] As a result, German filmmaker Wolfgang Staudte was able to shoot his film *Die Mörder sind unter uns* (*The Murderers Are among Us*) at DEFA between March and August 1946, at a time when filmmakers in the West could only dream of German production. Ironically, Staudte had intended this film to be made in the West but was tired of waiting for a U.S. license. No wonder that to Pommer, East German film reconstruction offered a somewhat threatening picture shortly after his arrival:

> They have assembled every branch of the film industry in one inter-locking organization. Raw stock manufacture, film production and distribution are monopolies, and film theatres have had to sign 5 year contracts with the Russian-owned distribution company. They have built a powerful industry along the lines of the old Ufa, and if the zonal boundaries are ever dropped, they will be in perfect position to absorb the weak, decentralized industry in the U.S. Zone. The final result may well be a Russian-dominated industry releasing the kind of films they approve throughout at least the Russian and U.S. Zones.[25]

The specter of communism was only one of several difficulties the western Allies were up against one year into German occupation. In the U.S. zone budgetary restraints soon rendered the slow pace of democratization, handicapped from the start by time-consuming denazification scrutiny, unrealistic. With few accomplishments to show for the first postwar year's efforts, military policy was headed toward failure. A military report revealed that "the film program had served little in the reeducation of the Germans, had held Americans up to public ridicule, and had hurt the reputation of the American film industry in Germany."[26] For the Americans, the conspicuous mixture of political, ideological, and economic motives led to critical self-inspection, questioning their *raison d'être* in Germany: "What was our aim? To purge German movies of Nazism? To show the Germans American films? To revive distribution of

24. See Spiker, *Film und Kapital*, 240; and Roeber and Jacoby, *Handbuch*, 91.
25. Letter from E. Pommer to Winston.
26. Gladwin Hill, "Our Film Program in Germany, II: How Far Was It a Failure?" *Hollywood Quarterly*, 2:2 (1947): 135.

American commercial film in Germany?"[27] If Germany was to have a chance at self-government and if its film industry was to exist at all, Americans had to change course drastically.

Eric Pommer, U.S. Military Government Film Control Officer

Given the enormous task U.S. military officials were facing in rebuilding postwar Germany's film industry, it is surprising that they did not initially look to Pommer, whose knowledge and expertise in the international film arena were no secret and were desperately needed in 1945.[28] Their first choice was U.S. émigré Billy Wilder, who went to Germany but soon resigned and returned to the States after realizing the overwhelming dimensions of this task. As his successor he suggested Pommer to ICD. Having given "the problem a great deal of thought," Pommer agreed to take on the task of reconstructing the German film industry in the American-occupied zone and sector. Starting in mid-1946, it was to be for six months, a year perhaps. His wife Gertrude preferred to stay in California. His decision made, Pommer wrote to his future employer while still in California: "I felt it was my duty to put, without hesitation, my knowledge and expertise at the disposal of the Information Control Division, especially as I am in full accord with their aims as explained to me by Billy Wilder."[29]

Such a step took considerable courage. Many ex-Germans shared the anguish expressed by Felix Gilbert about his own return to postwar Germany: "After having worked so hard to cut myself off from the past, I shied away from the stress involved in seeing the past come to life again."[30] Returned émigré Hans Mayer, for instance, spoke of a Germany that had become foreign to him (*deutsche Fremde*).[31] Pommer's decision placed him among the few

27. Hill, "Our Film Program in Germany, II," 131.

28. Such an invitation was not issued from Germany for anyone in the film industry. The exception was the Austrian film industry whose Willi Forst invited filmmakers to return home. Pem (Paul Marcus), "Gedenkansprache für Erich Pommer," *Hamburger Filmgespräche* III (Hamburg: Hamburger Gesellschaft für Filmkunde, 1967), 39.

29. Letter from E. Pommer to Davidson Taylor, Chief of Film-Theatre-Music Control Section, 24 October 1945, E. Pommer Collection.

30. Gilbert, *European Past*, 193.

31. Hans Mayer, *Ein Deutscher auf Widerruf: Erinnerungen*, vol. 1 (Frankfurt/Main: Suhrkamp, 1982), 324.

able to see again the country of their birth as early as 1946. Contrary to the practice of assigning émigrés to European military duty, the occupation powers made a civilian's return to Europe virtually impossible, requiring a two-year waiting period before granting a visa request.[32] To use Pommer's words of October 1946, the Allied powers and Germany were – technically speaking – still in a "state of war" prohibitive to all travel and trade.[33] In his memoirs, German author Carl Zuckmayer, also a U.S. émigré, recalled the legal obstacles:

> Now, after all the years without home ties, and with barely a hope to return, "the long wait" really started. For in the first post-war years it was practically impossible to go to Germany, unless one belonged to the troops of the occupation powers or was consigned a special task by them. The occupation law isolated Germany and Austria from the world ... [34]

But the return to Germany was a mixed blessing, and not only for Pommer. "I hope that both of us will never regret my coming over here," were the prophetic words he wrote to his wife shortly after his arrival in Germany.[35] His words reflected the lingering doubts and traumatic experience preceding his decision to revisit his native Germany. It was no secret that Germans and other Europeans in United States exile were critical of persons willing to return. As German actor Fritz Kortner explained, returnees had to contend with the reproaches of fellow émigrés in the States, especially after the disclosure of atrocious Nazi crimes led to increased anti-German sentiment among émigrés.[36] This certainly hit Pommer whose friends apparently felt "he should not have lent himself" for the position of film control officer.[37]

32. It is noteworthy that the article, "Hollywood Luminaries in a Mass Migration to European Film Studios," in *Variety* of 10 July 1946, listed only one German returnee, E. Pommer. All others were French, British, and American, headed for studios in London and Paris, except Max Reinhardt's Austrian-born widow, Helene Thimig, who was returning to Austria.

33. Letter from E. Pommer to Mr. Karol, Paris, 10 October 1946, E. Pommer Collection.

34. Carl Zuckmayer, *Als wär's ein Stück von mir* (Vienna: Thomas F. Salzer, S. Fischer Verlag, 1967), 540.

35. Letter from E. Pommer to his wife and son, 29 July 1946. Pommer left Washington, DC, after his State Department briefing on 30 June 1946. A few days later he was transferred to the Department of the Army, Office of Military Government for Germany (U.S.) and stationed in Berlin. Pommer's personal travel itinerary from 1946–1953, 25 August 1953, J. Pommer Collection.

36. Fritz Kortner, cited in Hartmut Goege, "Die Remigration deutschsprachiger Filmregisseure nach 1945," unpubl. M.A. thesis, Univ. Münster, 1986, 28.

37. "Billige Dekoration," *Der Spiegel*, 7 November 1951.

But Germans at home were no less critical. They often caused those who returned to Germany, even for a short time, to feel unwelcome. According to Frank Stern, "it was not enthusiasm which greeted the conquering armies; rather, they were faced with deliberate ignorance, contempt, pride and guilt. . ."[38] Such pervasive resentment toward returnees prompted German-born film historian Lotte Eisner, who had made Paris her home, to travel to postwar Germany as a French woman rather than a German. Like Stern's, her impression was that "no one wanted to be reminded of the guilt of the fathers, and *Heimkehrer* [returnees] from exile were not looked upon favorably."[39] Marlene Dietrich, Pommer's star of *Der blaue Engel* and a U.S. immigrant since 1930, experienced German anger as late as 1960, first, because she went to the United States, second, because she did not return after the war, and third, because she did return.[40] U.S. film director Douglas Sirk, well-known at Ufa under his German name Detlef Sierck, returned but left Germany again, deeply depressed. Apparently,

> he discovered "no profound break" with the past, a total failure to confront recent history. Criticism was reserved for those who had left the fatherland. He felt the movie industry had been destroyed, first by the Nazis, then by the American occupying forces.[41]

And yet, Pommer volunteered his services. Perhaps he experienced what German philosopher Theodor W. Adorno, himself a returned émigré to Germany, called a sense of continuity and loyalty to one's own past. "It is an ancient tradition," Adorno felt, "that those who are arbitrarily and blindly driven out of their homeland by tyranny return after its down-fall."[42] To many who had found a home in the States, the end of the war seemed to bring a strong sense of obligation to lend a helping hand abroad. Pommer's wartime correspondence with friends expelled from Germany had often reflected his anguish over his family's relatively easy life in the States while fellow-Germans in exile elsewhere were less fortunate. In early 1941 he had written to close

38. See Stern, Introduction to *The Whitewashing of the Yellow Badge*, XIII.
39. Lotte H. Eisner, *Ich hatte einst ein schönes Vaterland: Memoiren* (Heidelberg: Wunderhorn, 1984), 323.
40. Seydel, *Marlene Dietrich*, 271.
41. Anthony Heilbut, *Exiled in Paradise: German Refugee Artists and Intellectuals in America, from the 1930s to the Present* (New York: Viking Press, 1983), 335.
42. Theodor W. Adorno, "On the Question: 'What Is German'?" *New German Critique*, 36 (fall 1985), 125.

friends in British exile, expressing feelings German émigrés everywhere shared. He wrote in English, not German:

> We believed you when you said that it was not so easy to settle down and write from over there. But you are wrong when you assume that it must be very easy for us to write very often to you in view of the fact that we still live here just like in peace time and enjoy the Californian sun. During the last several months Gertrude as well as myself again and again sat down and started to write you. Those letters were never sent because we were afraid of your reaction when you would receive letters from friends who had nothing else to tell you but of their daily little worries and stories and gossip about their mutual friends ... We believed that talking about our still secure life might hurt you, only to find out that you would consider it as a good diversion.[43]

Possibly he was guided in his decision to return, like Adorno, by the urge "to do some good in Germany, to work against the embitterment, against the repetition of the catastrophe."[44] But Pommer was also eager to repay his adopted country for having welcomed him in times of need. "It would give me," he wrote while still negotiating his control officer tasks, "the opportunity I have long desired to be useful to our country, which became a new home for me and my family."[45] And after arriving in Berlin, Pommer wrote to his wife: "It is a fine feeling to know that after such a long time, that one is useful again. I honestly believe that I can be successful here and also accomplish for the future what I hope for."[46] Not surprisingly, given Pommer's loyalty to both countries, a German journalist was convinced that Pommer accepted the position because he felt his film industry authority and expertise could sway Washington's politics.[47]

For many in exile, the emotionally charged decision to revisit their roots was also propelled by economic considerations, evoking not only understandable apprehension but also unjustified criticism. For early returnees like former Ufa film director Ludwig Berger, there was the fear of being perceived a "protégé of the U.S. occupation power."[48] Hollywood success, some émigrés feared,

43. Letter from E. Pommer to Lore and Maurice Cowan, 31 January 1941. Lore was the widow of German film director Paul Leni, J. Pommer Collection.

44. Adorno, "On the Question: 'What Is German'?" 126.

45. Letter from E. Pommer to Heinz Roemheld, Chief of the Film-Theatre-Music Control Section of ICD, 29 September 1945.

46. Letter from E. Pommer to his wife and son, 29 July 1946.

47. Pem, "Begegnungen mit Erich Pommer."

48. Dagover, *Ich war die Dame*, 106.

might be counterproductive to a favorable welcome in Europe should they want to return.[49] Fritz Lang and Marlene Dietrich both had successful careers in Hollywood but, once back in Germany, they experienced hostility from those who were eager to send them "home" to the States.

It was also not unusual to accuse returning émigrés of opportunism, arguing that the ones who wanted to return for good had been unable to launch a successful Hollywood career.[50] A German newspaper implied, for instance, that Pommer was pursuing a German career in 1951 because he failed in Hollywood, whereas others, like Fritz Lang and cinematographer Karl Freund, did not need to return because "they were successful in Hollywood."[51] In fact, few émigrés achieved success after their return, as Hartmut Goege's study of expatriates returning to Germany demonstrated. Most remained in Germany only briefly and few had the desire to stay. Max Ophüls was one of few exceptions. As a native of the sometimes French- and sometimes German-held Saarland region and equally at home in two cultures, he was well received back in France. An attempted second career in Germany might have been rewarding but was interrupted by his death. His widow, Hilde Ophüls, expressed his strong wish to return from overseas in these words: "When *La Ronde* was completed, we finally did what we had desired and feared for so long. We visited Germany … I believe it was during this trip that we decided to remain in Europe for good."[52]

Pommer had last seen Berlin in 1933. Experiencing Berlin in August 1946 was devastating. His letter, written from Berlin to his wife and son in California speaks for itself:

> The first impressions I got of this utterly destroyed town and its inhabitants were so dreadful that, despite all efforts, I could not put them down on paper. Whatever you may have seen in the newsreels gives you only a feeble impression of the real extent of the destruction of Berlin. Great efforts are made to clear up the rubble. After a year of hectic work at least the streets look clean

49. Goege, "Remigration," 38.

50. This view was also held by Hermann Kosterlitz (known as Henry Koster in the U.S.) who declined offers to direct in Germany and signed with 20th Century-Fox. Curt Siodmak refused to return, claiming: "During my years in exile I learned that someone who is successful professionally, will continue to be, even though he will endure set-backs from time to time." See Goege, "Remigration," 31–32.

51. Perforator (Albert Schneider), "Bayerischer Filmuntersuchungsausschuß," *Deutsche Woche*, 17 October 1951. Lang, of course, did return to Germany, but not until later.

52. Ophüls, *Spiel im Dasein*, 237.

again. If possible at all, rebuilding will take many, many years; but at the moment materials are not available and a real initiative does not exist. Berlin still has about 2,000,000 inhabitants. With few exceptions, they are underfed and have lost everything except for the shabby clothes they are wearing. Nobody knows where and how they subsist.[53]

Pommer's apprehensions about facing hostility were, at least in the beginning, overcome by an initially welcoming reception. West German filmmakers, condemned to professional idleness by the occupation powers, allegedly welcomed him with open arms, "like men at sea looking for the Pole star."[54] The older generation of filmmakers saw him as film's "miracle doctor" and not as U.S. Army officer.[55] Work could be resumed, as some expressed, "as if nothing had happened."[56] But carrying out directives, which Pommer had thought fairly simple on first hearing them, turned into a seemingly impossible mission:

> Rebuild the German film industry. Open motion picture theatres. Keep them supplied with films. And keep those blacklists handy. No Nazis. Well, the only trouble was that the industry, especially its most important center, Berlin, was almost completely destroyed. And the only Germans able to do the rebuilding were a deep dark black. . .[57]

His work as motion picture control officer in Germany was obstructed by immense problems.[58] There were endless obstacles to German film production: the lack of funds, the virtually untouchable Ufi assets, the prohibition of vertical company formation, the

53. Letter from E. Pommer to his wife and son, 18 August 1946.
54. Erich Kästner, "Gespräch mit Erich Pommer," *Neue Zeitung*, 15 July 1946.
55. Manfred Barthel, *So war es wirklich: Der deutsche Nachkriegsfilm* (Munich and Berlin: F.A. Herbig, 1986), 25.
56. Curt Riess, *Das gibt's nur einmal* (Hamburg: H. Nannen Verlag, 1958), 86.
57. Report from E. Pommer to Winston.
58. The Film Production Control Office placed Pommer in charge of new film production in the U.S. zone. He was to draft a policy to guide studios, film producers and all others involved in production, and was to advise the director of ICD in all matters regarding reconstruction policy. He was fully responsible for approving scripts and all major contracts, supervising new productions and studio operations, and censoring new productions. He supervised the financial arrangements of producers, studios, and distributors concerning new films. The most politically charged task was the screening of potential film producers. Supervising production therefore was based on the assurance that only "acceptable" actors, directors, etc. were employed and that military government policies were not violated. Office of the Director of Information Control, Task Assignment List for Eric Pommer, NMI, ODIC/566, E. Pommer Collection.

scrutiny of license applicants, the control over themes and content of films, and the unlimited import of foreign films.[59] "We had to begin to rebuild, literally," Pommer reported in 1947.[60] His hope to overcome the lack of raw film stock, for instance, by enlisting the help of the United States, as he expressed in initial interviews with the West German press, did not come to pass.[61] At the end of 1946, France had produced ninety-six films;[62] the Allies only two, one in the Soviet and one in the British sector.[63]

In Germany's western zones, film production was not the highest priority, given the country's destruction and people's needs. As Gilbert described conditions:

> The chaotic situation in Germany made restoration of the bare necessities of an orderly life the most urgent task. The rebuilding of roads and houses, the repair of sewers, of water, gas, and electricity lines, the reestablishment of communications that would allow provision of food and transportation of building materials: all had the highest priority.[64]

To Pommer, lack of the most basic physical necessities and initial absence of financial support from the States made OMGUS aspirations for reconstructing the German film industry seem ludicrous. He felt that "to be able to turn the crank of production, I would have to get a hold of everything that is lacking in

59. Roeber and Jacoby, *Handbuch*, 194.

60. DENA-Sonderdienst 3.

61. Pommer reported on the raw film stock situation: "Raw stock is another critical problem. The factories in the Russian Zone produce 10 million meters of film each month, but to date practically none of it has found its way into the legitimate markets in the U.S. Zone. It is interesting to note that this 10 million meters monthly is manufactured with 50% of the original machinery in Wolfen. The other 50% was moved to the Ukrain [*sic*], and there set up and put to work." Report from E. Pommer to Winston. Wolfen is the seat of the raw film stock factory Agfa. Germany's yearly need of raw film stock had reached 32 million meters by 1949. It was then supplied by Perutz (Munich), Gevaert (Antwerp), and Thümer (West-Berlin, through the East German factory Agfa in Wolfen). Roeber and Jacoby, *Handbuch*, 372.

62. Erich Kästner, "Filmindustrie und Zweizonenmarkt," *Die Neue Zeitung*, 7 March 1947.

63. The film *Sag die Wahrheit* (*Tell the Truth*), produced by the newly formed Studio 45 company in Berlin's British sector, premiered on 20 December 1946 in West Berlin. This speedy release was possible because three-fourths of *Sag die Wahrheit* had been completed during the war by Terra-Filmkunst (Ufi). The late date on which the film rights were purchased (1 October 1946) reveals to what extent the film already existed. Roeber and Jacoby, *Handbuch*, 206.

64. Gilbert, *A European Past*, 201.

Germany today."[65] Here is his own account of his frustrations in film production:

> Let's see what we are up against in what was once one of the greatest film producing countries. A good script is the first hurdle – and there are practically no usable script-writers left in Germany. The set designers can change the entire intent of the picture. The electricians who light the sets can spoil it. The cameraman can ruin the picture as well as the actors who play in it. A good non-Nazi cast is very difficult to assemble, and you all know what actors can do to a picture. And if one of the few usable directors develops ulcers – an occupational disease – the picture goes out the window. If, by a combination of miracles, the picture is finished, then the bombed-out laboratories can spoil the quality of the negative when they develop it. They get another chance to spoil it when they print it. Then the cutter gets hold of the film, and if he isn't good, the picture isn't good. You must remember that practically all of these people are "artists" – that's in quotes – and "geniuses" – also in quotes – and present not only practical, but also temperamental problems. Egotism, jealousy, ambition, hysteria – and fear – all have to be knocked out of them without leaving scars. Not an easy job for the few underfed, timid producers we have been able to dig up. The topper is that when you finally get a good film into a German movie house, the projection machines are so bad that the picture loses half its effect.[66]

In the face of Germany's postwar chaos, he questioned such notions as artistic creativity in film production, asking: "How can we speak of a reconstruction of the German film industry"? Priorities lay elsewhere: "It is, after all, not enough to provide raw film stock – and food. Authors need first of all cigarettes and coffee, and they have become currency in Germany. As long as I can't give them something to smoke or something stimulating to drink everything is hopeless."[67]

West Germany's only standing film studios were the Bavaria-Film studios in Munich-Geiselgasteig, at Pommer's arrival still being used to garage U.S. Army trucks. In 1947 he managed to get the U.S. military Government to release Ufi *Konzern* funds for their reconstruction.[68] Once trailing in scope behind Tempelhof and

65. Pem, "Begegnungen mit Erich Pommer."
66. Report from E. Pommer to Winston.
67. Pem, "Gedenkansprache," 38.
68. Pleyer, *Deutscher Nachkriegsfilm*, 42. The liquidation of Ufi funds did not begin until 1950, after Pommer's control officer position for the military government had already ended. In September 1949, the Allies formulated the "Lex Ufa" as the basis for Ufi's reprivatization and disentanglement. See Spiker, *Film und Kapital*, 242.

Neubabelsberg and considered somewhat provincial during Berlin's reign as film capital, the Munich studios took off. In 1948 the Russian blockade of Berlin forced Pommer to move his headquarters entirely to Munich, eventually turning Geiselgasteig, with Fritz Thiery's efforts, into West Germany's most modern studios.[69] Outside Munich, films were frequently shot entirely outdoors at first, to compensate for primitive studio conditions, and the studios themselves were often makeshift facilities. Production budgets had to stay under RM 500,000 per film: "This means no films with elaborate sets and, for some time to come, no technicolor film."[70]

The first film produced in the Geiselgasteig studios, *Zwischen Gestern und Morgen* (*Between Yesterday and Tomorrow*), was proof that production was at last under way. The refurbished studios enabled filmmaker Harald Braun to rebuild an old Munich hotel and use it as movie set, with noticeable results. As Pleyer commented, "the film that premiered on 11 December 1947 in Munich displayed the technical perfection that marked most German films during the Third Reich because it was produced in a well equipped studio."[71] But not all new films showed a perfection that could stand comparison with earlier times. For example, Helmut Käutner's first postwar film, *In jenen Tagen* (*In Those Days*), lacked technical quality because he had to rely on raw film pieces obtained on various black markets in exchange for food and cigarettes.[72]

Germany's poverty, however, did not discourage Pommer. Instead, he saw a challenge to raise film production to high artistic levels:

> Germany is poor. It's the great chance for the reputable German film. We must want the essential. All pomp and spectacular wizardry has to disappear. Mass movies? No. Stars? Not really necessary. The decisive factor is the script. The idea. The development of the idea. Poverty can have a productive effect.[73]

There was no doubt in his mind that the German film industry would rebound after physical and regulatory obstacles were removed. He pointed to *Caligari* as proof that small budgets and

69. Letter from Leo Mayer, Perutz Company in Munich, to Josef Baumgartner, Bavarian Parliament Delegate, 6 March 1953, J. Pommer Collection.

70. Friedrich Luft, "Erich Pommer, der Film und die Zukunft," *Der Tagesspiegel*, 26 July 1964.

71. Pleyer, *Deutscher Nachkriegsfilm*, 42.

72. Goege, "Remigration," 25.

73. Riess, *Das gibt's nur einmal*, 87.

enormous material constraints could result in excellence.[74] He saw a chance for new German films to excel through the exploration of new themes and endorsed movies that confronted issues of today and tomorrow, without dwelling on the past: reconstruction problems, refugee relocation, returning prisoners of war, democratic education of Germany's youth, and women's roles.[75] He rejected escapist movies, arguing that they were supplied *en masse* from abroad. All ten production teams licensed by early 1947 suggested films that dealt with current problems.[76] Pommer intensely believed that artistic film production could be guaranteed only through strict division between licensed, privately funded production groups on the one hand and the trustees or studio directors supplying the studios, technical means, and work force on the other.[77] The producer should have the financial and artistic responsibility. "We are giving technical help, but we are not responsible for the artistic contents of U.S.-licensed films," he declared.[78] It was Pommer, the producer of earlier times again, granting a license to those producers who were able to assemble a complete team that assured artistic success.[79]

More than ever he was convinced that the German film must become part of the larger international system to survive and prosper: "Neither the German nor the Austrian market alone will suffice to support a worthwhile German language picture industry," he declared in his first postwar German year.[80] He suggested the exploration of other German language production and distribution outlets, including countries like Sweden and Switzerland. Despite widespread anti-German sentiment, especially in the United States, he fought for the export of German films, claiming:

> The political and spiritual reorientation of the German people is, of course, our primary object, but there is another important

74. Dora Fehling, "Künftig nur künstlerische Filme; Erich Pommer: Aufbau aus eigener Kraft," *Telegraf*, 28 July 1946.

75. Dorle Lutz, "Erich Pommer und der deutsche Film," *Schwäbische Landeszeitung*, 13 August 1946.

76. Friedrich Luft, "Die Filmproduktion in der US=Zone," *Die Neue Zeitung*, 20 January 1947.

77. Kästner, "Gespräch mit Erich Pommer;" and Lutz, "Erich Pommer und der deutsche Film."

78. Roger Manvell and Heinrich Fraenkel, *The German Cinema* (New York: Praeger Publishers, 1971), 108.

79. Lutz, "Erich Pommer und der deutsche Film."

80. "German Film Industry Needs More Teuton Outlets to Live, Sez Pommer," *Variety*, 4 December 1946.

angle. Films make large sums of money – a fact that has just about ruined films as an art form, which may not be of great importance at the moment. Because of this ability to make money, films have been given an important place on the export program, and are expected to help buy much food for the Germans, and badly needed raw material.[81]

Pommer's export plans and his accelerated efforts to put German production back on its feet gave a signal the MPEA could not ignore. Evidently the battle over Germany's market could be won only if Pommer were replaced by a film control officer less favorably inclined toward postwar Germany and more agreeable toward Hollywood. While Pommer's correspondence with his family in California reflected his adamant position about returning to the States when his year was up, a storm was brewing behind his back that could stand comparison with the best of Hollywood's screen thrillers. On 18 January 1947, the *New York Times* reported an interview with MPEA Vice-President Irving Maas who "decried" German film growth and demanded a slower pace in reconstructing the industry in Germany.[82] "Nazi propaganda poison so deeply pervaded the whole German mentality," Maas argued, "that extreme measures must be taken to provide the necessary mental catharsis." Not surprisingly, he recommended that Germans should be fed "heavy doses of all pictures except those of their own making." Fighting back, Pommer successfully defended his and the U.S. military's position, receiving total clearance not only from ICD Director General McClure but also from U.S. military Governor General Lucius Clay.

But in February, a letter marked "personal and confidential" reached Maas's desk, signed by the MPEA representative in Berlin, Robert Vining. Presented by Vining as the record of an "exact conversation" he supposedly had with Pommer in Berlin, it was nothing but the continuation of a smear campaign already started by the MPEA in the U.S. press. The incrimination of Pommer was appalling. The bragging, arrogant, and coarse person whose opinions and language Vining attributed to Pommer was a man who simply never existed, in the audiotapes he left behind, in the numerous private and professional letters he wrote throughout his career, or in the memory of those who knew him best. According to

81. Report from E. Pommer to Winston.
82. "German Film Growth Decried by U.S. Aide," *New York Times*, 18 January 1947. See also Fehrenbach, *Cinema in Democratizing Germany*, 58–68.

Vining, Pommer called the British officials in Germany "fools" and Darryl Zanuck, Vice-President of 20th Century-Fox "a Nebraska boy" without a "world outlook" who "talks through his hat"; and he referred to the U.S. film industry as making "stupid and repeated mistakes" and to himself as "smart." The highlights of Vining's letter can speak for themselves:

> I only get in really good licks at night when all of the important men of the German business come to my house and we talk business sometimes until two and after. Not only Germans come, I have the decartelization boys, the economics boys, other key people of OMGUS come to dinner. And let me tell you frankly your real enemies are these boys because I have convinced them that in rebuilding the German industry I can get them millions in export credits ... At my secret meetings I hear all my old friends have to say and let me tell you this for your own good, if there is one thing they are united on it is a determination that the old days and conditions when Ike Blumenthal, Al Aronson and all the rest of the boys rode roughshod over this German market are gone forever, they will never come back, even if I have to lick them again as I did once. I am a famous producer, but production is not what I really enjoy it is getting into foreign markets ... I've got the German film business right in my pocket, and there it is going to remain.[83]

Alarmed by the negative U.S. press and unaware of the existence of Vining's letter, Pommer's son John felt compelled to alert his father by cable from the States "to take immediate steps to correct impression that program solely your doing and to clarify your future intentions of not considering a private position there."[84] His warning came none too soon, preparing his father for an article *Variety* published only a week later. It was a conspicuous reiteration of parts of the Vining letter and interpreted Pommer's action in Germany as revenge for unfair treatment he had allegedly received during his years in Hollywood:

> Behind the recent move toward permitting export of German pix into the United States and other countries – a move that has generated almost worldwide resentment and anger – is considerable personal feeling. It's aimed by Hollywood at Erich Pommer and by Erich Pommer at Hollywood ... Charge in American film circles is that Pommer volunteered to take on the task of revitalizing the German industry in a mixture of personal ambition and spleen –

83. Letter from Robert E. Vining to Irving A. Maas, 9 February 1947, E. Pommer Collection.
84. Cable from J. Pommer to his father, 30 April 1947.

mostly spleen. It's being said in Hollywood that Pommer took something of a kicking around during his years there – a kicking around that some admit may have been unfair – and that he's now out to prove that almost single-handedly he can make the German industry a further threat to Hollywood's world preeminence.[85]

The fight was on, Pommer's wife wrote to him in May, urging him to fight back. The chance soon came, during a hearing before the Deputy Secretary of the Army in Washington, DC.[86] In the end, OMGUS declared the Vining letter a fiction and vindicated Pommer, who remained in office, his policy position confirmed by Deputy Secretary of War, Petersen, and General Clay. On the whole, Pommer was satisfied, especially after an agreement was reached between OMGUS and Eric Johnston, head of the Motion Picture Association of America (MPAA). Regarding the Association's export branch, the MPEA, Pommer wrote to his family:

> As to my personal relations with the MPEA, Mr. Johnston and his retinue treat me more than correct; you might say, more than friendly. Still, it is perfectly clear to me that this friendship is only superficial, and that I continue to be anything but popular with these gentlemen. The next months will demonstrate the degree to which the MPEA is ready to forget and forgive the defeat that it unquestionably suffered.[87]

In September of that year Pommer's wife joined him in Germany. Her letters to their son in California made repeated references to her husband's health. "I try to watch over Eric's health if he will let me," she wrote. "He does not look too good; his blood sugar is too high. It is impossible to change it until I can put him on a strict diet." And two months later: "At the last examination his heart showed an enlargement, so he is getting some injections at the moment."[88] But more battles still lay ahead, this time initiated by the German front.

A major aspect of his work in Germany, the settlement of the film control issue, was yet to be done. As liaison officer between the British, French, and Soviet film organizations, Pommer faced the enormous task of negotiating for unified censorship legislation based on the U.S. model. This model was the Hays Code,

85. "Pommer's 'Kicking Around' in H'wood Said to Influence His German Pic Plans," *Variety*, 7 May 1947.

86. Letter from J. Pommer to Wolfgang Jacobsen, Kinemathek Berlin, 9 July 1986. J. Pommer Collection.

87. Letter from E. Pommer to his wife and son, 14 July 1947.

88. Letters from Gertrude Pommer to her son, 29 September and 15 November 1947.

"established in the United States by the Motion Picture Distributors' Association of America as a self-regulating mechanism to preempt the bothersome intervention of local American officials, educators, and clergy who sought to censor films on the basis of political or moral considerations."[89] It soon became apparent that not only the Soviets but also the British and the French, protecting their own economic and political interests, opposed this model. Consensus, though reluctantly agreed upon, was finally reached among the western Allies by the sheer lure of economic support. The implementation of the Marshall Plan rendered British and French resistance to the American model futile. The currency reform of 1948 further united the western Allies; the division of East and West was now complete. French resistance continued to flare up until Pommer (U.S.), George Dessauer (British), and Marcel Colin-Reval (French) were able to set the parameters for the Tripartite Film Committee formed toward the end of 1948.[90]

But implementation of the U.S. film control model in Germany was an entirely different matter, requiring complicated negotiations with film industry members and, what was to have the most lasting effect on Pommer's future, with local power groups and the church. In order to combat the latter's anticipated resistance to losing authority over film matters, Pommer's first step in implementing the film industry's self-censorship system was the formation of the German Producers' Association (Verband Deutscher Filmproduzenten) in the British/U.S. bizone in the spring of 1947; the position of vice-president was handed to Eberhard Klagemann. At their initial meetings, centering as they did on the industry's need to move toward self-censorship, Pommer and Klagemann successfully convinced German producers of the importance and strength of the U.S. model: the commitment of film firms, distribution channels, and theater owners to abide by the voluntary censorship code, thereby giving a three-fold guarantee to the state.[91] As Heide Fehrenbach, author of *Cinema in Democratizing Germany*, concluded, the specter of both government and church meddling in film affairs finally convinced the German producers to support the U.S. model. But the battle with government and church authorities, especially in conservative Catholic Bavaria, was yet to come.

89. Fehrenbach, *Cinema in Democratizing Germany*, 71. See pp. 69–91 for a thorough account of the German film industry on the road to self-censorship.

90. Fehrenbach, *Cinema in Democratizing Germany*, 74.

91. Ibid., 76.

During the reconstruction of the Bavaria Film studios in Munich, Pommer repeatedly met with the Bavarian Ministers of Economics and Culture. It became increasingly clear to him that they were making efforts to carve out a voice in film censorship matters for Bavaria. To the consternation of OMGUS officials there were closed door attempts to establish a preproduction censorship committee and efforts to change the composition of the film review board. As Fehrenbach pointed out, the proposal for the constitution of the industry's Council of Voluntary Censorship, the Freiwillige Selbstkontrolle der Filmwirtschaft (FSK), increased the representation of the "public sector" (*öffentliche Hand*) but retained an absolute majority of film producers. After repeated breakdowns in negotiation, a compromise was finally reached, with the film industry keeping the majority and Bavaria's Minister of Culture succumbing, though declaring the result temporary.[92] Pommer was no longer in Germany to see the culmination of his work as film control officer. Convinced that his work was complete, he had resigned after three years of service and returned home to the States. The Office of Voluntary Censorship (FSK) opened in Wiesbaden in the British zone on 15 July 1949. But the wrath of the Bavarian authorities thwarted by his censorship policies was to haunt Pommer for years to come.

From the start, Pommer's role in postwar Germany was controversial. Americans and Germans on both continents resented his involvement in the industry. For Pommer, returning to Germany dressed in a U.S. Army uniform was a no-win situation. In his complicity with Allied policies, he appeared in 1946 as conqueror, an image the U.S. press reinforced with headlines like "Pommer Heading for Germany to Make Indoctrination Films."[93] Probably he could not foresee the pervasive hostility he would experience from two continents in his capacity as film control officer. Some Americans suspected him of betrayal and opportunism; some Germans regarded him as both defector and conqueror, all of them insinuating that Pommer did not know which side he represented. According to Stuart Schulberg: "The Germans often claimed that Pommer was holding back the German film industry in order to keep the territory safe for U.S. motion picture interests – while the Americans, through the MPAA, continually accused

92. Fehrenbach, *Cinema in Democratizing Germany*, 83.
93. "Pommer Heading For Germany to Make Indoctrination Films," *Variety*, 27 February 1946.

him of subverting U.S. interests in order to build a powerful competitor there."[94]

The Allies' order to prevent a new film monopoly in West Germany outraged Germans and weighed heavily on Pommer. He was accused of being "the father of film-decartelization," responsible for separating production, distribution, and exhibition, thus stunting the industry. Moreover, some said he "proudly" referred to himself by that name.[95] The Germans' bias was especially evident in the accusation that he not only approved of decartelization, but also directed it at Ufa, the company he had helped build in the 1920s. The implication was that, as an American, he now felt pleasure in such destruction.[96] All available evidence shows that Pommer vehemently resisted decartelization and even hoped to change the American government's position on this matter. Anyone as familiar with Weimar cinema as Pommer knew that a vertical company structure with control over production, distribution, and exhibition by one company provided the basis for a successful national cinema. He understood from experience that only ownership of one's own theaters guaranteed exhibition. Willy Haas, a Weimar Germany scriptwriter, wrote in his memoirs that Pommer "fought like crazy" against giving up guaranteed exhibition.[97] As John Pommer explained:

> In a way my father was a victim of the Consent Decree policy that he himself introduced in postwar Germany despite his better judgment. It was detrimental to the Hollywood major studios. But at least they controlled production and distribution whereas in the Germany of the 1950s the distributor was king, without really knowing the business.[98]

In light of such resentment, the overt and covert attacks were not surprising. In the end, after leaving military duty in Germany in May 1949, rewards did not come from many sources except the U.S.

94. Letter from Stuart Schulberg to Herbert G. Luft, 7 March 1960, J. Pommer Collection.

95. "Der Vater der Film-Dekartellisierung," *Oberbayerisches Volksblatt*, 12 January 1952.

96. "Der Vater der Film-Dekartellisierung." See also Perforator (Albert Schneider) who accused Pommer of obstructing the recovery of German national film production for which he was "the appropriate man by virtue of his former association with Ufa." Perforator, "Bayerischer Filmuntersuchungsausschuß."

97. Willy Haas, *Die literarische Welt: Erinnerungen* (Munich, 1960), 98.

98. Quoted from a letter from J. Pommer to Heide Fehrenbach, author of *Cinema in Democratizing Germany*, 26 July 1993, J. Pommer Collection.

military government in Germany.[99] Colonel William C. Rogers, chief of the U.S. Army's Film-Theatre-Music Division in Bavaria, unconditionally acknowledged Pommer's accomplishments:

> Eric Pommer was the single rallying point around which the post-war film industry in Germany centered. When he arrived in Germany there was no film industry. By the time he left, there was a film industry and a flourishing one … As Eric Pommer's work proceeded, all sections of the film industry came to life … and a whole section of life in Germany owed its being to him … Pommer was the only one who had a concept of the place of the German film in international circles. The film industry could not flourish as a German activity only. There had to be international exchange of persons as well as international distribution of films. He was personally responsible for the first inter-governmental agreements for the exhibition of postwar films outside of Germany.[100]

Eric Pommer, Independent Producer

In the early 1950s, Pommer returned again to West Germany, this time as a civilian. The press chronicled his activities with increasing viciousness. His return as civilian seemed to confirm the suspicions voiced by the press when Pommer first set foot in Germany after the war. An article in *The Film Daily* in late 1946 had been typical:

> Meanwhile, reports reached Washington that Pommer may emerge as the top figure in the revived German / Austrian film industries, with strong interests in production, distribution, and exhibition branches. Although Pommer's job, ostensibly, is to get the German & Austrian pix industries running once again, there is widespread belief that he may remain in Germany, in a private capacity, once the industry is fully returned to private ownership.[101]

Undoubtedly Pommer had entertained independent production plans while on military duty in Germany. When discovering German actress Hildegard Knef, for instance, he had predicted an

---

99. See letter from Gordon E. Textor, Director of ICD, to E. Pommer, 10 May 1949, E. Pommer Collection.

100. Excerpts from a letter written by retired Colonel William C. Rogers, 27 January 1969, obviously intended to defend Pommer's work in Germany. Addressee not named. J. Pommer Collection.

101. *The Film Daily*, 18 December 1946.

international career for her: "You will launch a career," he allegedly told her. "Until I'll be producing again, I would like to advise you. It would be a pity if you were to make wrong decisions."[102] And Knef did star in Pommer's first three postwar productions in the Federal Republic, *Nachts auf den Straßen* (*The Mistress*), *Illusion in Moll* (*Illusion in a Minor Key*), and *Eine Liebesgeschichte* (*A Love Story*). But while it was true that Pommer planned to resume his career as independent producer after completing his military assignment, these plans were initially intended to be U.S. based but coproduced with European countries.

For this purpose, Pommer, his wife, and his son formed a California corporation named Eric Pommer Films, Inc. after his return to the States in 1949. Each owned one-third of the company. At the same time Pommer became partner with U.S. film director Dorothy Arzner in their newly formed, albeit short-lived, Signature Productions. As John Pommer explained:

> Initially our intent was to produce English-language films in Europe in coproduction with German production companies. We were unable to attract proper financing in the United States and Eric Pommer decided to produce German-language films, while I continued my career in California as assistant director and production manager. I also handled the EPF [Eric Pommer Films] affairs in this country.[103]

One of Pommer's plans was a remake of *The Blue Angel* with Marilyn Monroe in the Marlene Dietrich part. He contacted Darryl Zanuck because Monroe was under contract to 20th Century-Fox. He envisioned the harbor of Marseilles as background for an elderly Charles Boyer and Monroe as an American singer. Though Pommer was turned down, he may have sparked Zanuck's interest in the story, as became evident later.

When none of Pommer's plans for U.S.-produced films materialized, he finally, regretfully, as his son confirms, settled for production in Germany. But these plans also caused difficulties because occupation guidelines prohibited the production of German

102. Hildegard Knef, *Der geschenkte Gaul* (Vienna, Zurich, Munich: Verlag Fritz Molden, 1970), 164.

103. Letter from J. Pommer to author, 19 January 1995. Among the plans were screen adaptations of an Albert Maltz novel, *The Cross and the Arrow*; of a Carl Zuckmayer play, *Des Teufels General* (*The Devil's General*), and a spy story involving the character of Lanny Budd. Unfortunately, extensive negotiations with several American production companies, including David Selznick's SRO and Sol Lesser's Thalia Productions, led nowhere.

language films by American companies in Germany. Until 1953 these regulations also prohibited ownership of a German company by a U.S. citizen. While keeping Eric Pommer Films as distribution channel for German-produced films outside Germany, Pommer and his German production assistant, Elizabeth Weljaminoff, formed the Intercontinental Film GmbH in Munich in October 1951. As with Mayflower, he again selected a company name that reflected the international nature of its intent; his first choice, "Transatlantic," was not available. In 1953, after restrictions were lifted, Weljaminoff sold her 10 percent ownership share to Pommer.

There were additional obstacles for a U.S. citizen producing in Germany in the early fifties. Intercontinental had to coproduce its first film with a company owned exclusively by German citizens. *Nachts auf den Straßen* was therefore coproduced with Neue Deutsche Film GmbH (NDF) of Munich and shot in the Geiselgasteig studios. These restrictions were no longer in effect for Pommer's subsequent Intercontinental films. In addition to regulatory restrictions there were budgetary restraints, as his choice of actors and directors proved. While he showcased the young Hildegard Knef in three of his four postwar films, he shrewdly counted on the box office appeal of former Ufa stars and provided a come-back for Hans Albers and Sybille Schmitz. Pommer never worked with his former Ufa film directors again but chose relative newcomers to direct his films, Rudolf Jugert for the first three and Laslo Benedek for the last. He recalled his friend Fritz Rotter, a former German writer and lyricist from Hollywood to work on his films, and he gave returned émigré Carl Zuckmayer a chance as scriptwriter.

Such apparent indications of a tight budget notwithstanding, his first postwar film, *Nachts auf den Straßen*, distributed by Allianz-Film, was a critical success. Critics took it as proof that German film production was on its way up and that German films had a chance again in and outside Germany.[104] The West German magazine *Der Spiegel* expressed some amazement over the fact that a veteran like Pommer was still able to make films.[105] With *Nachts auf den Straßen* Pommer proved that ability decisively, using a minimal budget of DM 900,000 and capitalizing on nonfinancial resources like the German Autobahn for his sets, thereby partially circumventing Germany's film funding deficiency.[106] He

104. Karl Eiland, "Der deutsche Film hat wieder Chancen," *Westdeutsche Allgemeine*, 29 January 1952.
105. "Billige Dekoration," *Der Spiegel*, 7 November 1951.
106. See "Billige Dekoration."

further cut expenses by reducing the pay of his male protagonist Hans Albers, giving him a profit share instead. *Nachts auf den Straßen* was awarded the German Film Prize of 1953 for "Best Motion Picture of the Year [1952]" at the Berlin Film Festival. It was a promising start.

But problems were soon to begin. Pommer, the independent producer, was haunted by the very policies he had facilitated as control officer a few years earlier. This fact was publicized with glee.[107] One newspaper article intimated that Pommer elected to coproduce *Nachts auf den Straßen* with the U.S.-licensed Neue Deutsche Filmgesellschaft in Munich after realizing that he would have difficulty obtaining production funds on his own. He was accused of having opted for coproduction precisely to obtain Federal guaranteed credits (*Bundesbürgschaften*) since, unlike NDF's licensee, he lacked the required German citizenship. He was also criticized for his alleged unwillingness to channel his current profits from re-release of his Ufa films *Der blaue Engel* and *Der Kongreß tanzt* into his first Intercontinental-produced film.[108] A favorable report in *Der Spiegel* a few weeks later refuted this criticism and pointed out that Pommer's restitution from these Ufa films was indeed the financial basis for *Nachts auf den Straßen*.[109]

It was only a small step to accusing Pommer of intending to revoke his American citizenship for economic reasons.[110] On the German Council of Voluntary Censorship's third anniversary, for instance, *The Motion Picture Herald*'s Berlin correspondent stated, "now 63, Mr. Pommer says he wishes to return to Germany for good."[111] And a German correspondent for *Sight and Sound*, visiting Pommer at the Geiselgasteig studios during filming of *Nachts auf den Straßen* in 1952, reported:

107. See Perforator (Albert Schneider), "Bayerischer Filmuntersuchungsausschuß."

108. Perforator (Albert Schneider), "Bayerischer Filmuntersuchungsausschuß." The 1951 agreement with ULC (the Ufa Liquidation Committee) gave Pommer his proper participation receipts on *all* films of the Erich Pommer Produktion back to his last pre-Hitler payment. However, due to the currency reform of 1948, the amounts due for the years prior to the reform were discounted by the conversion rate from Reichsmark to Deutsche Mark. See 1951 Vereinbarung über die Abgeltung der Ansprüche des Herrn Eric Pommer auf Einspielergebnisse aus den Filmen seiner Produktion (agreement regarding Eric Pommer's restitution claims over profits from his films).

109. "Billige Dekoration."

110. Perforator (Albert Schneider), "Bayerischer Filmuntersuchungsausschuß."

111. Volkmar von Schulsdorf, "Germans Plan Trade Bank," *The Motion Picture Herald*, 20 September 1952.

The 63-year old Pommer is a victim of political circumstances, which have forced him from emigration to re-emigration. This doesn't mean that Mr. Pommer had to return to Germany to earn his livelihood as producer, but it was like the semi-conscious voice that persuaded well-known emigrants to start life again where it was once forcibly interrupted.[112]

And finally, Pommer, Thiery, and other former Ufa friends were drawn into ugly intrigue when the Federal government, preparing for the dismantlement of the Ufi assets, offered the now economically prospering Bavaria-Film company for sale. They were charged with trying to assume economic control of Germany's now most successful film enterprise.[113]

Pommer was viciously attacked by Josef Baumgartner, the newly formed Bavaria Party's (*Bayernpartei*) first chairman. As delegate to the Bavarian Parliament (*Landtag*) he clearly used and abused his immunity from lawsuits to besmirch Pommer for his own political aggrandizement, not unlike McCarthy in the infamous U.S. political witch hunts of the same period. Not surprisingly, Baumgartner was the same Bavarian government official, who, in his capacity as Bavarian Minister of Agriculture, had outraged U.S. military officials in the spring of 1947. As staunch adversary to the "collective guilt principle" imposed on Germans, he opposed virtually every major policy of the U.S. or the bizonal agency and also made no secret of his strong antisemitism. In a meeting of Christian Socialist Union members, covered in the *New York Times*, he declared, "… almost the greatest difficulty is in the fact – I hope we are among ourselves – that today almost only third and fourth rate Americans are here in Germany."[114] When asked how he felt about the fact "that the majority of the important Americans here consist of Freemasons and Jews," which explained certain attitudes toward Bavaria and the church, he answered that, for economic recovery, Germany could never do without the Jews, especially those in business in the States and the rest of the world. But he expressed vehement objection to the Jews in Bavaria who had arrived from the East.

With such strong resentment toward both Americans and Jews, Baumgartner's willingness to believe unfounded accusations

112. Gerd Treuhaft, "Pommer in Germany," *Sight and Sound*, 21: 4 (April/June 1952): 144.
113. Letter from E. Pommer to Dr. Josef Baumgartner, 26 February 1953, E. Pommer Collection.
114. "Bavarian Resists Allies' Food Plan," *New York Times*, 3 April 1947.

directed at Pommer, who was a Prussian to boot, was not surprising.[115] Pommer countered the attack with a letter showing that the state of Bavaria had benefited substantially from his earlier work as film control officer. He also pointed out that, within the context of the U.S. Military rules and guidelines he had to follow, he had stretched the size, power, and international viability of the Bavaria-Film redevelopment to its maximal limits, thereby most earnestly representing German rather than American interests.[116] He wrote to Baumgartner: "If you had taken just a little time to inform yourself about the postwar history of the Geiselgasteig facilities you would have realized without difficulty that their reconstruction was the opposite of a 'Morgenthau' plan."[117]

Not inclined to throw in the towel, Pommer persisted in producing in Germany despite repeated difficulties. After *Nachts auf den Straßen* followed two more films with Hildegard Knef, *Illusion in Moll* and *Eine Liebesgeschichte*. The former, a melodrama, did not stir up new controversy – but the latter was a can of worms, decried by antiwar groups in the young Republic. It was based on Carl Zuckmayer's novel about eighteenth-century Germany under the reign of Frederick the Great, specifically, about an event during the year following the Seven Years' War (1756–63) that confirmed Prussia's military power over Austria. Far from being a "war monger," the confessed pacifist Pommer had been drawn to the story for its "interesting human and romantic, albeit old-fashioned, conflict."[118] As he had done with *Nibelungen* in Germany

115. Following Baumgartner's speech, the War Department intervened, OMGUS filed a report, and General Clay criticized Baumgartner at a press conference. The latter presented ten sworn affidavits from members present at the CSU meeting in Munich that he had not made those statements. U.S. demands to dismiss Baumgartner from office or take him to court evaporated because the U.S. government considered it unwise to oust a minister who was in charge of feeding people. See Stern, *The Whitewashing of the Yellow Badge*, 289–91.

116. Walter Pröhl, managing director of Bavaria-Filmkunst GmbH, confirms this view in a letter to Pommer's son: "... the German cinema, and the film city Geiselgasteig especially, has lost a friend. He did everything in the postwar years to facilitate Geiselgasteig film activity, despite his US Film Control Officer tasks to dismantle large *Konzern* enterprises." Letter from Pröhl to J. Pommer, 16 May 1966, J. Pommer Collection.

117. Letter from E. Pommer to Dr. J. Baumgartner. Henry Morgenthau Jr., President Roosevelt's Secretary of the Treasury, is known for his highly controversial recommendations for Germany's postwar development, including Germany's reduction to an agrarian state with minimal industrial potential. Roeber and Jacoby, *Handbuch*, 86; and *Funk & Wagnalls New Encyclopedia*, 16, Joseph Laffan Morse, ed. (New York: Funk & Wagnalls, 1973), 449.

118. Letter from J. Pommer to author, 17 June 1995.

and with *Fire over England* and *Troopship* in Britain, he intended *Eine Liebesgeschichte* to revitalize national identity. But he was blamed for using poor judgment in choosing a military subject in postwar Germany.

Perhaps he erred; his film certainly touched a raw nerve at a time when the vast majority of Germans, still haunted by devastating Nazi ideology, seemed in no condition to accept notions of military duty.[119] Pommer and Zuckmayer's most vicious personal attacker went so far as to accuse them of opportunism, comparing them with Nazi Germany's most prestigious film director, Veit Harlan, who had acquired notoriety by producing the antisemitic *Jud Süss* (*Jew Suss*).[120] Pommer was further reprimanded for producing a film that could damage Germany's reputation outside its borders. The visual quality of the film, however, was undisputed. Introducing a new technology to the German public, Pommer shot *Eine Liebesgeschichte* in Garutso-Plastorama, the invention of a Russian immigrant to the United States, which facilitated scenes of exceptional depth of field on a wide-screen hitherto unknown to the German public in pre-cinemascope times.[121] Pommer's efforts were rewarded with the 1954 Berlin award for best photography.

After Allianz-Film and Deutsche London Film, Pommer chose Schorcht-Verleih for the next four films to be produced at Intercontinental Film. The first one, *Hoch über Kaprun*, though promising at first, ended in disaster. It was a monumental film project, a fictionalized rendition of the building of the Austrian power station Kaprun, which was financed by the United States. The American High Commission in Vienna enthusiastically supported Pommer's project because "the vast dimensions of a Pommer-film, based on [Jürgen] Thorwald's novel, apparently guaranteed the best chance for audience success, not only in Germany but in the United States as well."[122] However, Pommer soon found himself caught between two political rivals, this time the Americans and Austrians. The Americans welcomed Pommer's proposed film, *Hoch über Kaprun*, as powerfully demonstrating and justifying millions of Marshall Plan dollars invested in the Austrian power

119. "Was ist da passiert? Der neue Pommer-Film," *Aufbau*, 28 May 1954.

120. Letter from Michael Heinze-Mansfeld to E. Pommer and Zuckmayer, 6 May 1954, J. Pommer Collection.

121. Other German producers, especially Peter Ostermayr and Richard Koenig, also used the Garutso-Plastorama system. A few years later, computer technology produced lenses that rendered the system obsolete. Letter from J. Pommer to Wolfgang Jacobsen, 9 July 1986, J. Pommer Collection.

122. "Leiche im Beton," *Der Spiegel*, 4 August 1954.

station. The Austrians, however, were incensed by the novel's sensationalism. They felt it to be an insult to Austria, considered the Thorwald film version to be morally and politically unacceptable, and feared it would produce unfavorable publicity, especially in view of Pommer's intended German and English language international distribution. The Austrians won this battle by refusing Pommer permission to shoot on location. According to *Der Spiegel*, Austria favored a politically less harmful *Heimatfilm*, a trivialized version entitled *Das Lied von Kaprun* (*The Song of Kaprun*), to be produced by an insignificant production company called Süddeutscher Film. Acknowledging Pommer's reputation, *Der Spiegel* immediately called it a match between "David" Süddeutscher Film and "Goliath" Pommer.[123]

The second film to be distributed by Schorcht was *Kinder, Mütter und ein General*, based on Herbert Reinecker's novel *Hau ab mit Heldentum* (*Good Riddance to Heroism*) serialized in a German magazine. It tells the story of five mothers near the end of the Second World War. They live on the eastern border; the Russian troops are approaching. They travel to their boys' school to get them home, only to find out that their sons have run away to join the army. The mothers follow them all the way to the front, causing profound reactions, from buck privates to the general commanding the division. Against orders, the company commander takes his unit back and is placed on house arrest. The general sends the company to the front as replacement, and the boys face certain death. The mothers are forgotten.

Intended to be Pommer's definitive antiwar statement in 1955, the film should have appeared earlier, at the time of *Eine Liebesgeschichte*. But one single year in postwar German developments made a crucial difference, and the political changes from 1954 to 1955 took their toll on *Kinder, Mütter und ein General*. In 1955 the West German government, represented by its first postwar Chancellor Konrad Adenauer, received the Allies' permission to reestablish an army (*Bundeswehr*). The result was a most unwelcome climate for an antiwar film such as Pommer's and, according to John Pommer, strong governmental pressure on distributor Kurt Schorcht to stop a film that was ready for release. John Pommer stated: "Over the protest of the director and Eric Pommer, Kurt Schorcht insisted on added scenes wherein the sons remain united with their mothers, which totally negates the film's

123. "Leiche im Beton."

theme."[124] Schorcht then released the film with the new ending and without proper advance advertising and promotion, thereby accepting a considerable financial loss. He placed the film in as few theaters as possible, pulled it from distribution before word of mouth could attract more moviegoers, and refused to enter it in the Cannes Film Festival.

In Germany the film was a financial disaster, unable to recoup its negative cost, which had been unduly inflated by shooting the second ending. It fared better in non-German markets but, as John Pommer put it, financial success for a German language film depended on the German market, especially in those days. But critically, the film was a success, gaining prizes in and outside Germany. In Germany, *Kinder, Mütter und ein General* was declared "Film of the Month" by the Evangelical Film Guild (*Evangelische Filmgilde*) in February 1955; veteran actress Therese Giese won the Best Actress award (*Filmband in Silber*) for her role as one of the mothers. Pommer was able to release the film in Belgium in its original version and with a proper advertising campaign. Under the title *Mothers Are Always Forgotten*, it received the Belgian Critic Award (*Grand Prix de l'Union de la Critique de Cinéma*) in Brussels in 1955. It won over competition with *La Strada, Blackboard Jungle,* and *Bad Day at Black Rock*. The prize did not sway distributor Schorcht. As John Pommer explained,

> Schorcht did not even attempt to extend that success to France. Director Laslo Benedek happened to be in Europe when *KMG* was about to be released in France. He reported to Eric Pommer that he had to "fight like a lion" to get the proper ending into at least the first release print and that Schorcht demonstrated "total apathy."[125]

In the United States, *Kinder, Mütter und ein General* was recognized as outstanding foreign film and awarded the Golden Globe from the Hollywood Foreign Press Association in 1956. It took Pommer's one-hundredth birthday to enable German audiences to see the film in its original version in the Federal Republic. In 1989 the Berlin Film Festival staged a retrospective of Pommer's films. Upon John Pommer's request, the only existing original copy of *Kinder, Mütter und ein General* was retrieved from storage at the University of Southern California (USC) and shown at the festival.

124. Letter from J. Pommer to author, 19 January 1995. See also "Kriegsfilm: Der versöhnliche Ausklang," *Der Spiegel*, 9 March 1955.
125. Letter from J. Pommer to author, 19 January 1995.

Despite the critical acclaim of the film, Pommer was unable to enlist sufficient economic support. He did not want to release it in the States in the 1950s unless it was properly dubbed, for which he needed, but lacked, the relatively small capital of $45,000.[126] He considered showing *Kinder, Mütter und ein General* in its original version in U.S. art movie houses but dismissed this alternative as economically unprofitable.[127]

Mounting difficulties and increasing age and health problems eventually forced Pommer to give up his German plans. His deteriorating health became a serious factor in 1956 when he traveled to the States on what was supposed to be no longer than a short trip to find a U.S. distributor for *Kinder, Mütter und ein General*. Despite his serious illnesses – diabetes since 1928, colon cancer surgery followed by colostomy in 1933, and coronary thrombosis in 1941 – he so far had managed to keep up a remarkably energetic work pace. He had been able to control his diabetes through proper diet, which also helped him lose weight. During the Russian blockade of Berlin he was unable to obtain the food he needed and had to switch to insulin. Now, at age sixty-seven, all these were taking their toll.[128] As a result, he was unable to realize his project *Schatten hinter fremden Fenstern* (*Shadows at Foreign Windows*). It was an adventure story involving a U.S. sailor unjustly accused of a crime who is being hunted against the background of the Hamburg harbor and its redlight district, the Reeperbahn, until he can prove his innocence. Pommer was hoping to interest an important U.S. star in this film, which he intended to shoot in two languages.[129]

But a foot infection, aggravated by his diabetes, worsened and prevented his return to Europe. By the fall of 1956 it had become so serious that he almost died of sepsis. It eventually led to the amputation of the diseased leg above the knee, rendering any future production plans in Germany futile. At age seventy-one Pommer was no longer willing to prepare for combat. A letter written in 1961 to his friend Budd Rogers, a producers' representative in New York, said it all:

> I have been doing a lot of thinking, ... and reached a decision in regard to "Kinder, Mütter" ... [It] has now been available in this

126. Virginia Wolff, "Besuch bei Erich Pommer," *Aufbau*, 10 May 1957.
127. Ibid.
128. Letter from J. Pommer to author, 19 October 1986.
129. Letter from J. Pommer to author, 5 August 1993.

country for almost 5 years and has made, partially with your kind help, the rounds. During this time my contention that the German film can regain even approximately the place it once held in the US market has been proven wrong, at least until now. Things might have been different if the German film industry would have realized much more than it did the multiple difficulties it was bound to reencounter in this market after the long Nazi period. The German film industry failed so far in providing even the smallest kind of consolidated public relations budget and campaign, as this was done, for example, by the French and the Italians. Or the Germans could have designed at least a small part of their program for foreign consumption, as we did in the old days. I therefore have come to the conclusion that it will be best to clear my desk of all matters of the past and I hope then to be able to go on to some new activities.[130]

At Intercontinental-Film, business transactions were wound down in the Federal Republic. Unable to collect from the bankrupted Allianz-Film, the distributor of Pommer's first two postwar films, Pommer and Eric Pommer Films made a number of loans to alleviate the company's cash flow problems.[131] Living in California, Pommer was not informed on time that Intercontinental-Film was assessed back-taxes in the amount of DM 8,000 on the profit of *Nachts auf den Straßen*. The assessment and decree, advising the company of its rights to appeal, were erroneously mailed to coproducer Neue Deutsche Film and not forwarded to California on time. On 23 April 1958, Intercontinental-Film was stricken off the Commercial Register. With Pommer unable to return to Germany, the company had to be liquidated.

Occasionally during his last years in California the German press published reports alluding to his retirement in poverty and dependence.[132] These reports were greatly exaggerated, especially in light of the settlement Pommer received from Ufa. In 1958 Pommer was approached by Ufa regarding buyout of his participation in the proceeds from films of Erich Pommer Produktion. According to John Pommer, Ufa's move was possibly occasioned by Pommer's earlier suggestion to Darryl Zanuck to remake *The Blue Angel*

130. Letter from E. Pommer to Budd Rogers, 5 February 1961, quoted in letter from J. Pommer to author, 6 July 1993.

131. Letter from J. Pommer to author, 19 January 1995.

132. See, among other sources, Wolf, "Besuch bei Erich Pommer"; "Begegnung mit einer Persönlichkeit: Erich Pommer sieht auf 50 Jahre Filmarbeit zurück," *Der neue Film*, 19 March 1959; Robert G. Scheuer, "Zum Vermächtnis des großen, verkannten Produzenten: Berlinale 66: Erich Pommer-Retrospektive," *Filmblätter*, 21 May 1966; and Knef, *Der geschenkte Gaul*, 456.

because Zanuck now approached Ufa about the rights to the film. Expecting vast profits, Ufa did not want to share them with Pommer and started negotiations. In 1959 Pommer accepted a lump sum payment in lieu of future profits from any of his films. Darryl Zanuck produced a remake of *The Blue Angel*, again using a German background. The film was disappointing, not least to Ufa.[133]

The Ufa settlement enabled the Pommers to purchase their first house since 1941. There they lived modestly, but comfortably, off their German and American social security pensions for about a year, until July 1960 when Pommer lost his wife; they had been married for almost half a century. Being disabled, he moved into his son's house where he could enjoy his grandchildren. There were visitors, often asking for advice, including actors like Heinz Rühmann and Romy Schneider, actor / director Maximilian Schell, director Hellmuth Käutner, and various other members of the film industry. He received frequent inquiries from legal departments in Germany requesting his aid regarding film rights. He was asked by Sol Lesser to volunteer in the establishment of the Hollywood Film Museum, which was not accomplished until many years later. He advised his son and friends on film and television projects. He was active until the end, working on the research and development of a documentary television series to be entitled *From Potsdam to Bonn* and, allegedly, busy writing his memoirs. He never lost his positive attitude or his sense of humor, which had carried him through many battles.

His death in 1966 – six years after his wife's – did not elicit a public retelling of his story as is normally expected for a person of Pommer's cultural influence and public visibility. This fact was honestly discussed by Robert Scheuer in an article called "In Memoriam of the Great, Misjudged Producer."[134] Arguing that the German cinema still feeds on Pommer's films while denying Pommer that satisfaction, Scheuer called for rehabilitation and correction rather than honor. Pommer's son, responding to this call, clarified his father's retirement away from Germany as follows:

> He left Germany because he felt unable, due to his illness, to fight the sins of commission and negligence on *Kinder, Mütter und ein General* with sufficient energy. The illness finally subsided after an amputation. I don't believe I have to stress that the circumstances

---

133. Letter from J. Pommer to author, 19 September 1995.
134. Scheuer, "Zum Vermächtnis des großen, verkannten Produzenten."

which caused the film's failure in Germany ... prevent, to a large degree even now, that the German cinema gets back on its feet.[135]

Honor did come to Pommer in 1959 when the Federal Republic of Germany awarded him the Officer's Cross of the Order of Merit (*das große Bundesverdienstkreuz*) for his fifty years of motion picture achievements. But not until 1989, his hundredth birthday anniversary, did a retrospective of his films take place in Berlin. These honors do not hide the fact that this producer who once had a reputation for "spending too much" died in relatively modest circumstances, as did many of his compatriots who left Germany in 1933. Fate denied him the luxuries his groundbreaking contribution to the international film industry should have afforded him.

135. Letter from J. Pommer to Robert G. Scheuer, editor of *Filmblätter*, 31 May 1966, published in *Filmblätter*, 18 June 1966.

CONCLUSION

From its beginning in Germany in 1889, Erich Pommer's life was marked by war and peace. Two world wars overshadowed him, demanding sacrifices and dealing wounds that left lifelong scars. His life, from its small-town bourgeois beginnings to its closure across the Atlantic, does not yield a neatly structured biography. In the wake of the Second World War, wavering between two continents was the mark of a forced émigré.

As a film producer, however, he hardly knew peace. When peace followed war, those periods, as his professional experiences proved, were far from restful. At its centenary, the cinema worldwide is looking back on battles fought over ideological, cultural, and, primarily, economic dominance. Erich Pommer's life and career cannot be seen in the bright light of continuous adventure and golden opportunity, and certainly not in terms of accumulated wealth.

Pommer's repeated starts from scratch, his life and career pattern of peaks and valleys, his detours, successes, and failures, were always set in motion by historical, political, and economic forces. As Klaus Kreimeier pointed out:

> The film production of an epoch is, to a larger extent than the traditional spheres of the cultural super structure, on one hand, intertwined most closely with the dominating political forms, with the conditions of the political system, and its ideological manifestations. On the other hand, it reflects the dominating economic conditions and is as such closer to the social basis than, say, the work of an esoteric lyricist or that of an "avant-garde" composer.[1]

1. Klaus Kreimeier, quoted in Keiner, *Thea von Harbou*, 11.

The power of these forces on the film industry is apparent through all stages of the history of German film, which, to a large degree, is Pommer's history as well. They shaped his work, especially in the film industry of Germany's two republics, controlling him and, at other times, endowing him with control. As George Kubler claimed, "times and opportunities differ more than the degree of talent."[2] During the 1920s and early 1930s, and to some extent the late 1940s, Pommer possessed the traits which, in Kubler's view, must complement talent to form the effective tools for profitable engagement under challenging conditions: physical energy, reasonably durable health, and powers of concentration. In the 1950s some of these began to wane. The Weimar period towers above all as a period in which, to use Kubler's phrase, Pommer's genius unfolded in the "fortuitous keying together of disposition and situation into an exceptionally efficient entity."[3]

Unlike any other émigré from the German film industry, Pommer was given this opportunity a second time. The fact that he was not sufficiently recognized for rebuilding the postwar industry from the ashes in no way diminishes his contribution. To Pommer, his work as film control officer was one of the finest achievements of his career, and his few independently produced postwar films were critically acclaimed to boot. But German journalist Paul Marcus (Pem) looked at only part of the dilemma in his assessment of Pommer's career after 1945:

> The fact that Pommer was not able to demonstrate to the new German film industry once again how to make films with world-wide perspectives cannot be attributed to his age, but to the animosity brought towards him; he was made responsible for the U.S. film policies for whose execution he was merely the facilitator.[4]

All this was true, as the last chapter showed. Wars might be won when fighting a nation, an industry, an institution, or an individual. The battle against time, however, could not be won, by Pommer or his contemporaries.

Those who built Weimar Germany's film industry could not expect to embark on a second career in the 1950s with the same physical and spiritual energy they had possessed three decades

---

2. George Kubler, *The Shape of Time: Remarks on the History of Things* (1962; New Haven and London: A Yale Paperbound, 1978), 8.
3. Ibid.
4. Pem (Paul Marcus), "Begegnungen mit Erich Pommer."

earlier.[5] Many recognized that their work belonged to a bygone era and abstained from trying. When German producer "Atze" Brauner expressed an interest in Fritz Lang, Weimar Germany's most celebrated film director, Lang was wise enough to realize that it was merely to exploit him for remaking his Weimar films; a profitable, as it turned out, but critically condemned venture for both producer and director.[6] Anthony Heilbut, writing on exiled artists and intellectuals in Hollywood, felt that "Lang's episode was the saddest of all" because he considered the German postwar work given to Lang to be "hack assignments."[7] Lang's indictment of his native Germany was extreme:

> The people with whom one has to work there are unbearable. It is not enough that they break promises, written or not. Moreover, the film industry – if one can apply that name at all to the pathetic remnant of a film production that once made the country world famous – is run today by former lawyers, SS-men, and export people of God knows what.[8]

Undoubtedly, Lang was seen as a legend from the distant past. The New German Cinema was creating its own celebrities. Filmmaker Werner Herzog, one of these, naively wondered how "absolutely forgotten" Fritz Lang was in Germany at the time of his death:

> I believe that hardly anyone here knew that he was still alive. I have pondered the question: Are we now fatherless, I mean the younger ones who are making films now? And then it occurs to me more and more that is what we have been from the very beginning, for Fritz Lang had been chased from our midst so far that he was not alive, but a figment, a myth.[9]

5. Film producer and director Joe May, for instance, fully realized that a return to Germany would have meant starting from scratch at age seventy. After his initial Hollywood success he was boycotted by Universal and, instead, opted for a Viennese restaurant in Hollywood which he opened with financial support from Billy Wilder. Goege, "Remigration," 34.

6. Lang made three remakes for Artur ("Atze") Brauner's CCC-Company in West Berlin's French sector: *Die 1,000 Augen des Dr. Mabuse* (*The 1,000 Eyes of Dr. Mabuse*), *Der Tiger von Eschnapur* (*The Tiger of Bengal*), and *Das Indische Grabmal* (*The Hindu Tomb*). "Atze" Brauner, *Mich gibt's nur einmal* (Frankfurt/Main: Fischer Taschenbuch, 1978), 132. Lang had directed the first *Mabuse* films for Pommer at Ufa. He had written the scripts for *Tiger* and *Grabmal* in 1920, only to lose out as film director to Joe May.

7. Heilbut, *Exiled in Paradise*, 336.

8. Goege, "Remigration," 85.

9. Letter from Werner Herzog to Lotte Eisner, quoted in Eisner, *Ich hatte einst ein schönes Vaterland*, 300.

"In Europe a new generation had grown up," recalled Robert Siodmak, another of Pommer's Ufa film directors during the early 1930s: "Hardly anyone knew my name, and I had to start at the beginning."[10] By the same token, postwar moviegoers were hardly aware of films like *Caligari* or *Faust, Nibelungen* or *Metropolis*. Older Germans still reminisced about *Der blaue Engel* or *Der Kongreß tanzt* but associated them with their music or their stars. Pommer's monumental Weimar film achievements were largely forgotten; nobody paid attention to producers anyway. And here he was in Germany, highly visible, an American producing in the country of his birth where he was once a pioneer. Pommer found himself between two worlds in more than a geographic sense; he was caught in the power game between two political forces and caught between two eras.

But not only the creative teams of Pommer's Weimar years were missing. The cultural conditions determining Weimar Germany could not be transferred to the Federal Republic, as some returning émigrés might have expected. Postwar Germany lacked the Weimar film industry's structural advantages, and filmmakers missed the degree of autonomy they had enjoyed there in the 1920s. Pommer, accustomed to business opportunities of Ufa magnitude, knew what a detrimental effect the prohibition of vertical company and industry structures would have on the revival of film in postwar Germany. In the absence of such a foundation he faced the same funding and distribution obstacles to his own films in the 1950s that continue to stunt German filmmaking today. John Pommer wrote about his father's postwar productions: "He never again had the degree of control that encompassed distribution, choice of theatres, final say over promotion and advertising."[11]

Pommer's own assessment of the postwar German film industry, looking back at his personal achievements and disappointments, was not encouraging to young German filmmakers. He felt that "despite the economic wonder, the German film industry manages to waste the many opportunities which were handed to it practically on a golden platter."[12] That view was shared by film director Helmut Käutner who wrote to Pommer in 1965, a year before Pommer's death:

10. Goege, "Remigration," 62.

11. Letter from J. Pommer to author, 5 November 1988.

12. Jürgen Kasten, "Filmkunst als Markenartikel," *Neue Zürcher Zeitung*, 31 March 1989.

Whatever you provided at the time was misunderstood as much as it remained unutilized. The consequence is an economic and intellectual crisis whose dimensions seem to me deadly ... The present reasons are even more paralyzing after political reasons have somewhat subsided.[13]

As an insider, producer "Atze" Brauner summarized the feelings of the first postwar German filmmaker generation well: "The fine twenties and thirties will not repeat themselves because there is no basis."[14]

13. Letter from Helmut Käutner to E. Pommer, 24 January 1965, J. Pommer Collection.
14. Letter from Artur ("Atze") Brauner to E. Pommer, 23 April 1963, J. Pommer Collection.

APPENDIX A

Biography of John E. Pommer

John E. Pommer was born in 1916 in Berlin, Germany, and educated in Berlin, Beverly Hills, and London. He also attended UCLA but went to work before obtaining a degree.

He started in 1934 in the Editorial Department of Fox Film Corporation, working on Will Rogers, Charlie Chan, Jane Withers, and early Shirley Temple films. In 1936 he started as assistant director for London Film Productions. After a brief interlude as sound effects and music editor, he joined RKO Radio Pictures in 1939 and thereafter worked only as assistant director or production manager. Except for four years in the U.S. Signal Corps during the Second World War and one year for 20th Century-Fox in Germany as production manager on Anatole Litvak's *Decision before Dawn*, he remained with RKO until the company ceased production in 1952. Thereafter he worked freelance for Four Star, CBS, Desilu, Superman, Flying A, Revue, Hal Roach, Loretta Young, and other television companies. In 1957 he returned to Germany as production manager of Stanley Kubrick's *Paths of Glory*.

In 1961 he joined Bing Crosby Productions as Production Executive and was appointed Vice-President in Charge of Production in 1965. In 1969 the company was sold to Cox Broadcasting Corporation of Atlanta. He remained with the company until it ceased production in 1979, when he retired. During this period he supervised production of television, including the "Ben Casey" and "Hogan's Heroes" series and a number of motion pictures, the last of which was *The Great Santini*.

He worked with many directors, including William Dieterle, Robert Flaherty, John Ford, Garson Kanin, Alexander Korda, Lewis Milestone, and Jean Renoir. Actors included Jean Arthur, Joan Bennett, Ethel Barrymore, Charles Bickford, Charles Boyer, Ronald Colman, Robert Cummings, Kirk Douglas, Irene Dunn, Robert Duvall, Cary Grant, Van Heflin, Miriam Hopkins, Walter Huston, Elsa Lanchester, Charles Laughton, Gertrude Lawrence, Thomas Mitchell, Pat O'Brien, Maureen O'Hara, Dick Powell, Robert Ryan, Spencer Tracy, Claire Trevor, and Robert Young.

Outstanding pictures included *Kitty Foile* with an Academy Award to Ginger Rogers, *The Farmer's Daughter* with an Academy Award to Loretta Young, and *All That Money Can Buy*.

In the 1960s and 1970s he served on the Board of Trustees of the pension and health plans of the Motion Picture Industry, the Actors and the Directors Guilds, and was the first Chairman, Selection and Admissions Committee, of the Directors Guild Assistant Directors Training Plan.

In 1950 he married the German actress Heidi Scharf. She was born in Delitzsch near Leipzig, Germany, attended the Ballet School of the Leipzig Opera, and studied modern dance with Mary Wigman. Her first engagement was with the Corps de Ballet of the Dresden Opera. After moving to Berlin she modeled and continued studying ballet with Tatiana Gsovsky. She became part of the Deutsche Tanzbühne, an organization that combined ballet with modern dance but six months later was shut down by Propaganda Minister Josef Goebbels for performing "degenerate art." She then joined the Film Academy at the Neubabelsberg Studios. Goebbels personally ordered that she not be assigned any important parts because she "looked too American."

In early 1946 *Life Magazine* ran several pages of pictures under the title "Speaking of Pictures: German Girl Dances in Berlin Ruins" that drew attention to her. She worked for a year at DEFA as dance teacher and later played in several films, including the ingenue with Hans Albers in *Und über uns der Himmel*. After the Berlin Blockade she moved to Munich where she played the second female lead to Margot Hielscher in *Hallo Fräulein*. She also sang and danced in Munich cabarets, such as *Die Schaubude* and *Barberina*.

The couple raised a daughter, Nina Brehm, who is a management consultant in Louisville, Kentucky; and a son, Eric S. Pommer, an attorney in Ventura, California.

APPENDIX B

American Films in Germany

The various sources providing information about films shown in Germany throughout the silent era often contradict one another. Some figures are based on censorship records, others on production, distribution, and exhibition data. The tables in this Appendix reflect these different categories.

The following sources were consulted: *Film Daily Year Book of Motion Pictures* (FDYB) 1925, 1927, and 1928; *Lichtbild-Bühne*, 7 June 1918; *Variety*, 26 October 1927; Hanno Hardt, Elke Hilscher, and Winfried B. Lerg's *Presse im Exil*; Rahel Lipschütz's 1931 dissertation, *Der Ufa-Konzern*; and Hans Traub's 1943 history of Ufa, *Die Ufa*.

Following the stabilization of the German mark at the end of 1923, foreign film companies resumed film export to Germany. *Film-Kurier* reported in late 1924 that the German public was astonished to find that "America's filmic art" did not begin with cowboys and end with Charlie Chaplin, but that America was intentionally producing "super" pictures especially for the broad masses (*Film-Kurier*, export edition, 30 December 1924). The 1925 German market still held "no allurement" for American producers but the popularity of U.S. films was expected to improve with better economic conditions (*FDYB* 1925: 653). From 1 September 1925 to 31 August 1926, 204 German and 286 U.S. feature films were shown in Germany (*FDYB* 1927: 941).

TABLE 1
Distribution of German and U.S. films according to the censorship records
(*FDYB* 1927: 940; *FDYB*, 1928: 961)

Period	German Films	U.S. Films
1 Jan. 1925 – 31 Dec. 1925	380	351
1 July 1925 – 30 June 1926	218	246
1 Jan. 1926 – 31 Dec. 1926	186	218
1 Jan. 1927 – 31 Mar. 1927	59	71

TABLE 2
Films distributed in Germany (*Presse im Exil*, 62):

Year	Films Distrib.	German Films	Foreign Films	Foreign films' US %
1926	487	185	302	44%
1927	525	242	283	36%
1928	517	224	293	38%
1929	416	183	233	34%
1930	284	146	138	29%
1931	278	144	134	31%
1932	213	132	81	26%
1933	206	114	92	31%

During the silent period from 1923 to 1928, the average number of long feature films circulating on the German market was 500. Of these, German companies produced between 240 and 250. Ufa produced an annual average of 14 films in the 1920s' second half (*Der Ufa-Konzern*, 33–37). The following table shows Ufa's contribution to Germany's films.

TABLE 3
Ufa's contribution to German film production (*Der Ufa-Konzern*, 33–37)

Year	German-Produced	Ufa-Produced
1912	52	—
1918	1,317	269
1923	253	39
1926	185	12
1927	243	15
1929	183	13
1931	142	19

APPENDIX C

Filmography

This filmography lists films produced by Erich Pommer's companies (Decla, Decla-Bioscop, Intercontinental, Mayflower) and those Pommer produced or supervised while associated with other companies (Eclair, Ufa, London Film Productions, Fox, Paramount, RKO).

This filmography does not claim to be complete. Several circumstances obfuscate the record. In Germany, there were no producer credits until the late 1920s. Production reports, even in the *Ufa Magazin*, and advertisements did not list producers. Company consolidation in Weimar Germany often complicates accurate company attribution, as is the case with Uco/Decla/Bioscop/Ufa. From 1923–26, when Pommer was in charge of feature film production at Ufa, the filmography also includes those films assigned by Ufa to unaffiliated companies. Known available data regarding these (D-Film, Dea-Film, Carl-Froehlich-Film, Licho-Film, May-Film, Stern-Film, etc.) are far from complete.

The following sources were consulted: film credits, newspapers, magazines, and trade press publications, primarily *Film-Kurier*, *Lichtbild-Bühne*, *Kinematograph*, *Schaubühne/Weltbühne*, and *Tage-Buch*. Gerhard Lamprecht's eleven volumes, *Deutsche Stummfilme 1903–1931*, provided details for the earliest films. In addition, autobiographies and biographies of Pommer's team of film directors, scriptwriters, stars, and production staff were helpful, but the authors often copied data, including errors, from one another, contradicting earlier press information. For the later period, Ufa files were the most reliable source. Siegfried Kyser's early filmography, compiled with Erich Pommer himself, contained much

valuable data, and Pommer's son, John E. Pommer, generously
helped with dates and information. Additional reliable entries can
be found in other sources, primarily in Wolfgang Jacobsen's *Erich
Pommer: Ein Produzent macht Filmgeschichte.*

Abbreviations

P   premiere
W   script
D   director
C   cinematography
S   set design
M   music
A   actors

ECLAIR (Vienna, Austria)

Zu Pferd auf dem Riesenrad / A Cheval sur la Grande Roue
       (Marcel Vandal, coproducer)
       P   1913
Das Geheimnis der Luft / Le Mystère de l'Air
       (Marcel Vandal, coproducer)
       P   1913

DECLA (Berlin, Germany)

Berlin im Kriegsjahr 1915
       P   1915
Der Glaube siegt
       P   Apr. 1915 (?)
       W   Carl Schönfeld
       D   Carl Schönfeld
Die Masuren
       P   1915
       D   Nunek Danuky
       A   Anna von Palen
Brot
       P   24 Apr. 1915
       W   Rudolf del Zopp
       D   Rudolf del Zopp
       A   Hans Ahrens
Carl und Carla
       P   Apr. 1915, Marmorhaus
       W   Felix Stern
       D   Carl Wilhelm
       C   Friedrich Weinmann

    A   Lisa Weise, Carl Beckersachs, Gustav Botz, Olga Engl, Maria Lux, Paul Schwaiger, Max Zilzer, Werner Klatt

Die Goldquelle

    P   1915

    W   Carl Schönfeld

    D   Carl Schönfeld

    A   Carl Schönfeld, Lilly Nador, Albert Paul

Der Barbier von Filmersdorf

    P   1915

    W   Carl Wilhelm (based on an idea by Oscar Sabo)

    D   Carl Wilhelm

    A   Oscar Sabo, Wolfgang Zilzer

O diese Männer

    P   1915

    W   Carl Schönfeld

    D   Carl Schönfeld

    A   Rudolf Essek, Ilse Remo, Klein-Nelly, Olga Limburg, Else Roché (=Roscher)

Ein unbeschriebenes Blatt

    P   1915

    W   Joseph Delmont

    D   Joseph Delmont

    A   Fritz Achterberg

Ein Schrei in der Nacht (Alwin Neuß series)

    P   Dec. 1915, Marmorhaus

    W   Alwin Neuß (from an idea by Paul Rosenhayn)

    D   Alwin Neuß

    A   Alwin Neuß, Eddie Seefeld, Aenne Köhler, Reinhold Pasch, Adolf Suchanek

Das Gewissen (Alwin Neuß series)

    P   14 Jan. 1916, Prinzeßtheater

    W   Robert Reinert

    D   Alwin Neuß

    A   Alwin Neuß, Andreas von Horn

Die Stimme des Toten (Alwin Neuß series)

    P   Feb. 1916, Tauentzienpalast

    W   Robert Reinert

    D   Alwin Neuß

    A   Alwin Neuß, Bruno Kastner

Das Licht im Dunkeln (Alwin Neuß series)

    P   1916

    D   Alwin Neuß

    A   Alwin Neuß

Ein Zirkusmädel

    P   1916

    D   Carl Wilhelm (?)

    A   Lisa Weise, Carl Beckersachs

Streichhölzer, kauft Streichhölzer! (Alwin Neuß series)

    P   1916, Marmorhaus

    W   Ruth Goetz (from an idea by Alwin Neuß)

D   Alwin Neuß
C   Friedrich Weinmann
A   Hella Moja, Max Köhler, Andrae Lebius (= Aenderly Lebius),
       Emmy Flemmich, Kurt Busch, Gustav Heppner, Neumann-Ernest,
       Lo Vallis, Curt Bois, William Huch

Der Weg der Tränen (Alwin Neuß series)
P   1916
W   Ruth Goetz (based on an idea by Alwin Neuß)
D   Alwin Neuß
C   Friedrich Weinmann
A   Hella Moja, Albert Paul, Charly Berger, Harry Lamberts-Paulsen

Dynamit (Alwin Neuß series)
P   May 1916
W   William Kahn, Edmund Edel
D   Alwin Neuß
A   Alwin Neuß, Bruno Kastner

Der Thug / Im Dienste der Todesgöttin (Alwin Neuß series)
P   Oct. 1916, BTL Potsdamerstraße
D   Alwin Neuß
A   Alwin Neuß, Willi Kaiser-Heyl

Der Tod des Erasmus
P   1916, Marmorhaus
D   Otto Rippert
A   Hella Moja, Leo Connard, Albert Paul, Josef Danneger

Und wenn ich lieb', nimm dich in acht
P   1917
D   Otto Rippert
A   Hella Moja, Hans Adalbert Schlettow

Komtesse Hella
P   1916, Marmorhaus
D   Otto Rippert (?)
A   Hella Moja

Die Spinne (Tom Shark detective series)
P   2 Feb. 1917
W   Paul Otto
D   Alwin Neuß
A   Alwin Neuß, Leo Connard, Laurence Köhler, Curt Bois, Leopold
       Thurner, Wolfgang Zilzer

Der Schwur der Renate Rabenau
P   1917
W   Karl Schneider
D   Otto Rippert
A   Hella Moja, Magnus Stifter, Anna von Palen, Leo Connard

Das Lied des Lebens (Alwin Neuß series)
P   1917
W   Karl Schneider
D   Alwin Neuß
A   Alwin Neuß, Lore Rückert, Rita Clermont, Willi Kaiser-Heyl

Der Club der Neun (Alwin Neuß series)
P   1916/17
D   Alwin Neuß
A   Alwin Neuß, Harry Lamberts-Paulsen
Der Jubiläumspreis (Alwin Neuß series)
P   1917
D   Alwin Neuß
A   Alwin Neuß
Die Faust des Schicksals (Alwin Neuß series)
P   1917
W   Paul Otto
D   Alwin Neuß
A   Alwin Neuß, Willi Kaiser-Heyl, Ressel Orla, Käte Haack
Die Königstochter von Travankore
P   1917
W   Martin Berger
D   Otto Rippert
C   Carl Hoffmann
A   Hella Moja, Heinrich Peer (?), Paul Rehkopf
Das Spiel vom Tode (Alwin Neuß series)
P   1917
W   Paul Otto (based on *Das Chagrinleder* by Honoré de Balzac)
D   Alwin Neuß
A   Alwin Neuß, Käte Haack, Lu Synd, Kurt Bobeth-Bolander, Leo
       Connard, Harry Lambert-Paulsen, Paul Passarge
Das Defizit (Tom Shark detective series)
P   1917
W   Paul Rosenhayn
D   Alwin Neuß
A   Alwin Neuß
Das Buch des Lasters
P   1917
W   Henriette Lachmann
D   Otto Rippert
C   Carl Hoffmann
A   Eva Speyer, Käte Haack, Theodor Loos, Georg John
Zwei blaue Jungen (Alwin Neuß series)
P   24 Nov. 1917, Berlin
Die Kraft des Michael Argobast (Alwin Neuß series)
P   Jan. 1918, Marmorhaus
W   Paul Otto (based on the novel by Erich Wulffen)
D   Alwin Neuß
A   Alwin Neuß
Arme Lena
P   1918
W   Julius Urgiss
A   Ressel Orla, Josefine Dora
Baroneßchen auf Strafurlaub
P   1918
W   Gebhard Schätzler-Perasini

D   Otto Rippert

A   Hanne Brinkmann, Hans Albers, Ferry Sikla, Jenny Marba

Clown Charly (Alwin Neuß series)

P   1918, Mozarthaus

D   Alwin Neuß

M   Giuseppe Becce

A   Alwin Neuß, Karl Falkenberg

Das Glück der Frau Beate

P   1918

D   Otto Rippert (?)

A   Ressel Orla, Emil Birron

Der Wilderer (Alwin Neuß series)

P   1918, Mozartsaal

D   Alwin Neuß

M   Guiseppe Becce

A   Alwin Neuß

Der Cowboy (Alwin Neuß series)

P   1918, Mozartsaal

D   Alwin Neuß

M   Guiseppe Becce

A   Alwin Neuß, Max Laurence

Der Weg, der zur Verdammnis führt Part I: *Das Schicksal der Aenne Wolter*

P   Nov. 1918, Prinzeßtheater

W   Julius Sternheim

D   Otto Rippert

C   Carl Hoffmann

A   Charlotte Böcklin, Guido Herzfeld, Karl Falkenberg, Kurt Ehrle, Frieda Lemke, Tony Tetzlaff, Hedwig Golmick, Maria Forescu, Martha Orlanda, Emil Albes, Clementine Plessner

Die Frauen des Josias Grafenreuth

P   1918

D   Otto Rippert

A   Ressel Orla

Die Krone des Lebens

P   1918

D   Otto Rippert (?)

A   Ressel Orla, Fritz Spira

Das bemooste Haupt (Alwin Neuß series)

P   1918

D   Alwin Neuß

A   Alwin Neuß, Victor Senger

Das Lied der Mutter (Alwin Neuß series)

P   Jan. 1919

W   Julius Sternheim

D   Alwin Neuß

C   Carl Hoffmann

A   Alwin Neuß, Tony Tetzlaff, Marta Daghofer (=Lil Dagover)

Die Bettler GmbH (Alwin Neuß series)

P   1918/1919

W   Fritz Lang

D   Alwin Neuß
A   Alwin Neuß, Fred Selva-Goebel, Fritz Achterberg, Otto Paul, Marta Daghofer (=Lil Dagover)

Die Rache ist mein (Alwin Neuß series)
P   1918/19
W   Fritz Lang
D   Alwin Neuß
A   Alwin Neuß, Otto Paul, Arnold Czempin, Helga Molander, Marta Daghofer (=Lil Dagover), Hanni Rheinwald

Der Voluntär (Alwin Neuß series)
P   1919
W   Max Jungk
D   Alwin Neuß
T   Hermann Warm
A   Alwin Neuß, Leopoldine Konstantin, Lil Dagover, Franz Arndt, Karl Falkenberg

Die blonde Lo (women's series)
P   1919
W   Julius Sternheim
D   Josef Coenen
A   Carola Toelle, Lil Dagover, Paul Morgan

Der Weg, der zur Verdammnis führt Part II: *Hyänen der Lust*
P   7 Mar. 1919, Marmorhaus
W   Julius Sternheim
D   Otto Rippert
C   Willy Hameister
A   Charlotte Böcklin, Grete Weixler, Emil Albes, Clementine Plessner, Albert Paul, Käte Haack, Margarete Frey, Max Hochstätter, Ilse Wilke, Heinz Willy Kaiser, Guido Herzfeld, Margarete Kupfer, Rosa Murger, Eduard Eysenck, Marie von Bülow

Halbblut
P   3 Apr. 1919, Marmorhaus
W   Fritz Lang
D   Fritz Lang
C   Carl Hoffmann
A   Ressel Orla, Carl de Vogt, Gilda Langer, Paul Morgan, Carl Gerhard Schröder

Die Insel der Glücklichen (earlier title: *Die Augen der Maske*) (women's series)
P   1919 (?), Marmorhaus
W   Wolfgang Geiger
D   Josef Coenen
C   Paul Holzki (?)
S   Carl Ludwig Kirmse, Hermann Warm
A   Carola Toelle, Werner Krauß, Paul Otto, Käte Roeven, Magnus Stifter, Ally Kay-Kolberg (?)

Wolkenbau und Flimmerstern
P   1919
W   Wolfgang Geiger, Fritz Lang
A   Margarete Frey, Karl-Gerhard Schröder, Albert Paul, Ressel Orla

Der Herr der Liebe
    P   Sept. 1919, Richard-Oswald-Lichtspiele
    W   Leo (Oscar?) Koffler
    D   Fritz Lang
    C   Emil Schünemann
    S   Carl Ludwig Kirmse
    A   Carl de Vogt, Gilda Langer, Erika Unruh, Fritz Lang

Das ewige Rätsel (women's series)
    P   Oct. 1919, Marmorhaus
    W   Wolfgang Geiger
    D   Josef Coenen
    S   Carl Ludwig Kirmse
    A   Carola Toelle, Werner Krauß, Josef Ewald, Paul Otto

Die Spinnen (adventure series) Part I: *Der goldene See / Die Abenteuer des Kay Hoog*
    P   3 Oct. 1919, Richard-Oswald-Lichtspiele
    W   Fritz Lang
    D   Fritz Lang
    C   Emil Schünemann, Karl Freund
    S   Hermann Warm, Otto Hunte, Carl Ludwig Kirmse,
          Heinrich Umlauff
    A   Ressel Orla, Carl de Vogt, Georg John, Lil Dagover, Paul Morgan,
          Harry Frank, Rudolf Lettinger

Die Pest in Florenz (world class series)
    P   23 Oct. 1919, Marmorhaus
    W   Fritz Lang
    D   Otto Rippert
    C   Willy Hameister, Emil Schünemann
    S   Hermann Warm, Walter Reimann, Walter Röhrig, Franz Jaffé
    M   Bruno Gellert
    A   Theodor Becker, Marga Kierska, Erich Bartels, Juliette Brandt,
          Erner Hübsch, Otto Mannstaedt, Anders Wikman, Karl Bern-
          hard, Franz Knaak, Hans Walter, Auguste Prasch Grevensberg

Harakiri
    P   Dec. 1919, Marmorhaus
    W   Max Jungk (based on the play *Madame Butterfly* by John
          Luther Long and David Belasco)
    D   Fritz Lang
    C   Max Faßbaender
    S   Heinrich Umlauff
    A   Lil Dagover, Paul Biensfeldt, Georg John, Rudolf Lettinger,
          Meinhart Maur, Niels Prien, Harry Frank, Herta Hedén, Erner
          Hübsch, Käte Küster, Josef Römer, Loni Nest

Die Frau mit den Orchideen
    P   1919
    W   Fritz Lang
    D   Otto Rippert
    C   Carl Hoffmann
    A   Werner Krauß, Carl de Vogt, Gilda Langer

Totentanz
    P   1919
    W   Fritz Lang

D	Otto Rippert
A	Sascha Gura, Werner Krauß

Die Ehe der Frau Mary (women's series)

P	1919
W	Wolfgang Geiger (Emilie Goerck ?)
D	Josef Coenen (?)
A	Carola Toelle, Erika Unruh, Carl de Vogt, Gertrud Wolle, Loni Nest

Das neue Kanaan (world class series)

P	1919
W	Gernot Bock-Stieber

Opfer

P	14 Jan. 1920, Marmorhaus
A	Carola Toelle, Werner Krauß, Rudolf Lettinger, Wilhelm Diegelmann, Henri Peters-Arnolds, Max Kronert, Jaro Fürth, Ferdinand Robert, Josef Rehberger, M. Marlinsky

Das Kabinett des Dr. Caligari (world class series)

P	26 Feb. 1920, Marmorhaus
W	Carl Mayer, Hans Janowitz
D	Robert Wiene (Rudolf Meinert, production head)
C	Willy Hameister
S	Hermann Warm, Walter Reimann, Walter Röhrig
A	Lil Dagover, Conrad Veidt, Werner Krauß, Friedrich Feher, Hans Heinz von Twardowski, Rudolf Lettinger, Ludwig Rex, Elsa Wagner, Henri Peters-Arnolds, Hans Lanser-Ludolff

Der falsche Schein (women's series)

P	1919
W	Based on a story by Rudolf Strauß
D	Emil Justitz
S	Carl Ludwig Kirmse
A	Carola Toelle, Robert Scholz, Claire Creutz

Die Tänzerin

P	1919
W	Based on the play by Mennbert Lenghel
A	Leopoldine Konstantin

Die Spinnen (adventure series) Part II: *Das Brillantenschiff* (original title: *Das Sklavenschiff*)

P	Feb. 1920, Theater am Moritzplatz
W	Fritz Lang
D	Fritz Lang
C	Emil Schünemann, Carl Freund
S	Hermann Warm, Otto Hunte, Karl Ludwig Kirmse, Heinrich Umlauff
A	Ressel Orla, Carl de Vogt, Georg John, Paul Morgan, Rudolf Lettinger, Thea Zander, Reiner-Steiner, Friedrich Kühne, Edgar Pauly, Meinhart Maur, K.A. Römer, Paul Biensfeldt, Gilda Langer

Frauenruhm (former title: *Um Ruhm und Frauenglück*) (women's series)

P	1919
W	Alfred Schirokauer (based on his novel)
D	Ernst Fiedler-Spies

A   Carola Toelle, Adalbert Lenz, Josef Römer, Hermann Vallentin, Rudolf Lettinger, Ernst Pröckl, Rudolf Forster, Lia Eibenschütz

Der siebente Tag

P   1920

W   Robert Liebmann based on the comedy by Rudolph Schanzer and Ernst Welisch

D   Ernst Stahl-Nachbaur

C   Adolf Otto Weitzenberg

W   Franz Meiwers

A   Carola Toelle, Paul Mederow, Gustl Beer, Adele Sandrock, Ernst Rotmund, Käthe Nevil, Franz Weber, Ernst Pohl, Cläre Harten, Erhard Siedel, Ilse Wilke, Fritz Beckmann, Theo Siegmund, Hedwig von Lorée

Hoppla, Herr Lehrer

P   25 Feb. 1920, Marmorhaus

W   Curt Wolfram Kiesslich

A   Curt Wolfram Kiesslich, Emil Sondermann, Mizzi Linder, Juliette Brandt, Marlis Rottach, Franz Baumann

Morel, der Meister der Kette Part I: *Die Kette*

P   Mar. 1920

W   (based on *Glanz und Elend der Kurtisanen* by Honoré de Balzac)

D   Conrad Wiene (?), Louis Ralph

A   Louis Ralph

Morel, der Meister der Kette Part II: *Glanz und Elend*

P   2 Apr. 1920

W   (based on *Glanz und Elend der Kurtisanen* by Honoré de Balzac)

D   Conrad Wiene (?), Louis Ralph

A   Louis Ralph, Rudolf Forster, Marietta Palto

Johannes Goth (women's series)

P   May 1920, Marmorhaus

W   Carl Mayer

D   Karl Gerhardt

C   Adolf Otto Weitzenberg

S   Franz Seemann

A   Carola Toelle, Werner Krauß, Ernst Stahl-Nachbaur, Claire Creutz, Josef Rehberger, Loni Nest

Die Frau im Himmel

P   Aug. 1920, Marmorhaus

W   Johannes Guter, Walter C. Lierke

D   Johannes Guter

A   Lil Dagover, Werner Krauß, Alfred Abel, Robert Scholz, Lothar Müthel, Hans Brockmann

Ein sterbendes Geschlecht (world class series)

P   1920

W   Robert Wiene

D   Karl Gerhardt

C   Willy Hameister

S   Hermann Warm

DECLA-BIOSCOP (Berlin)

Das lachende Grauen
P   1920
W   Carl Mayer
D   Rudolf Meinert
A   Uschi Elleot

Aus dem Leben zweier Freundinnen und ihrer Freunde
P   1920
D   Julius Sternheim

Das tötliche Schweigen (Carola Toelle series)
P   Aug. 1920, Decla-Lichtspiele
W   Elisabeth Braunhofer
D   Artur Holz
C   Adolf Otto Weitzenberg
A   Carola Toelle, Heinz Stieda, K.A. Römer, Friedel Köhne, Erika
     Unruh, Julius Brandt, Nien Sön Ling

Der Januskopf
P   26 Aug. 1920, Marmorhaus
W   Hans Janowitz
D   F.W. Murnau
C   Karl Freund, Carl Hoffmann
S   Heinrich Richter
A   Cornad Veidt, Margarete Schlegel, Willy Kaiser-Heyl, Margarete
     Kupfer, Gustav Botz, Jaro Fürth

Genuine
P   2 Sept. 1920, Marmorhaus
W   Carl Mayer
D   Robert Wiene
C   Willy Hameister
S   César Klein, Bernhard Klein, Kurt Hermann Rosenberg
A   Fern Andra, Ernst Gronau, Harlad Paulsen, Albert Bennefeld, John
     Gottkowt, Hans Heinz von Twardowski, Lewis Brody

Maulwürfe
P   Sept. 1920
W   Ernst Fiedler-Spies
D   Artur Holz
C   Paul Holzki
S   Franz Seemann
A   Carl Bernhard, Anna Burmeester, Frieda Steding, Walter Wolffgram,
     Alexander v. Antalffy, Arthur Schröder, Charles Lievre, Alfred Haase,
     Alfons Hess, Senta Eichstaedt, Rudi Thaller

Die Tophar-Mumie
P   14 Oct. 1920, Marmorhaus
W   Friedel Köhne
D   Johannes Guter
C   Wilhelm Schwäbl
S   Franz Seemann
A   Ellen Bargi, Josef Klein, Friedrich Kühne, Rudolf Hochbauer, Albert
     Bennefeld, Paul Mederow

Der Richter von Zalamea
P 28 Oct. 1920, Marmorhaus
W Ludwig Berger (based on the drama *El Alcalde de Zalamea*
   by Pedro Calderon)
D Ludwig Berger
C Adolf Otto Weitzenberg
S Hermann Warm, Ernst Meivers
A Lil Dagover, Albert Steinrück, Agnes Straub, Lothar Müthel,
   Heinrich Witte, Hermann Vallentin, Max Schreck, Hellmuth Krüger,
   Elisabeth Horn, Ernst Legal, Ernst Rotmund, Armin Schweitzer

Das Blut der Ahnen (luxury class series)
P Nov. 1920, Decla-Lichtspiele, Unter den Linden
W Robert Wiene, Johannes Brandt
D Karl Gerhardt
C Willy Hameister
S Hermann Warm
A Lil Dagover, Maria Zelenka, Harald Paulsen, Robert Scholz, Lili
   Alexandra, Josef Rehberger, Jaro Fürth

Die Jagd nach dem Tode (Decla adventure series) Part I: *Die verbotene Stadt*
P 1920, Decla-Lichtspiele
W Robert Wiene, Johannes Brandt
D Karl Gerhardt
C Paul Holzki
S Hermann Warm
A Lil Dagover, Nils Chrisander, Kurt Brenkendorf, Bernhard Goetzke,
   Paul Rehkopf

Die Nacht der Königin Isabeau
P Nov. 1920, Marmorhaus
W Robert Wiene
D Robert Wiene
C Willy Hameister
S Winckler-Tannenberg
A Fern Andra, Hans Heinrich von Twardowski, Elsa Wagner, Fritz
   Kortner, Lothar Müthel, John Gottowt, Albert Lind, Alex. Moissi

Die sieben Todsünden
P 1920
W (based on *Verbrecher GmbH* by Fedor von Zobeltitz)
D Heinrich Peer
A Manja Tzatschewa, Mich. Vakkonyi, Johannes Riemann, Heinrich
   Peer, Erner Hübsch

Das Zeichen des Malayen (detective series)
P 1920
W Carl-Heinz Boese
D Carl-Heinz Boese
A Kurt Brenkendorff, Ally Kay, Alexander von Antalffy

Die Kwannon von Okadera (first Uco-Film production)
P 2 Dec. 1920, Marmorhaus
W Ludwig Wolff (based on his novel in *Berliner Illustrirte*
   Zeitung)
D Carl Froelich

S   Ernst Meivers
A   Lil Dagover, Werner Krauß, Marija Leiko, Robert Forster-Larrinaga, Alina von Mielewska, Max Adalbert, Hans Junkermann, Leonhard Haskel, Paul Morgan, Hanna Gath

Das Haupt des Juarez (Decla masterworks series)
P   9 Dec. 1920, Decla-Lichtspiele, Unter den Linden
W   Wolfgang Geiger
D   Johannes Guter
C   Adolf Otto Weitzenberg
S   Hermann Warm (Rudolf Meinert, art director)
A   Sascha Gura, Adele Sandrock, Josef Delmore, Wilhelm Diegelmann, Josef Klein, Lothar Müthel, Else Kupfer, Eduard von Winterstein, Hermann Vallentin

Joseph in Ägypten
P   1920
W   Artur Holz

Morjane
P   1920
W   Rudolf Saklikower (drama, Villiers de l'Isle Adams)

Toteninsel (Bioscop luxury class series)
P   7 Jan. 1921, Ufa-Theater, Kurfürstendamm
W   Walter Supper, Carl Froelich
D   Carl Froelich
C   Adolf Otto Weitzenberg
S   Hermann Warm, Walther Röhrig
A   Lil Dagover, Bernhard Goetzke, Walter Janssen, Gertrud von Hoschek, Olga Wotan, Robert Vogel, Carl Gentner

Das Geheimnis von Bombay (earlier title: *Das indische Panoptikum*)
P   Jan. 1921, Marmorhaus
W   Rolf E. Vanloo, Paul Beyer
D   Artur Holz
C   Adolf Otto Weitzenberg
S   Robert Herlth, Walter Röhrig
A   Lil Dagover, Conrad Veidt, Hermann Böttcher, Bernhard Goetzke, Nien Sön Ling, Lewis Brody, Gustav Oberg, K.A. Römer

Die Dreizehn aus Stahl
P   14 Jan. 1921, Decla-Lichtspiele, Unter den Linden
W   Wolfgang Geiger, Johannes Guter
D   Johannes Guter
C   Adolf Otto Weitzenberg
S   Franz Seemann
A   Carl de Vogt, Claire Lotto, Camillo Trimbacher, Georg Schnell, Lo Wedekind, Josef Klein, Rudolf Prasch, Fritz Zimmermann, Paul Hallström, Lore Busch, Nien Sön Ling, Rudolf Hofbauer, Auguste Prasch-Grevenberg. K.A. Römer

Das Medium (women's series) Berliner Film Manufaktur GmbH, Berlin
P   1921, Decla-Lichtspiele
W   Max Jungk
D   Hermann Rosenfeld
C   Max Faßbaender

S   Artur Günther
A   Lil Dagover, Werner Krauß, Bruno Harprecht, Erra Bognar, Karl
     Armster, Frieda Richard, Fred Selva-Goebel, Frieda Lehndorff, Harry
     Berber, Edgar Klitsch
Kämpfende Herzen (also known as *Die Vier um die Frau*)
P   Feb. 1921, Marmorhaus
W   Rolf E. Vanloo, Fritz Lang, Thea von Harbou
D   Fritz Lang
C   Otto Kanturek
S   Ernst Meiwers, Hans Jacoby
A   Carola Toelle, Hermann Böttcher, Lilli Lohrer, Anton Edthofer, Robert
     Forster-Larrinaga, Harry Frank, Ludwig Hartau, Leonhard Haskel,
     Paul Rehkopf, Gottfried Huppertz, Rudolf Klein-Rogge, Lisa von
     Marton, Erika Unruh, Paul Morgan, Edgar Pauly, Gerhard Ritterband
Die Jagd nach dem Tode (Decla adventure series) Part III: *Der Mann im Dunkeln*
P   18 Feb. 1921, Decla-Lichtspiele, Unter den Linden
W   Robert Wiene, Johannes Brandt
D   Karl Gerhardt
C   Paul Holzki
S   Hermann Warm
A   Nils Chrisander, Robert Scholz, Kurt Brenkendorf, Bernhard
     Goetzke, Isa Marsen (=Marsa), Paul Hansen, Renée Pélar,
     Rudolf Hilberg
Die treibende Kraft (Fern Andra series)
P   Mar. 1921
W   Ola Alsen (from Victorien Sardou)
D   Zoltan Nagy
C   Adolf Otto Weitzenberg
S   Franz Seemann, Hans Jacoby
A   Fern Andra, Tronier Funder, Magda Madeleine, Lya de Putti,
     Erling Hanson, Hermann Böttcher
Irrende Seelen (also known as *Sklaven der Sinne*) (Russo-Film)
P   3 Mar. 1921, Marmorhaus
W   Carl Froelich, Walter Supper (from *The Idiot* by Dostojevsky)
D   Carl Froelich
C   Axel Graatkjaer
S   Robert Herlth, Walter Röhrig
A   Asta Nielsen, Alfred Abel, Walter Janssen, Lyda Salmonova, Guido
     Herzfeld, Leonhard Haskel, Elsa Wagner, Marga von Kierska,
     Auguste Prasch-Grevenberg, Erika Unruh, Frieda Richard, Lydia
     Savitzky, Ernst Rotmund, Sylvia Torf, Wassily Wronsky, Adolf
     Edgar Licho, Lilly Doneckar, Maria Connard, Simon Konarsky,
     Eugenia Eduardowa
Schloß Vogelöd (Uco-Film)
P   7 Apr. 1921, Marmorhaus
W   Carl Mayer (based on the novel by Rudolf Stratz)
D   F. W. Murnau
C   Fritz Arno Wagner, Laszlo Scheffer
S   Hermann Warm

A   Olga Tschechowa, Arnold Korff, Lulu Keyser-Korff, Paul Bildt, Lothar Mehnert, Paul Hartmann, Hermann Vallentin, Julius Falkenstein, Robert Leffler, Victor Blütner, Walter Kurt Kuhle, Loni Nest

Der Roman der Christine von Herre
P   30 Sept. 1921, UT Kurfürstendamm / UT Nollendorfplatz
W   Ludwig Berger (based on a novella by Heinrich Zschokke)
D   Ludwig Berger
C   Karl Freund
S   Rudolf Bamberger, Franz Seemann
A   Agnes Straub, Werner Krauß, Paul Hartmann, Julius Falkenstein, Ernst Legal, Heinrich George, Marie Ferron, Max Schreck, Sybill Morel, Ilka Grüning, Adele Sandrock

Die Jagd nach dem Tode (Decla adventure series) Part IV: *Die Goldmine von Sar-Khin*
P   Oct. 1921 (?)
W   Robert Liebmann
D   Karl Gerhardt
C   Paul Holzki
S   Hermann Warm
A   Nils Chrisander, Robert Scholz, Kurt Brenkendorf, Bernhard Goetzke, Isa Marsen (=Marsa), Paul Hansen, Renée Pélar

Der Erbe der van Diemen (also known as *Das rätselhafte Testament*)
P   1921, Decla-Lichtspiele
W   Max Jungk, Julius Urgiss
D   Bruno Ziener
C   Carl Hoffmann
S   Heinrich Richter
A   Adolf Edgar Licho, Melitta Ferrow, Ernest Winar, Maud Marion, Norbert Wicki, Adolphe Engers, Hans Felix, Fritz Beckmann

Um den Sohn
P   1921
W   (based on the novel by Artur Landsberger)
D   Frederik Larsen
C   Willy Goldberger
S   Fritz Lederer
A   Carola Toelle, Robert Scholz, Ernst Hoffmann, Ilka Grüning, Emmy Sturm, Ernst Stahl-Nachbaur, Mary Zucker, Hedda Kemp, Paul Westermeier, Karl Huszar, Julius Brandt, Max Ruhbeck, Albert Patry, Frieda Richard, Harry Berber

Das Spiel mit dem Feuer
P   1921, Marmorhaus
W   (based on an idea by Julius Horst and Alexander Engel)
D   Robert Wiene, Georg Kroll
C   Fritz Arno Wagner
S   Robert Herlth, Walter Röhrig
A   Diana Karenne, Wassily Wronsky, Anton Edthofer, Hans Junkermann, Otto Treptow, Leonhard Haskel, Karl Platen, Emil Heyse, Max Kronert, Lucia Tosti, Viktor Blum, Ossip Runitsch, Emil Birron

Das Mädchen, das wartete
P   1921
W   F. Carlsen (based on a novel by James Barr)

D   Frederik Larsen
C   Willy Goldberger
S   Fritz Lederer
A   Carola Toelle, Robert Scholz, Albert Steinrück, Ressel Orla, Fred Selva-Goebel, Karl Huszar, Fritz Schulz, Anton Edthofer(?), Ernst Stahl-Nachbaur (?)

Der müde Tod

P   6 Oct. 1921, UT Kurfürstendamm
W   Fritz Lang, Thea von Harbou
D   Fritz Lang
C   Fritz Arno Wagner, Erich Nitzschmann, Hermann Saalfrank
S   Robert Herlth, Walter Röhrig, Hermann Warm
M   Guiseppe Becce (Mozartsaal)
A   Lil Dagover, Bernhard Goetzke, Walter Janssen, Hans Sternberg, Carl Rückert, Max Adalbert, Wilhelm Diegelmann, Erich Pabst, Hermann Picha, Karl Platen, Paul Rehkopf, Max Pfeiffer, Georg John, Grete Berger, Lydia Potechina, Eduard von Winterstein, Erika Unruh, Rudolf Klein-Rogge, Lothar Müthel, Edgar Pauly, Lina Paulsen, Lewis Brody, Karl Huszar, Paul Biensfeld, Paul Neumann

Die schwarze Pantherin (Russo-Film)

P   14 Oct. 1921, Decla-Lichtspiele, Unter den Linden
W   Hans Janowitz, Johannes Guter (based on Wynnytschenko's play)
D   Johannes Guter
S   Erich Czerwonski, Hans Jacobi
A   Elena Polewitzkaja, Xenia Desni, Eugen Burg, Georg Jurowsky, Lydia Potechina

Der ewige Fluch

P   Oct./Nov. 1921
W   Fritz Wendhausen, Paul Beyer
D   Fritz Wendhausen
C   Paul Holzki
S   Hermann Warm
A   Rosa Valetti, Charlotte Schultz, Rudolf Forster, Margarete Schlegel, Karl Etlinger, Charles Willy Kayser, Emil Heyse, Max Kronert

Violet

P   11 Nov. 1921, Tauentzienpalast
W   Julius Sternheim, Artur Holz (based on the Ullstein-novel *Der Roman einer Mutter* by Kurt Aram)
D   Artur Holz
C   Paul Holzki
S   Erich Czerwonski
A   Olga Tschechowa, Hans Kuhnert, Adele Sandrock, Eugen Burg, Bogumil Miler, Emmi Ennering, Paul Gerhardt, Hedwig Karna, Maria Dona, Willi Hendrichs, Hans Rohden, Loni Nest

Zirkus des Lebens (probably also known as *Bürger Hollyoal*) (adventure series)

P   15 Dec. 1921, Marmorhaus
W   Hans Janowitz, Franz Schulz
D   Johannes Guter
C   Axel Graatkjaer
S   Hermann Warm

A   Werner Krauß, Greta Schröder-Matray, Gustav May, Paul Richter,
      Josef Klein, Rudolf Klein-Rogge, Emil Heyse, Lydia Potechina,
      Philipp Manning, Vicky Werckmeister

Der Mord in der Greenstreet
P   1921
W   Friedrich Eisenlohr, Erwin Baron
D   Johannes Guter
C   Erich Nitzschmann
S   Franz Seemann
A   Lil Dagover, Sophie Pagay, Georg Jurowsky, Emil Heyse, Wassily
      Wronsky, Erwin Barron, Hugo Flink

Die Intrigen der Madame de la Pommeraye (Russo-Film)
P   20 Jan. 1922, Tauentzienpalast
W   Fritz Wendhausen, Paul Beyer (based on motifs from Diderot)
D   Fritz Wendhausen
C   Carl Hoffmann
S   Robert Herlth, Walter Röhrig
A   Olga Gsowskaja, Alfred Abel, Paul Hartmann, Margarete Schlegel,
      Grete Berger

Bardame
P   24 Feb. 1922, Marmorhaus
W   Johannes Guter
D   Johannes Guter
S   Erich Czerwonski
A   Xenia Desni, Olga d'Org, Lydia Potechina, Paul Hartmann, Robert
      Scholz, Hermann Thimig, Charlotte Ander, Anton Edthofer, Elsa
      Wagner, Lina Paulsen, Wilhelm Diegelmann, Leonhard Haskel, Karl
      Huszar, Rudolf Lettinger

Tiefland (Licho-Film)
P   1922
W   (based on the opera by Eugen d'Albert)
D   Adolf Edgar Licho
C   Karl Hasselmann, Friedrich Weinmann
S   Hermann Krehan
M   Werner Richard Heymann
A   Lil Dagover, Michael Bohnen, Ilka Grüning, Paul Hansen, Martha
      Angerstein-Licho, Ida Perry

UFA (Silent)

Dr. Mabuse, der Spieler Part I: *Dr. Mabuse, der Spieler – Ein Bild der Zeit* (Uco-Film)
P   27 Apr. 1922, Ufa-Palast am Zoo
W   Fritz Lang, Thea von Harbou (based on the novel by
      Norbert Jacques)
D   Fritz Lang
C   Carl Hoffmann
S   Carl Stahl-Urach, Otto Hunte, Erich Kettelhut, Karl Vollbrecht
A   Rudolf Klein-Rogge, Bernhard Goetzke, Alfred Abel, Aud Egede
      Nissen, Gertrude Welcker, Paul Richter, Robert Forster-Larrinaga,
      Hans Adalbert Schlettow, Georg John, Karl Huszar, Grete Berger,
      Julius Falkenstein, Lydia Potechina, Julius E. Herrmann, Karl Platen,

Anita Berber, Julie Brandt, Auguste Prasch-Grevenberg, Adele
Sandrock, Max Adalbert

Dr. Mabuse, der Spieler Part II: *Inferno – Menschen der Zeit* (Uco-Film)
P   26 May 1922, Ufa-Palast am Zoo
W   Thea von Harbou
D   Fritz Lang
C   Carl Hoffmann
S   Otto Hunte, Erich Kettelhut, Karl Vollbrecht
A   see Part I

Luise Millerin (Froelich-Film)
P   21 Aug. 1922, Ufa-Palast am Zoo
W   Walter Supper, G. W. Pabst (based on the play *Kabale und Liebe* by
Friedrich Schiller)
D   Carl Froelich
C   Kurt Lande, Vilmos Fényes
S   Robert Herlth, Walter Röhrig, Hans Sohnle, Professors Lhotka
and Frick
A   Lil Dagover, Paul Hartmann, Walter Janssen, Gertrud Welcker,
Friedrich Kühne, Fritz Kortner, Werner Krauß, Ilka Grüning,
Reinhold Schünzel

Der Taugenichts
P   1 Sept. 1922, UT Kurfürstendamm
W   Walter Supper, G. W. Pabst, Carl Froelich (based on the novel
Aus dem Leben eines Taugenichts by Josef von Eichendorff)
D   Carl Froelich
C   Vilmos Fényes
S   Robert Herlth
A   Erhard Siedel, Julia Serda, Valérie von Martens, Gustav Waldau,
Hans Junkermann, Hans Thimig

Phantom (Uco-Film)
P   13 Nov. 1922, Ufa-Palast am Zoo
W   Thea von Harbou, Hans Heinrich von Twardowski (based on the
novel by Gerhart Hauptmann)
D   F.W. Murnau
C   Axel Graatkjaer, Theophan Ouchakoff
S   Hermann Warm, Erich Czerwonski
M   Leo Spieß
A   Alfred Abel, Frieda Richard, Aud Egede Nissen, Hans Heinrich von
Twardowski, Karl Etlinger, Lil Dagover, Grete Berger, Anton Edthofer,
Ilka Grüning, Lya de Putti, Adolf Klein

Der Ruf des Schicksals (Dea-Film)
P   1922
W   Johannes Brandt (based on the novel *Die Kusine aus Amerika* by
Kurt Aram)
D   Johannes Guter
A   Xenia Desni, Fritz Kortner, Ernst Hofmann

Der steinerne Reiter (Decla)
P   23 Jan. 1923, UT Kurfürstendamm
W   Thea von Harbou, Fritz Wendhausen
D   Fritz Wendhausen

C   Karl Hoffmann, Günther Rittau
S   Heinrich Heuser
M   Guiseppe Becce
A   Rudolf Klein-Rogge, Lucie Mannheim, Paul Biensfeldt, Otto Framer, Gustav von Wangenheim, Georg John, Fritz Kampen, Grete Berger, Wilhelm Diegelmann, Emil Heyse, Emilie Unda, Hans Sternberg, Annie Mewes, Martin Lübbert

Ein Glas Wasser (also known as *Das Spiel der Königin*) (Decla-Bioscop)
P   1 Feb. 1923, Ufa-Palast am Zoo
W   Ludwig Berger, Adolf Lantz (based on the comedy *Le verre d'eau* by Eugene Scribe)
D   Ludwig Berger
C   Günther Krampf, Erich Waschneck
S   Hermann Warm, Rudolf Bamberger, Erich Czerwonski
M   Bruno Scholz
A   Mady Christians, Lucie Höflich, Rudolf Rittner, Hans Waßmann, Bruno Decarli, Hugo Döblin, Helga Thomas, Hans Brausewetter, Max Gülstorff, Franz Jackson, Henry Stuart

Die Prinzessin Suwarin (Uco-Film)
P   Apr. 1923, Tauentzienpalast
W   Thea von Harbou (based on a novel by Ludwig Wolff, published in *Berliner Illustrirte Zeitung*)
D   Johannes Guter
C   Günther Krampf, Otto Baecker
S   Erich Czerwonski
A   Lil Dagover, Heinrich Schroth, Xenia Desni, Alfred Abel, Georg Jurowsky, Lucie Mannheim, Rudolf Klein-Rogge, Guido Herzfeld, Ernst Pröckl, Anton Edthofer, Heinrich Gotho

Die Austreibung (Decla-Bioscop)
P   23 Oct. 1923, UT am Kurfürstendamm
W   Thea von Harbou (based on the play by Carl Hauptmann)
D   F.W. Murnau
C   Karl Freund
S   Rochus Gliese, Erich Czerwonski
M   Joseph Vieth
A   Carl Goetz, Eugen Klöpfer, Ilka Grüning, Lucie Mannheim, Wilhelm Dieterle, Aud Egede Nissen, Robert Leffler, Jacob Tiedtke, Emilie Kurz

Der Wetterwart (Froelich-Film)
P   1923
W   H. Huxhol, C. Bauermann
D   Carl Froelich
C   Tober and Vilmos Fényes
S   Hanns Sohnle, Otto Erdmann
A   Mady Christians, Albert Steinrück, Hans Brausewetter, Julius Falkenstein

Seine Frau, die Unbekannte (Decla-Bioscop)
P   19 Oct. 1923, Tauentzienpalast
W   Benjamin Christensen
D   Benjamin Christensen

C   Frederik Fuglsang
S   Hans Jacoby
A   Lil Dagover, Willy Fritsch, Maria Reisenhofer, Maria Wefers,
    Mathilde Sussin, Edith Edwards, Karl Platen, Martin Lübbert,
    Karl Falkenberg, Paul Rehkopf, Jaro Fürth
Der verlorene Schuh (Decla-Bioscop)
P   5 Dec. 1923, Ufa-Palast am Zoo
W   Ludwig Berger (based on the fairy tale *Cinderella* and motifs
    by E.T.A. Hoffmann and Brentano)
D   Ludwig Berger
C   Günther Krampf, Otto Baecker
S   Rudolf Bamberger, Heinrich Heuser
M   Guido Bagier
A   Helga Thomas, Paul Hartmann, Mady Christians, Lucie Höflich,
    Olga Tschechowa, Frieda Richard, Hermann Thimig, Leonhard
    Haskel, Max Gülstorff, Paula Conrad-Schlenther, Emilie Kurz,
    Werner Hollmann, Georg John, Karl Eichholz, Margarete Kupfer,
    Isolde Kurtz
Der Evangelimann (Union-Film)
P   4 Jan. 1924, Tauentzienpalast
W   Hermann Kienzl, Holger Madsen (based on the opera by
    Hermann Kienzl)
D   Holger Madsen
C   Fredrik Fuglsang
S   Botho Höfer
A   Hanni Weiße, Paul Hartmann, Elisabeth Bergner, Heinrich Peer,
    Jacob Feldhammer
Die Finanzen des Großherzogs (Union-Film)
P   1 or 7 Jan. 1924, Ufa-Palast am Zoo
W   Thea von Harbou (based on the novel by Frank Heller)
D   F.W. Murnau
C   Karl Freund, Franz Planer
S   Rochus Gliese, Erich Czerwonski
A   Alfred Abel, Mady Christians, Harry Liedtke, Robert Scholz,
    Aldolphe Engers, Hermann Vallentin, Julius Falkenstein, Guido
    Herzfeld, Ilka Grüning, Max Schreck, Hugo Block
Die Nibelungen Part I: *Siegfrieds Tod* (Decla-Bioscop)
P   14 Feb. 1924, Ufa-Palast am Zoo
W   Fritz Lang, Thea von Harbou (based on *Die Nibelungen* and
    Norse Sagas)
D   Fritz Lang
C   Carl Hoffmann, Günther Rittau, Walter Ruttmann
S   Otto Hunte, Karl Vollbrecht, Erich Kettelhut
M   Gottfried Huppertz
A   Paul Richter, Margarethe Schön, Hanna Ralph, Gertrud Arnold,
    Theodor Loos, Hans Carl Müller, Erwin Biswanger, Bernhard
    Goetzke, Hans Adalbert Schlettow, Georg John, Frieda Richard,
    Georg Jurowski, Hardy von Francois
Die Nibelungen Part II: *Kriemhilds Rache* (Decla-Bioscop)
P   24 Apr. 1924, Ufa-Palast am Zoo
W   Thea von Harbou

D   Fritz Lang
C   Carl Hoffmann, Günther Rittau
S   same as Part I
M   same as Part I
A   same as Part I, and Rudolf Klein-Rogge, Hubert Heinrich, Rudolf Rittner, Grete Berger

Michael (Decla-Bioscop)

P   26 Sept. 1924, Ufa-Theater am Kurfürstendamm
W   Thea von Harbou, Carl-Theodor Dreyer (based on the novel by Hermann Bang)
D   Carl-Theodor Dreyer
C   Karl Freund
S   Hugo Häring
M   Hans Joseph Vieth
A   Walter Slezak, Benjamin Christensen, Nora Gregor, Alexander Murski, Grete Mosheim, Didier Aslan, Robert Garrison

Komödie des Herzens (Union-Film)

P   30 Sept. 1924, Tauentzienpalast
W   Peter Murglie (= F.W. Murnau and Rochus Gliese)
D   Rochus Gliese
M   Giuseppe Becce
A   Lil Dagover, Nagel Barrie, Colette Brettel, Ruth Weyer, Alexander Murski

Mein Leopold (BB-Film of Ufa)

P   1 Oct. 1924, Ufa-Palast am Zoo
W   (based on the play by Adolf L'Arronge)
D   Heinrich Bolten-Baeckers
C   Schattmann, Böttjer
S   Erich Czerwonski
A   Arthur Krausneck, Walter Slezak, Käthe Haack, Georg Alexander, Leo Peukert, Renate Rosner, Lotte Steinhoff, Paula Conrad

Der letzte Mann

P   23 Dec. 1924, Ufa-Palast am Zoo
W   Carl Mayer
D   F.W. Murnau
C   Karl Freund, Robert Baberske
S   Robert Herlth, Walter Röhrig
M   Giuseppe Becce
A   Emil Jannings, Hermann Vallentin, Maly Delschaft, Emilie Kurz, Georg John, Max Hiller, Hans Unterkirchner, Olaf Strom, Erich Schönfelder, Emmy Wyda

Der Turm des Schweigens (Decla-Bioscop)

P   29 Jan. 1925
W   Curt J. Braun
D   Johannes Guter
C   Günther Rittau
S   Rudi Feld
A   Xenia Desni, Hanna Ralph, Nigel Barrie, Fritz Delius, Hermann Leffler, Philipp Manning, Avrom Morewsky

Zur Chronik von Grieshuus (also known as *Um das Erbe von Grieshuus*) (Union-Film)
P   2 or 11 Feb. 1925, Ufa-Palast am Zoo
W   Thea von Harbou (based on the novel by Theodor Storm)
D   Arthur von Gerlach
C   Fritz Arno Wagner, Carl Drews, Erich Nitzschmann
S   Robert Herlth, Walter Röhrig, Hans Poelzig
M   Gottfried Huppertz
A   Lil Dagover, Arthur Kraußneck, Paul Hartmann, Rudolf Rittner, Gertrud Welcker, Rudolf Forster, Gertrud Arnold, Hans Peter Peterhans, Josef Peterhans, Ernst Gronau

Pietro, der Korsar
P   19 Feb. 1925, Ufa-Theater Turmstraße und Alexanderplatz
W   Arthur Robison (based on the novel by Wilhelm Hegler)
D   Arthur Robison
C   Fritz Arno Wagner, George Schneevoigt, Rudolf Mayer
S   Albin Grau
A   Aud Egede Nissen, Paul Richter, Rudolf Klein-Rogge, Frieda Richard, Fritz Richard, Walter von Allwörden, Georg John, Lydia Potechina, Edith Edwards, Jacob Tiedtke

Der Begleitmann
P   1924/25
D   Johannes Guter
A   Lillian Hall-Davies, Ossi Oswalda, Willi Fritsch, Ernst Hoffmann

Dekameron-Nächte/Decameron-Nights (Wilcox-Film-Ufa Coproduction)
P   20 Mar. 1925, Tauentzienpalast
D   Herbert Wilcox
C   Theodor Sparkuhl
S   Norman G. Arnold
M   Guiseppe Becce
A   Xenia Desni, Hanna Ralph, Lionel Barrymore, Werner Krauß, Randel Ayrton, Bernhard Goetzke, Albert Steinrück, Ivy Duke, Georg John, Samson Thomas

Der Sprung ins Leben (Messter-Film)
P   1925
D   Johannes Guter
A   Xenia Desni, Walter Rilla, Paul Heidemann

Tatjana (Messter-Film)
P   1925
W   Robert Dinesen (based on a story by Harriet Block)
D   Robert Dinesen
C   Carl Drews
S   Jack Winter
A   Olga Tschechowa, Robert Dinesen, Paul Hartmann

Eifersucht (Stern-Film of Ufa)
P   1925 (?)
W   Paul Czinner
D   Karl Grune
C   Karl Hasselmann
S   Karl Gröge
A   Lya de Putti, Werner Krauß, Georg Alexander

Die gefundene Braut
P   28 Apr. 1925, Tauentzienpalast
W   Heinrich Brandt
D   Rochus Gliese
C   Günther Rittau
S   Kurt Radtke, Kurt Kahle
M   Guiseppe Becce
A   Xenia Desni, André Mattoni, Walter Slezak, Jenny Jugo, Lydia
          Potechina, Emilie Kurz, Alexander Murski, Elsa Wagner, Karl Brose,
          Max Schreck, Walter Wener, Cali Kaiser-Lin

Blitzzug der Liebe
P   6 May 1925, Ufa-Palast am Zoo
W   Robert Liebmann (based on the novel by Karl Hans Strobl)
D   Johannes Guter
C   Carl Hoffmann
S   Rudi Feld
A   Ossi Oswalda, Willy Fritsch, Lillian Hall-Davis, Nigel Barrie,
          Jenny Jugo, Ernst Hofmann, Josefine Dora, Karl Platen, Georg John,
          Werner Westerhol, Philipp Manning

Die Prinzessin und der Geiger/The Blackguard (Ufa-Gainsborough Pictures, London,
    coproduction)
P   4 Sep. 1925, Ufa-Theater Nollendorfplatz
W   Alfred Hitchcock (based on the novel *The Blackguard* by Ramond Paton)
D   Graham Cutts
C   Theodor Sparkuhl
S   Alfred Hitchcock
A   Jane Novak, Walter Rilla, Bernhard Goetzke, Rosa Valetti, Dora
          Bergner, Fritz Alberti, Robert Scholz, Loni Nest, Frank Stanmore,
          Alexander Murski, Robert Leffler

Eine anständige Frau (Davidson-Film [D-Film] of Ufa)
P   1925 (?)
W   Paul Rosenhayn
D   Pau Ludwig Stein
C   Kurt Courant
S   Walter Reimann
A   Liane Haid, Harry Liedtke, Alfons Fryland, Mary Mascott

Liebesfeuer (Davidson-Film [D-Film] of Ufa)
P   11 Sept. 1925, Tauentzienpalast/Ufa-Theater, Turmstraße/
          Ufa-Palast, Königstadt
W   Wilhelm Thiele (based on an idea by Jolanthe Marés)
D   Paul Ludwig Stein
C   Kurt Courant
S   Walter Reimann
A   Liane Haid, Alfons Fryland, Walter Rilla, Paul Biensfeld

Der Farmer aus Texas (May-Film of Ufa)
P   1925 (?)
W   Joe May and R. Vewor (based on Georg Kaiser's comedy
          Kolportage)
D   Joe May
C   Karl Drews and Frenquells
S   Paul Leni

A   Lillian Hall-Davis, Willy Fritsch, Pauline Garon, Edward Burns, Mady Christians, Christian Bummerstadt, Hans Junkermann

Der Tänzer meiner Frau (Felsom-Film of Ufa)

P   1925 (?)
W   Alexander Korda and Adolf Lantz
D   Alexander Korda
C   Oertel
S   Paul Leni
A   Maria Korda, Willy Fritsch, Victor Varkonyi, Lea Seidl, Hans Junkermann, Livio Pavanelli, Olga Limburg, Hermann Thimig

Liebe macht blind

P   2 Oct. 1925, Mozartsaal
W   Robert Liebmann (based on the skid *Die Doppelgängerin* by Viktor Leon)
D   Lothar Mendes
C   Werner Brandes
S   Hans Jacoby
A   Lil Dagover, Conrad Veidt, Lillian Hall-Davis, Georg Alexander, Jenny Jugo, Alexander Murski

Das Mädchen mit der Protektion

P   1925
W   Willy Haas
D   Max Mack
C   Günther Krampf
S   Kurt Kahle, Kurt Radtke
A   Ossi Oswalda, Willy Fritsch, Nora Gregor, Adele Sandrock, Oreste Bilancia, Paul Morgan, Karl Etlinger, Hugo Döblin, Wilhelm Diegelmann, Hans Junkermann, Georg Baselt

Das Fräulein vom Amt (also known as *Liebe und Telefon*) (Sternheim-Film of Ufa)

P   15 Oct. 1925, Tauentzienpalast
W   Heinrik Galeen, Adolf Lantz
D   Hanns Schwarz
C   Fritz Arno Wagner
S   Erich Czerwonski
M   Giuseppe Becce
A   Mary Johnson, André Mattoni, Margarete Lanner, Alexander Murski, Willi Kaiser-Heyl, Karl Platen, Frieda Richard, Paul Biensfeld, Fritz Richard, Hugo Döblin, Lydia Potechina

Die Frau mit dem schlechten Ruf

P   1925
W   based on the novel *The Woman Who Did* by Grant Allen (?)
D   Benjamin Christensen
C   Carl Hoffmann
S   Hans Jacoby
A   Lionel Barrymore, Alexandra Sorina, Gustav Fröhlich, Henry Vybart, Herta Müller, Daisy Campell, Fritz Richard, Frieda Richard, Walter Bruckmann, Eugenie Teichgräber

Der Herr ohne Wohnung (BB-Film of Ufa)

P   1925
D   Heinrich Bolten-Baeckers
A   Georg Alexander

Der Mann seiner Frau (Mestro-Film of Ufa)
P 1925
W Alfred Halm (based on an idea by Hans Lüdtke)
D Felix Basch
A Lucie Doraine

Varieté
P 16 Nov. 1925, Ufa-Palast am Zoo
W Ewald André Dupont (based on the novel *Der Eid des Stefan Huller* by Friedrich Holländer)
D Ewald André Dupont
C Karl Freund
S O.F. Werndorff
M Ernö Rapée
A Emil Jannings, Maly Delschaft, Lya de Putti, Alice Hechy, Georg John, Kurt Gerron, Paul Rehkopf, Warwick Ward

Ein Walzertraum
P 18 Dec. 1925, Ufa-Palast am Zoo
W Robert Liebmann, Norbert Falk (based on the novella *Nux, der Prinzgemahl* by Hans Müller, and the operetta *Ein Walzertraum* by Felix Dörmann, Leopold Jacobson, and Oscar Strauß)
D Ludwig Berger
C Werner Brandes
S Rudolf Bamberger
M Ernö Rapée
A Willy Fritsch, Mady Christians, Xenia Desni, Lucie Höflich, Lydia Potechina, Mathilde Sussin, Julius Falkenstein, Jacob Tiedtke, Carl Beckersachs

Mein Freund, der Chauffeur
P Jan. 1926, Tauentzienpalast
W Hans Behrendt, Erich Waschneck (based on the novel *Der Blitzchauffeur* by C. N. and A. M. Williamson)
D Erich Waschneck
C Friedel Behn-Grund
S Carl Ludwig Kirmse, Botho Höfer, Bernhard Schwidewski
A Oskar Marion, Hans Albers, Alice Kempen, Barbara von Annenkopf, Olly Orska-Bornemann, Ferdinand von Alten

Der Wilderer (also known as *Weidmannsheil*)
P 20 Jan. 1926
W Johannes Meyer
D Johannes Meyer
C Gustave Preiss, Paul Krien
S Hans Sohnle, Otto Erdmann
A Helga Thomas, Rudolf Rittner, Heinrich Schroth, Carl de Vogt

Tartüff
P 26 Jan. 1926, Gloria-Palast
W Carl Mayer (based on the comedy by Molière)
D F.W. Murnau
C Karl Freund
S Robert Herlth, Walter Röhrig
M Giuseppe Becce

A   Emil Jannings, Lil Dagover, Werner Krauß, Lucie Höflich, André Mattoni, Rosa Valetti, Hermann Picha

Diebstahl des Herzens (also known as: *Herrn Filip Collins Abenteuer*)
P   Feb. 1926, Gloria-Palast
W   Robert Liebmann (based on the novel *Collins Abenteuer* by Frank Heller)
D   Johannes Guter
C   Karl Hoffmann, Günther Krampf
S   Rudi Feld
A   Georg Alexander, Ossi Oswalda, Adolf Edgar Licho, Elisabeth Pinajeff, Alexander Murski, Paul Biensfeld, Karl Platen, Karl Victor Plagge, Hans Junkermann

Manon Lescaut
P   15 Feb. 1926, Ufa-Palast am Zoo
W   Artur Robison, Hans Kyser (based on the novel by Abbé Prévost)
D   Artur Robison
C   Theodor Sparkuhl
S   Paul Leni
M   Ernö Rapée
A   Lya de Putti, Wladimir Gaidarow, Eduard Rothauser, Fritz Greiner, Hubert von Meyerinck, Frieda Richard, Emilie Kurz, Lydia Potechina, Theodor Loos, Trude Hesterberg, Marlene Dietrich, Siegfried Arno, Olga Engl

Karriere (also known as *Der rosa Diamant*)
P   8 Mar. 1926
W   Franz Schulz, Hans Rameau (based on the comedy *Karriere* by Richard Keßler)
D   Rochus Gliese
C   Fritz Arno Wagner
S   Egon Eiermann
A   Xenia Desni, Rudolf Klein-Rogge, Wilhelm Dieterle, Ginette Maddie, Hans Rameau, Adolf Zurmühl, Alice Hechy

Das Mädchen mit dem Löwenhaupt
P   1925 (?)
W   Thea von Harbou (based on Wilhelm Speyer's novel in *Berliner Illustrirte Zeitung*)
D   Rochus Gliese
A   Xenia Desni

Der Geiger von Florenz
P   10 Mar. 1926, Gloria-Palast
W   Paul Czinner
D   Paul Czinner
C   Adolf Schlasy, Arpad Viragh
S   Erich Czerwonski, O. E. Werndorff
M   Giuseppe Becce
A   Elisabeth Bergner, Conrad Veidt, Nora Gregor, Walter Rilla, Grete Mosheim, Ellen Plessow

Die Brüder Schellenberg
P   22 Mar. 1926, Ufa-Palast am Zoo
W   Willy Haas, Karl Grune (based on the novel by BernhardKellermann)

D   Karl Grune
C   Karl Hasselmann
S   Karl Görge, Kurt Rahle
M   Ernö Rapée, Werner Richard Heymann
A   Conrad Veidt, Lil Dagover, Liane Haid, Henry de Vries, Werner Fuetterer, Bruno Kastner, Eugen Klöpfer, Julius Falkenstein, Wilhelm Bendow, Erich Kaiser-Titz, Paul Morgan, Frieda Richard, Jaro Fürth

Die drei Kuckucksuhren
P   25 May 1926, Gloria-Palast
W   Robert Liebmann (based on the novel by Georg Mühlen-Schulte)
D   Lothar Mendes
C   Fritz Arno Wagner
S   Hans Jacoby
A   Lillian Hall-Davis, Nina Vanna, Nils Asther, Eric Barclay, Albert Steinrück, Hermann Vallentin, Paul Graetz

Die Boxerbraut
P   9 Sept. 1926, Ufa-Palast am Zoo
W   Robert Liebmann
D   Johannes Guter
C   Theodor Sparkuhl
S   Erich Czerwonski
A   Xenia Desni, Willy Fritsch, Hermann Picha, Teddy Bill, Harry Lamberts-Paulsen, Alice Kempen, Lovis Brody

Der Mann im Feuer
P   23 Sept. 1926, Ufa-Palast am Zoo
W   Armin Petersen, Erich Waschneck (based on an idea by Curt J. Braun and Heinrich Brandt)
D   Erich Waschneck
C   Werner Brandes, Friedel Behn-Grund
S   Botho Höfer
M   Werner Richard Heymann
A   Rudolf Rittner, Helga Thomas, Olga Tschechowa, Henry Stuart, Kurt Vespermann, Jacob Tiedtke

Sein großer Fall
P   30 Sept. 1926, Ufa-Palast am Zoo
W   Wilhelm Thiele, Fritz Wendhausen
D   Fritz Wendhausen
C   Werner Brandes
S   Hans Jacoby
M   Werner Richard Heymann
A   Alexander Murski, Christa Tordy, Olga Tschechowa, Rudolf Forster, Carl Ebert, Andr. Behrens-Klausen, Hans Adalbert von Schlettow, Wilhelm Bendow, Emil Heyse, Nikolai Malikoff

Faust
P   14 Oct. 1926
W   Hans Kyser (based on the script *Das verlorene Paradies* by Ludwig Berger, and the drama by Johann Wolfgang von Goethe)
D   F.W. Murnau
C   Carl Hoffmann
S   Robert Herlth, Walter Röhrig

A   Gösta Ekmann, Emil Jannings, Camilla Horn, Frieda Richard, Wilhelm Dieterle, Yvette Gilbert, Eric Barclay, Hanna Ralph, Werner Fütterer

Metropolis

P   10 Jan. 1927, Ufa-Palast am Zoo
W   Fritz Lang, Thea von Harbou
D   Fritz Lang
C   Karl Freund, Günther Rittau, Eugene Schüfftan
S   Otto Hunte, Erich Kettelhut, Karl Vollbrecht
M   Gottfried Huppertz
A   Brigitte Helm, Alfred Abel, Gustav Fröhlich, Rudolf Klein-Rogge, Fritz Rasp, Theodor Loos, Erwin Biswanger, Heinrich George, Olaf Storm, Hanns Leo Reich, Heinrich Gotho

UNITED STATES I (Paramount)

Hotel Imperial/Hotel Stadt Lemberg

P   31 Dec. 1926, Paramount on Broadway
W   Jules Furthman (based on the novel by Lajos Biro)
D   Mauritz Stiller
C   Bert Glennon
A   Pola Negri, James Hall, George Siegmann, Nicholas Bouszanin, Max Davidson, Michael Vavitsch, Otto Fries

Barbed Wire/Stacheldraht

P   1927
W   Jules Furthman (based on the novel *The Woman of Knochaloe* by Hall Caine)
D   Rowland Lee
C   Bert Glennon
A   Pola Negri, Clive Brook, Einar Hansen, Clyde Cook, Gustav von Seyfferlitz, Claude Schlingwater

UFA (Silent) (Erich Pommer Produktion)

Heimkehr (earlier title: *Carl und Anna*)

P   29 Aug. 1928, Gloria-Palast
W   Fred Majo, Fritz Wendhausen (based on the novel *Carl und Anna* by Leonhard Frank)
D   Joe May
C   Günther Rittau
S   Julius von Brosody, Arthur Schwarz
A   Dita Parlo, Lars Hansen, Gustav Fröhlich, Theodor Loos, Philipp Manning

Ungarische Rhapsodie

P   6 Nov. 1928, Ufa-Palast am Zoo
W   Fred Majo (=Joe May), Hans Szekely
D   Hanns Schwarz
C   Carl Hoffmann
S   Erich Kettelhut
A   Dita Parlo, Willy Fritsch, Lil Dagover, Fritz Greiner, Gisela Bathory, Erich Kaiser-Titz, Leopold Kramer, Andor Heltai, Harry Hardt, Oswaldo Valenti

Die wunderbare Lüge der Nina Petrowna
- P   15 Apr. 1929, Ufa-Palast am Zoo
- W   Hans Szekely
- D   Hanns Schwarz
- C   Carl Hoffmann
- S   Robert Herlth, Walter Röhrig
- M   Willy Schmidt-Gentner
- A   Brigitte Helm, Franz Lederer, Warwick Ward, Harry Hardt, Ekkehard Arendt, Michael von Newlinski, Lya Jan, Franz Schafheitlin

Asphalt
- P   1929
- W   Fred Majo (=Joe May), Rolf E. Vanloo (based on a film-story by Vanloo)
- D   Joe May
- C   Günther Rittau
- S   Erich Kettelhut
- A   Betty Amann, Gustav Fröhlich, Albert Steinrück, Else Heller, Hans Adalbert Schlettow, Hans Albers, Arthur Duarte, Paul Hörbiger, Trude Lieske, Karl Platen, Rosa Valetti

UFA (Sound) (Erich Pommer Produktion)

Medodie des Herzens (earlier title: *Sonntags um 1/2 4*)
- P   16 Dec. 1929, Ufa-Palast am Zoo
- W   Hans Szekely
- D   Hanns Schwarz
- C   Günther Rittau, Hans Schneeberger
- S   Erich Kettelhut
- M   Werner Richard Heymann, Viktor Gertler, Paul Abraham
- A   Dita Parlo, Willy Fritsch, Ilka Grüning, Annie Moves, Gerö Maly, Marosa Simon, Tomy Andrey, Lazlo Körmendy

Liebeswalzer
- P   7 Feb. 1930, Gloria-Palast
- W   Robert Liebmann, Hans Müller
- D   Wilhelm Thiele
- C   Werner Brandes, Konstantin Tschet
- S   Erich Kettelhut
- M   Werner Richard Heymann, Paul Godwin Band
- A   Lilian Harvey, Willy Fritsch, Georg Alexander, Julia Serda, Karl Ludwig Diehl, Hans Junkermann, Lotte Spira, Viktor Schwannecke, Karl Ettlinger, Rudolf Biebrach, Willy Prager, Marianne Winkelstern, Emmy von Stetten

Der blaue Engel
- P   1 Apr. 1930
- W   Carl Zuckmayer, Karl Vollmöller, Robert Liebmann (based on the novel *Professor Unrat* by Heinrich Mann)
- D   Josef von Sternberg
- C   Günther Rittau, Hans Schneeberger
- S   Otto Hunte, Emil Hasler
- M   Friedrich Holländer

A   Marlene Dietrich, Emil Jannings, Rosa Valetti, Kurt Gerron, Hans
     Albers, Karl Huszar, Eduard von Winterstein, Carl Balhaus, Wilhelm
     Diegelmann, Gerhard Bienert

Die Drei von der Tankstelle

P   15 Sept. 1930, Gloria-Palast
W   Franz Schulz, Paul Frank
D   Wilhelm Thiele
C   Franz Planer
S   Otto Hunte
M   Werner Richard Heymann
A   Lilian Harvey, Willy Fritsch, Oskar Karlweis, Heinz Rühmann, Fritz
     Kampers, Olga Tschechowa, Kurt Gerron, Felix Bressart, Gertrud
     Wolle, Leo Monosson

Liebling der Götter

P   13 Oct. 1930, Gloria-Palast
W   Robert Liebmann, Hans Müller
D   Hanns Schwarz
C   Günther Rittau, Konstantin Tschet
S   Erich Kettelhut
M   Willy Schmidt-Gentner, Karl May
A   Emil Jannings, Renate Müller, Olga Tschechowa, Hans Moser, Max
     Gülstorff, Eduard von Winterstein, Willy Prager, Oskar Sima, Truus
     von Alten, Lilian Ellerbusch

Der Einbrecher

P   16 Dec. 1930, Gloria-Palast
W   Robert Liebmann, Louis Verneuil
D   Hanns Schwarz
C   Günther Rittau, Konstantin Tschet
S   Erich Kettelhut
M   Friedrich Holländer
A   Lilian Harvey, Willy Fritsch, Ralph Arthur Roberts, Heinz Rühmann,
     Oskar Sima, Gertrud Wolle, Kurt Gerron, Paul Henkels

Der Mann, der seinen Mörder sucht

P   5 Feb. 1931
W   Robert Siodmak, Ludwig Hirschfeld, Kurt Siodmak, Billie Wilder
     (based on the play *Jim, der Mann mit der Narbe* by Ernst Neubach)
D   Robert Siodmak
C   Konstantin Tschet
S   Robert Herlth, Walter Röhrig
M   Friedrich Holländer
A   Heinz Rühmann, Lien Deyers, Raimund Janitschek, Hans Leibelt,
     Hermann Speelmanns, Friedrich Holländer, Gerhart Bienert,
     Wolfgang von Waltershausen

Ihre Hoheit befiehlt

P   3 Mar. 1931, Mannheim
W   Robert Liebmann, Paul Frank, Billie Wilder
D   Hanns Schwarz
C   Günther Rittau, Konstantin Tschet
S   Erich Kettelhut
M   Werner Richard Heymann

A   Käthe von Nagy, Willy Fritsch, Reinhold Schünzel, Paul Hörbiger, Paul Heidemann, Karl Platen, Fritz Spira

Voruntersuchung

P   20 Apr. 1931
W   Robert Liebmann (based on a play by Max Ahlsberg and Otto Ernst Hesse)
D   Robert Siodmak
C   Konstantin Tschet, Otto Becker
S   Erich Kettelhut
A   Gustav Fröhlich, Albert Bassermann, Hans Brausewetter, Charlotte Ander, Annie Markart, Edith Meinhard, Oskar Sima, Julius Falkenstein, Heinrich Gretler, Hermann Speelmanns, Jakob Tiedtke, Gerhart Bienert

Bomben auf Monte Carlo

P   31 Aug. 1931
W   Hans Müller, Franz Schulz (based on the novella *Montecarloi tortenet* by Heltai Jenö)
D   Hanns Schwarz
C   Günther Rittau, Konstantin Tschet
S   Erich Kettelhut
M   Werner Richard Heymann
A   Hans Albers, Anna Sten, Heinz Rühmann, Ida Wüst, Karl Ettlinger, Kurt Gerron, Peter Lorre, Otto Wallburg

Der Kongreß tanzt

P   20 Oct. 1931, Ufa-Palast am Zoo
W   Robert Liebmann, Norbert Falk
D   Eric Charell
C   Carl Hoffmann
S   Robert Herlth, Walter Röhrig
M   Werner Richard Heymann
A   Lilian Harvey, Willy Fritsch, Conrad Veidt, Otto Wallburg, Carl Heinz Schroth, Lil Dagover, Alfred Abel, Alfred Gerasch, Adele Sandrock, Margarete Kupfer, Julius Falkenstein, Max Gülstorff, Paul Hörbiger

Stürme der Leidenschaft

P   22 or 23 Jan. 1932, Ufa-Palast am Zoo
W   Robert Liebmann, Hans Müller
D   Robert Siodmak
C   Günther Rittau
S   Erich Kettelhut
M   Friedrich Holländer, Gerard Jacobson
A   Emil Jannings, Anna Sten, Trude Hesterberg, Frank Nicklisch, Otto Wernicke, Hans Deppe, Hans Reimann, Julius Falkenstein, Anton Pointner, Wilhelm Bendow, Hermann Vallentin

Der Sieger

P   23 Mar. 1932, Gloria-Palast
W   Robert Liebmann, Leonard Frank
D   Hans Hinrich, Paul Martin
C   Günther Rittau, Otto Baecker
S   Erich Kettelhut
M   Werner Richard Heymann

A   Hans Albers, Käthe von Nagy, Julius Falkenstein, Hans Brausewetter, Frieda Richard, Max Gülstorff, Ida Wüst, Adele Sandrock, Willi Domgraf-Fassbender, Hans Deppe

Quick

P   8 Aug. 1932, Ufa-Palast am Zoo
W   Hans Müller (based on the play by Felix Gandera)
D   Robert Siodmak
C   Günther Rittau, Otto Baecker
S   Erich Kettelhut
M   Werner Richard Heymann, Gerard Jacobson, Hans Otto Borgmann
A   Lilian Harvey, Hans Albers, Willi Stettner, Albert Kersten, Paul Hörbiger, Carl Meinhard, Paul Westermaier, Käthe Haack

Ein blonder Traum

P   23 Sept. 1932, Gloria-Palast
W   Walter Reisch, Billie Wilder
D   Paul Martin
C   Günther Rittau, Otto Baecker, Konstantin Tschet
S   Erich Kettelhut (?)
M   Werner Richard Heymann, Gerard Jacobson
A   Lilian Harvey, Willy Fritsch, Willi Forst, Paul Hörbiger, Trude Hesterberg, Hans Deppe, Wolfgang Heinz

Ich bei Tag und du bei Nacht

P   29 Nov. 1932, Gloria-Palast
W   Robert Liebmann, Hans Szekely
D   Ludwig Berger
C   Friedel Behn-Grund
S   Otto Hunte
M   Werner Richard Heymann
A   Käthe von Nagy, Willy Fritsch, Amanda Lindner, Julius Falkenstein, Elisabeth Lennartz, Albert Lieven, Friedrich Gnas, Anton Pointner, Eugen Rex, Ida Wüst, Rudolf Platte

FP1 antwortet nicht

P   22 Dec. 1932, Ufa-Palast am Zoo
W   Walter Reisen (based on the novel by Kurt Siodmak)
D   Karl Hartl
C   Günther Rittau, Konstantin Tschet, Otto Baecker
S   Erich Kettelhut
M   Allan Gray, Hans-Otto Bergmann
A   Hans Albers, Sybille Schmitz, Paul Hartmann, Peter Lorre, Hermann Speelmanns, Paul Westermeier, Arthur Peiser

Ich und die Kaiserin (earlier titles: *Marquis von S./Vermächtnis*)

P   22 Feb. 1933, Gloria-Palast
W   Robert Liebmann, Paul Frank, Walter Reisch, Felix Salten
D   Friedrich Holländer
C   Friedel Behn-Grund
S   Robert Herlth, Walter Röhrig
M   Friedrich Holländer, Franz Wachsmann
A   Lilian Harvey, Mady Christians, Conrad Veidt, Heinz Rühmann, Friedel Schuster, Hubert von Meyerinck, Julius Falkenstein, Paul Morgan, Hans Hermann Schaufuss, Hans Deppe

FRANCE (Fox-Europa, Paris)

On a volé un Homme
P   13 Mar. 1934, Marignan-Pathé, Paris
W   Hans Wilhelm, René Pujol
D   Max Ophüls
C   René Guissart
M   Bronislaw Kaper, Walter Jurmann
A   Lily Damita, Henry Garat, Fernand Fabre, Charles Fallot, Pierre
      Pierade, Lucien Callamand, Robert Goupil

Liliom
P   27 Apr. 1934, Cinéma Agricultures / Cinéma Bonaparte Ciné
      Opéra, Paris
W   Fritz Lang, Robert Liebmann, Bernhard Zimmer (based on the play
      by Ferenc Molnar)
D   Fritz Lang
C   Rudolf Maté, Louis Née
S   Paul Colin, René Renoux
M   Jean Lenoir, Franz Waxmann (=Wachsmann)
A   Charles Boyer, Madeleine Ozeray, Florelle, Alexandre Rignault,
      Robert Arnoux, Roland Poulin, Viviane Romance, Henri Richaud,
      Rosa Valetti, Lily Latté

UNITED STATES II (20th Century-Fox)

Music in the Air
P   13 Dec. 1934, Radio City Music Hall, New York
W   Howard I. Young, Billy Wilder (based on the Broadway Show by
      Jerome Kern and Oscar Hammerstein)
D   Joe May
C   Ernest Palm
M   Franz Waxmann (=Wachsmann)
A   Gloria Swanson, John Boles, Douglas Montgomery, June Lang,
      Marjorie Main, Reginald Owen, Al Shean, Roger Imhof

GREAT BRITAIN

Fire over England (London Film Productions, Alexander Korda)
P   1 Mar. 1937, Leicester Square Theatre, London
W   Clemence Dane and Sergei Nolbandov (based on the novel by
      A.E.W. Mason)
D   William K. Howard
C   James Wong Howe
S   Lazare Meerson
M   Richard Addinsell
A   Flora Robson, Raymond Massey, Morton Selten, Tamara Desni,
      Vivien Leigh, Laurence Olivier, Leslie Banks
Farewell Again U.S. title: *Troopship* (London Film Productions, Alexander Korda)
P   5 May 1937, Tradeshow, London
W   Wolfgang Wilhelm, Clemence Dane, Patrick Kirwan
D   Tim Whelan

C   James Wong Howe
M   Richard Addinsell
A   Flora Robson, Leslie Banks, Robert Newton, Sebastian Shaw,
     Patricia Hilliard, Edward Lexy, Gertrude Musgrowe
Vessel of Wrath U.S. title: *The Beachcomber* (Mayflower)
P   24 Feb. 1938, Regal Theatre, Marbel Arch, London
W   B. van Thal (based on the novel *Vessel of Wrath* by Somerset Maugham)
D   Erich Pommer
C   Jules Kruger
S   Tom Morahan
M   Richard Addinsell
A   Charles Laughton, Elsa Lanchester, Robert Newton, Tyrone Guthrie
     Dolly Mollinger, Rosita Garcia, Fred Gropes
St. Martin's Lane (also known as *London after Dark*) U.S. title: *Sidewalks*
  of London (Mayflower)
P   24 June 1938, Folkeston Astoria
W   (based on the story by Clemence Dane)
D   Tim Whelan
C   Jules Kruger
S   Tom Morahan
M   Arthur Johnston, Caroll Gibb
A   Charles Laughton, Vivien Leigh, Rex Harrison, Tyrone Guthrie, Basil
     Gill, David Barnes, Larry Adler, Gus McNaughton, Bert Cormack,
     Edward Lexxy
Jamaica Inn (Mayflower)
P   12 May 1939, Regal Theatre, London
W   Sidney Gilliat, Joan Harrison, J.B. Priesley (based on the novel by
     Daphne du Maurier)
D   Alfred Hitchcock
C   Harry Stradling, Bernard Knowles
S   Tom Morahan
M   Eric Fenby
A   Charles Laughton, Maureen O'Hara, Robert Newton, Emlyn
     Williams, Leslie Banks, Frederick Piper, Marie Ney

UNITED STATES III (RKO)

Dance, Girl, Dance
P   23 Aug. 1940
W   Tess Slesinger, Frank Davis (based on a novel by Vicky Baum)
D   Dorothy Arzner
C   Russell Metty
S   van Nest Polglase, Darrell Silvera
M   Edward Ward, Chester Forrest, Robert Wright
A   Maureen O'Hara, Lucille Ball, Louis Hayward, Virginia Field, Mary
     Carlisle, Ralph Bellamy, Edward Brophy, Paul Esmond, Walter Abel,
     Harold Huber, Maria Ouspenskaya, Katherine Alexander
They Knew What They Wanted
P   25 Oct. 1940
W   Roland Ardrey (based on the play by Sidney Howard)
D   Garson Kanin

C   Harry Stradling
M   Alfred Newman
A   Charles Laughton, Carole Lombard, Frank Fay, William Gargan, Harry Carey, Joe Bernard, Janet Fox, Karl Malden, Victor Kilian, Lee Tung-Foo

POSTWAR GERMANY (Intercontinental-Film)

Nachts auf den Straßen (Intercontinental-NDF=Neue Deutsche Filmgesellschaft coproduction)
P   15 Jan. 1952, Turmpalast, Frankfurt/Main
W   Helmuth Käutner, Fritz Rotter
D   Rudolf Jugert
C   Vaclav Vich
S   Ludwig Reiber
M   Werner Eisbrenner
A   Hans Albers, Hildegard Knef, Lucie Mannheim, Marius Goring, Heinrich Gretler, Karin Andersen, Martin Urtel, Hans Reiser, Gertrud Wolle

Illusion in Moll
P   18 Dec. 1952, Theater am Karlstor, Munich
W   Fritz Rotter
D   Rudolf Jugert
C   Vaclac Vich
S   Ludwig Reiber
M   Friedrich Meyer
A   Hildegard Knef, Hardy Krüger, Herbert Hübner, Sybille Schmitz, Nadja Tiller, Maurice Teynac, Gaby Fehling, Anneliese Born, Albrecht Schönhals, Lina Carstens

Eine Liebesgeschichte
P   25 Feb. 1954, Theater am Aegi, Hanover
W   Axel Eggebrecht, Carl Zuckmayer (based on a novel by Zuckmayer)
D   Rudolf Jugert
C   Hans Schneeberger
M   Werner Eisbrenner
A   Hildegard Knef, O.W. Fischer, Viktor de Kowa, Karl Ludwig Diehl, Mathias Wiemann, Claus Biederstaedt, Maria Paudler, Reinhold Schünzel

Kinder, Mütter und ein General
P   4 Mar. 1955, Passage, Hamburg
W   Herbert Reinecker (based on his novel *Hau ab mit Heldentum*)
D   Laslo Benedek
C   Günther Rittau, Günter Senftleben
S   Erich Kettelhut, Johannes Ott
M   Werner Eisbrenner
A   Hilde Krahl, Therese Giehse, Ursula Herking, Alice Treff, Bernhard Wicki, Claus Biederstaedt, Maximilian Schell, Ewald Balser, Klaus Kinski, Beate Koepnick, Hans-Christian Blech, Marianne Sinclair

BIBLIOGRAPHY

Numerous articles from German newspapers, journals, periodicals, and magazines consulted for this book are only listed in the footnotes of individual chapters. The Bibliography lists mainly articles authored by Erich Pommer or those referring to his name in their titles.

Adorno, Theodor W. "On the Question: 'What Is German?'" *New German Critique* 36 (fall 1985): 121–31.

Allen, Robert C. and Douglas Gomery. *Film History, Theory and Practice.* New York: Alfred A. Knopf, 1985.

"Am Wrack der Ufa." *Das Tage-Buch,* 2 April 1927.

Anderson, Curt I. C. *Über die deutsche Fimindustrie und ihre volkswirtschaftliche Bedeutung unter Berücksichtigung ihrer internationalen Beziehungen.* Ph.D. diss., Univ. Munich, 1927. Munich: Weiss, 1929.

Andrew, Dudley. "Sound in France: The Origins of a Native School." *Yale French Studies* 60 (1980): 94–114.

Arnheim, Rudolf. "Betrübliche Filme." *Die Weltbühne,* 12 January 1932.

Bagdanovich, Peter. *John Ford.* Berkeley: Univ. of California Press, 1970.

Balio, Tino, ed. *The American Film Industry.* Madison: Univ. of Wisconsin Press, 1976.

Barthel, Manfred. *So war es wirklich: Der deutsche Nachkriegsfilm.* Munich and Berlin: F.A. Herbig, 1986.

"Bavarian Resists Allies' Food Plan." *New York Times,* 3 April 1947.

Baxter, John. *The Cinema of Josef von Sternberg.* New York: A.S. Barnes, 1971.

———. *The Hollywood Exiles.* New York: Taplinger Publishing Company, 1976.

———. *Hollywood in the Thirties.* New York: Paperback Library, 1970.

"Begegnung mit einer Persönlichkeit. Erich Pommer sieht auf 50 Jahre Filmarbeit zurück." *Der neue Film,* 19 March 1959.

"Bei der Ufa machte man das so: Kino – das große Traumgeschäft." *Der Spiegel.* 20 parts. 9 September 1950–7 January 1951.

Berger, Ludwig. "Der Film kommt durch die Hintertür: Gedanken zur Situation der westdeutschen Produktion." *Tagesspiegel,* 13 March 1966.

———. *Theatermenschen: So sah ich sie.* Velber/Hanover: Friedrich Verlag, 1962.

———. "Tonfilm muß nicht Dreck sein." *Das Tagebuch,* 10 August 1929.

———. *Wir sind vom gleichen Stoff aus dem die Träume sind.* Tübingen: Wunderlich Verlag Hermann Leins, 1953.

"Berlin capital viennoise." *Les Cahiers de la Cinémathèque*, 13, 14, 15 (1975): 169–75.

"Billige Dekoration." *Der Spiegel*, 7 November 1951.

Blumenberg, Hans-Christoph, ed. *Robert Siodmak: Zwischen Berlin und Hollywood: Erinnerungen eines großen Regisseurs*. Munich: Goldmann Verlag, 1980.

————. "100 Years of Movies – or the Story of Monsieur Cinema at a Child's Birthday Party, *Deutschland*, 3 (June 1995): 63–66.

Board of Governors of the Federal Reserve System. *Banking and Monetary Statistics*. Washington, DC: National Capitol Press, 1943.

Bock, Hans-Michael, ed. *CineGraph: Lexikon zum deutschsprachigen Film*. Munich: edition text + kritik, 1984, continuing.

———— and Michael Töteberg, eds. *Das Ufa-Buch*. Frankfurt/Main: Zweitausendeins, 1992.

Bordwell, David. *The Films of Carl-Theodor Dreyer*. Berkeley, Los Angeles, London: Univ. of California Press, 1981.

Brauner, Artur ["Atze"]. Letter to Erich Pommer, 23 April 1963. J. Pommer Collection.

————. *Mich gibt's nur einmal*. Frankfurt/Main: Fischer Taschenbuch Verlag, 1978.

Bremer, Heinz. Letter to Erich Pommer, 1 June 1959. J. Pommer Collection.

Brennicke, Ilona and Joe Hembus. *Klassiker des deutschen Stummfilms, 1910–1930*. Munich: Goldmann Verlag, 1983.

Bucher, Felix. *Screen Series Germany*. London: A. Zwemmer Ltd., New York: A.S. Barnes, 1970.

Budd, Mike, ed. *The Cabinet of Dr. Caligari: Texts, Contexts, Histories*. New Brunswick and London: Rutgers Univ. Press, 1990.

Buscombe, Edward. "Notes on Columbia Pictures Corporation, 1926–41." *Screen*, 16 (autumn 1975): 65–82.

Caligari und Caligarismus. Berlin: Deutsche Kinemathek, 1970.

Callow, Simon. *Charles Laughton: A Difficult Actor*. London: Methuen, 1987.

Chersi Usai, Paolo and Lorenzo Codelli, ed. *Before Caligari: German Cinema, 1895– 1920*. Edizioni Biblioteca dell'Immagine, 1990.

Correll, Ernst Hugo. "Die Arbeit des Produktionsleiters." *Die Woche*, Sonder-Nummer "Der Tonfilm," 4 July 1931.

Dagover, Lil. *Ich war die Dame*. Munich: Franz Scheekluth-Verlag, 1979.

Das Cabinet des Erich Pommer: Ein Produzent macht Filmgeschichte. 1989. 16 mm. Munich: Klick Film GmbH.

"Das große Bilderbuch des Films." *Film-Kurier*, n. d.

"Das Welt-Echo des 'letzten Mannes'." *Film-Kurier*, 17 April 1925.

Davy, Charles, ed. *Footnotes to the Film*. London: Lovat Dickson Ltd. Readers' Union Ltd., 1937.

"Der leitende Genius der Ufa-Decla." *Der Kinematograph*, 18 May 1924.

"Der Sinn der Kipho: Die Ansprache Erich Pommers." *Film-Kurier*, fifth supplement, 26 September 1930.

"Der stumme Film ist erledigt: Gespräch mit dem Produktionsleiter der 'Ufa,' Erich Pommer." *Die Filmwoche*, 12 March 1930.

"Der Vater der Film-Dekartellisierung: Erich Pommer und die Entflechtung der Ufa." *Oberbayerisches Volksblatt*, 12 January 1952.

"Der Wendepunkt." *Lichtbild-Bühne*, 16 February 1924.

"Deutsch-französischer Filmaustausch: Ufa-Etablissement L. Aubert." *Film-Kurier*, 22 May 1924.

"Die Beendigung des Nibelungenfilms." *Lichtbild-Bühne*, 18 March 1924.

"Die internationale Filmkonferenz in Paris: Äußerungen Direktor Erich Pommers." *Film-Kurier*, 12 July 1922.

"Die Münchener 'Siegfried'-Premiere." *Süddeutsche Filmzeitung*, 14 March 1924.

"Die Nibelungen." *Süddeutsche Filmzeitung*, 14 March 1924.

"*Die Nibelungen* in München." *Film-Kurier*, first supplement, 15 March 1924.

Die rechte Hand des Kaufmanns. Teismans Kontorhandbuch. Essen: Verlag W. Gandert, n. d.

"Die schlechten USA-Filme." *Abendpost Hannover*, 14 August 1947.

"Die siebente und achte Großmacht: Erich Pommer an die Presse." *Film-Kurier*, 23 May 1925.

"Die tollen zwanziger Jahre." Alfred Neven Du Mont, ed. *Magnum*, 35 (April 1961).

Diederichs, Helmut H. "Die Anfänge der deutschen Filmkritik 1909 bis 1915 unter besonderer Berücksichtigung der Zeitschrift 'Bild und Film'." Ph.D. diss., Johann Wolfgang Goethe-Univ., Frankfurt/Main, 1983.

Dittmar, Peter. *F.W. Murnau*. Ph.D. diss., Freie Univ. Berlin, 1962. Berlin: Ernst Reuter, n. d.

Dost, Michael, Florian Hopf, and Alexander Kluge. *Filmwirtschaft in der BRD und in Europa: Götterdämmerung in Raten*. Munich: Carl Hanser Verlag, 1973.

"Drei neue Ufafilme: Dazu 2 Pommer-Filme und 6 Auftragsfilme." *Film-Kurier*. 15 April 1926.

Eggebrecht, Axel. *Der halbe Weg: Zwischenbilanz einer Epoche*. Reinbek: Rowohlt, 1975.

──────. "Deutscher Filmfrühling 1927." *Die Weltbühne*, 10 March 1927.

──────. "Film im Februar." *Die Weltbühne*, 15 March 1927.

──────. "Film im Jahreswechsel." *Die Weltbühne*, 11 January 1927.

──────. "Filmdämmerung?" *Die Weltbühne*, 9 February 1926.

──────. "Filmkunst und Filmgeschäft." *Die Weltbühne*, 2 March 1926.

──────. "Filmsommer 1926." *Die Weltbühne*, 10 August 1926.

──────. "Filmwinter 1926." *Die Weltbühne*, 7 December 1926.

Eibel, Alfred. *Fritz Lang: Choix de textes établi par Alfred Eibel*. Paris: Présence du Cinéma, 1964.

Eiland, Karl. "Der deutsche Film hat wieder Chancen." *Westdeutsche Allgemeine*, 29 January 1952.

"Ein Jahr deutscher Tonfilm: Imposante Leistung der deutschen Film-Industrie." *Film-Kurier*, 27 September 1930.

Eisner, Lotte H. *Fritz Lang*. New York: DaCapo Paperback, 1986.

──────. *Ich hatte einst ein schönes Vaterland: Memoiren*. Heidelberg: Wunderhorn, 1984.

──────. *The Haunted Screen: Expressionism in the German Cinema and the Influence of Max Reinhardt*. Berkeley and Los Angeles: Univ. of California Press, 1973.

──────. Letter to author, 27 March 1979.

──────. *Murnau*. Berkeley and Los Angeles: Univ. of California Press, 1973.

Elsaesser, Thomas. *New German Cinema: A History*. London: Macmillan Education Ltd., British Film Institute Cinema Series, 1989.

──────. "Pathos and Leave-Taking: The German Emigrés in Paris During the 1930s." *Sight and Sound* 53: 4 (autumn 1984): 278–83.

Eric Pommer Collection [E. Pommer Collection]. Los Angeles, CA: Doheney Library, Gifts and Exchange, University of Southern California.

"Eric Pommer Leaves F. P.; Couldn't Agree on Story." *Variety*, 26 January 1927.

"Erich Pommer im Vorstand der Ufa: Kurswechsel bei der Universum-Film AG." *Lichtbild-Bühne*, 10 February 1923.

Erich Pommer Obituary. *Der Spiegel*, 16 May 1966.

"Erich Pommer ou le 4e Reich." *Cahiers du Cinéma* 180 (July 1966).

"Erich Pommer scheidet aus der Spitzenorganisation." *Film-Kurier*, 28 January 1926.

"Erich Pommer zurückgetreten." *Film-Kurier*, 22 January 1926.

"Erich Pommers Abreise." *Film-Kurier*, 6 April 1926.

"Erich Pommers Pariser Brief." *Film-Kurier*, 27 March 1925.

"Europäische Film-Entente … ? Erich Pommers Pariser Eindrücke – Französisch-deutsche Aussprache – Die Atmosphäre klärt sich – Eine internationale Interessengemeinschaft?" *Lichtbild-Bühne*, 1 July 1922.

Fehling, Dora. "Künftig nur künstlerische Filme; Erich Pommer: Aufbau aus eigener Kraft." *Telegraf*, 28 July 1946.

Fehrenbach, Heide. *Cinema in Democratizing Germany: Reconstructing National Identity after Hitler*. Chapel Hill: Univ. of Carolina Press, 1995.

Feld, Hans. "Er machte Filmgeschichte." *Der neue Film*, 58: 20 (1959).

Film Daily Year Book. 1922–1929.

Filmarchitektur. Robert Herlth. Munich: Deutsches Institut für Film und Fernsehen, 1965.

Ford, Charles. "Grandeur and Decadence of Ufa." *Films in Review* 4: 6 (June-July 1953): 266–68.

Frank, Nino. "30 ans de cinéma: Confidences d'Erich Pommer." *Pour vous*, 11 February 1937.

"Fritz Langs Pariser Erfolg." *Film-Kurier*, first supplement, 26 March 1925.

Funk & Wagnells New Encyclopedia, 16. Joseph Laffan Morse, ed. New York: Funk & Wagnells, Inc., 1973.

Fürstenau, Justus. *Entnazifizierung: Ein Kapitel deutscher Nachkriegspolitik*. Neuwied and Berlin: Luchterhand, 1969.

Gabler, Neal. *An Empire of Their Own: How the Jews Invented Hollywood*. New York: Crown Publishers, 1988.

"German Film Growth Decried by U.S. Aide," *New York Times*, 18 January 1947.

"German Film Industry Needs More Teuton Outlets to Live, Sez Pommer." *Variety*, 4 December 1946.

Gilbert, Felix. *A European Past: Memoirs, 1905–1945*. New York and London: W.W. Norton and Company, 1988.

Goege, Hartmut. "Die Remigration deutschsprachiger Filmregisseure nach 1945." M.A. thesis, Univ. Münster, 1986.

Gomery, Douglas. "Economic Struggle and Hollywood Imperialism: Europe Converts to Sound." *Yale French Studies*, 60 (1980): 80–93.

——. "Tri-Ergon, Tobis-Klangfilm, and the Coming of Sound." *Cinema Journal*, 16: 1 (fall 1976): 51–61.

—— and Janet Staiger. "The History of World Cinema: Models for Economic Analysis." *Film-Reader*, 4 (spring 1979): 35–44.

Green, Abel. "Germans Slam Hollywood: Reinhardt with Molnar – Pommer." *Variety*, 7 May 1930.

Großmann, Stefan. "Erich Pommers Sturz." *Das Tage-Buch*, 30 January 1926.

Guback, Thomas H. *The International Film Industry: Western Europe and America since 1945*. Bloomington: Indiana Univ. Press, 1969.

Haas, Willy. "Der Tag der großen Premiere, 'Der letzte Mann' im Ufa-Palast am Zoo." *Film-Kurier*, 24 December 1924.

——. *Die literarische Welt: Erinnerungen*. Munich: 1960.

——. "Die Überraschungen im Auslandsgeschäft." *Film-Kurier*, 30 March 1922.

——. "Haben wir einen internationalen Überblick?" *Film-Kurier*, 9 January 1924.

Hardt, Hanno, Elke Hilscher, and Winfried B. Lerg, eds. *Presse im Exil: Beiträge zur Kommunikationsgeschichte des deutschen Exils, 1933–1945*. Munich, New York, London, Paris: K.G. Saur, 1979.

Haskell, Molly. "Epic! Heroic! American!" *The New York Times Book Review*, 23 October 1988.

Heilbut, Anthony. *Exiled in Paradise: German Refugee Artists and Intellectuals in America, from the 1930s to the Present*. New York: Viking Press, 1983.

Heining, Heinrich. *Goethe und der Film*. Baden-Baden: Neue Verlags-Anstalt, 1949.

Heinrichs, Fritz. "Die Entwicklung der Tonfilmindustrie." *Technik und Wirtschaft*, 23: 10 (October 1930): 269–73.

Hellmich, Hanns. "Die Finanzierung der deutschen Filmproduktion." Ph.D. diss., Schlesische Friedrich-Wilhelm Univ., Breslau, 1935.

Hembus, Joe. *Der deutsche Film kann gar nicht besser sein*. Bremen: Carl Schünemann, 1961.

Hempel, Rolf. *Carl Mayer: Ein Autor schreibt mit der Kamera*. Berlin: Henschelverlag Kunst und Gesellschaft, 1968.

Herking, Ursula. *Danke für die Blumen: Damals; Gestern; Heute*. Munich, Gütersloh, Vienna: C. Bertelsmann, 1973.

Herzberg, G. [Georg]. "50 Jahre Ufa. Ein bedeutsames Kapitel deutscher Geschichte." *Film-echo/Filmwoche*, 1 March 1968.

Higham, Charles. *Charles Laughton: An Intimate Biography*. Garden City, NY: Doubleday, 1976.

Hill, Gladwin. "Our Film Program in Germany, II: How Far Was It a Failure?" *Hollywood Quarterly*, 2: 2 (1947): 131–37.

"Hollywood Luminaries in a Mass Migration to European Film Studios." *Variety*, 10 July 1946.

Horak, Jan-Christopher. *Anti-Nazi Filme der deutschsprachigen Emigration von Hollywood, 1939–1945*. Münster: MAkS Publikationen, 1985.

——. "Ernst Lubitsch and the Rise of Ufa, 1917–1922." M.A. thesis, Boston Univ., 1973.

——. *Fluchtpunkt Hollywood: Eine Dokumentation zur Filmemigration nach 1933*. Münster: MAkS Publikationen, 1986.

——. *Middle European Emigrés in Hollywood (1933–1945): An American Film Institute Oral History*. Beverly Hills: Louis B. Mayer Foundation, n.d.

Huaco, George A. *The Sociology of Film Art*. New York and London: Basic Books, Inc., 1965.

"Impressionen rund um den Film, IV: Erich Pommer." *Der Film*, 15 March 1930.

"International Co-Operation (As Eric Pommer Sees It)." *Variety*, 3 August 1927.

"Internationalisierung des Films ist nur noch eine Frage der Zeit. Erich Pommer gibt in Hollywood ein Interview: 'Die Zusammenarbeit Europas mit Amerika bringt den Aufschwung der Weltfilmproduktion.'" *Film-Kurier*, 10 September 1927.

"Interview mit Louis Aubert." *Film-Kurier*, 24 May 1924.

Jacobs, Lewis, ed. *The Compound Cinema: The Film Writings of Harry Alan Potamkin*. New York: Teachers College Press, 1977.

Jacobsen, Wolfgang. *Erich Pommer: Ein Produzent macht Filmgeschichte*. Berlin: Argon-Verlag, 1989.

———. Letter to author, 19 September 1988.

Jäger, Ernst. "Nicht zur Veröffentlichung: Vergeßnes, Bekanntes und Indiskretes aus deutscher Filmgeschichte." 45 parts. *Der neue Film* (January 1954 ff.)

Jahrbuch der Filmindustrie, 1923/24. Berlin: Verlag der *Lichtbild-Bühne*, 1924.

Jahrbuch der Filmindustrie, 1926/27. Berlin: Verlag der *Lichtbild-Bühne*, 1927.

Jahrbuch der Filmindustrie, 1928. Berlin: Verlag der *Lichtbild-Bühne*, 1928.

Jay, Martin. *Permanent Exiles: Essays on the Intellectual Migration from Germany to America*. New York: Columbia Univ. Press, 1985.

Jewell, Richard B. and Vernon Harbin. *The RKO Story*. New York: Arlington House, Octopus Books, Ltd., 1982.

John E. Pommer Collection [J. Pommer Collection]. Camarillo, CA.

Joseph, Robert. "Our Film Program in Germany, I: How Far Was It a Success?" *Hollywood Quarterly*, 2: 2 (1947): 122–30.

———. "Gespräch mit Erich Pommer." *Die Neue Zeitung*, 15 July 1946.

Kallmann, Alfred. *Die Konzernierung in der Filmindustrie, erläutert an den Filmindustrien Deutschlands und Amerikas*. Ph.D. diss., Univ. Jena, 1932. Würzburg: Triltsch, 1932.

Kanin, Garson. *Hollywood: Stars and Starlets, Tycoons and Fleshpeddlers, Moviemakers and Moneymakers, Frauds and Geniuses, Hopefuls and Has-Beens, Great Lovers and Sex Symbols*. New York: Limelight Editions, 1984.

Karasek, Hellmuth. *Billy Wilder: Eine Nahaufnahme*. Hamburg, Hoffmann & Campe, 1992.

Kasten, Jürgen. "Filmkunst als Markenartikel." *Neue Zürcher Zeitung*, 31 March 1989.

Kästner, Erich. "Filmindustrie und Zweizonenmarkt." *Die Neue Zeitung*, 7 March 1947.

Käutner, Helmut. Letter to Erich Pommer, 24 January 1965. J. Pommer Collection.

Kayser, Ulrich. "Die deutsche Filmindustrie: Entwicklung, Aufbau und volkswirtschaftliche Bedeutung." Ph.D. diss., Univ. Tübingen, 1921.

Keiner, Reinhold. *Thea von Harbou und der deutsche Film bis 1933*. Studien zur Filmgeschichte 2. Ph.D. diss., Philipps-Univ., Marburg/Lahn, 1983. Hildesheim, Zurich, New York: Georg Olms Verlag, 1984.

Kessler, Frank, Sabine Lenk, and Martin Loiperdinger, eds. *Kintop 1: Früher Film in Deutschland*. Basel, Frankfurt/Main: Stroemfeld/Roter Stern, 1993.

———. *Kintop 3: Oskar Messter: Erfinder und Geschäftsmann*. Basel, Frankfurt/Main: Stroemfeld/Roter Stern, 1994.

Klär, Karl. *Film zwischen Wunsch und Wirklichkeit*. Wiesbaden: Verlagsgesellschaft Feldt & Co., 1957.

Knef, Hildegard. *Der geschenkte Gaul*. Vienna, Zurich, Munich: Verlag Fritz Molden, 1970.

Kohner, Frederick. Erich Pommer Biography. Foreign Film Seminar, USC, n. d. John E. Pommer Collection.

———. *The Magician of Sunset Boulevard: The Improbable Life of Paul Kohner, Hollywood Agent*. Palos Verdes, CA: Morgan Press, 1977.

Kovacs, Steven. "What Is a Producer, Anyway?" *Sight and Sound* (spring 1985): 89–93.

Kracauer, Siegfried. *From Caligari to Hitler: A Psychological History of the German Film*. Princeton, NJ: Princeton Univ. Press, 1947.

Kreimeier, Klaus. *Die Ufa-Story: Geschichte eines Filmkonzerns*. Munich and Vienna: Carl Hanser Verlag, 1992.

"Kriegsfilm: Der versöhnliche Ausklang." *Der Spiegel*, 9 March 1955.

Kubler, George. *The Shape of Time: Remarks on the History of Things*. New Haven and London: A Yale Paperbound, 1978.

Lamprecht, Gerhard. *Deutsche Stummfilme, 1903–1931*. 11 vols. Berlin: Deutsche Kinemathek, 1967–70.

Lanchester, Elsa. *Charles Laughton and I*. New York: Hartcourt, Brace and Co., 1938.

———. *Elsa Lanchester By Herself*. New York: St. Martin's Press, 1983.

Langfeld, W. Letter to Erich Pommer, 19 August 1964. J. Pommer Collection.

"L'apport allemand." *Les Cahiers de la Cinémathèque*, 13/14/15 (1975): 204–10.

"L'effort Allemand." *Les Cahiers de la Cinémathèque*, 13/14/15 (1975): 121–24.

"Leiche im Beton." *Der Spiegel*, 4 August 1954.

Lejeune, C.A. *Cinema*. London: Alexander Maclehose & Co., 1931.

Leonhard, Rudolf. "Filmindustrie und Avantgarde." *Illustrierter Telegraf*, 3 May 1948.

"Le parlant en Allemagne." *Les Cahiers de la Cinémathèque*, 13/14/15 (1975): 47–49.

Lipschütz, Rahel. *Der Ufa-Konzern: Geschichte, Aufbau und Bedeutung im Rahmen des deutschen Filmgewerbes*. Ph.D. diss., Univ. Berlin, 1932. Berlin: Energiadruck, 1932.

Lorenzen, Dagmar and Ulrike Weinitschke. "'Les Nibelungen' de Fritz Lang a Harald Reinl." *Les Cahiers de la Cinémathèque*, 42/43 (summer 1985): 106–12.

Luft, Friedrich. "Die Filmproduktion in der US-Zone." *Die Neue Zeitung*, 20 January 1947.

Luft, Friedrich. "Erich Pommer, der Film und die Zukunft." *Der Tagesspiegel*, 26 July 1946.

Luft, Herbert G. "Erich Pommer: Germany's Greatest Film Producer Became Such Through Charm and Assiduity." *Films in Review*, 10: 8 (October 1959): 457–69.

———. "Erich Pommer: Part II." *Films in Review*, 10: 9 (November 1959): 518–33.

Lüthge, B.E. "Die Entente in Tempelhof." *Film-Kurier*, 3 July 1919.

Lutz, Dorle. "Erich Pommer und der deutsche Film." *Schwäbische Landeszeitung*, 13 August 1946.

MacCann, Richard Dyer. "Erich Pommer: Film Leadership on the Old Scale." *Christian Science Monitor*, 27 October 1959.

———. "The Television Critic's Hidden Agenda." Symposium and Conference on Television Criticism: Public and Academic Responsibility. April 1985. Iowa City: The Univ. of Iowa.

Maibohm, Ludwig. *Fritz Lang: Seine Filme – sein Leben*. Munich: Wilhelm Heyne Verlag, 1981.

Manvell, Roger, introd. *Masterworks of the German Cinema*. New York, Evanston, San Francisco, London: Harper & Row, Icon Editions, 1973.

——— and Heinrich Fraenkel. *The German Cinema*. New York: Praeger Publishers, 1971.

Manz, H.P. *Ufa und Deutscher Film*. Zurich: Sanssouci Verlag, 1963.

May, Joe and Hanns Schwarz. "Was ist ein Produktionsleiter?" *Film-Kurier*, 4 May 1928.

Mayer, Hans. *Ein Deutscher auf Widerruf: Erinnerungen*. 2 vols. Frankfurt/Main: Suhrkamp, 1982.

Mayne, Judith. *Directed by Dorothy Arzner*. Bloomington and Indianapolis: Indiana Univ. Press, 1994.

Messter, Oskar. *Mein Weg mit dem Film*. Berlin-Schöneberg: Max Hesses Verlag, 1936.

Mitry, Jean. *Histoire du cinéma: III, 1923–1930*. Paris: Editions universitaires, 1973.

Monaco, Paul. *Cinema and Society. France and Germany During the Twenties*. New York, Oxford, Amsterdam: Elsevier, 1976.

"Mosse- und Ullsteinfilme." *Das Tage-Buch*, 27 November 1920.

Mühsam, Kurt and Egon Jacobson. *Lexikon des Films*. Berlin: Verlag der *Lichtbild-Bühne*, 1926.

Muller, Joseph-Emile. *Lexikon des Expressionismus*. Cologne: Verlag M. DuMont Schauberg, 1974.

Neale, Steve. "Art Cinema as Institution." *Screen*, 22: 1 (1981): 11–39.

Negri, Pola. *Memoirs of a Star*. Garden City, NY: Doubleday, 1970.

"Nibelungen-Dämmerung." *Lichtbild-Bühne*, 20 March 1924.

"Nochmals Caligari." *Der Film*, 13 August 1922.

Oertel, Rudolf. *Filmspiegel: Ein Brevier aus der Welt des Films*. Vienna: Wilhelm Frick Verlag, 1941.

Olimsky, Fritz. *Tendenzen der Filmwirtschaft und deren Auswirkung auf die Filmpresse*. Ph.D. diss., Univ. Berlin, 1931. Berlin: *Berliner Börsen-Zeitung*, 1931.

Ophüls, Max. *Spiel im Dasein: Eine Rückblende*. Stuttgart: Henry Govert Verlag, 1959.

Parsons, Louella O. "Laughton, Pommer Bring Their Mayflower Unit to Hollywood," *Los Angeles Examiner*, 20 October 1939.

Pecker, Alexandra. "Marcel Vandal & Erich Pommer, Pionniers de l'entente Franco-Allemande: Vers une nouvelle formule de diplomatie internationale." *Comoedia*, 9 February 1933.

Pem (Marcus, Paul). "Begegnungen mit Erich Pommer." *Morgen*, 28 March 1959.

———. "Ein Leben für den Film: Zum 75. Geburtstag Erich Pommers am 20. July." *Berliner Allgemeine*, 17 July 1964.

———. "Gedenkansprache für Erich Pommer. *Hamburger Filmgespräche, III*. Hamburg: Hamburger Gesellschaft für Filmkunde, 1967.

Perforator (Schneider, Albert). "Bayerischer Untersuchungsausschuß. Die seltsamen Wandlungen des Erich Pommer." *Deutsche Woche*, 17 October 1951.

Petley, Julian. *Capital and Culture: German Cinema, 1933–45*. London: British Film Institute, 1979.

Pinthus, Kurt. "Die Film-Krisis." *Das Tage-Buch*, 7 April 1928.

——. "Ein großer, teurer, schlechter und ein kleiner, billiger, guter Film." *Das Tage-Buch*, 25 December 1926.

——. "Lemberg und Metropolis." *Das Tage-Buch*, 15 June 1927.

Pleyer, Peter. *Deutscher Nachkriegsfilm, 1946–1948.* Münster: Verlag C. J. Fahle, 1965.

"Pommer bleibt in Berlin." *Film-Kurier*, 24 November 1927.

"Pommer Co-Producer With Sol Lesser." *To-Day's Cinema*, 7 November 1950.

"Pommer Dissatisfied; May Walk out on M-G." *Variety*, 23 March 1927.

"Pommer Gets Western." *Variety*, 6 April 1927.

"Pommer Heading For Germany to Make Indoctrination Films." *Variety*, 27 February 1946.

"Pommer Moving." *Variety*, 20 July 1927.

"Pommer to Reich as Screen Head," *Motion Picture Herald*, 164: 3 (20 July 1946): 43.

"Pommer und Paramount." *Film-Kurier*, 27 February 1926.

"Pommer with M-G-M; Can Handle Greta." *Variety*, 9 February 1927.

Pommer, Erich. "Artistical Form and Sound-Film Problems of International and National Films." *Der Film*, international ed., 14: 11 (June 1929): 16a–17a.

——. "Bedeutung der Konzerne in der Filmindustrie." *Das Tage-Buch*, 11 September 1920.

——. "Der deutsche Film hat Weltgeltung." *Reichsfilmblatt*, 20 February 1932.

——. "Der internationale Film." *Film-Kurier*, 28 August 1928.

——. "Der Tonfilm beherrscht Wien." *Film-Kurier*, 5 April 1930.

——. "Der Tonfilm und seine Technik." *Reichsfilmblatt*, 15 February 1930.

——. "Dichter und Tonfilm." *Der Querschnitt*, 11: 1 (January 1931): 46. Republished in *Weimarer Republik: Manifeste und Dokumente zur deutschen Literatur, 1918–1933.* Anton Kaes, ed. Stuttgart: J. B. Metzlerische Verlagsbuchhandlung, 1983.

——. "Eine Erklärung." Letter to *Berliner Tageblatt*, 1 April 1930.

——. "Film, Filmgeschäft und Weltmarkt." *Der Film*, 23 May 1928.

——. "Geschäftsfilm und künstlerischer Film." *Der Film*, 10 December 1922.

——. "Hands across the Sea in Movie Development." *New York Times*, 16 January 1927.

——. "Internationale Film-Verständigung." *Das Tage-Buch*, 15 July 1922.

——. Interview. By Petko Kadiev and Siegfried Kyser. 1964. Audiotape. E. Pommer Collection.

——. "Künstlerische Unterhaltungsfilme." *Reichsfilmblatt*, 20 April 1929.

——. Letter to Josef Baumgartner, 26 February 1953. E. Pommer Collection.

——. Letter to Karl Freund, 15 January 1965. J. Pommer Collection.

——. Letter to Pem (Paul Marcus), 22 March 1964. J. Pommer Collection.

——. Letters to Lore and Maurice Cowan, 31 January 1941 and 19 May 1964. J. Pommer Collection.

——. Manuscript for Alfred Eibel. 1964. E. Pommer Collection.

——. "The Origin of Dr. Caligari." *Art in Cinema Society*. Art in Cinema: A Symposium on the Avant-garde Film. New York: Arno Press, 1968.

——. "Praktische loyale Einfuhrpolitik." *Film-Echo*, supplement to *Der Montag/Berliner Lokalanzeiger*, 31 July 1922.

——. Report to Carl Winston, 23 August 1947.

——. "Richtlinien der neuen Produktion." *Film-Kurier*, second supplement, 27 September 1930.

——. "Visuelle Handlung oder Milieu." *Reichsfilmblatt*, 30 March 1929.

——. "Was deutsche Fachleute sagen." *Film-Kurier*, 10 June 1919.

——. "Was für den Filmexport geschehen muß." *Film-Kurier*, 1 January 1922.

——. "Wie eine Tonfilm-Szene gedreht wird." *Die Filmwoche*, 9 April 1930.

——. "Wir und die anderen." *Film-Rundschau*, supplement to *Tägliche Rundschau*, 23 July 1922.

Pommer, Erich and RKO Radio Pictures, Inc. Summary of Contract, 1 April 1940. E. Pommer Collection.

Pommer, John E. Letter to August Arnold, 23 May 1966. J. Pommer Collection.

——. Letter to Wolfgang Jacobsen, 9 July 1986. J. Pommer Collection.

——. Letter to Robert G. Scheuer, 31 May 1966. "Nochmals: In Sachen Pommer." *Filmblätter*, 18 June 1966.

——. Letters to author, 1984–1995.

——. Personal interview. 7 January 1985.

"Pommer's 'Kicking Around' in H'wood Said to Influence His German Pic Plans." *Variety*, 7 May 1947.

"Pommers Ausscheiden aus der Ufa." *Lichtbild-Bühne*, 23 January 1926.
"Pommers Reise nach Amerika." *Lichtbild-Bühne*, 30 September 1924.
Porges, Friedrich. "Erich Pommers Goldenes Jubiläum." *Aufbau*, 30 April 1959.
———. "Nur das Beste ist gut genug für das Publikum: Ein Leben für den Film, Gespräch mit dem fünfundsiebzigjährigen Erich Pommer. *Die Welt*, 25 July 1964.
———. "Tragödie der Filmarbeit." *Film-Kurier*, 10 January 1924.
Pröhl, Walter. Letter to John E. Pommer, 16 May 1966. J. Pommer Collection.
Rauthe, Johann Friedrich. "Der Aufbau der deutschen Film-Industrie unter besonderer Berücksichtigung der Konzentrationsbewegung der neuesten Zeit." Ph.D. diss., Friedrich-Wilhelms-Univ. Berlin, 1922.
"Reden und Trinksprüche beim Nibelungen-Bankett." *Film-Kurier*, 18 February 1924.
Riess, Curt. *Das gab's nur einmal: Die große Zeit des deutschen Films*. 3 vols. Frankfurt/Main, Berlin, Vienna: Ullstein Sachbuch, 1985.
———. *Das gibt's nur einmal*. Hamburg: H. Nannen Verlag, 1958.
Roeber, Georg and Gerhard Jacoby. *Handbuch der filmwirtschaftlichen Medienbereiche*. Pullach/Munich: Verlag Dokumentation, 1973.
Roger, Gerhard. "Pommer – Producer, Preusse, Pionier. 'Mr. Erich' ist fünfzig Jahre beim Film!" *Filmblätter*, 28 March 1959.
Rotha, Paul. *The Film Till Now: A Survey of World Cinema*. New York: Twayne Publishers, 1963.
———. "It's in the Script." *World Film News* (London), 3: 5 (September 1938): 204–205.
Sattig, Ewald. *Die deutsche Filmpresse*. Ph.D. diss., Univ. Leipzig, 1937. Breslau: Brehmer and Minuth, 1937.
Saunders, Thomas. "History in the Making: Weimar Cinema and National Identity?" Conference Paper, Univ. of Illinois at Chicago, October 1988.
———. *Hollywood in Berlin: American Cinema and Weimar Germany*. Berkeley and Los Angeles: Univ. of California Press, 1994.
———. "Politics, the Cinema, and Early Revisitations of War in Weimar Germany," *Canadian Journal of History*, 23 (April 1988): 25–48.
Scheuer, Robert G. "Zum Vermächtnis des großen, verkannten Produzenten; Berlinale 66: Erich Pommer-Retrospektive." *Filmblätter*, 21 May 1966.
Schivelbusch, Wolfgang. *Vor dem Vorhang: Das geistige Berlin, 1945–1948*. Munich and Vienna: Carl Hanser Verlag, 1995.
Schöning, Jörg, ed. *London Calling: Deutsche im britischen Film der dreißiger Jahre*. Munich: edition text + kritik, 1993.
Schulberg, Stuart. Letter to Herbert G. Luft. J. Pommer Collection.
———. Letter. *Films in Review*, 10: 10 (December 1959): 632.
Seydel, Renate. *Marlene Dietrich: Eine Chronik ihres Lebens*. Berlin: Henschelverlag, 1984.
——— and Allan Hagedorff. *Asta Nielsen: Ihr Leben in Fotodokumenten, Selbstzeugnissen und zeitgenössischen Betrachtungen*. Munich: Universitas Verlag, 1981.
Siemsen, Hans. "Deutsch-Amerikanischer Filmkrieg." *Die Weltbühne*, 1 September 1921.
Singer, Kurt. *The Laughton Story: An Intimate Story of Charles Laughton*. Philadelphia and Toronto: John C. Winston, 1954.
———. "Film-Übersicht." *Die Weltbühne*, 6 April 1922.
———. "Noch immer Kino." *Die Weltbühne*, 24 November 1921.
Spiker, Jürgen. *Film und Kapital*. Berlin: Verlag Volker Spiess, 1975.
Staiger, Janet and Douglas Gomery. "The History of World Cinema: Models for Economic Analysis." *Film Reader*, 4 (1979).
Stern, Frank. *The Whitewashing of the Yellow Badge: Antisemitism and Philosemitism in Postwar Germany*, trans. William Templer. Oxford, New York, Seoul, and Tokyo: Pergamon Press, 1992.
Straschek, Günter Peter. *Handbuch wider das Kino*. Frankfurt/Main: edition Suhrkamp 446, 1975.
Strohm, Walter. *Die Umstellung der deutschen Filmwirtschaft vom Stummfilm auf den Tonfilm unter dem Einfluß des Tonfilmpatentmonopols*. Ph.D. diss., Univ. Freiburg/ Breisgau, 1935. Freiburg: Kehrer, 1934.
Swanson, Gloria. *Swanson on Swanson*. New York: Random House, 1980.
Tabori, Paul. *Alexander Korda*. London: Oldbourne Book Co., 1959.
The Cabinet of Dr. Caligari. A Film by Robert Wiene, Carl Mayer, and Hans Janowitz. Classic Film Scripts. New York: Simon and Schuster, 1972.

123

Thomas, Bob. "Alfred Hitchcock: The German Years." *Action* (January-February 1973), 23–25.
Thompson, David. *A Biographical Dictionary of Film*. New York: William Morrow and Co., 1976.
Thompson, Kristin. *Exporting Entertainment: America in the World Film Market, 1907–34*. London: British Film Institute, 1985.
Traub, Hans. *Die Ufa: Ein Beitrag zur Entwicklungsgeschichte des deutschen Filmschaffens*. Berlin: Ufa-Buchverlag GmbH, 1943.
Treuner, Hermann, ed. *Filmkünstler: Wir über uns selbst*. Berlin: Sybillen Verlag, 1928.
Truffaut, François. *Hitchcock*. New York: Simon and Schuster, A Touchstone Book, 1967.
Tudor, Andrew. *Image and Influence: Studies in the Sociology of Film*. New York: St. Martin's Press, 1974.
Ufa Files R109I. Koblenz: Bundesarchiv, Federal Republic of Germany.
Ufa Magazin. Berlin, 1926.
Ufa Publicity Booklet. Berlin, 1923.
Uricchio, William. "German University Dissertations with Motion Picture Related Topics, 1910–1945." *Historical Journal of Film, Radio and Television*, 7: 2 (1987): 175–90.
Von Cziffra, Géza. *Kauf dir einen bunten Luftballon: Erinnerungen an Götter und Halbgötter*. Munich and Berlin: F.A. Herbig Verlagsbuchhandlung, 1975.
Von Eckardt, Wolf and Sander L. Gilman. *Bertolt Brecht's Berlin: A Scrapbook of the Twenties*. Garden City, NY: Anchor Books, 1975.
Von Ossietzky, Carl. *Rechenschaft: Publizistik aus den Jahren 1913–1933*. Bruno Frei, ed. Berlin and Weimar: Aufbau-Verlag, 1970.
Von Sternberg, Josef. *Fun in a Chinese Laundry: An Autobiography*. New York: Macmillan Publishing Co., 1965.
Von Zglinicki, Friedrich. *Der Weg des Films: Die Geschichte der Kinematographie und ihrer Vorläufer*. Berlin: Rembrandt-Verlag, 1956.
Walker, Alexander. *Vivien: The Life of Vivien Leigh*. New York: Weidenfeld & Nicolson, 1987.
"Was bedeutet das Kontingent für uns? Ein Interview mit Erich Pommer: Das Kontingent in Frankreich?" *Lichtbild-Bühne*, 22 March 1924.
Waxmann, Franz. Letter to Herbert G. Luft. 4 October 1959. John E. Pommer Collection.
Weisz, Christoph, ed. *OMGUS-Handbuch: Die amerikanische Militärregierung in Deutschland, 1945–1949*. Munich: R. Oldenbourg Verlag, 1994.
"Wichtige Veränderungen in der 'Ufa.' Direktor Erich Pommer übernimmt die Oberleitung der gesamten Produktion." *Film-Kurier*, 8 February 1923.
Williams, Alan. *Republic of Images: A History of French Filmmaking*. Cambridge, MA and London: Harvard Univ. Press, 1992.
Williams, J. Danvers. "Laughton's New Boss." *Film Weekly*, 27 February 1937.
———. "Mr. Pommer's Experiment." *Film Weekly*, 10 December 1938.
Wolff, Victoria. "Besuch bei Erich Pommer." *Aufbau*, 10 May 1957.
Wollenberg, H.H. *Fifty Years of German Film*. London: The Falcon Press Ltd., 1948.
Zierold, Norman. *Garbo*. New York: Stein and Day, 1969.
Zuckmayer, Carl. *Als wär's ein Stück von mir*. Vienna: Thomas F. Salzer, 1966. S. Fischer Verlag, 1967.

INDEX